PRINCIPLES OF EDUCATION,

DRAWN FROM

NATURE AND REVELATION,

AND APPLIED TO

FEMALE EDUCATION IN THE UPPER CLASSES.

BY

THE AUTHOR OF "AMY HERBERT"

AND OTHER TALES;

"THE FIRST HISTORY OF ROME;" "NIGHT LESSONS FROM SCRIPTURE;" "HISTORY OF THE EARLY CHURCH;" ETC. ETC.

Elizabeth M. Sewell.

TWO VOLUMES IN ONE.

NEW YORK:

D. APPLETON AND COMPANY,

443 & 445 BROADWAY.

1866.

PREFACE.

THIS volume is the result not of theory, but of experience. If it had been otherwise, it would never have been offered to the world. Education is too important a matter for theory. The risks of mistake are too fatal.

But when the Providence of God has forced upon us the practical consideration of a particular subject, and given us opportunities for testing the principles on which we have acted, it can scarcely be presumptuous to bring the conclusions at which we have arrived—whether through success or failure—into a definite form that may possibly be useful to others.

And there are occasionally periods in life when, after having waited in the earnest hope that some other person would give utterance to opinions and facts generally ignored, though fully known, we are at last urged to speak ourselves, from the sense of a necessity which no longer admits of delay.

Under a feeling of this kind some things contained in

the following pages have been written. Whether what has been said is true or false, wise or unwise, the world must judge: but the one sole desire of the writer has been to base the principles of education upon the teaching of God in Nature and Revelation.

It is this teaching alone which can make any advice authoritative. But we must all gain strength and confidence in the work of education by discovering—if we are able to do so—that the laws for the training and government of children, which we have gathered from general opinion and tradition, or worked out by personal experience and the efforts of our individual intellect, are really no other than those primary laws upon which the One Great Ruler of all has based His own Government, and which are only *not* seen and acknowledged generally, because they work so naturally and uniformly that we submit to without being conscious of them.

BONCHURCH, *May* 15, 1865.

CONTENTS.

CHAPTER VII.

LOVE EXHIBITED IN TENDERNESS AND SYMPATHY.

CHAPTER VIII.

REPROOF.

CHAPTER IX.

FORGIVENESS.

CHAPTER X.

ADVICE.

CHAPTER XI.

TRAINING.

CHAPTER XII.

CONFIDENCE AND RESPONSIBILITY.

CHAPTER XIII.

HUMAN FAITH.

CHAPTER XIV.

RESPECT.

CHAPTER XV.

TRUTH.

CHAPTER XVI.

EDUCATION IN JUSTICE AS THE ANTIDOTE TO SELFISHNESS.

CHAPTER XVII.

EDUCATION IN JUSTICE AS THE ANTIDOTE TO PREJUDICE AND ILLIBERALITY.

CHAPTER XVIII.

PRIDE.

CHAPTER XIX.

PRIDE (*continued*).

CHAPTER XX.

VANITY.

CHAPTER XXI.

TEMPER.

CHAPTER XXII.

PURITY.

CHAPTER XXIII.

LOVE.

CHAPTER XXIV.

FRIENDSHIP.

CHAPTER XXV.

THE PRINCIPLE OF RELIGION.

CHAPTER XXVI.

DEFINITE RELIGIOUS INSTRUCTION.

CHAPTER XXVII.

DEFINITE RELIGIOUS INSTRUCTION (*continued*).

CHAPTER XXVIII.

SCHOOLS AND PRIVATE PUPILS.

CHAPTER XXIX.

SCHOOLS AND PRIVATE PUPILS (*continued*).

CHAPTER XXX.

GOVERNESSES IN FAMILIES.

CHAPTER XXXI.

THE TRAINING OF GOVERNESSES.

CHAPTER XXXII.

INSTRUCTION.

CONCLUSION.

PRINCIPLES OF EDUCATION.

CHAPTER I.

THE OBJECT OF EDUCATION.

It is written in the Book of Ecclesiastes, "there is no new thing under the sun."[1] That which we call new is but a fresh combination of old materials—a fresh deduction from facts previously known. And if this is true in politics, science, and art, so is it much more true in morals. For morality is a system, not, like the discoveries of science, perfected through the workings of different minds in different ages, but complete in itself from its very commencement. To the commandments of God nothing can be added, and from them nothing can be subtracted. Education, therefore, which, according to the usual acceptation of the word, may be termed the guiding or leading of the young mind in the way which will best enable it to obey the commandments of God, can by no possibility be founded upon any principles in the nineteenth century which were not equally in existence, and equally binding, at the time when, after the Fall, man's present state of probation began. Of every book upon education it may justly be said, "that which is true is not new, and that which is

[1] Eccles. i. 9.

new is not true." And from this consideration it would at first sight follow, as a natural consequence, that to bring before the world any remarks upon a subject acknowledged to be thus exhausted, must be not only useless but wearisome. If we can only say what others have said before us, why waste our time in the repetition? There is but one answer to this objection. Every age, and every phase of society, has its own characteristics, its own dangers, and its wn fallacies, and will therefore necessarily view the subject of education in a manner peculiar to what may be called its own idiosyncrasies.

In the days of chivalry, education was carried on through the medium of the training which pages and squires received in the castles of the feudal barons, and the instruction given to young maidens by the lady who presided over the mysteries of leechcraft, and the intricacies of tapestry-work. A book upon education, written at the time of the Crusades, if such could be found, even though it might embody the soundest principles, would, except by a few thoughtful persons, be regarded merely as a literary curiosity. It would have little or no influence upon the present generation, simply because, however true, it would not meet its necessities. And in a similar though in a less degree, the educational books even of a hundred years ago are likely to be regarded rather as quaint than instructive.

The remarks addressed to our great-grandfathers and grandmothers, as they sat in upright chairs, never resting against the backs, seem misapplied to us, as we lounge upon sofas, or luxuriate in every imaginable form of easy position. The cautions needful in days when drinking was a fashionable vice, and coarseness of thought and action was openly tolerated, are inapplicable to a state of society in which self-restraint is demanded by the laws of society, and language, however insidious and suggestive, must, as a first requirement, be polished.

The age of railroads and electric telegraphs has needs as it has duties of its own; and before any ideas upon education

can affect the generation of the day, they must be clothed in the words to which it is accustomed to hearken, and illustrated by the allusions with which it is familiar.

But whilst this reason for the repetition of old truths under new forms certainly exists, the fundamental fact that the object of education has in all ages been recognized to be the same, remains unaltered; and it is consequently evident, that before any advantage can be derived from an inquiry into the principles on which education is to be conducted, it must be thoroughly understood what the object is at which it aims. Theories and systems may be clever, ingenious, and plausible; they may even produce results highly satisfactory in a certain sense; but if those results are not such as were sought for, the theories and systems must be confessed to be failures.

To educate rightly is, as it has been said, to guide and lead the young mind in the way which will best enable it to obey the commandments of God. This will probably be acknowledged by all serious and thoughtful persons as an explanation fundamentally correct, although there may be differences of opinion as to the mode of its expression.

Will it be considered a startling assertion to add, that this is in reality only a secondary object?—that there is another for which we must and do work every hour, every moment, in the secrecy of our hearts, in the depths of our privacy, amid the turmoil of business and the distractions of pleasure, in the haunts of vice and in the sanctuary of God?—an object which on this side of the grave we can never know; which, if we did know, we could never hope to understand; but which is true, enduring, unalterable, as the Eternal Counsels of the Almighty, since it belongs to an Omniscience which has foreseen the end of every human being from the beginning; and according to that foreknowledge, though not apart from human will, has prepared the sphere in which throughout Eternity he shall fulfil the purpose for which not earth only, but the universe—not man alone, but the angels, were created.

Bishop Butler remarks that, in considering the constitution

of this present world, "we must acknowledge that as there is not any action or natural event, which we are acquainted with, so single and unconnected as not to have a respect to some other actions and events; so, possibly, each of them, when it has not an immediate, may yet have a remote natural relation to other actions and events, much beyond the compass of this present world."[1] And he adds, that further thought will "lead us to consider this little scene of human life, in which we are so busily engaged, as having a reference, of some sort or other, to a much larger plan of things. Whether we are any way related to the more distant parts of the boundless universe into which we are brought, is altogether uncertain; but it is evident that the course of things which comes within our view is connected with somewhat past, present, and future, beyond it. So that we are placed, as one may speak, in the middle of a scheme, not a fixed, but a progressive one; every way incomprehensible; incomprehensible, in a manner, equally with respect to what has been, to what now is, and what shall be hereafter."[2]

Being thus incomprehensible, we might suppose that a conviction, however strong, of the existence of such a scheme, would exercise but little influence on our actions at present. We may possibly, probably even certainly, be working for the completion of some mighty purpose of the Most High; but if we know not what it is, it must be to us as if it were not. Such would be the first hurried reasoning of our minds. Yet more careful consideration will, in all likelihood, bring us to a different conclusion. The conviction that every individual redeemed through the Blood of Christ has a place marked out for him, duties to be performed, trusts to be fulfilled, purposes for which he is to work in the life on which he will enter at the Resurrection, though it may not directly influence our conduct with regard to our earthly life, must and ought to do so as regards our preparation for Heaven. And

[1] Analogy, Part I., chap. vii. [2] Analogy, Part I., conclusion.

looking upon education as but another term for such preparation, one effect which it will probably have will be that of destroying our confidence in systems, as distinguished from principles.

The present age is one which may peculiarly be called the age of systems. Everything undertaken, more especially if it refers to the training of the young, is to be carried on upon some definite plan. This is a fact so commonly recognized, that one of the formulas of inquiry used, when persons are anxious to gain information from those who undertake to educate, is what system they pursue? It is the vaguest of all vague questions. It may mean—Do you give your lessons in French or English? Is your aim classical or scientific? Have you paid teachers, or do you instruct yourself? Or, it may also mean—Do you trust to discipline as your motive power, or do you depend wholly upon love? Do you carry out strictly the doctrines and rules of the Church; or, on the other hand, do you profess to be a so-called Liberal, recognizing all creeds and all sects without distinction? And as the question is vague, so, necessarily, the answers given will be vague; but the very fact that the inquiry is thought necessary proves that the existence of systems is recognized as a fundamental basis of education.

And why should it not be?

The answer will best be given by examining into the aim and the advantages of system. A system is a mode of action by which it is supposed we shall be able to attain, in the most direct manner and the most perfect degree, some specified object. If a young man intends to enter the army, he is sent to a military college; there he is instructed in certain branches of knowledge, and drilled according to certain rules. Whether he is vicious or virtuous, clever or dull, a fixed system is provided, and upon that he is trained. The one object is to make him a good soldier; and if a hundred young men present themselves, in the course of the year, as destined for the army, the same rules, with regard to military duties, will be applied to

all alike. The aim is clear, the system has been well considered, and the result is, therefore, upon the whole, satisfactory.

So it is with all other professions—with all trades and occupations. Give a definite object, and a system is not only desirable, but necessary; perfection cannot be attained without it.

But if, as it has been suggested with regard to the training of the young, we know nothing of our ultimate object; if the purpose for which we are to labour is hidden; if the results to be finally produced are utterly beyond our comprehension,—then are systems not aids, but stumbling-blocks; not good, but infinitely mischievous.

This may be seen more clearly if we consider that in the idea of a definite and peculiar moral system of education there is always involved the exaltation of some one guiding principle above, if not apart from, others.

As, with the heathen Stoic, indifference to worldly enjoyments was recognized as the one chief element of goodness, and with the Christian Jesuit obedience is considered the virtue to which all others must bow; so, in the present day, we sometimes hear of love, or reverence, or honour, or the sense of duty, without reference to rewards, spoken of as the mainsprings by which the whole machinery of education is to be worked. And being, as they are, principles excellent in themselves, we may perhaps have wondered why it is that in almost all cases the peculiar systems based upon them are found in the end to fail.

May it not be for this reason? A system, whatever it may be, must, so far as it is a system, act without regard to the varieties of character; it must aim at producing the same tone of mind in every individual subjected to its influence; and the first elementary truth in education—because lying at the foundation, as it would appear, of all God's dealings with man, and all His purposes for him—is that we are neither required, nor intended, to have the same tone of mind. Har-

mony, not melody, is the object of creation; and if we strive for melody, we shall but end in producing discord.

But it may, perhaps, be said, the command given us is, "Be ye perfect, even as your Father which is in heaven is perfect."[1] If, therefore, the perfection of God consists, as we know it does, in the equal balance of all His attributes, is it not each man's duty to strive, so far as he may, to attain a similar balance in his own character?

Unquestionably; and yet it is most probably true that the actual attainment of such an equal balance by every human being would be inconsistent with the mysterious purposes of God in creation.

For we must remember that there are two kinds of perfection—perfection in degree, and perfection in kind. God alone is perfect in degree; His creatures are only perfect in kind. All goodness, all power, all beauty, are included in the idea of the one great Maker and Father of all. To His children He gives certain portions of this perfection, so that they may exhibit different phases of it; and this distinguishing gift—whether energy, or love, or generosity, or the spirit of self-sacrifice, or whatever it may be—is essential, as marking the kind of perfection for which the individual is destined. But as, in consequence of human imperfection, every strong natural inclination has a tendency to exaggeration, and consequently to sin, therefore this peculiar characteristic requires to be balanced by others, to be checked and trained—not in order to annihilate it, for that would be attempting to thwart the will of God in its creation—but that it may be kept in such just proportion as to fit it for the work to which it is destined. We see the use of such strong tendencies, and yet the necessity of keeping them in due proportion to the rest of the character, in the working of human affairs. A man is, we will suppose, gifted with certain qualities which enable him to plan and carry out a wise and benevolent work. Without these he-

[1] St. Matt. v. 48.

could not have succeeded; and yet these very same qualities, if not controlled and balanced, will in the end outgrow their usefulness, and ultimately mar the very object which at first they helped to attain. To aim at a perfectly equal balance of character is therefore absolutely necessary, whilst, at the same time, to attain it is impossible. There is a book from which we draw our wisest maxims of morality, and which we profess to make our chief guide in education, that might—if we would give ourselves the trouble to examine it—lead us to some very manifest conclusions upon the subject. The Bible has many offices to perform; none, perhaps, may be more important, in a secondary degree, than that of setting before us the mode in which the All-Wise God has seen fit to train individual characters. And when we look into it with this idea in our minds, one fact strikes us at the outset—that whatever such training may have been, it did in no way tend to destroy the marked distinction in intellect, temper, affection, between man and man. Abraham, Joseph, Moses, Samuel, David, Hezekiah, Jeremiah, St. Peter, St. Paul, St. John—how separately, how vividly, they stand forth before us! How evident is the action and reaction of their natural dispositions, and the circumstances in which they were placed! How entirely are they the same persons—exhibiting the same special characteristics throughout the whole course of their lives!

This will be seen more plainly if we examine one or two instances more minutely. Joseph, Moses, and St. Paul were persons who filled most prominent parts in the history of God's dealings with man. They were trained, if the expression may with reverence be permitted, under the especial Eye of God, with a view to their filling very important offices on earth. Let us consider how far such training affected their distinct individuality.

CHAPTER II.

SCRIPTURE CHARACTERS.

THE character of Joseph is one felt more easily than it can be described; but that human affection, both quick and deep, was its distinguishing trait, will scarcely be disputed. Sensitive, clinging, sympathizing, open-hearted, we follow the course of his eventful life with a continually recurring pang that one apparently so little fitted to endure sorrow should have been compelled so largely to partake of it.

The marked characteristics of his disposition exhibit themselves from the very commencement of his history. He was the child of Jacob's old age, and his confiding gentleness was doubtless fostered by the tenderness lavished upon him by his father—both for his own sake and for the memory of his mother. When he dreamed a wonderful dream, and his childish imagination was excited by it, the brothers who hated him were the persons to whom he turned for sympathy; when sent on his solitary journey to seek for tidings of them, no feeling of dread seems to have entered his heart; and when they carried out their cruel plans, and sold him to the Ishmaelites, there was no upbraiding: only in the anguish of his soul he besought them, and they would not hear.

He was brought down into Egypt—a captive—the victim of a wrong which might well have turned every gentle feeling into rankling bitterness; but adversity had no such power over him. Destined to be the ruler of a great nation, his

warm affections were yet in no way to be uprooted: they needed only to be governed; and when the temptation which presented itself was resisted, the strength which his principles had by that resistance acquired was a safeguard for his future life.

There is no need to continue the story in detail. Even if we have read it at no other time, we have probably, year by year, as the appointed Sunday lesson occurred, looked for it as for the "very lovely song of one that hath a pleasant voice."[1] We have watched the rise of Joseph from a prison to a palace, the successive interviews with his brethren, the yearning of his heart towards them, the anxious thought for his father, and the burst of overpowering feeling, which "the Egyptians and the house of Pharaoh heard," when at length the long hidden secret was revealed. It is all known to us, all familiar, though sacred as the prayers of our infancy. But in its sacredness we may not forget its human truthfulness. Joseph was a man "subject to like passions as ourselves"; and the character impressed upon him at his birth remained with him, and can be traced till his death. If we would know whether years and prosperity could chill the warmth of his affections, we may think upon the grief evinced for his father's death, the mourning "with a great and very sore lamentation,"[2] commemorated even by the people of the land; and the tenderness which expended itself doubtless upon Ephraim's children of the third generation, as well as upon the children of "Machir the son of Manasseh," who "were brought up upon Joseph's knees."[3]

Such was the individuality of Joseph, perhaps the most interesting of all the characters in the Old Testament. That he was a wise ruler, just and true, serving his earthly sovereign as he served his God, and that the events of his early life fitted him for the office he was to fulfil, are facts equally important and instructive. But the point which we are now called upon

[1] Ezek. xxxiii. 32. [2] Gen. l. 10. [3] Gen. l. 23.

to remark is, that in training him, as no doubt God in His wisdom did train him, to be the ruler of Egypt, his distinctive qualities were left untouched, or, at least, were only guided and cultivated. There were features of his character which, when developed by circumstances, fitted him for the post he was to occupy in Egypt; but there were also other and more striking characteristics, educated by an inner discipline, which, unless we conceive them to have had no object—an idea inconsistent with the infinite wisdom of the Creator—must have been given him with a view to some duty or office connected with a higher and more enduring existence.

As Joseph lived, so he died, and so he will rise again. Can it be that his love, his tenderness, his sympathy, shall be without purpose in Eternity?

Moses comes before us with a very different claim upon our interest. We are told, in the Book of Numbers, that he was the "meekest of men"; but probably the comment which we all make upon the words is that of wonder. We think of Moses striking the rock in his impatience, and it would seem that he was not meek.

Yet we must remember that meekness does not necessarily imply insensibility or slowness of feeling, but only strict self-control, united with unselfishness and sympathy. The most excitable person may, with such counteracting qualities, become the meekest; self-control keeping the eager impulse under subjection, until unselfishness and sympathy have had time to make themselves heard, and by placing the irritating circumstances in a just light, to remove or soften the cause of offence.

Self-control is, however, a hard lesson; and until it is thoroughly acquired, a person born with an impetuous temperament will be liable to sudden outbreaks of wrath. Moses at the beginning of his career, and at its conclusion, appears, in this respect, like two distinct persons; and yet examination seems to show that he never lost his natural excitability. For it must be remembered that God has not implanted in our nature any passion which, necessarily and irresistibly, leads us to sin.

Unjustifiable anger is doubtless a great offence, but the quick feelings and the energy of disposition which, when distorted and exaggerated, constitute sinful anger, are in themselves innocent, and may even be productive of great good. Moses, impetuous by nature, became "the meekest of men," that is, he learnt to control his distinctive feelings, so as not to indulge them on wrong occasions, or in a wrong degree; but the characteristics still remained. They had a work to do on earth, and have doubtless a work to do also in the unseen world; and whatever may be the mysterious connection between the glorified body and the renewed soul, and whatever the effect of matter upon mind, we may not think that when we meet the great Hebrew lawgiver, before the judgment seat of our Redeemer, it will be in any form, or with any qualities, but those which shall enable us at once to recognize him in his distinct individuality.

We will cursorily glance at his history as an evidence of what has been asserted.

On the very first occasion when Moses is brought before us in Scripture, his impetuosity, quick sympathy, and unselfishness, though mingled with singular timidity, are exhibited. He spied an Egyptian smiting a Hebrew, and he slew the Egyptian, and hid him in the sand. The following day he interfered in a quarrel between two of his own countrymen, and then in alarm fled from Egypt. In Midian he again appeared in a similar character, as the champion of the daughters of Reuel, in their contest with the shepherds.

During the whole period of the wonderful intercourse between the Almighty and the chosen deliverer of Israel, the impetuosity of Moses' character was displayed continually. When the miracles, which he was enabled to work, failed of their effects upon the king's heart, he ventured to expostulate with God, in words which could only have been suggested by the disappointment of an impatient spirit. The overtasking of his own powers, when, at the very outset of the journey through the wilderness, he undertook himself to decide the

quarrels which arose amongst the people, is an evidence that his was no naturally calm and prudent mind. The appeal made by his father-in-law, "Thou wilt surely wear away, both thou, and this people that is with thee: for this thing is too heavy for thee,"[1] shows the consciousness entertained by those who watched him, of the eagerness, which would almost necessarily tend to exaggeration in action; whilst the ready compliance with Jethro's suggestion is a proof of the control which he was learning to exercise over his own impulses.

The circumstances which followed the giving of the law are another and very striking testimony to the impetuosity of Moses' character. When he descended the mount, and heard the voices of the people shouting in their idolatrous worship, his "anger waxed hot, and he cast the tables (of the law) out of his hands, and brake them beneath the mount."[2] It was a just anger—more than just—it was holy; but it was anger still, and the punishment inflicted upon the people is in accordance with it. Moses burnt the calf in the fire, and "ground it to powder, and strawed it upon the water, and made the children of Israel drink of it." And when he had thus humbled them to the dust, he gave the fierce command to the sons of Levi, "Go in and out from gate to gate throughout the camp, and slay every man his companion, and every man his neighbour."[3]

The prayer which followed that terrible vengeance is surely also the prayer of no calm mind. "Oh, this people have sinned a great sin, and have made them gods of gold. Yet now, if Thou wilt forgive their sin: and if not, blot me, I pray Thee, out of Thy book which Thou hast written."[4] Neither was it a quiet unimpassioned spirit which could have dared to utter that awful request—"I beseech Thee, shew me Thy Glory"[5]—immediately after the exhibition of the Almighty's vengeance. That such a request was, in its measure,

[1] Exod. xviii. 18. [2] Exod. xxxii. 19. [3] Exod. xxxii. 20, 27. [4] Exod. xxxii. 31, 32. [5] Exod. xxxiii. 18.

granted, is a sufficient proof, if any were needed, that ardent feelings, however enthusiastic, are, when duly controlled, acceptable in God's sight, if only they are directed into their legitimate channel.

In singular contrast with the great jealousy exhibited by Moses for the honour of the Almighty—a jealousy which was again shown in the case of the rebellion of Korah—is the fact that in the one instance in which his private actions were condemned, his conduct was such as to cause the comment to be inserted which has given rise in many minds to so much astonishment—"Now the man Moses was very meek, above all the men which were upon the face of the earth."[1]

Yes, Moses was meek. He had controlled and subdued himself to meekness where his own honour was at stake; but when the glory of his God was concerned he was still what he was at his birth—zealous, ardent, even hasty, in his impulses and his actions; and God, as it would seem, did not will that it should be otherwise.

And yet, for an angry word and a hasty action, Moses was denied the one great longing of his life—he was forbidden to enter the Promised Land.

There must have been some overpowering cause for a discipline so severe, and so rigidly carried out. It may be that when men have all but attained the self-restraint which converts their natural characteristics into settled virtue, God is pleased to test and purify them more thoroughly in order that every remaining particle of dross may be purged away, and they may be fully fitted for their work in another state. From the day when the decree was given—"Because ye believed Me not, to sanctify Me in the eyes of the children of Israel, therefore ye shall not bring this congregation into the land which I have given them"[2]—the life of the eager-hearted leader of Israel must have been one long struggle between the impatient yearnings of his natural disposition and the submission demanded by God.

[1] Numb. xii. 3. [2] Numb. xx. 12.

We see it throughout the whole of the Book of Deuteronomy. It is a book containing no mere repetition of laws: it is the outpouring of the strongest patriotism, of the most ardent longing for a people's welfare; but it is also the revelation of a secret bitterness of regret in the heart of Moses, which betrays itself in the constantly recurring reference to the punishment that had fallen upon him. "The Lord was angry with me for your sakes, saying, Thou shalt not go in thither."[1] "And I besought the Lord at that time, saying, O Lord God, ... I pray Thee, let me go over, and see the good land that is beyond Jordan, that goodly mountain, and Lebanon."[2] "But I must die in this land, I must not go over Jordan: but ye shall go over and possess that good land."[3] He was not to enter. He was but to gaze from afar on a picture the foreground of which alone was clearly discernible. The deep valley of the Jordan intervened between him and "that good land." From the heights of Pisgah he could catch but a glimpse of Gilead and the distant hills of Naphtali; and though Jerusalem, the destined centre of his nation's glory, may have been visible through the opening of the descent to Jericho, yet the limits of the country of his hope—"the utmost sea and the desert of the south"—were hidden from him.

And yet so much had he dwelt upon it in imagination, that he speaks of it in the language of one to whom every feature of the landscape and every production of the soil were familiar. "The Lord thy God bringeth thee into a land of brooks and waters that spring out of valleys and hills; a land of wheat, and barley, and vines, and fig-trees, and pomegranates; a land of oil-olive, and honey; a land wherein thou shalt eat bread without scarceness; a land whose stones are iron, and out of whose hills thou mayest dig brass."[4] And even when directing them as to the solemn ceremonies by which their entrance into their inheritance was to be marked, he turns aside,

[1] Deut. i. 37.
[2] Deut. iii. 23, 25.
[3] Deut. iv. 22.
[4] Deut. viii. 7–9.

as it were, to mark the distinctive outline of the scenery to be connected with it. Ebal and Gerizim—the mountains of blessing and of cursing—were fixed for ever in the knowledge of the people by the description given, lingeringly and tenderly, as though they belonged rather to a home of memory than of promise. "Are they not on the other side Jordan, by the way where the sun goeth down, in the land of the Canaanites, which dwell in the champaign over against Gilgal, beside the plains of Moreh?"[1]

To see the land of this vivid faith, to approach so near, even to its border, and yet to be debarred from entering, was a punishment the severity of which can never be appreciated till we realize the distinctive characteristics of the man on whom it was inflicted. Yet, after the long tempestuous life, and the one bitter disappointment, the last blessing of Moses shows a fulness of confidence and rest which brings with it the conviction that the imperfection of human impetuosity had at length been subdued into an exulting trust; and that the meekest, yet, perhaps, the most eager-hearted of men, was ready for his work in a future and a sinless world. "There is none like unto the God of Jeshurun, who rideth upon the heaven in thy help, and in His excellency on the sky. The Eternal God is thy refuge, and underneath are the everlasting Arms: and He shall thrust out the enemy from before thee; and shall say, Destroy them. Israel then shall dwell in safety alone: the fountain of Jacob shall be upon a land of corn and wine; also his heavens shall drop down dew. Happy art thou, O Israel: who is like unto thee, O people saved by the Lord, the shield of thy help, and who is the sword of thy excellency! and thine enemies shall be found liars unto thee; and thou shalt tread upon their high places."[2]

"So Moses the servant of the Lord died there in the land of Moab, according to the word of the Lord. And He buried him in a valley in the land of Moab, over against Beth-peor; but no man knoweth of his sepulchre unto this day."[3]

[1] Deut. xi. 30. [2] Deut. xxxiii. 26–29. [3] Deut. xxxiv. 5, 6.

One more illustration of the marked differences between the best of men may be taken from the characters belonging to the Christian dispensation. Moses and St. Paul were both impulsive, earnest, energetic; both laboured devotedly for the service of their Almighty Lord; both were permitted to contribute largely to the establisment of His Kingdom upon earth. Yet we feel that they were essentially unlike. In what did this dissimilarity consist?

Perhaps the first and most obvious distinction may be found in a characteristic in St. Paul, which we are often inclined utterly to condemn, so rarely is it controlled sufficiently to work for good. For want of a better term, it may be called self-reliance. Now, it is evident that this quality may lead a man to presumption; it may induce him to lean on his own understanding, rejecting the counsels of God. But it is also certain, though perhaps not at once equally evident, that without it no great work of good can in this world be carried out; unless, as in the case of Moses, it may please God visibly to interpose His own power, and exhibit it the more through the very weakness of the instrument He vouchsafes to employ.

If St. Paul had not been an Apostle, he must still have been a distinguished man. He had opinions, purposes, determinations of his own; he was by nature bold. Comparing him with Moses, and imagining him placed in the same position, we feel that his character must have exhibited itself differently. The commands of God would have been equally obeyed by both; but where Moses shrank back with timid reluctance, St. Paul would, as we cannot but imagine, have thrown the energy of his will into the work, and confronted its difficulties with exultation. In Moses, impetuosity was the excitement of a moment; in St. Paul, it was the burning ardour of a life. Throughout the whole career of the great Hebrew Lawgiver, we are continually carried back to the Almighty as the immediate Director of his determinations. So strongly, indeed, is this displayed that, without the fact of this guidance, it would seem impossible for Moses, being what he was, to have done what

he did. He might have felt for his countrymen, he might have committed some hasty act in their defence; but by nature he was, as it appears, timid in working out his wishes, however strong might be the impulse which awakened them. Even if he had been capable of forming laws for the Israelites, he was clearly not capable of an act so bold as that of carrying them out of Egypt; still less of leading them through the wilderness, and bearing with their murmurs and their rebellions for forty years.

St. Paul might have done it; for St. Paul, as a man, feared no difficulties, and had a steadiness of aim which nothing could alter. And if St. Paul had been left in the darkness of Juadism, he might have been Antichrist in the independence of his dauntless spirit, and the strength of his wonderful intellect. Is it in the least necessary that such independence and strength should be crushed, before the sinful human creature is admitted into the presence of his Maker? A cursory glance at St. Paul's life would seem to teach us otherwise.

The outset of his history shows the power of independent thought and action, excited in a wrong cause. It was this which made him turn aside from the gentler counsels of Gamaliel, and take part in the condemnation of Stephen; and the same characteristic, when sanctified by the Spirit of God, led him afterwards openly to give up the prejudices of his birth and education, fearlessly to proclaim salvation to the Gentiles, and without regard to the consequences to carry on the controversies which that act necessarily involved. And it is very remarkable that the interposition of the Almighty appears in scarcely any instance exerted to check this independence of character. Whilst, in the case of Moses, even the minutest details of law and conduct were regulated by special command, in that of St. Paul a freedom of conduct was permitted which the Apostle himself plainly recognises. We see it in his missionary journeys, begun, indeed, by express command, but carried out in conformity with human plans, and only in one instance interrupted by the command not to preach in Bithynia,

but to go at once to Europe. The circumcision of Timothy, and the omission of the same rite in the case of Titus, were the decisions, as it would evidently seem, of human judgment. The opinions respecting the advisability of marriage under certain circumstances, sent to the Corinthian Church, were expressly stated to be, in some points, the result of his own consideration of the subject; whilst in explaining his conduct, or in excusing himself when blamed, St. Paul constantly brings forward reasons which would have been worse than needless if an express command had been issued in each separate case. Thus, he says, speaking of his change of mind with reference to his intended visit to Corinth, "When I therefore was thus minded, did I use lightness? I call God for a record upon my soul, that to spare you I came not as yet unto Corinth." [1] And so in another place, "I determined this with myself, that I would not come again to you in heaviness." [2] And once more, "Have I committed an offence in abasing myself that ye might be exalted, because I have preached to you the gospel of God freely? In all things I have kept myself from being burdensome unto you, and so will I keep myself." [3]

In these and in many other instances, we see plainly that the Apostle, converted by a miracle, and divinely inspired, was yet permitted, within certain limits, to carry out the counsels of God in the mode which seemed to his own judgment the best and wisest; though we must not forget that whilst asserting this in the plainest way, he adds, "I think also that I have the Spirit of God." [4]

At what point the Divine guidance and the peculiarities of the human mind met, it is as impossible for us to decide, as it is to discover which of our thoughts are given us by the direct interposition of the Holy Spirit, and which are the result of what may be termed natural causes. The only fact of importance to the present subject is, that the independent working of St. Paul's vigorous character was in no way crushed by the

[1] 2 Cor. i. 17, 23. [2] 2 Cor. ii. 1.
[3] 2 Cor. xi. 7, 9. [4] 1 Cor. vii. 40.

obedience required by his Christian profession, or by the fact of his Divine inspiration. And as scope was given to this vigour in action, so was it also permitted in thought. St. Paul's intellect, his originality, and, if the expression may, without irreverence, be used, his worldly wisdom, are exhibited in his public addresses as well as in his written Epistles. Looking at his speeches, made under different circumstances, we are at once struck by their variety, their definite aim, and the boldness with which every point that can be turned to advantage is seized upon. In his speech to the Athenians, perhaps the most remarkable of all, the line of his argument is Christian only in a very remote degree. Addressing a heathen people, he reasons upon the principles of natural religion, and from them leads the way gradually to revelation. When addressing his own countrymen, he gives the story of his conversion at length, and enlists their attention, at the very opening of his speech, by declaring his adherence to the strictest principles of their law. But when he speaks to Felix, the profligate heathen, he passes over the miraculous portion of his story, and in his defence lays the chief stress upon his love of law, peace, and order; at the same time strongly asserting his own innocence—a form of self-respect according well with the Roman sense of dignity. In the presence of Agrippa, again, he becomes a different person. He sinks the public character, and appeals to the king individually. One they were in the foundation of their faith, one in their reverence for the prophets, and their expectation of a Messiah. Why should they not be one in the hope of resurrection and salvation? Neither did the Apostle neglect to seize any point which might fairly be turned to his own advantage. Before the Roman officer he claimed the privileges of a Roman citizen, and thus secured himself from the degradation of scourging. When Pharisees and Sadducees were mingled in one council, he declared himself "a Pharisee, the son of a Pharisee," [1] and immediately divided the

[1] Acts xxiii. 6.

assembly. When threatened by the Jews, he, without hesitation, appealed to the Roman emperor. In all this there was the working of a mind which had a power of rapid judgment and quick decision that must, under any circumstances, have been remarkable, but which is singularly striking when we see it exhibited in one whose miraculous conversion, and whose dedication to a special office as an inspired teacher, would, it might have been supposed, subdue, if not utterly crush, the action of the merely natural reason.

There is no need to carry out these illustrations any further. What has been said may indeed to many appear to be merely a repetition of self-evident facts; and yet, how far do we find these facts acted upon? How many thoughtful parents have loved an ideal child, and formed for it, even before its birth, an ideal system of education! How many, instead of accepting their children as they have been given them, with all their distinctive traits, have, by the power of imagination, invested them with qualities which they did not possess, but which it was considered right that they should possess; and acting upon that preconceived determination, forced them into professions or positions in life for which they were unsuited, and thus fatally marred their prospects! It is the case with almost all, more or less. We make ourselves our children's Providence, and then marvel that we fail to attain the object for which we have laboured. Regardless of the characteristics which God has implanted in them, and which must be intended for the accomplishment of His purpose, we bend and coerce in order to form the character and the life according to our own ideas of what is best, and then sit down in disappointment, and lay the blame on the child, if we dare not attribute it to our Maker.

And yet it will be said all education must be unsound which does not propose for itself some object; and the highest of all objects must be that of living a life in accordance with God's Will. If, therefore, we strive to educate our children in conformity with God's Will, we must be doing right. Most per-

fectly true; but the mistake we make is in confounding God's Will with God's command. His Will, with regard to each individual, is the object or purpose, the final cause, of that individual's creation. His commands are the laws by which He teaches us how this object may best be attained. The knowledge of God's commands does not, therefore, as we are apt to think, give us a knowledge of His Will with regard either to ourselves or to others; if it did, we should be obliged continually to go counter to the Providential circumstances of life in order to place our children in the position in which we should have reason to think they would be least exposed to the temptation to disobey those commands. A boy with an ardent desire for the life of a soldier could never, for instance, by Christian parents, be allowed to become a soldier, because it is universally acknowledged that the military profession is open to the risk of great evil; and the very fact of the longing for such a life would imply that the boy had sympathies and tendencies that would peculiarly expose him to this evil. Heavy as is the responsibility of a parent now, it would in that case be increased tenfold; for all future contingencies, as well as all present claims, would have to be weighed, before we could venture to take a single step toward setting forth our children in life, with the expectation of a blessing to accompany them.

God does indeed give us commands. We know them, and must work according to them. But He does not reveal to us His Will—meaning by His Will His purposes and intentions; we may not, therefore, search irreverently into what that Will may be; but we must watch the distinctive characteristics of our children, and the circumstances in which He has placed them, and applying to them the commands as best we may, we must leave the result in God's Hands; being quite sure that whether failure or success may attend our earthly projects, there can be but one end, and that God's end, brought out in the future.

And if we would be assured that this acceptance of individual characteristics is our only safe guide in education, we may

consider briefly the effect of the contrary—the systematic principle.

A child, we will suppose, is eager, affectionate, yet hasty in judgment, and passionate in temper. Our system, perhaps, is sternness and justice. We think it right to repel feeling; and we can and do repel it—externally. But the impetuosity and temper break forth when the child escapes our control, and the results are a hundred-fold more fatal than they could possibly have been if we had accepted the character as the indication of God's Will for the child's future destiny, and sympathized with, and trained, instead of attempting to repel it.

Again, another child may be reserved, cold in manner, shy, and exclusive. Our system, perhaps, is that of openness and confidence. We insist upon unreserve; we display our own feelings, and expect a similar exhibition in return. In all probability we shall fail in our wish; but if we succeed, we shall have gained only an outward victory: the natural tone of mind will return when the external influence is withdrawn, and by the necessary law of reaction its peculiarities will be exaggerated.

Or, to take one more example, we rely perhaps upon obedience—absolute obedience. If we insist upon it we shall have it, and the result will at first be eminently gratifying; for without obedience the very idea of education is an absurdity. But if we train the child upon obedience only, without reference to other principles, it will become, if weak, an automaton; if strong, a hypocrite. Either the will, from force of habit, will succumb through life to every more powerful will with which it comes in contact; or, equally from force of habit, the natural disposition will be concealed, and the character will be made to appear that which may for the moment be most to the advantage of the individual.

A system, indeed, even supposing it to be good for one, cannot possibly be good for all: there are no doubt faults which must in each be alike uprooted, yet even with regard to them the mode of dealing must in every case be a subject of separate study.

But the characteristics of which we have been speaking are by no means necessarily faults, though they are very likely to become such. If they are to be ignored or crushed by system, then is man's wisdom very different from God's. Where shall we find the rigidity of system in the government of the Almighty?

Ten laws contain the commands of God for the conduct of the whole human race, though they are to be amplified and applied to every condition and circumstance according to man's reason and judgment. And these have been condensed by our Redeemer into two, which whosoever should be enabled to keep in all their fulness, would be exalted to the purity of an angel: "Thou shalt love the Lord thy God with all thy heart, and with all thy soul, and with all thy strength, and with all thy mind; and thy neighbour as thyself."[1]

We want no other principles. These, and these only, are the perfect revelation of God, and whatever laws may be deduced from them are but phases and portions of the great whole. As the several rays of colour merge in the pure light; as the various attributes of the All-Holy One blend into one infinite perfection; so the various forms of our duty to God are contained in the first of these commands, and those connected with our duty to man in the second. And when we base education upon any one phase of good instead of that which embraces all goodness, we act as did the heathen when they deified the attributes of the Almighty, and, placing them on His Throne, fell down and worshipped each man the god of his own choice—the principle which was most akin to the desire of his own heart.

The effect of that idolatry upon the morals of mankind—the inextricable confusion which it occasioned—is too well known to be enlarged upon. But we may be certain that a false principle will work a fatal result as surely now as it did then.

[1] St. Luke x. 27.

CHAPTER III.

PRINCIPLES AND RULES

We have arrived at this conclusion: that the object of education is the carrying out of God's Will for the individual; that the purpose of this Will is hidden from us in the Eternal counsels of God; but that the direction in which we are to work is pointed out to us by the peculiar endowments of character and of intellect with which every person is gifted; whilst the principles which are to guide us are contained in the two great commands—to love God wholly, and to love our neighbour as ourselves.

We now come to the more difficult and intricate questions which concern the application of these laws to particular cases.

When we look at the various conditions of man's life on earth, it is evident that this application of the two fundamental laws must involve secondary laws, such as those contained in the Decalogue, whilst these again must be subdivided to meet the needs of civil, ecclesiastical, and domestic government. It is of the latter only—that is, of the laws required for domestic government—that we have now to speak.

Were we angels, we should need none but fundamental law; for angels, as Hooker says, "beholding the Face of God, in admiration of so great excellency, they all adore Him; and being rapt with the love of His Beauty, they cleave insepara bly for ever unto Him. Desire to resemble Him in goodness

2

maketh them unweariable, and even insatiable in their longing to do by all means all manner of good unto all the creatures of God, but especially unto the children of men."[1] And the nearer a man approaches to the life of an angel upon earth, the less he will find himself oppressed by the restraints of moral secondary laws. They are but exemplifications of the two great primary laws, and as such he can not only reconcile himself to them without difficulty, but even cease to feel that they are laws, so far as the notion of law implies restraint.

To attempt, however, to go through life without secondary laws of some kind, marked and well considered, would be to act against the dictates of reason, and also to set aside the example which God Himself has given us in His own dealings with His creatures. For the example of these secondary laws and the principle of their right application is to be found in the mode in which God has, at two different periods of the world's history, been pleased to teach the people whom He has set apart for Himself, under the Jewish and under the Christian dispensations.

When the Jews were led out of Egypt, they were a nation in infancy. Long subjection had crushed all strength of mind, all settled force of purpose, all power of abstraction. Like children, they could be ruled only by the visible. Earthly objects, earthly gratifications, were their sole ideas of reward. Impatient of disappointment—led away by the temptations of sense—it required the actual symbols of God's presence to keep Him in their remembrance. When Moses remained in the mount, they called upon Aaron to make them a god, for unless they saw their deity they could not believe in him. When water failed them, they murmured; when food became scarce, they forgot the miseries of slavery, and groaned for the flesh-pots of Egypt. Miracles made only a momentary impression upon them, for, like children, so limited were their powers of thought and reasoning, that miracles themselves became natural to them.

[1] Eccles. Pol., Book I.

To give none but abstract laws to such a people would have been absolutely unavailing; as unavailing as it would be to preach to a little child of that eternal Law, the origin of all law, "which hath been of God, and with God everlastingly—that Law, the Author and Observer whereof is one only God, to be blessed for ever." [1]

For a nation in its infancy, therefore, not only general secondary laws, but temporary laws, or rules of various descriptions, were essential. They required limitations, warnings, minute directions, instantaneous punishments; for by these only could their earthly and narrow minds be kept in the right path. If left to themselves, they must have been the prey of their own passions, and succumbed to their own weakness. And we find that in training them God did thus deal with them. He marked out distinctly the path in which they were to tread. He gave them directions for their daily use. He interposed with cautions at every step. He made their religion one of outward observances, which, even if they failed to recognize as having a spiritual meaning, yet stamped upon their hearts indelibly the consciousness of an unseen God whom they were to obey; and every infraction of those rules was punished without delay. And so He led them on, step by step, until they were established in their own land; and then, by slow degrees, He relaxed this visible interposition, and though He still made His rules binding upon them, He taught them the bitter consequences of disobedience rather by the experience of natural punishments, than by the immediate infliction of His judgments.

The history of the Jews under the Judges is the history of a nation whose physical powers are developing, whilst the moral and intellectual powers are, as it were, in abeyance. The constant strife, the rough hardihood, the summary vengeance of which we read, all speak of such a period. God from time to time interposed for their deliverance, but it would seem as if He had willed that they should work out for them-

[1] Eccles. Pol., Book I.

selves those laws of civil government without which a people can be but barbarians. Like children at school, they had their contests for might over right, and were compelled to recognize the necessity of government by the sufferings which its absence brought upon them. Under the Kings their intellectual powers were enlarged, civilization spread; wealth, and luxury, and earthly splendour formed part of the national greatness. But moral advancement was left far in the background. That was a time for solemn rebukes and prophetic threatenings; but there were no new laws, and actual miraculous interpositions were rare, and given rather as warnings to those who had forsaken God, than as encouragements to those who served Him. Elijah and Elisha were prophets in Israel; for Judah—more faithful—needed not such visible reminders of the Almighty's power.

But the Jews, as a nation, failed to respond to the care lavished upon them. They did the work predestined for them in the counsels of God, but their will was not one with His, and they were cast off. And then began a new dispensation—one which was to embrace the whole human race.

It was a dispensation commenced under different circumstances, at a more advanced period of the world's growth. Learning, art, and civilization had arrived at a point which, even in these days of professed advancement, can scarcely be said to be surpassed. The writers of that period are still our teachers; the works of its sculptors and architects are still our models. Mankind were adults, and the education of childhood was unsuited to them.

And therefore, when God vouchsafed once more to reveal His commands, it was in a different way. The laws promulgated by our Blessed Lord took the form of principles. The rules for their application it was left to the Christian Church to work out for itself, though directly guided at first, as we cannot doubt, by the Spirit of God.

The truth of this statement has already been illustrated by the life of St. Paul; but it is evidenced throughout the whole

of the New Testament, and is confirmed by the history of mankind from that period to the present day. We, in our ignorance and blindness, doubtless are often inclined to wish it had been otherwise. In the midst of the controversies which meet us on every side, we long for more certain guidance, and lament that the points in dispute had not been clearly defined at the very outset of Christianity.

But putting aside the fact that nations, like individuals, when cultivated in intellect, will always make use of their powers to reason away laws instead of obeying them; and that no rules, however stringent, will be sufficiently clear to bind those who have arrived at a period when the will is opposed to restraint; it is sufficient for our present purpose to remark what the Almighty, in His inscrutable wisdom, has evidently pointed out to us by His government of the world, namely, that a more perfect obedience, a purer morality, a higher tone of thought are to be attained by leaving the will and the judgment free—when reason and intellect have prepared the way for that freedom—than by any system of rules, however perfect, or any directions for guidance, however wise. With rigid rules, clearly defined ceremonies, absolutely commanded, we might doubtless have had a more perfect exhibition of the exterior of Christ's Church on earth. But that Church is ultimately destined for Heaven; and the quarrying and polishing of each separate stone, which is to form part of "the Building not made with hands," is undoubtedly carried on through the medium of those sharp collisions and frictions which mar the perfection of its present beauty.

When religion was to be taught to the Jews in their ignorance, God allowed them to make no mistakes. When it was to be taught to the whole world in its intelligence, men were educated by the very means of their mistakes.

The deduction, as regards the education of individuals, is evident:

Rules for children; principles for adults.

Is there any axiom more true? May we not also ask, Is there any axiom more neglected?

Let us inquire of those who are commissioned for a time to take the place of parents—tutors and governesses—what is the frequent complaint made against the young people approaching to manhood and womanhood who are committed to their charge. Is it not that they fail in obedience, dutifulness, and respect to their parents? And what is too often the regret, the sorrow—we will not call it complaint—of these young persons, when they speak of their parents? Is it not that, as the expression is, they cannot get on with them—they are afraid of them—they think them fidgety, interfering, particular? It may seem a very hard thing to say; for there is no ideal to which the world clings more tenaciously than to that of the reciprocal affection and duty between parents and children—most especially between mothers and daughters. Every young mother believes that her little girl will grow up to be her cherished companion, and friend, and comfort: not because she is educated rightly, but simply because she is her daughter; and every child dreams of a mother who is to be its visible guardian angel: not because she is wise, and just, and tender, but because, in the imagination of a child, the office of such a visible guardian angel necessarily belongs to its mother.

To say that the existence of this hallowed affection can ever be a mere dream of the imagination, will be at once to raise an outcry of surprise and indignation. In asserting such a possibility, it may be said, we put aside the fact that the relation between a mother and her child is recognized as sacred by God, and deny the evident intentions of His Providence. If a mother's love and a child's grateful duty are not realities of natural affection, where can we look for anything on which, in this disappointing world, our yearning hearts may rest? The love between a mother and child is, indeed, most sacred. God forbid that we should not think it so! It is the manifest intention of Providence that, in every case, it should exist. It

would be folly to deny it. But there are many other things, with regard to which the intention is evident—so evident, indeed, that it is impossible for any reasoning being to doubt it—whilst yet the failures are far more numerous than the fulfilment. Mankind are intended to be happy and healthy; but misery and sickness are the portion of nine-tenths of the human race.

Man's will, man's folly, are allowed, in a very awful manner, to mar the merciful intentions of Providence; and, perhaps, in no way do they work more fatally than in the relation between parents and children.

"My little one is such a darling, I cannot help spoiling it!" The words sound almost sweet when uttered by a young mother. They speak of love, self-sacrifice, tenderness: yet are they the most cruel words which could ever escape her lips.

Not help spoiling it! Then she cannot help disobeying the positive injunction of God, neglecting the example He has Himself given. She cannot help laying up in store for her child, sin and sin's punishment; in this world, bitter regret, suffering, shame—it may be remorse, which shall never be repentance; and in the world to come——? If it were permitted us to question the unhappy ones for whom even a Redeemer's love is unavailing, how many, do we think, might be numbered amongst them, who were once—spoilt children? Rules for children—strict rules! We cannot say it to ourselves too often. Not severe rules, not given—that were a most grievous mistake—with any severity of manner; but definite rules, on the infraction of which punishment shall instantly be inflicted. The first of the Israelites, in the wilderness, who broke the rigid law of the Sabbath, died for his offence. God was then teaching a nation of children. When He afterwards gave His commands to the intelligent world, the Redeemer proclaimed the abrogation of the external rule, and declared that "the Sabbath was made for man, and not man for the Sabbath." [1]

[1] St. Mark, ii. 27.

This brings us to the second part of the axiom—Principles for adults.

What do we see, in the present day, with regard to its application to young persons?

It will, perhaps, be said, it does not concern them. They are not adults. True; but they are rapidly becoming such. The precise age when a youth becomes morally a man, or a young girl a woman, it may be difficult to determine. It will vary according to character. But no one will say that young people of fifteen, sixteen, or seventeen are, strictly speaking, children or can wisely be treated as such. And, perhaps, no one actually professes to do so. The theory is, that as the mind enlarges, the judgment may be left more free. A right theory, consistent with common sense, and—as we have pointed out—with the dealings of God with man. But when we come to practice, what do we find? These children, such darlings that it was impossible not to spoil them—are they darlings still? They can no longer be taken into their mother's lap, and fondled and coaxed. Their fits of infantine passion have become settled ill temper. Their petty wilfulness has been trained into disobedience. Their shyness and timidity have been carefully nursed into vanity and affectation. Their childish whims have been converted into selfishness. What is to be done with a disobedient, vain, affected, selfish, ill-tempered girl of, we will say, fifteen? Talk to her of principles; she has no notion of what you mean! Principles are understood by their application. Their meaning is to be learnt by degrees—by the help of rules and examples. There is no royal road for instruction in principles, any more than for instruction in any other branch of learning; and, as the young girl has the mind of a child, she must, it is supposed, be treated accordingly. She is placed therefore under a strict governess; she is watched, scolded, punished, debarred from amusement, and taught to look upon herself as hopelessly wicked, and, in consequence, forced back upon the solitude of her own heart; and, meeting with no sympathy, she naturally

shelters herself under a reserve, which is considered only another symptom of a cold heart. At length, considered totally unmanageable, she is sent away from home. If in this new sphere a better life should dawn upon her, will it not, probably, be years before her affections can be drawn towards the mother who so miserably spoilt her in childhood, and so hopelessly misunderstood her in youth?

Or, take another instance, not uncommon. We will suppose a child not to have been so utterly spoilt, but only over-petted, taught to think much of herself, to put herself forward, to give her opinion unasked, to be, in fact, conceited and wilful. These faults will assuredly not decrease as years advance. What we are apt to call conceit and wilfulness is often only the natural result of a too rapid growth of the intellectual, as compared with the moral, powers. Minds outgrow their strength just as bodies do.

A clever girl, or even one who is not exactly clever, but who has been brought forward, and allowed to act and speak at twelve as if she were twenty, will naturally, at fifteen or sixteen, form opinions of her own, and think herself competent to decide upon all questions with which she is, or is not, concerned. And this is very unpleasant to a parent. Little children, if forward and disagreeable, can be sent up into the nursery, and put out of sight; but a forward girl is an offence to a mother's vanity. She must be spoken to sharply—snubbed, as it is called; and the young lady is very quick to discern what snubbing means, and to resent it. So she becomes disobedient and disrespectful, and the mother talks to her of duty, and obedience, and self-control, and, finding her words unavailing, becomes angry, and loses the respect of her child, and then follows a *scene;* and the gulf between the parent and the child, which has long been slowly opening, becomes wider; perhaps so wide, that it can never thoroughly close again. Who is to blame? The daughter, surely! She is no longer a baby. She is quite aware that she ought to obey and be respectful to her mother, and she has sense enough to see that

her mother has right on her side. She ought to understand acting upon principle. Yes, indeed, she ought: she has arrived at the right age; but, then, whose duty was it to teach her to apply principle? Who ought, in childhood, to have educated her by rules based upon principle, and, through them, to have led her childish mind to the comprehension of the principle itself?

Let the fallow ground be first furrowed by careful and well-observed rules, and in those furrows we may drop the seeds of principles, with the certainty that they will produce a good and a plentiful crop; but, if we allow the ground to become hard and clotted, we may cast our principles upon it, but we must look to their being borne away upon the winds.

Or, once more. We will suppose a child to have been well and carefully brought up, made to obey, checked when forward, taught to be considerate and respectful, and then to have arrived at the age when reason and thought begin to develop themselves. A strong will, a clear intellect, and acute observation, are perhaps exhibited early, and the mother recognizes the fact with pride. But the habit of rule is strong within her. She likes power—she has the self-confidence resulting from success. Her child is so charming; it is evident that the education has so far been successful, and how, then, can rules be laid aside? The young girl is so young, she must make mistakes; her mother must know best what is good for her. And the thought of having a heart, simple, unstained by the world, absolutely dependent upon one, is so very tempting both to affection and to vanity! The mother, therefore, continues her supervision. She expects to know every thought of her young daughter's mind, as in the days when the little child prattled at her knee. She thinks it right to be acquainted with everything connected with her correspondence and her young friendships. Conversations must be repeated, letters must be read; and in order to insure this, rules must be laid down. But the rules are irksome, simply because they are

rules. The daughter has no friendship which her mother would disapprove. She neither writes nor receives letters of which she is ashamed; but she detests supervision. And she is beginning to differ from her mother upon some abstract points. She has opinions, tastes of her own; and she wants to express them freely. It would seem disrespectful, and it would certainly be painful, to state these opinions to her mother, because she knows that they are supposed always to be of one mind; so she longs to write and speak to others—to have the pleasure of thinking, and perhaps, in some cases, acting independently. But these rules, these restraints and limitations, meet her at every turn. It is grievous to say, but her mother, good and excellent though she may be, is gradually assuming the character of a warder set over her, to watch that she does not escape from prison. Not that she really desires to escape; only she would like to feel that she might do so.

This is by no means an uncommon case; and it may be met with not only when girls are young, but when they are past what may be called youth, and yet are inmates of their mother's home. To govern adults, or those approaching to the age, by rules, is to ignore the first principles of reason, and utterly to destroy the happiness of domestic intercourse. When persons have reached what are called years of discretion, freedom is as essential to their moral, as air is to their physical, strength.

It is not, however, to be supposed that what has been here said, implies that at any fixed age, such as fifteen, sixteen, seventeen, or at any precise subsequent period, government by rules may be laid aside, and government by principles adopted. It is a question of degree. The little child of two or three must be absolutely governed by rules, because it is only by means of temporary rules that it can be taught to submit itself to primary fixed laws. It can understand obedience; it cannot understand the love of God: obedience, therefore, is, for the time being, its primary law. The adult man or wo-

man must (speaking of domestic life only) be left to the absolute government of principles, for if we attempt to lay down rules for young men and young women, we shall infallibly estrange their affections. Between these two points there are many degrees, varying according to circumstances; and the part of wisdom in education is gradually to relax our rules, so that the perfectly obedient child may pass into the happy liberty of well principled youth, and the perfect freedom of full age, without any abrupt transition, but only with the consciousness that the strict yet loving government by rule exercised by a parent in infancy, has been succeeded by that much stricter, much sterner government by principle, which every human being must exercise over himself, if he would pass through this world with the respect of his fellow creatures, and enter upon the next with the approbation of his Maker.

It would seem scarcely necessary to add that in thus advocating the enforcement of rules for children, it is presupposed that they are rules based upon principle. Subjection to rules of any kind will indeed train the young mind to the habit of obedience, but it will never train it to goodness. The slave obeys the rule of his tyrannical master, but the moment he is left to himself, he obeys nothing but his own impulses. The test of the wisdom of our rules is the ease with which we may dispense with them when once the principle upon which they were based is firmly established. It is singular to remark how very few rules and what very rare punishments are required in the government, even of a child, who has in infancy been trained to strict obedience, based upon principle. The little one who, when a year and a half old, finds that it never has what it cries for, will require but a very small amount of checking and thwarting in its wishes when it is three or four; because by that time it will fully have learnt that most difficult of all lessons to an indulged child—to take "No" for an answer.

So, again, the child of three, who, when told to go or come, refuses, and finds that an instantaneous punishment, however

slight, follows its refusal, will need no threatening and scolding at five or six to compel it to obey. The child of five or six who finds that certain rules are laid down for its conduct, and that on the transgression of those rules a penalty is always inflicted, will, by the time it is nine or ten, keep a rule as strictly in its mother's absence as in her presence. At that age the irksomeness of obedience is lessened, because the child is quite able to understand the principle on which obedience rests; to see that it obeys its parents because they are the vicegerents of God, exercising authority from Him, and therefore claiming submission as a religious right. The sacredness of obedience once established, the parents' wishes, as well as their commands, become sacred. The child, though often unknown to itself, begins to act from a feeling of duty. "Such an action is not right, because my mother would disapprove; therefore I will not do it."

Once fairly establish this idea of duty in the mind, and rules are comparatively needless, and at thirteen or fourteen the child is scarcely conscious of them. She goes and comes, she writes and speaks freely; and though a few dirctions may be necessary as guides and landmarks, there is no necessity to enforce them. The child enforces them upon herself. At fifteen or sixteen her task becomes more difficult: she is learning to rule herself instead of to be ruled; and now the mother's duty changes. She is not so much called upon to command, as to counsel and advise; and because the child's will is one with hers, there is no need for severity in this office of adviser. Sympathy, tenderness, consideration, the full exhibition of that marvellous depth of affection which God has implanted in a mother's heart, all may be displayed with little or no check from external rules. And if we ask for the result, we may find it in the perfect confidence, the reverent devoted affection on the part of the child, and the loving delight and deep satisfaction on the part of the mother, which make the relationship between them perhaps the happiest, as it is certainly the holiest, of which our nature in its earthly affections is capable.

Is this an ideal picture? It need not be so: God intended it to be a reality. It is our own folly which makes it an ideal. We strive, it may be, to be strict, just, true, unselfish, and indulgent in our dealings with our children. But we begin with indulgence and end with strictness, instead of beginning with strictness and ending with indulgence; and the result is fatal.

If it be asked, why do we thus act? the answer will sound severe, but it will be very true. Because we are selfish. We love ourselves better than our children. There is nothing more tempting to a woman's tenderness than her little child of two years old; it is tempting even to those who are not mothers. The soft round cheek, the bright complexion, the silky hair, are so inviting to the eye, the broken words are so sweet to the ear, the tottering steps appeal so trustingly for help, and the first demonstrations of awakening love are so inexpressibly winning, that it requires a self-denial greatly beyond that to which we have at all accustomed ourselves, to look grave or check, much more to punish. But ought it not to be equally difficult to check, reprove, or punish the disobedient girl of thirteen or fourteen? Her face is still young and fair, her voice is still sweet, her steps are tottering on a far more dangerous path; her love, when awakened, is a far more valuable treasure than that of the unconscious little one. Yes, but she is disrespectful, passionate, disobedient; she makes us angry; she vexes us. There lies the secret; it is self, after all.

An unselfish mother will punish her little child, though it may wring her heart to do so. She will never fear chilling its infant heart by wise strictness; for a mother's tenderness will make amends in an instant for the suffering inflicted. Very little children will bear a large amount of moral coercion, just as they will a large amount of physical coercion. It belongs to their age; to be compelled to obey is natural, and they never resent it; and it is the feeling of resentment which makes enforced obedience injurious to the moral character.

And so, also, an unselfish mother, if by any unhappy weak-

ness she should have failed, by wise rules, to train her child to obedience in infancy, will be patient and forbearing when the consequences of that neglect are displayed in youth.

She will not then insist upon laying down rules, thwarting, and restraining. It is too late; restraints which would have been light in childhood, are felt to be very heavy in youth. They will but increase irritability, and widen the difference. The mother has "sown the wind," and she must be prepared to "reap the whirlwind;" happy only if, by gentleness, love, sympathy, she can at length so far regain her child's affections as to win her confidence, and at last, through God's mercy, awaken principle.

But this, in almost all cases, is found to be a work that must be devolved upon others. Training away from home is required to mend what mistaken indulgence has marred. And after all, it will only be *mending*—the mark of imperfection will remain most probably for life.

Alas! that so few will think of this. Alas! that a direction the most obvious, the most reasonable, and, upon the whole, the most likely to be acknowledged in words, of all which God has given to guide us in education, should be so neglected, that it requires pages of expostulation and illustration to enforce it;. and that, after all which can be said, it is probable that scarcely one in twenty will ever fully carry out into practice the axiom—Rules for children; principles for adults.

CHAPTER IV.

OBEDIENCE.

THE first object of a mother in educating her little child must, as it has been shown, be the enforcement of obedience. There is much to be said as to the principles on which this enforcement is to be based; but we will first inquire what is commonly understood by obedience.

A young mother will declare, "I always make my child attend to what I say. I had a struggle with it yesterday for a quarter of an hour, but I was the conqueror in the end."

A struggle of a quarter of an hour! Does that mean that the mother was coaxing, urging, entreating, threatening for a quarter of an hour? Then she was all that time teaching her child what a power it had over her. She was instructing it in the strength of its own will, the effect of its pertinacity. True, she gained her own way, as it is called, at last; but she let the child know that it had a way also, and one which its mother found it very difficult to resist. And children are much more keen than we are apt to imagine, and they very soon learn that if they can but hold out long enough, they will bring matters to a compromise, and so gain their object under another form.

This is not the notion of obedience given us in the Bible. God does indeed warn, entreat, threaten His people beforehand; but the act of disobedience once committed, punishment follows immediately.

Delay in obedience is disobedience. This truth ought to be implanted in the mind of a little child, even for its personal safety. It runs across the road when a carriage is coming: the mother calls it back; it obeys, and is saved; it disobeys, and is knocked down. There are many things analogous to this in morals. No one can tell what the effect of such delay may be. But one thing is certain, that instantaneous obedience is the only kind of obedience worthy of the name, and that years of miserable conflict between the mother and the child—conflict inevitably tending to the diminution of affection—will be spared if it can be attained. Instead of insisting upon a child's doing what it is told, punish it, however gently, because it does not do so, and there will be no need to insist on another occasion.

"My dear, I never speak twice," was the rule of one of the tenderest, most devoted of mothers; and her children blessed her for it throughout their whole lives.

And this mode of enforcing obedience by punishing disobedience will meet many very difficult cases, in which a child is unquestionably wilful, and yet in which it is quite out of the mother's power to make it do what is commanded. To refuse to speak, or to say a lesson, is the most common mode of tormenting with an obstinate child; and the mother deems it necessary to carry out her commands, and begins with entreating, continues with threatening, and ends with prolonged punishment; and after all, perhaps, the child is victor upon the one subject in dispute. But why give it the opportunity? Punish it at once because it refused, and the whole question is set at rest, and without any struggle over the contested point. It must be owned this sounds stern, and as disobedience is a child's frequent fault, it may be supposed that the result of such a mode of training would be constant punishment.

But there is a caution to be given on the other hand—one without which it must be allowed that such a style of education will be severe. If we never allow our children to disobey us, we must take care what commands we lay upon them.

To come when called is an act in the power of every child, however young. To speak to a stranger is not really so; for the shyness belonging to its age stands in the way, and without meaning to be disobedient, the child cannot instantly overcome the feeling. In the one case obedience may safely be insisted upon; in the other, it is unwise to provoke a contest, and therefore the wish should be expressed rather as a request than a command. So, again, a little child *can* repeat after us any word which we may utter, and to refuse will be direct disobedience, and must be punished as such; but it *cannot* always remember a letter which it has learnt, and therefore, when we suspect it of obstinacy, instead of insisting upon its remembering, we shall do well to exact some little penalty for forgetfulness, and let the matter pass. In all cases the one great point to be observed is to enforce what we command, and therefore not to weaken our own authority by unnecessarily commanding what we cannot enforce.

And when we speak of punishment, it must be remembered that every look or movement which expresses displeasure is more or less punishment to a very little child. The mere holding up of a finger, or looking grave, or speaking quickly and decidedly, will be felt to be such, and a rap on the hand will be actual severity, and be recollected for hours. And even as children grow older, sharp, instant punishments will be found to be more efficacious, and less irritating to the temper, than penalties which are delayed, though the latter may in themselves be more gentle. To express decided anger, and send a child to her room for a couple of hours, makes a marked impression, and opens the door for sorrow and forgiveness, and the rest of the day may then be spent cheerfully. But to look calmly sad, to give a grave lecture, and say that the child must go to bed only half an hour before her usual time, makes the whole day a penance. The sense of being, as it were, under a cloud, deadens the wish to do better, and that must be a singularly good child who does not feel that it is

scarcely worth while to try and improve, when punishment must follow at any rate.

With children and their parents, as with the parents and their God, without the sense of forgiveness there will be no real desire of amendment; and it is only by slow degrees and under certain circumstances (which may hereafter be considered) that any of us learn to dissociate the ideas of punishment and anger.

But as the child's mind opens, and reason develops, it will become necessary not only to exact and enforce obedience, but to show the grounds upon which the duty rests; and here we must look beyond the natural authority which God has delegated to parents, and inquire what is the origin of all law; for we may be sure that if we educate upon any principle short of the highest, if we base our actions upon any truth which is not fundamental, we shall in the end find that we have been reasoning upon a fallacy, and that error in practice is the result.

That the authority delegated to parents is not the original basis of a child's duty of obedience, is at once evident from the fact that there may be cases in which to disobey a parent may be right. A wicked father, we will suppose, commands his child to steal. The child's duty is to refuse. But if the parent's commands were fundamentally binding, refusal could, under no circumstances, be permissible.

There must, then, be something higher than a parent's authority—a law upon which that law rests; and if the mother, whilst enforcing obedience, desires also to enforce principle, she must continually lead the child's mind beyond herself, and show that her commands are imperative because derived from the obligation of a superior law. Or, in other words, that *Law*, not *Will*, is the fundamental principle of moral government. This assertion carries us back very far, even to a point at which human reason fails—the mystery of the Being and Acts of the Most High.

"They err," says Hooker, "who think that of the Will of

God to do this or that, there is no reason besides His Will. Many times no reason known to us; but that there is no reason thereof I judge it most unreasonable to imagine, inasmuch as He worketh all things, not only according to His own Will, but *the counsel of His own Will.* And whatsoever is done with counsel or wise resolution, hath of necessity some reason why it should be done, albeit that reason be to us in some things so secret, that it forceth the wit of man to stand, as the blessed Apostle himself doth, amazed thereat: '*O the depth of the riches both of the Wisdom and Knowledge of God! how unsearchable are His Judgments, and His Ways past finding out.*' That Law eternal, which God Himself hath made to Himself, and thereby worketh all things whereof He is the Cause and Author, ... how should either men or angels be able perfectly to behold? . . . . Nor is the freedom of the Will of God any whit abated, let, or hindered by means of this; because the imposition of this Law upon Himself is His own free and voluntary act."[1]

In this great mystery, the eternal obligation of Law, is doubtless to be found the primary necessity for the punishment of sin, so that, as it would seem, even the mercy of an Infinite God could not pardon without an atonement.

And as the Almighty teaches us this truth by the doctrines of revelation, so it is the one constant lesson conveyed to us by His working in nature. The first thing a child learns by his own experience is, that when he transgresses certain physical laws he inevitably incurs punishment. If he puts his hand too near the fire, he is scorched; if he runs out into the rain, he is wet; if he runs carelessly, he falls down. These varied forms of suffering are the fixed result of the transgression of certain physical laws.[2]

And so, as the child grows up, and its mind opens to the perception of the moral government of God, the same lesson is enforced by the observation of what are called the natural re-

[1] Eccles. Pol., Book I. [2] Butler's Analogy, Part I. chap. ii.

sults of human actions. Intemperance, it is seen, brings disease; carelessness in worldly affairs entails ruin; falsehood and dishonesty are followed by distrust and civil punishment. The consequences of the actions here mentioned may not be universal, or in all cases inevitable, but the general law is sufficiently marked for the instruction of mankind; and no one who suffers from the natural result of his own misconduct is allowed to impugn the justice of Providence. For neither the child nor the adult will usually regard the consequences of evil conduct as punishments inflicted by the direct Will of God; though unquestionably they are so, since it is God who made the law, and affixed the penalty. The lesson which men chiefly learn from such experiences is that Law, whether physical or moral, is in itself sacred, and may not be transgressed with impunity.

One great distinction between moral and physical law must, however, be remarked. Moral law is absolutely one with the Will of God, and therefore is in its nature immutable. Physical law is only the result of that Will, and therefore may be altered whenever the Almighty, in His infinite Wisdom, shall think fit to do so. Truth, justice, benevolence, must always be included in the moral law of the universe, because they belong to the Nature of the Deity; but it is quite possible to conceive a state in which the physical laws of nature shall be so changed, as that fire may fail to burn, and water to drown.

As regards our present condition, however, the effect of both moral and physical law is the same, and we find, therefore, that the idea of abstract law meets us at every turn. We feel it before we recognize it. We act upon it without in the least understanding what it is which compels us to do so. For instance, the majority of men in a state will often for years quietly submit to laws manifestly injurious and unjust. What induces them to do so? It is not physical force; for if all who suffered from the laws would rise against them, no power could withstand their efforts. Neither is it subjection to the will of any one man, for these laws are the work of many men, the

production of centuries; and a people who will rise against any single hard law, enacted by the will of some individual man, will submit almost uncomplainingly to a great many hard laws received as an heirloom, and in which there is not apparently the working of any present will. The principle which keeps them in subjection is simply that of obedience to abstract law; the strongest, the most enduring of all principles, because, whatever may be the form under which it is exhibited, it is essentially one with the Will of God.

And we shall find by experience that the mind of the youngest child, whose reason is beginning to exercise itself, can be influenced by this truth, because the mind, like the body, is in a child as perfect in kind as it is in a full-grown man; and all the appeals which can naturally and rightly be made to the highest principles in man, may, in a lesser degree, and under a different form, be made to the highest principles in a child.

"I should like to let you have this pleasure, but I said that, if you were naughty, you should not have it, and therefore you cannot."

That is a very common simple speech; hundreds of mothers, who are trying to bring up their children well, may have uttered it. But very few, probably, have ever looked into the deep, the wonderfully deep principle involved in it.

"I should like to do it;" there is the will. "I said that if you were naughty you should not have it;" there is the law: "therefore you cannot;" there is the submission to law: and Law as opposed to Will. And when we look into the government of God, as made known to us in revelation, may we not, without irreverence, say that something of the same kind is discoverable?

"O Jerusalem, Jerusalem, thou that killest the prophets, and stonest them which are sent unto thee, how often would I have gathered thy children together, even as a hen gathereth her chickens under her wings, and ye would not! Behold, your house is left unto you desolate." [1]

[1] St. Matt. xxiii. 37, 38.

Who shall say that the Lord of all *could* not have saved Jerusalem if He had so willed? Who shall say that a love so unutterably tender *could* not have influenced that Will in favour of the chosen city? But there was something beyond love, beyond will—something which men will hereafter be compelled to acknowledge, it may be to their everlasting woe—the supremacy of Law. "Hath he said, and shall he not do it? or hath he spoken, and shall he not make it good?" [1]

It is only when the sacred obligation of abstract law is fully recognized, that any person can be safely entrusted with the task of putting that law into practice. The mother who governs her child upon Will has as many rules for its guidance as there are circumstances which call for her interference. She has no fear of making a law, because she has no fear of breaking it. She threatens and promises at random, because she knows that it is at her own option to break or to keep her word. And the result is, naturally, the wreck of all firm principle. The thought of punishment is without terror; the prospect of reward is without allurement. With no certainty before it, the moral nature of the child rests upon shifting sand, and is drifted in every direction, according to the accidental gusts of passion or impulse. The sternest discipline of unbending severity, so long as it is just, is better than such an education. Yet the mother who is most strict in adherence to her own laws will be the least likely to be severe in her legislation. Her threatenings will be few, as her promises will be cautious, for her law is made in order that it may be kept, therefore she will be careful in framing it.

The effect of the assertion of Law upon the mind of a child is very remarkable. It is as if the mother appealed to a principle to the sanctity of which its little heart at once responded. It will beg and implore, and even be pettish and disrespectful, so long as the refusal is based upon Will; but the very moment the idea of Law is suggested, it sinks in-

[1] Numb. xxiii. 19.

stinctively into acquiescence. And the mother gains the respect of her child by the fact of this subjection of her own will, even though the law, to which she bends, may be one which she herself has made. There is nothing nobler, indeed, than the submission to abstract law, of one who has it in his power to command; for such submission is the most dignified form of obedience. He who knows not how to obey Law, knows not, indeed, how to govern; and for this reason, that such obedience is but another form of government, even that of self by self, and before we can hope to rule others wisely, we must be able to rule ourselves.

CHAPTER V.

OBEDIENCE (*continued*).

But it may be asked, How is this principle of obedience to Law as distinct from obedience to Will to be inculcated, in the course of that every-day training by which a child's mind is formed? The question may be answered by searching more deeply into the moral government of God, as displayed in his dealings with his creatures.

There are two objects which are the aim of wise government: the discouragement of vice, and the encouragement of virtue. The first of these objects is to be attained by punishment, the latter by reward. God punishes the drunkard by disgrace and illness; He rewards the industrious man by respect and prosperity.

But the failure in obtaining reward is also a punishment; and it follows, therefore, that if a man will not be industrious, he will be punished as surely as the drunkard, only it will be negatively instead of positively.

Now, in these cases, it will be seen that both punishments and rewards are, what are called, natural; that is, they are stated, fixed, or settled.[1] No man is, or ought to be, angry with Providence, when, having omitted to sow his seed, he fails to reap the harvest. The mind aquiesces in a result which is known beforehand; and, even if a law be considered in itself severe, yet the carrying it out is recognized as just.

[1] Butler's Analogy, Part I. chap. i.

This truth is easy of application with regard to education, and it may be acted upon early and successfully.

A child, we will suppose, has certain lessons to learn; if repeated correctly, some fixed though trifling reward is to be obtained. It may be merely a ticket, or a good mark. But when the lesson is learnt imperfectly, the reward is lost. A very slight punishment it is; so slight, indeed, that the child scarcely recognizes that it is punishment; yet it is felt, and the result is greater attention for the future. In this instance, as in that of the husbandman, there is no sense of resentment; the fact that the penalty was natural or fixed takes from it the sting. Child and man, alike, are unconsciously influenced by a sense of the eternal obligation of abstract law.

And natural punishments have this great advantage, that they not only remove any suspicion of personal anger on the part of the inflictor, but they also open the door for mercy and consideration; so that the actual contriver of the punishment comes to be looked upon as its benevolent mitigator. We see this also in nature. An improvident man loses the blessings he might have secured, and brings himself into difficulties. They are the natural punishment of his improvidence, and he acknowledges this. But God sends him friends who assist him, and his heart is touched with gratitude, and he is brought to own the benevolence of the very Being who, in fact, inflicted the suffering.

So a child, by forgetfulness, naturally loses some settled reward; but upon consideration of the circumstances, the mother interposes, and, though she will not bestow the reward which has been lost, she gives something which makes the disappointment less, and the child is full of love and thankfulness. Or, again, even where positive punishment is inflicted, the fact of making it natural takes away half its sting. Suppose two children to be equally untidy in their habits: on a certain occasion one is punished in some unexpected mode, according to its mother's will, and feels herself injured and resentful; the other accepts, as a natural consequence, a fixed amount of for-

feit, and is vexed with herself, but never considers for an instant that she is treated hardly. Such natural laws may, indeed, be foolishly multiplied or misapplied; but whatever blunders we may make, either in forming or in carrying them out, will, we may be assured, be infinitely less prejudicial to the moral character of our children, than those which result from punishments or rewards unwisely given as occasion arises. It may even be said that an education carried on with perfect temper, perfect judgment, yet without general fixed rules, will be less efficacious in forming the character for life, than one greatly inferior to it in these respects, but in which definite rules are laid down and fixed, and natural punishments follow as the consequence of their infraction.

The one is the government of Will—wise and good indeed, but nevertheless only Will. The other is the government of Law, and when the impression of the authority of Will is removed from the mind, the impression of the authority of Law will remain.

But the pressure of natural laws is most felt when the will begins to be exercised. Very little children have not the power or opportunity of running counter to either physical or moral laws, except in a slight degree. They are for the most part moved by the will of others. The establishment of domestic natural laws belongs, therefore, more to the schoolroom than to the nursery. Natural laws also are intended for the guidance of daily conduct, to keep us right in lesser matters. They do not provide for greater contingencies. A man who commits a great crime is not punished by natural, but civil law; although civil law, when strictly examined, will be found to be in one sense natural also[1]—that is, the fact of punishment by a civil tribunal is natural, though the precise extent of the punishment is not. In like manner, a child committing some great offence, or exhibiting some remarkable goodness, must be punished or rewarded in some extra degree. But, in every case, the object of a wise government will be the same,

[1] Butler's Analogy, Part I. chap. ii.

to stamp upon the mind the idea of a moral law apart from the will of the ruler, and to which all must alike submit.

It is this idea which, when carried out in all the varied ramifications of human obligation, produces at last the principle of duty; and the superiority of the obedience based upon this recognition, over that which rests merely upon necessity, or even affection, is obvious to all.

But, it will perhaps be said, by thus showing the obligation of abstract law, are we not in danger of encouraging a formal obedience, which will in the end produce a spirit of self-righteousness? Is not the obedience of a Christian based upon love rather than upon law?

In answer to this, it must be remembered that what we are discussing here is only the right theory of education, so far as it is placed in our own power. We can make a child obedient to law. We cannot fill its little heart with love to God. But if we do our part, trusting to our Master's aid, and praying to Him for guidance, we may be quite sure that God will do His.

And let it be granted—though only for the sake of argument—that a child brought up in strict obedience to law, may, when he grows up to man's estate, be in danger of regarding that obedience with complacency, instead of humbling himself before God for his unworthiness; is therefore obedience to law a sin? Because a man may pride himself upon his justice, his truth, and integrity, are justice, truth, and integrity evil? "Shall we continue in sin, that grace may abound? God forbid!" [1]

But the true statement of the case is very different. The man who piques himself upon his obedience to the moral law, does so simply because he does not know what that law involves. We are accustomed to speak of the moral law as limited to the obvious commands of the decalogue; or, at least, as including only those more extended applications of them which our Blessed Lord has given us in his Sermon on

[1] Romans vi. 1, 2.

the Mount. But, as Bishop Butler has plainly shown, the revelation of Himself which God has been pleased to make in Christianity, extends the moral law much beyond this. "The office of our Lord being made known, and the relation He stands in to us, the obligation of religious regards to Him is plainly moral, as much as charity to mankind is; since this obligation arises before external command, immediately out of that His office and relation itself."[1] The same may be said of the office of the Holy Spirit, and of all the duties which necessarily arise from the truths made known to us by revelation. They are all moral, all based upon eternal, immutable law; all therefore to be obeyed.

And let any one, be he child or man, strive heartily to obey that law, and where will be his self-complacency? Is not the truest saint most often the deepest penitent, because in his earnest striving to fulfil the law, he awakens to the consciousness of the frequency of his transgressions?

The principle of obedience to law, as law, is undoubtedly the only sure basis of moral goodness. But we do not find this truth practically admitted. What are the openly acknowledged wishes of the generality of parents—mothers especially? One longs that her little one may fully return her affection. Another exults in the thought that her child will be absolutely dependent upon her for happiness. A third trusts that, in consequence of a wise system of education, her children and herself may always be one in feeling, principle, and opinion. But how few look upon the immortal beings to whom they have given birth as endued with independent wills, destined to walk in independent paths, and therefore requiring, above all things, the guidance not of a mother's will, or a father's law, but of those eternal principles of right, which are adapted to every variety of character, and every conjunction of circumstances.

And yet, after all which can be said in favour of a character thus based upon submission to abstract law, or in other

[1] Butler's Analogy, Part II. chap. i.

words to duty, it must be owned that it is not very attractive to the imagination. There are even persons who honestly own that they dislike the idea of duty; who would prefer to see a child acting upon impulse; who put comparatively little value upon a kind action, when it is prompted by a sense of right, instead of a sudden emotion. A hasty consideration of such asserted preferences would induce a calm-minded person to turn from them as unreasoning folly. But it may be questioned whether they strictly deserve the name. Duty—such as these persons picture it to themselves—is a very cold, dry, almost a repulsive principle. It never raised any human being to the elevation of a saint, and it would in vain knock for admittance at the gates of Heaven. And why? Because it is not duty, but only a portion of it. Men take a part for the whole, and marvel because the distorted image they have formed does not attract their reverence. God, indeed, tells us to follow duty, and we suppose that we obey Him, when we strictly honour our parents, control our tempers, are strictly pure, rigidly honest, true in word and deed. But does not God also tell us to trust our salvation to our Redeemer—to give our hearts to Him? Does He not call upon us to be tender, sympathizing, repentant, and humble? Is the proud man obedient to God's law merely because he never infringes the law of external morality? Is the selfish man ruled by duty, because he walks uprightly in the sight of his fellow-men, and so never falls into open sin? Duty is a very large word, infinitely larger than our thoughts can imagine, for it is coextensive with the perfections of the Almighty. "Thy commandment," says the Psalmist, "is exceeding broad." Once only has mankind been permitted to see its full exemplification. Who will dare to say that the character of the Saviour of the world would have been more winning to our affections, if He had been less obedient, less devoted to duty?

It is, indeed, a cruel mistake we make, when we allow anything short of abstract duty, in its perfection, which is therefore duty to God, to be the ground of our children's

moral actions. Their affection for ourselves may apparently produce equally good results for a time ; but there will surely come a point at which, like the efforts of the Egyptian magicians, the power of love's sorcery will fail. Time and change of circumstances tell sadly even upon the tenderest of earthly feelings ; and though it be granted, as well it may be, that the beginnings of duty in the mind of a child are generally cold, and devoid of that direct recognition of God which converts moral into religious principle, yet it is a great unkindness to allow the early, impressible days of childhood to pass, without the formation of those habits of obedience to law which, when the heart is more awakened, will make the ways of religion "pleasantness, and all her paths peace." The one continually recurring lamentation of those who in later years have turned from sin to godliness, is the weakness of their resolution. Now the very strength, the bone and sinew of resolution, is obedience to abstract law—to law, even though self-imposed. The child who is made to do what he has said he will do, simply because he has said it, who is obliged to keep his promise because he made it, who is taught that he is bound by an engagement because it is an engagement, may have but little thought of religion, and no conscious love to God. But when at length he does open his eyes to the reality of his position in this world, when he does seek to live for Heaven and Eternity, those habits of submission to abstract right and obligation will be of more worth to him than all the excitement of feeling, however intense, because they will, through God's grace, enable him to keep his resolutions. They are the means, the appointed channels, through which a blessing is bestowed upon his efforts to do God service.

And—which is particularly to be remarked—they are absolutely independent of intellectual power. Strength of mind, consistency, firmness of purpose, are to be found in the uneducated, the otherwise weak and even deficient in intellect. The little child may and often will possess them, when the man whom nations admire is wanting in them. "How can I do

this great wickedness, and sin against God?"[1] *Can*, meaning not impossibility as regards the will, for which, in the case of temptation, there is no *can ;* but the moral impossibility of breaking a law.

This is the great safeguard for all; but if we wish it to be effectual, it must be acquired early. Let the seed-time of childhood pass, and it may never be ours. And what life is without it—how wasted, shattered, it may be utterly ruined and degraded—we may each ask ourselves, if not from the sorrowful testimony of our own conscience, yet from the memory of some wrecked life, which will surely recur to us, when we tell to ourselves the tale of the spoilt children of impulse, whose course we have watched from their cradle to their sad, perhaps even dishonoured, grave.

[1] Gen. xxxix. 9.

CHAPTER VI.

JUSTICE.

OBEDIENCE, based upon the recognition of abstract law, is, we have seen, the primary object of all sound education. But abstract law must, of necessity, be presented to the mind in various forms, in order that it may be rightly appreciated. So, light must be divided into the prismatic rays before we can avail ourselves of it for the purpose of life; and the first form under which the idea of abstract law must be brought before a child, so as to be available for its sound education, is that of justice.

That this principle lies at the foundation of all wisdom and goodness will at once be seen, if we consider that justice is but another word for practical truth. Men are unjust in their dealings, because in their actions they pretend to be what they are not, or to do what they do not do. They are unjust in their judgments, because those judgments are founded upon untruths. Justice, like law (from which indeed it is inseparable), appeals instantly and directly to the highest principles of man's being; and the sense of justice will always be found peculiarly keen in a child, because the nature made in the Image of God, though now distorted and degraded, has not, at that early age, been defaced by sophistry and self-interest.

In mature age, we become so accustomed to meet with injustice, and, if we are at all sincere with our own hearts, are so conscious of being guilty of it ourselves, that we learn to look upon it almost as a necessity. We instinctively resign

ourselves to it for the present, looking forward to the day when all shall finally be set right. And the very fact of the tenacity with which we cling to the prospect of this final restitution of all things to their true position, shows how entirely the sense of justice is a part of the original constitution of man's nature.

And thus we find that God's Justice was the first great attribute of His Being revealed to the Jewish nation in their condition of childhood. "The Lord your God is God of gods, and Lord of lords, a great God, a mighty, and a terrible, which regardeth not persons, nor taketh reward."[1] And as the sacredness of abstract law was declared when it was made known that "the soul which sinned should die," so the distinction between wilful sins and sins of negligence was the just modification of that law when applied to a race burdened with infirmity.

The same principle of strict justice was exhibited in a practical form in the very commencement of the education of the Jewish people. The first act of Moses, when he began his direct government of the Israelites, was to appoint judges, who were to hear and decide all cases of dispute, "able men, such as fear God, men of truth, hating covetousness."[2] None might take a gift from the rich, "for the gift blindeth the wise, and perverteth the words of the righteous;"[3] but neither might any "countenance a poor man in his cause."[4]

It was by judges that the Jews were ruled when owning no sovereign but the Almighty. And in after years, when the elders of Israel gathered themselves together, and demanded that Samuel should make them a king, their plea was that his sons walked not in their father's ways; that "they turned aside after lucre, and took bribes, and perverted judgment."[5]

So, again, the faithless request being granted, and Samuel about publicly to withdraw from his office, he ended his indignant, yet earnest, expostulation, with the question, "Whom

[1] Deut. x. 17. [2] Exod. xviii. 21. [3] Exod. xxiii. 8. [4] Exod. xxiii. 3. [5] 1 Sam. viii. 3.

have I defrauded ? whom have I oppressed? or of whose hand have I received any bribe to blind mine eyes therewith?"[1]

And they said, "Thou hast not defrauded us, nor oppressed us, neither hast thou taken aught of any man's hand."[2]

It would be useless to multiply illustrations. The constantly repeated charge of the prophets against the kings and priests of Israel and Judah, was that they "abhorred judgment, and perverted all equity."[3] And when those who would fain have purchased pardon by penance or sacrifice, inquired wherewith they should "come before the Lord, and bow" themselves "before the high God,"[4] they were answered by the solemn warning, "He hath showed thee, O man, what is good; and what doth the Lord require of thee, but to do justly, and to love mercy, and to walk humbly with thy God?"[5]

Justice first, mercy and humility afterwards; because without justice, mercy and humility must be unreal.

And does not the history of God's dealings with the Jews teach us the same lesson? His favoured servants, in so far as they sinned, met with no partial treatment. Jacob deceived his father, and was, in his turn, deceived by Laban. Moses followed the example of the Israelites, and—though but in one instance—showed impatience and faithlessness, and, like them, he died on "this side Jordan," and never entered upon the land of promise. David was the man after God's own heart—the man who, above all other men, loved his Maker with a fervour of devotion which seems scarcely to belong to human imperfection; but he committed a complicated, deadly sin, and though he repented, and was pardoned, yet from that hour the sword never departed from his house.

And so also, in like manner, as we may all have had occasion to observe, there are those whom God specially loves, whose characters are most in accordance with His own attributes; but the world moves on its appointed course, and its natural laws are not stayed in order to save them from suffer-

[1] 1 Sam. xii. 3. [2] 1 Sam. xii. 4. [3] Micah iii. 9.
[4] Micah vi. 6. [5] Micah vi. 8.

ing. The good man who acts unwisely is punished. The bad man who acts prudently reaps in this life his reward.[1]

Thus must it be with us in our government of our children, with respect to the rules which we lay down for them; for as obedience is the foundation of all virtue in the child, so justice is the foundation of all good government on the part of the parent. The history of our lives will probably be a convincing testimony, if any were required, to the truth of this assertion. Very few, probably, are they who, in looking back upon the days of their childhood, do not feel that in some instances they were treated unjustly. If they examine still more closely, they will, in all probability, find that this memory is a rankling one; that they cannot crush it, though they may turn aside from it. It will from time to time start up, chilling some thought of love, some fond recollection of early happiness. It calls, as it were, for expiation; it cannot be softened by the soothing influence of time; it can scarcely even be subdued by the teaching of charity. Such a memory is a very valuable lesson. It is better than any sermon. Parents educate their children unwisely, because they forget that they have ever been children themselves. They read books upon education, searching for principles and suggestions; and they do not see that God has written upon their own hearts truths to which the wisdom of philosophers is folly. The experience of a child is a guide for the instruction of a child. What we felt, and thought, and suffered, our children will feel, and think, and suffer like us; and if we bear about with us the memory of injustice, and feel that it has a voice, even now, crying from the depths of the past, let us, above all things, as we value our

[1] The writer has no wish to enter upon the very difficult and intricate inquiries connected with the perfection of God's moral government, seen imperfectly, as it must be, in this world. All that is here asserted is—that which every one who considers the question carefully must acknowledge—that certain rewards and certain punishments are in this world annexed to certain courses of conduct, and that whatever may be in other respects a man's virtues or vices, he is in those special instances rewarded or punished according to the natural laws which are alike for all.

children's love, their reverence, and their obedience, guard against injustice in ourselves.

Such an one is the mother's pet, and therefore, in her eyes, always in the right! It may be the eldest—the first awakener of her unextinguishable love; or the youngest—the plaything, who is indulged because it is the youngest; or the only boy, who is the mother's pride, because he is to be his father's representative. Whichever it may be, the result is the same. The balance of the family is upset by a sense of injustice, and the wisdom exhibited in other respects in the government of the children will fail to insure their goodness and their happiness.

And yet, it may be said, preferences must exist. One child is very tractable, another very much the reverse; it is impossible to feel alike to both. Perfectly true; but there is no injustice in preferring obedience to disobedience, good temper to bad. An unjust preference is founded upon some qualification apart from moral goodness. We are not answerable, indeed, for such a feeling, but we are very greatly answerable for showing it. It may be difficult for a mother to check her natural love, and punish the child in whom she delights, and reward the child who creates only an ordinary affection; but if she does not do so when necessary, she is sowing seeds of discord which will surely bear bitter fruit in Time, if not in Eternity. And even if the preference is justifiable—if it is founded upon moral worth—it will in no way allow with impunity of the slightest injustice. Children are very quick in discerning partiality, and the moment it is perceived they lose their respect and their confidence. We can all sympathize with this feeling; we are all indignant when we meet with prejudice and partiality; and yet strict justice is the very rarest of all qualities. Many things, indeed, go by the name of justice: unsparing strictness, for instance, a stern condemnation of anything which looks like wrong, an unbending adherence to a certain line of conduct. Men pique themselves upon such characteristics. They consider them indications of a firm, strong mind. They forget that God's Justice has reference to

times and circumstances, to opportunities and temptations; and that if our justice is to be like His, it must take all such considerations into account, or it will become injustice. Therefore it is that men are unjust. They are so not willingly, nor consciously, but because they are indolent or impatient, biassed by affection or interest. They decide without inquiry; they speak and act upon impulse. And parents are by no means exempt from these failings. They may have the greatest desire for their children's good, but they are not therefore free from selfishness. It requires time and trouble to investigate every little case brought before them. It perplexes the mind, and troubles the conscience. The mode adopted by the Irish judge who, having heard one side of a question, and being convinced by it, felt it a mere waste of time to listen to the other, suits with the press of occupation or amusement better than a careful search into facts, which may probably lead to the discovery of unpleasant truths.

And there are certain broad statements upon which it is always easy for haste or indolence to fall back when questions are complicated, or demand an inconvenient expenditure of time. A good child is always more likely to be in the right than a bad one; therefore it is supposed that the report of the former is safely to be admitted against the latter. This is an error common to persons who would shrink back, indignant, at the accusation of injustice. Or, if it should be a case of favouritism, the elder child, who is the pet, must necessarily know better than the younger one, who is not so. Or, on the other hand, elder children are always tyrannizing over the younger ones. Let any one of these assertions be firmly rooted in a mother's mind, and the hope of justice is vain, for every question is prejudged. The children know it to be so. They will not appeal to their mother, for they believe it to be useless. But natural instinct leads them to seek for justice amongst themselves. They establish a species of moral Lynch law, and strive to restore the balance of justice by injustice. The favourite is disliked, teased, perhaps persecuted. The

mother's preconviction is strengthened. Still greater partiality is shown, still greater revenge taken, and the result is a breach of family harmony which may last for years.

And all this time the mother is desirous of acting rightly. She even believes that she is doing so. The evidence of facts is before her, and it is in vain to dispute them. Only—she was in fault at the commencement, she began with injustice, and the end is discord.

It is not asserted that a family brought up upon a system of injustice will never turn out well. God uses the faults of parents and teachers as means of discipline for the children; and if only those could be expected to do rightly who are brought up upon right principles, the world would be in a much worse condition even than it is. But if children treated unjustly ever become religious and high-principled, it will be not because of their education, but in spite of it. And in scarcely any case will the parent receive that reward of affectionate respect, which is the only reward really to be valued.

It is a matter for very serious self-examination in all persons who have the care of children, especially all who are conscious of being themselves excitable, changeable, sensitive, carried away by impulse. A poetical temperament, verging upon that of a genius, is peculiarly liable to the aberration of moral principle which leads to injustice. Persons possessed of such a temperament make romances with regard to their children's characters. They idealize them; they never see them in their true colours. They are dazzled by what they think to be beauty, or talent, and upon these supposed gifts they engraft certain virtues, which, in all probability, do not exist at all, or at least only partially; and when called upon to decide some question concerning the children, it is upon this imaginary basis that they rest a decision, which, probably, in nine cases out of ten, will be unjust.

But indolence, impatience, and partiality are not the only sources of injustice. A preoccupied mind, or even the weakness and irritability consequent upon ill-health, will produce

the same results. To be strictly just requires, in fact, a very watchful and continual self-discipline ; and we must all know that to theorize upon a wise system of education for a child is easy, and to practise a similar system of education upon ourselves very difficult. And yet if we do not practise before we begin to theorize—still more, if we do not carry on that practice unremittingly—we may cast our books of instruction into the fire, and scatter our lessons of wisdom to the winds, for they can be of no avail to us. A sincere love of truth, calmness, patience, good sense, and self-control, all are essential to justice. How often are they to be found united in one character? How often do we meet with any person of whom it may be said " he or she is perfectly just"?

To act justly ourselves is, indeed, most difficult, and yet more difficult must it be to enforce the duty upon children. But this consideration must be left till we enter upon the inquiries connected with the necessity of education in truth, which is the foundation and corner-stone of justice.

CHAPTER VII.

LOVE EXHIBITED IN TENDERNESS AND SYMPATHY.

Abstract law, implicit obedience, strict justice! They are very dry-sounding, uninviting names. One can fancy a young mother assenting hastily to what has been said about them, because she does not know how to express her dissent; and then turning away, and secretly rejoicing, in the thought, "It is all very good, very right; it may succeed with some, but it does not suit me. My child shall be brought up upon a principle of love."

And is the young mother wrong? Is not God Love? If we are ever to be like Him, must we not each, in our measure, be now filled with Love? And when Faith shall be no longer needed, and Hope shall have become present joy, will not Love abide for ever?

The mother is right. Her instinct is a true one. If love is not named as the foundation stone of all right influence and guidance, it is because, in a mother's breast, it is presupposed always to exist. There is no need to tell her that she is to love. Nature has taught her the duty, and enabled her to perform it. But there is great need that she should be told how to show her love wisely; and great need, also, that others, who are entrusted with the task of education, and yet have no such maternal instinct to assist them, should be enabled so to regard the children entrusted to them, as to deal with them in the spirit of love, though they may not have the actual feeling of affection.

There is much talk of love in the present day. It is to be feared that a large portion of it is unreal. We see advertisements in the newspapers, which tell us that for twenty, thirty, or forty pounds a year, young people are to receive all the care and tenderness belonging to a home. We hear of the interesting charge which a governess undertakes, when she receives a pupil; and of the anxious solicitude of those who are appointed to stand in the place of parents. It is all very well. It may be very true. For twenty pounds a year, a child may receive the same amount of care and tenderness which it received at home, for there it will, perhaps, have had neither; a governess may look upon her pupil as an interesting charge; and those who stand in the place of parents may feel anxious solicitude. But experience, unfortunately, shows that a great deal of all this profession of feeling is mere educational cant, and the first thing for us all, if we would perform our task well—whatever it may be—is to look at it truly.

There is a light in which every child, for whom we are in any way responsible, may be regarded, which will at once awaken interest. The immortal soul is preparing for Heaven or for Hell, and we are called upon to assist in the preparation. But that thought is not one which will always be present to us.

There is another light, the light of our own past trials, our sufferings, and our sins, which will touch our hearts to the quick, when we look at the children standing at the entrance of the weary way which we have traversed, and think of their fearlessness, their ignorance, their bright expectations, and the certainty of their disappointment. But the matter-of-fact business of daily life leaves but little leisure for such considerations.

Education is no matter of romance, either for the mother or governess. It is a wearing, fretting, unexciting duty. It is conversant, indeed, with principles high as the heavens, perfect as God's perfection, and deep as the mystery of His Being; but those principles are exhibited under forms in which they

can often scarcely be recognized, even by persons who think most seriously. The irritation caused by forgetfulness, negligence, inattention, petty deceit, little vanities, hasty tempers—these are the trials which present themselves, and which must be met at the moment, without preparation, without reflection. Where is the romance of love which will withstand them? Where is the governess, or even the mother, who can, in such case, trust to her affection as her guide?

And yet without affection, law is powerless, justice has no lasting influence. What is to be done?

First, above everything, make no pretence. What we do not feel, let us not profess to show. If we have not the feeling of affection, flattering words and caresses are but shams; and no one is so quick as a child in discovering a sham, or in resenting it.

But there is a state of mind always connected with affection, and there are words and actions consequent upon affection, which yet may be so far dissociated from it as to be exhibited in perfect sincerity, where the actual feeling of affection, as it is commonly understood, does not, and cannot from circumstances, exist.

We see one who is a stranger to us, suffering; we are not perhaps acutely touched by the sight, yet we speak gently and tenderly—we show sympathy in our manner and words, and we do our utmost to relieve the suffering. No one accuses us of insincerity in this, though probably we could not have been more kind if the sufferer had been the dearest friend we possessed. The only distinction is, that in the one case tenderness and sympathy are the result of a mind trained to consider the needs of others, whilst in the other they would have been spontaneous.

And it is this phase of affection—this exhibition of tenderness and sympathy based upon principles as distinct from impulse—which will be found especially requisite if we would make the task of education easy and pleasant. It is the key by which to unlock the closed doors of the stubborn heart.

If we would know how to apply it wisely, we may once more look to the teaching of the Bible.

The first thing which strikes us in connection with the subject, is the different relationship in which God is exhibited to His creatures in the Jewish and in the Christian dispensation. To the Jews He was at first the great Lord of all, the Eternal Jehovah, observant of their misery, listening to their cry, and interposing to rescue them from suffering.

God spake unto Moses, and said unto him, "I have also heard the groaning of the children of Israel, whom the Egyptians keep in bondage; and I have remembered my covenant. Wherefore, say unto the children of Israel, I am the Lord, and I will bring you out from under the burdens of the Egyptians, and I will rid you out of their bondage, and I will redeem you with a stretched-out arm, and with great judgments." [1]

The power of God to protect and to save was the first lesson which the Jews had to learn. It was taught them by miracles, for miracles were the exhibitions of Omnipotence; and it was not until actual experience had convinced the Jews —if anything could convince them—that personal love and tenderness were mixed up with this Providential care, that Moses could make a still closer appeal to their feelings, and say, "Do ye thus requite the Lord, O foolish people and unwise? Is not He thy Father that hath bought thee? Hath He not made thee, and established thee? Of the Rock that begat thee thou art unmindful, and hast forgotten God that formed thee. And when the Lord saw it, He abhorred them, because of the provoking of His sons, and of His daughters. And He said, I will hide My face from them, I will see what their end shall be; for they are a very froward generation, children in whom is no faith." [2]

The title of Father thus claimed by Moses for the Sovereign Lord of all, is but seldom repeated in the Old Testament. David indeed says, "Like as a father pitieth his children, so

[1] Exod. vi. 5, 6. [2] Deut. xxxii. 6, 18, 19, 20.

the Lord pitieth them that fear Him."[1] And by the mouth of the prophet Jeremiah, the Almighty declares, "I am a Father to Israel, and Ephraim is my first-born."[2] And again, as in the prophecy of Malachi, "If then I be a Father, where is Mine honour?"[3] But the spirit of the Old Testament, it will scarcely be disputed, is that of the government of a just, and watchful, and loving Lord; apart from His people, and guiding them by His unerring wisdom, rather than by His personal sympathy.

Under the Gospel dispensation, the relationship between God and His people is instantly and marvellously altered. "My Father and your Father—my God and your God!" Who has ever heard these words, and pondered upon them, without a thrill of wondering love, which, could it but continue, would make every labour of obedience light, every pang of suffering easy to be borne? When He who was one with the Father became one also with us; when He "bore our grief and carried our sorrow," and was made "like unto us in all things," sin only excepted, our relationship to God became a new relation. "For ye have not received the spirit of bondage again to fear; but ye have received the Spirit of adoption, whereby we cry, Abba, Father."[4]

The duties which were difficult to the Jew became easy to the Christian. The obedience which required threatening, and warning, quick punishment, and present reward under the Old Testament, was the natural, almost involuntary impulse of the follower of Christ under the New.

Why, then, were not the Jews treated as the Christians? Why did not God vouchsafe to dwell visibly among them—to be one with them—to give them evidence of His personal sympathy and to win their obedience by the love of the human, rather than the awe inspired by the Divine Nature?

There must be an answer to that question, hidden amongst the unfathomable mysteries connected with God's scheme for

[1] Psalm ciii. 13. [2] Jer. xxxi. 9. [3] Mal. i. 6.
[4] Rom. viii. 15.

man's salvation, and especially with the fact that the time for His full revelation of Himself in "the Man Christ Jesus" was not yet fully come. Into this it would be presumptuous irreverence to inquire. But there is another answer lying on the surface of thought, which will be sufficient for the subject now under consideration. The Jews were a nation of children; and the first impression which it is necessary to imprint upon a child's mind, if we would permanently influence it for good, is that which is awe, when directed to God—reverence, when directed to man.

This is not in accordance with the theories of the present day. We have cast off our old notions of respect for age, authority, position. We believe that if such feelings are to be entertained at all, they must be the result of love, not its foundation. But the Bible and reason would seem to teach us otherwise. There can be no doubt that in dealing with the Jews, God first impressed them with the sense of His sovereignty, and His power; and then exhibited to them His tenderness, under the form of watchful care for their happiness. Even as Moses reminded them, "Thou shalt remember all the way which the Lord thy God led thee these forty years in the wilderness. Thy raiment waxed not old upon thee, neither did thy foot swell, these forty years. Beware that thou forget not the Lord thy God, who led thee through that great and terrible wilderness, wherein were fiery serpents, and scorpions, and drought, where there was no water; who brought thee forth water out of the rock of flint; who fed thee in the wilderness with manna, which thy fathers knew not, that He might humble thee, and that He might prove thee, to do thee good at thy latter end." [1]

It is true, no doubt, that in some peculiar instances a closer, more human sympathy, if the expression may be allowed, is observable. Moses, Samuel, and especially David, approached their Maker with a freedom of feeling which belongs almost to the Christian dispensation; but they were taken out of the

[1] Deut. viii. 2, 4, 11, 15, 16.

Jewish people—exalted above them. They were not in the condition of childhood, and, therefore, did not require its discipline. Their minds had reached that more advanced state in which tenderness is insufficient to satisfy the cravings of affection, but when the desire for personal sympathy is awakened, and the fulness of devotion is excited only as this desire is satisfied.

And does not reason teach us a somewhat similar lesson? A child is brought into the world perfectly helpless, and this helplessness lasts much longer than that of any of the animal creation. Its first experience connected with its fellow-creatures is that of absolute power. It lies in its nurse's arms, and whatever may be its feeble will, it is useless to exert it. Upon this follows the experience of watchful care; but it is a care exerted only for its physical wants, for as yet the child has no mental needs, and neither will it, as a general rule, have any which involve suffering, and demand aid, for several years. There may be precocious children of six or seven years of age, who begin to perplex themselves with all the difficulties belonging to sixteen or seventeen; but they are exceptions, and it is of the generality we would now speak. Young children do, indeed, think, that is, they ask puzzling questions, but not such as would show that their little minds are disturbed beyond the moment. Their griefs, like their joys, are either physical or imaginative. They have no real mental trials, and therefore sympathy, in the strict sense of the word, as implying mutual mental and moral comprehension, is not required by them.

But tenderness they do require, and that very greatly, for they are timid and nervous, and shrink from those who deal roughly with them; and so we find that gentle words and loving caresses are the teachings of nature—the instinctive impulse of a mother's affection. Yet this tenderness is not in the least incompatible with absolute authority on the one side, and a sense of reverence on the other. In fact, when persons try to lessen reverence by placing themselves on a level with their

little ones, instead of winning them, they are actually offending against natural instincts. The children were born powerless, in order that they might trust. They were born ignorant, in order that they might respect. They have as yet no mental development to enable them so to embrace the idea of God's Providence that it may be a support to them. This abstract idea is exhibited to them under a human form. Parents are a little child's Providence, and parents, therefore, are naturally intended to be loved, because they are reverenced—not reverenced because they are loved. This truth is by no means universally recognized.

We may sometimes see persons endeavouring to win their children's affections by making them their playfellows; by allowing them, as they say, to be perfectly free, or, in other words, to take liberties. We find mothers waiting upon their children; making themselves their slaves. We sometimes hear of a young mother's determination to do everything for her child with her own hands; not even to let a nurse dress it, because she desires to make it cling wholly to herself.

All this sounds well, but there is surely a fallacy in it, for the result is not quite in accordance with the intention. We do not find that these children, the engrossing object of their mother's affection when little, remain so entirely devoted to her when their minds enlarge. She has been their playfellow, their slave, their nurse; but she forgot that she was their mother, and the time has arrived when they have given up their infant games, when they are beginning to wait upon themselves, and no longer require a nurse, and of course they no longer require her.

And let a mother strive as she will to win her child's love by this unremitting attention to its little wants, she must, in the end, find herself incapable of contending with the superior attractions of a good nurse.

A baby, for instance, is sent for to the drawing-room. It is frightened by the sight of strangers, and turns instinctively to its nurse. A little child is ill and fretful, and it is soothed by

the home atmosphere of the nursery, and is, therefore, sent there. It feels pain, and immediately complains to the nurse. It is, in short, absolutely free with her, as it is with no one else. And mothers are sometimes distressed at this. They are even jealous of the affection shown the nurse. Nothing can be more absurd. It is the child's physical helplessness appealing to physical support; and so long as the mind is undeveloped, the instinct of helplessness will teach it to turn to the quarter from whence it can most readily obtain support. So, again, the mother attempts to be the child's playfellow, and for a time the little one is satisfied, whilst, exerting its infant tyranny, it compels its mother to amuse it; but give it a companion of its own age, and the mother is set aside. The one is a reality, the other a sham, and the child feels this instinctively.

The mistake in all these cases is that of confounding tenderness with sympathy. The former belongs to infancy, the latter to advanced childhood and youth. We cannot sympathize with a little baby, or even with a child of three or four years of age, for sympathy, in such cases, implies the being able to imagine ourselves in a state of infancy, to feel as the child feels. And even when the mind begins to open, and the moral nature to develop, sympathy must, at first, take the form of condescension, rather than of participation. The child's mind is formed for this; it does not expect more, and if more be attempted, the position assumed will be false, and reverence will be destroyed.

It must not, however, be supposed for a moment, that in saying this it is intended to imply that a mother should not always watch over the physical needs of her children, and when needful provide for them herself. There are very many cases in which the latter duty is a positive, and even a primary necessity. All that is meant is, that it is a mistake to suppose that by so doing a permanent hold upon their affections can be gained. No doubt, if she neglects them physically, she will lose their affections; but the reason will be because such neg-

lect is sinful, and the children unconsciously feel that it is so, and, therefore, cease to respect her.

A mother's real hold upon her children is mental and moral; and when, without attempting to be her child's playfellow, she insists upon respectful obedience; when she exercises her gentle authority so as to assist the awakening conscience; when she satisfies the desire for information by instruction, and charms the vivid imagination by poetry and healthy fiction; above all, when she directs her little one's thoughts to God, and by leading it to pray, opens the door of communication between the visible and the invisible world, and gives an outlet for those yearnings after the Eternal and the Infinite which lie hidden in the breast of a child, even as in that of a full-grown man, she is laying the foundation of a love which will last when physical needs have ceased; and which will be as much stronger and deeper than any affection based upon temporal necessity, as mind is superior to matter—Eternity to time—Immortality to death.

Such love is the love of reverence. But it is of slow growth, or, rather, its growth is for some time imperceptible; therefore, too often it does not satisfy a parent, and the love of companionship is accepted instead. And it demands self-control; and maternal feelings are very difficult of control. It needs sound judgment; and sound jndgment is the result of thought and observation. Much more easy is it to give way to feelings as circumstances arise; to be the child's playfellow one moment, and its impatient instructress the next; to be a slave to the little one's wishes when it happens to suit us, and to reprimand those wishes sharply when slavery happens not to suit us. We see the effect of such education amongst the lower orders. It requires no thought, no self-discipline; it is a kind of moral living from hand to mouth, which suits the poverty of our mental and spiritual endowments. The only misfortune is, that it must ultimately fail in attaining its end. The love produced by such a system will, like the seed sown upon stony ground, spring up quickly; but because there is no deepness

of earth—no foundation of reverence—it can have no root, and when the sun of life is up, and the scorching heat of selfishness and worldly temptations is felt, it will surely wither away.

There would seem to be little need to add the warning, that this enforcement of reverence must always be tempered by tenderness; and yet some persons are not tender. They mean to be very good and kind to their children, but they have naturally a cold, stiff manner, and they cannot overcome it. And there are others who really do not thoroughly interest themselves in their little ones until they have ceased to be little. They think them troublesome, and put them aside in the nursery, supposing that in due time, without any effort of theirs, they will come forth, ready to be operated upon by some theory of perfect education. The first case is a misfortune, but as it is nothing more, its effects will not be so permanently injurious. Children learn to read and understand coldness of manner, when it does not proceed from coldness of heart, and tenderness may be shown in many ways besides caresses or fondling words. But the second case is simply a sin, and it must expect sin's punishment. We may leave children to a nurse to be dressed, because it is probable that through life they must be more or less dependent for their bodily needs upon their inferiors in station; but if we leave them to her to be taught their little lessons, or guided in their prayers, we are abdicating the position of responsibility in which God has placed us; and as we have given up our duty, we must also give up our reward.

As a general rule, however, all persons are tender to babies and very little children; their helplessness awakens the feeling, and it is recognized as true, though there may be nothing like affection mixed with it. But there are two kinds of tenderness: one is the mere expression of natural instinct, the other the result of earnestness of thought and purpose. It is the latter only which can leave a permanent impression. The first association of ideas which a child should have with its mother should be that of being brought by her to think of

God. With that thought there will arise, even in the mind of the little one who can only lisp its prayer, the sense of sin whenever it has been naughty, and the entreaty for forgiveness; and with the assurance of forgiveness from the mother's lips there may be the expression of tenderness, deep, unspeakable—not the mere impulse of the moment, but that tenderness which will win the childish heart, and sink into its very being; and which will be read and understood unconsciously, through words, and looks, and tones, that to the careless observer may seem only to tell of respect and obedience. The child who associates the idea of its mother with its God, will reverence that mother even before it knows what reverence means; and one loving caress will then come with more power from her than a torrent of embraces from one who is but the minister to its little temper and fancies. Only let us have patience. Love is like every other of Heaven's natural gifts: it will bear fruit all the more richly because we give it time and opportunity to take root.

But we come now to sympathy—the second exhibition of the principle as apart from the impulse of love; and so much the more rare and difficult of attainment, as it requires self-restraint instead of self-indulgence; the control of impulse instead of the yielding to it. Tenderness, at least when shown to little children, is to most persons very easy, very pleasant. Sympathy, when exhibited towards youth, is difficult.

The dispensation of Christians is a dispensation of sympathy. The Divine nature was for a time concealed, and Christ took upon Himself really our griefs and cares, and became one with us. This assertion scarcely requires to be exemplified. In the New Testament the fact meets us at every turn. Let us see, but in one or two instances especially, how, by means of this human sympathy, our Redeemer educated His disciples—those who were the nearest and dearest to Him—those who were to be the Teachers of the World, the patterns for all ages.

"Let not your heart be troubled: ye believe in God, believe

also in Me. In My Father's house are many mansions: if it were not so, I would have told you. I go to prepare a place for you. And if I go and prepare a place for you, I will come again, and receive you unto Myself; that where I am, there ye may be also."[1]

"Ye are they which have continued with Me in My temptations. And I appoint unto you a kingdom, as My Father hath appointed unto Me; that ye may eat and drink at My table in My Kingdom, and sit on thrones judging the twelve tribes of Israel."[2]

"Father, I will that they also, whom Thou hast given Me, be with Me where I am; that they may behold My glory, which Thou hast given Me: for Thou lovedst Me before the foundation of the world."[3]

This is the exhibition of the sympathy of comprehension, a sympathy which can understand and appreciate the sorrows and the yearnings of others; and that, it must be remembered, at a time when the horror of coming agony and death might seem to render all such considerations impossible.

"This is my Body which is given for you: this do in remembrance of Me."[4] "My soul is exceeding sorrowful unto death: tarry ye here, and watch. Simon, sleepest thou? Couldest not thou watch one hour? Watch ye, and pray, lest ye enter into temptation. The spirit truly is ready, but the flesh is weak."[5] Here is the claim of reciprocal sympathy, and the exhibition of sinless human feeling which may be soothed by it.

It seems almost wrong to take these few instances as if they were all, whereas every act of our Blessed Lord was the expression of a sympathy personal and individual, as well as compassionate; but they may suffice to illustrate the two particular phases under which this virtue may be shown, and which, in our dealings with each other, and especially with young persons, we sometimes forget to distinguish.

[1] St. John xiv. 1–3. [2] St. Luke xxii. 28–30. [3] St. John xvii. 24.
[4] St. Luke xxii. 19. [5] St. Mark xiv. 34, 37, 38.

The sympathy of comprehension requires that we should throw ourselves into the circumstances and position of other persons, so as to realize in our minds what they are at the moment thinking or feeling. This is more difficult in the case of children and young persons than in those of our own standing. Memory is not so great an assistance to us in this task as we might expect. As life goes on, our early years are mapped out in large divisions, and we can recall general impressions, but details of feelings are lost to us. And even if we are able to remember, we find that it is an effort to do so. When called upon to act we are too busy, too hurried, to pause and consider what would have been the effect of similar conduct on ourselves in former years. A certain tone or manner perhaps irritated us then; or we were hardened instead of softened by reproaches; or we were indignant when particular regulations were made; or we felt ourselves unjustly treated by some special punishments. All this may have been true. But we say to ourselves, "We were young and foolish then; we know better now. It would be impossible to make the fancies of youth a rule for the government of mature years." It may be impossible, or at any rate it might be unwise, but certain it is, that if we cannot recall and do not carefully weigh these young and foolish fancies—if we cannot make allowance for them, and show our sympathy by consideration for them, even while perhaps we reprove and check them—we may enforce obedience upon our children or our pupils, but we shall never gain their love.

And so also with regard to imagination, longings, dreams, aspirations, morbid feelings: if we have forgotten that we ever had such ourselves,—if we can make no allowance for them, —if we avoid any mention of them, or turn from them with coldness or ridicule,—we shall, indeed, succeed in checking them, —that is, we shall shut them up,—and perhaps we shall think that we have crushed them; but they will only be withdrawn from our view to be raised as a barrier between us and the heart which we are seeking to influence, and when we strive to

enter that heart we shall find that its gates are closed against us.

Therefore it is that when the intellectual and moral faculties in children begin to develop themselves, so as to create definite needs, it becomes the duty of those who watch over them, to mark the form which those needs take, and to direct their government accordingly. But this is difficult—much more difficult than to dress and undress a baby, or to play hide and seek with a child of three years old. We are apt to talk as if moral culture was a task of such engrossing interest that no one could be wearied with it. But let us try to act as well as to talk. Let us find ourselves, worn in body and sorrowful in mind, forced to rouse all our energies, and listen to some tale of supposed hardship on the part of a child eleven or twelve years old; let us endeavour to throw ourselves fully into her feelings, to give her advice, to speak gently when our nerves are strung to a pitch of irritability, to be patient when the conversation is occupying the only leisure moments we could seize for rest or recreation. We shall not find our duty so engrossingly delightful as we had been apt to imagine. And neither shall we be so satisfied with our own powers of sympathy as to find any great satisfaction in exercising them. They who are the most earnestly desirous of using this power as a means of moral influence, are the most conscious of failure in effecting their purpose. Their words may be sinking into the heart of the hearer, but to themselves they will often sound dead and ineffective. They may appear to give a full attention to the confession of weakness, or the desire for counsel; yet they may be conscious in themselves of weariness and impatience. They may strive to be gentle and tender, but they will know their own imperfection of manner, and the very fear of repelling will increase what may be natural awkwardness. Above all things, they will desire to be true; and weariness, and deadness, and distraction, will frequently check the feeling of affection, even when it really exists, and make

them feel almost insincere when they attempt to show it. There is nothing delightful in all this.

To sympathize heartily, naturally, and constantly, a person must be thoroughly unselfish, and gifted with sound sense, exercised with tact and self-control. Need we wonder, then, that those who, acting upon the impulses of self-gratification, spoil their children of three years old; acting upon the same impulse, too often chill and repel their young daughter of thirteen? Such cases are very sad to watch—sad both for parents and children as regards the present, and still more sad because the effects of such estrangement are so fatal for the future. If a mother fails to win the confidence of her child, that confidence will be given elsewhere. But confidence cannot exist without sympathy, and sympathy cannot exist without unselfishness. We come back to the same point again and again. The root of bad education is selfish love. People often forget that there is such a thing. Love presupposes, to most minds, a feeling in which self is forgotten in the happiness of the person loved. But it is not so. Love is perhaps more often selfish, and therefore more often self-deceiving, than any other passion of the human heart. Even a mother's love may be selfish; and when it is, selfishness will be its recompense.

It is not said that this reciprocal neglect is right or justifiable. The faults of a mother can never justify the disobedience of a child. If the subject now to be discussed were the duty of children and young persons, a different view might be taken of the whole matter. But what is here said is addressed to parents, guardians, teachers, guides, and instructors of the young generally; and they are earnestly entreated to consider whether absence of sympathy may not be at the root of that lamentable failure in education which too often drives those just entering upon life, and about to encounter its fiercest temptations, to seek aid and counsel from any persons except those whom God has pointed out as their safest and most natural protectors.

It is not difficult to gain the hearts of those who are entrust-

ed to our care. A young mind—the mind of a girl especially—of eleven or twelve, of fifteen, sixteen, even seventeen or eighteen, is very impressible. The affections are strong, and very easily touched. Only show an interest in what interests them, and they will be found quite ready to open their hearts upon subjects of taste and amusement; and when the door of the heart is ever so little ajar, a kind word, or a little thoughtful act, will cause it to open still wider. A tone of sympathy in pain or disappointment will bring out the hidden sorrow; a reproof, given with encouragement instead of anger, will soften the proud spirit, and draw forth the penitent confession; and when once that point is reached the victory is all but won.

No, the difficulty is not with the children, but with ourselves. Young people will not trust us if we are not worthy to be trusted. They will not respect us if we are inconsistent. They will not love us if we are selfish and irritable. They will not listen to us when we bid them give their hearts to God, unless they see that we have first given Him our own.

But it may be said there are natural barriers, differences of temperament; want of self-confidence on the one hand, shyness and reserve on the other.

It is very true. No one can venture to assert that in every case tenderness and sympathy will open the heart which we are longing to gain, and yet the exceptions must be rare, if we take sympathy in its largest sense, as including reciprocity as well as comprehension of feeling.

When our Blessed Redeemer bade His disciples not to be troubled in their heart, but look forward to the "many mansions" in His Father's House, He showed that He understood, and would fain comfort, their secret grief. When He said to His chosen disciples that His soul was "exceeding sorrowful," and bade them "tarry and watch," He confessed His own human, though sinless, infirmity, and sought for consolation in the sense of human sympathy.

And who could resist such an appeal? Even looking to ourselves, are we not touched by the acknowledgment of suffer-

ing or anxiety on the part of one whom nature tells us to reverence and rest upon? And if called upon to confess a weakness, are we not ready at once to accept the counsel and to be influenced by the wishes of one who owns to have felt the power of a like temptation?

There may be great natural reserve, shyness, or pride in the child or the young girl whom we desire to direct aright, and for a long time the citadel of the heart may seem to hold out against us. We may even be unable to offer a comprehensive sympathy, because we are ignorant of what is passing in the mind. But if we can break down our own barriers (a very difficult undertaking with many people, and therefore never attempted), and speak of the difficulties or troubles which we have felt ourselves, the case must be indeed rare in which reserve will hold out against us.

And parents have a special opportunity of practising this reciprocal sympathy. They have the same temporal interests as their children. Their joys, sorrows, hopes, and fears, must be fundamentally derived from the same source. And we may often have remarked as a fact, though we may never have inquired into its cause, that the strongest affection between a mother and a daughter will be found where there has been some great common subject of anxiety. In the case of poverty, or anything approaching to poverty, the joint exertions of the mother and her child will seem to create a tie much stronger than natural affection. Great anxiety for any absent member of the family will produce the same effect. Anything, indeed, which brings the interests of the mother within the comprehension of the child, will have a tendency to produce this strong feeling.

There is a great lesson to be learnt from this. Too many mothers make playthings of their little ones in the nursery, and then send them to the schoolroom to live a life apart under the care of the governess; and after a certain number of years suppose they will come forth musicians, artists, historians, linguists, and, as a matter of course, affectionate and sympathetic

daughters. It is strange they do not see that, as regards information and accomplishments, they have sown the right seed, and therefore may expect an answering harvest; but that, as regards the feeling toward themselves, they have sown no seed at all.

What the child needed was to be made to feel one with her mother. But she has had no opportunity. They have lived separate lives. The mother has had her cares, but she has never even hinted at them, much less given the least idea that her young daughter's sympathy could be a comfort to her. Perhaps, indeed, some of these cares have been such as could not be told, but there are many little ways of keeping up affectionate interest without touching upon sorrows which probably only God can comfort. A very little child may be made to feel that her mother is soothed by having her with her; and may learn to delight in being useful to her. The love thus awakened is much stronger than that which results from any efforts of the mother to amuse or interest. More especially is this the case as years go on, and thought deepens. Whenever it is possible to confide in a young girl, to give her a share, either in sorrow or in joy, something is done toward strengthening affection; for in youth there is an actual craving for this sense of usefulness, this feeling of being helpful to some one.

A mistake is often made here—a grievous and fatal one. Kind, good, unselfish parents, or friends, weary themselves for the young; they sacrifice their own wishes, tastes, pursuits; they exert themselves in illness; they rush from one scene of excitement and amusement to another, and all to make those whom they so dearly love happy. But they cannot succeed. They are chasing a phantom, and it flies from them. The reality lies at their own door. Instead of making themselves useful to the young, if they would only make the young useful to them, they would be able to tell a very different tale. What these bright, gay, apparently thoughtless girls want is not amusement, but the feeling that they are necessary to the

friends they live with, necessary in the sense of usefulness and sympathy, as well as affection.

Doubtless there are difficulties in the way of this mutual understanding in every-day worldly matters between the heads of a family and its young members.

But there are difficulties everywhere. In fleeing from one kind, we do but encounter others. We may not exactly know how to make a young girl useful in the house, but we may begin by talking to her of our own occupations. We may distrust her prudence in important matters, but we may tell her our little perplexities. We may think it in vain to consult her when we cannot reckon her opinion of value, but the very fact of asking what she thinks will win her interest.

And if we do not thus attach her to home by giving her home cares as well as home pursuits, we shall find that these natural cravings for usefulness, the sense of responsibility, and the exercise of the intellect in some practical form, will find a vent elsewhere. If the daughters of a family do not share their mother's interests, they will share those of some other person, and who that person may be is a very grave question, involving unforeseen dangers. Girls' friendships are no light matter, though they are often treated lightly. They are subjects for great caution, and must cause considerable anxiety; yet they need never be feared so long as the daughter feels that the mother's cares are her cares—the mother's sorrows her sorrows.

For this is a tie more enduring than all others, because formed by God. He has moulded us into families, and though the members of those families may differ essentially in character, and be widely separated in the progress of life, yet, at the end, natural sympathy will be found to have survived all adventitious separations. No person is contented to die away from his relations, though he may be surrounded by his friends, and those friends may be far more congenial to his taste. The mother will ultimately cling to her child, and the child to her mother, though, from faults of temper and mistakes in educa-

tion, they may through life have jarred upon each other. But why should there be jars? Why should that holiest tie, which even the Lord of All vouchsafed to recognize, be ever loosened? Only let mothers meet their daughters, especially when advancing to womanhood, with sympathy, which shall be both comprehensive and reciprocal, and there will be little fear of reserve and estrangement.

Upon the subject of reciprocal sympathy, one more observation must, however, be made, which is applicable to all ages from childhood upwards.

To reprove is an essential part of the duty of parents, governors, teachers—all who have the care of others entrusted to them. But if reproof is ever to be effectual with the young, it must be the reproof which is softened by sympathy.

If we admonish, we must do it as those who have themselves felt the difficulty of obedience and self-control. If we advise, it must be as those who have had practical experience of the necessity of advice. And we must not only feel this, but say it.

Is it not a truth? Let us look into our own hearts.

Do we not need God's forbearance, His long-suffering patience? Are our own faults so easily subdued? Are we so pure-minded and simple, so attentive to our Lord's least wishes? Are we so grateful for all He has done for us? Are we so mindful of His warnings? Or rather does not conscience reproach us even by the very blame we cast upon others? Are there not times when we admonish severely, talk of self-discipline, and purity of heart, and sincerity of purpose; and, when the door is closed behind the child whose heart we have been striving to reach, find that we have cause to cast ourselves on our knees before our Maker, praying that He would pardon in us the very faults which we have been reproving, and grant to us, if it may be, even the same amount of simplicity and earnestness which we have the moment before pronounced to be so imperfect?

"We have not an High Priest which cannot be touched

with the feeling of our infirmities; but was in all points tempted like as we are, yet without sin. Let us, therefore, come boldly unto the throne of grace, that we may obtain mercy, and find grace to help in time of need."[1]

That was the character of Him who is educating each one of us for heaven.

May God teach us to be like Him!

[1] Heb. iv. 15, 16.

CHAPTER VIII.

REPROOF.

THE consideration of the necessity of sympathy has already brought us to the subject of reproof, but much more remains to be said upon this point, for it is with regard to reproof that mothers and daughters, governesses and their pupils, are most frequently antagonistic.

And, "very naturally," it will be said; "no one likes to be reproved." This is a broad assertion, the proof of which will perhaps be found upon examination to be somewhat wanting.

No one likes to be reproved! That is, no one likes another mortal, erring like himself, to assume a position of authority to which he has no claim, and to reprimand without having a right to do so. This is the first natural dislike to reproof.

Neither does any one like to hear his offences pointed out and condemned coolly and contemptuously, or with passionate reproaches, or irritation, or fretfulness of manner or tone.

Indifference, contempt, irritability, fretfulness can never be agreeable. But to dislike these things is not to dislike reproof, but the mode in which it is conveyed. As we attain that age so falsely called the age of discretion, and pass beyond it, we do indeed become more impatient of reproof in any form; but that is chiefly because we are unfortunately losing our sense of reverence for our fellow-creatures. Experience is beginning to show us their faults, and pride is whispering that our judgment and actions are as good as theirs, and therefore they have

no right to interfere with us. Women are especially sensitive to anything like reproof, because, except from their husbands, they so very seldom receive it. And when a husband reproves, the wife often considers herself at liberty to retaliate. The discipline which a man receives in his intercourse with the world—the reprimand, for instance, which a junior officer must, if necessary, patiently receive from his superior; a barrister from a judge; or, in fact, any man in a position of inferiority from the person who is placed above him—is for the most part unknown among educated women; and being thus untutored to submission, and consequently to reproof, they are proverbially difficult to govern.

But God did not make them so. A girl's nature is manageable. Her feelings are easily roused, her conscience is quickly worked upon; there is no stubborn hardness of heart which it is impossible to conquer. Instances may be brought forward as exceptions; but they must require greater proof than has ever yet been adduced, before they can be worthy of belief. Touch but the right spring, and we may venture to assert that there is no young girl who may not be brought to confess her faults, and not only to submit to reproof, but to be thankful for it.

But in order to this result, it must not be reproof given for the sake of reproof, because the temper of the reprover is excited or his command neglected. There are occasions, indeed, in which this kind of reproof is instinctive, and therefore necessary and useful; but these are exceptional cases referring to single exceptional acts. As Bishop Taylor says, "He who is angry with a servant's unwariness or inadvertency, or the remissness of a child's spirit and application to his studies, or on any sudden displeasure, is not guilty of prevaricating the sixth commandment, unless besides the object he add an inequality of degree, or unhandsome circumstances, or adjuncts. But since to reprove a sinning brother is, at the best, but an unwelcome and invidious employment, though it may also be understood to be full of charity, yet, therefore, we must not

make it to be hateful by adding reproach, scorn, violent expressions, scurrility, derision, or bitter invectives."

God's government of the Israelites was, indeed, carried on by the means of sudden and stern rebuke; but in their condition of childhood this was requisite, in order to impress upon them some definite idea either of the Almighty's power, or their own duty. And in the government of very little children, we also shall find ourselves compelled to have recourse to a quick tone, and an instantaneous punishment, for this is the only reproof which at that age can be understood. As the fault is one of act rather than of principle, so the reproof must be of like kind. But children verging upon youth require to have ideas recalled rather than impressed upon them, and anything like impatience or irritability in their case will be met by a feeling of resentment. We do indeed find, when examining our Lord's method of dealing with His disciples, that there were times when His censures were severe, sudden, and unsparing; but such censures were always either addressed generally, so that their severity was softened to the individual, or they were spoken to one for the benefit of many; and human nature is so constituted that, in the presence of others, we can better bear a few severe words than a lengthened appeal to our personal feelings. A young girl will submit to a stern rebuke before her companions; but she will writhe and wince, and at length shut herself up in sullenness, under a long lecture.

In illustration of what has been said, we may remark the mode in which our Saviour, as He was journeying to Jerusalem, addressed St. James and St. John, who desired to bring down fire from Heaven to consume the Samaritans. He turned and rebuked them, and said: "Ye know not what manner of spirit ye are of; for the Son of man is not come to destroy men's lives, but to save them." That was a special reproof, but though severe, it was quick, and uttered for the instruction of many.

So, again, under similar circumstances, He could say to

St. Peter in the presence of the disciples, "Get thee behind Me, Satan: for thou savourest not the things that be of God, but those that be of men;" but when, after the Apostle's fall, his heart was to be touched, so that it never should turn aside again, as Bishop Taylor reminds us, "our dearest Lord looked upon him when the sign was given with the crowing of the cock, and chid him into a shower of penitential tears." Yes, that is the true, the safe example of reproof, which shall be received humbly, and be remembered permanently. It must appeal to the affections.

With the mother this may be presumed to be natural and easy. With the governess it must require time, yet not necessarily any length of time. Those who have the care of the young will scarcely be disappointed if they calculate that a few weeks of firmness, justice, tenderness, and sympathy, will have so worked upon the heart as to make it open to kind reproof, and very thankful for helpful advice. It is even strange to watch how quickly a child's feelings may, through God's grace, be so touched as to prepare the way for the reception of the good seed. But it is unwise to attempt grave reproof until the ground is thus softened. To be blind for a time is wise, and very necessary, for if we begin to reprove too soon the heart will only become harder.

And when at length we see that the fitting moment is come, we shall at first often obtain our end more successfully if we use rather indirect means. The only reproof which our Lord gave in words to St. Peter, after the grievous denial, which might have been thought to have lessened His love, was indirect, and couched in the form of a question: "Simon, son of Jonas, lovest thou me?"

And a young girl whose pride will rebel at the direct assertion, from a comparative stranger, "You were guilty of such a fault," will respond very meekly to the question, "Would it not have been better if you had done otherwise?"

This may seem to some persons almost an insincere mode of treatment. It may appear to be ignoring facts, or at least

to be taking too lenient a view of them. The faults of the young are sins, and sin under any shape is *sinful*, and both in the Old Testament and the New is denounced unsparingly.

It is true. Sin is thus denounced; and, God forbid, that in speaking of it to young or old, to others or ourselves, we should ever deal with it differently from the Word of God! But if God hates sin, He loves the sinner. If it were not so, what hope would any one of us have of salvation? The same Saviour who, through the mouth of His Apostle, enumerated the works of the flesh, and has told us plainly that "they which do such things shall not inherit the kingdom of God,"[1] answered the accusation of the Pharisees against the woman taken in adultery, with the words, "Neither do I condemn thee—go and sin no more."

No words can be too strong to express the danger of indulged sin, for there is a voice in the secret heart which echoes their truth, but such warnings must be given at the right time and in the right way. When we have won the heart, we may say what we will of certain faults, and of the importance of conquering these, so long as we express what we really feel. If we only talk, as a matter of course, because we consider it to be a part of our business, we shall do better to be silent. Yet more, we may not only speak against these faults generally, but we may descend to details, and apply them to the individual; we may say, for instance, in plain words, "You were vain on such an occasion, selfish, passionate, proud, self-willed," conceited, or whatever the special fault may have been, and we shall find that after the first feeling of annoyance has passed, our words will be received thankfully. It is better, indeed, to be definite than general. A vague reproof calls up a spirit of self-justification and irritability, and is sometimes very disheartening; as, for instance, when a young girl is told, "You are so affected," or "so awkward," and is left to find out for herself in what particular way the affecta-

[1] Gal. v. 21.

tion or awkwardness exhibits itself. But in all cases, if we desire reproof to be well taken, there must be an unmistakable, simple, earnest interest in the welfare of the person we are addressing; and the consistency of our own conduct, the rigidness of our own self-discipline, must have shown that, however strict and unsparing we may be with others, we are much more so with ourselves. When this is the case, we may express ourselves as strongly as we think right, and so far from awakening resentment, we shall increase affection.

But we shall find also that this plainness of speech is more willingly endured when introduced gradually, in the course of a private general conversation, than when it is used in the form of a lecture from a superior to an inferior. There is a ground upon which we may all meet in common. Old and young, parent and child, governess and pupil, are all at school, all training for a future life. In administering a lecture we seem to put this truth aside. We unconsciously speak as if we stood on higher ground, apart from the temptations which are in reality common. The heart closes up then, and we cannot enter. If, however, we can descend from this position of superiority, and fairly recognize the fact that in spite of external differences we are really one; if we are able to draw out the half-spoken confession, to suggest the motives and feelings, which, it may be, the child herself only half understands; if we can say, "I know that when I was your age, I had such and such feelings, or acted in such and such a way," we give a sense of relief, of freedom to the burdened and wounded spirit; and the very plainness of our language becomes a soothing comfort.

To be known—understood; is it not what we all crave? Is it not often the root of a morbid desire for confession to men? Is it not the source of the unutterable rest which we feel in our confessions to God? We ask the friends who are dear to us as our own souls, to love us, though they know our faults, and as we repeat the words we feel that they are vain. No one knows us. No one can tell the history of our inner

lives. No one can see our secret impulses, our unworthy motives, our base self-deceit, our meanness and impurity in thought and feeling; and no one can recall the tale of those past transgressions, the guilt of which is blotted out, we trust, for Christ's sake, but the memory of which must one day face us before God's judgment seat.

We are not known, we cannot be known. As we advance on our lonely path, the conviction deepens day by day. We must bear with it—it is our trial, and our punishment. And so much the more as we strive to be true with ourselves, so much the more will the pain of in any way deceiving others, even though involuntarily, by appearing to be what we are not, become acute.

To tell what we are, and what we have been; to face the sorrow, the disappointment, perhaps the scorn and contempt, with the support of that one thought, at least I am no longer untrue; that is the yearning of the heart which has looked calmly in the face the contrast between its secret sins, and its profession of holiness. For this yearning there is no remedy, but to accept the approbation of men as our penance, and to turn from it to that Omniscient yet all Merciful Redeemer, "who knows all, yet loves us better than He knows."

But the young have these feelings only in their germ. They are conscious of having faults, but they cannot discriminate between them. They have impulses and motives which their moral sense teaches them are wrong, but they view them confusedly. They cannot classify them so as to understand how to deal with them; and when they attempt to speak of them, they confound natural and innocent feelings with the exaggerations which render them sinful. Not understanding themselves, they have a sense of self-dissatisfaction—a kind of self-suspicion, which destroys their peace, though it may not be an actual burden upon their hearts. The voice which tells them what it is which causes these uneasy feelings, is, therefore, a voice of comfort. To be saved the pain of explanation, and the attempt to confess what is not thoroughly under-

stood, is a great boon. At the first shock, indeed, there is a natural revulsion, but it quickly passes, and the relief of being thoroughly known, or of believing they are so, and yet loved and cared for, makes amends for any momentary suffering. They feel, as it were, set at liberty, able to speak, and ask advice, without restraint, and they are assisted in the confession of their difficulties by the light poured in upon their hearts, showing them whence those difficulties came.

And severe truths are also moral tonics, and we must all, more or less, acknowledge their strengthening power. There are occasions, indeed, in which what would otherwise be an injudicious dose may be administered with great effect.

Conceit is one of the few faults which may be reproved with an amount of plainness of speech inadmissible in most other cases. It is the result of moral or mental blindness. A veil hangs before the eyes, which prevents the truth from being seen; and though it may be removed roughly, the effect will be good.

Irony, also, is a species of reproof, which is sometimes efficacious, but it must be used with extreme caution. When applied to the correction of grave offences, it becomes satire, and is a censure so severe as only to be applicable to those rare cases in which a righteous indignation justifiably takes the place of sympathy.

When Ahab summoned Micaiah to his presence, and bade him tell whether the siege of Ramoth-Gilead could be undertaken with the hope of a blessing upon its result, the ironical answer, "Go, and prosper: for the Lord shall deliver it into the hand of the king," was felt instantly as a contemptuous reproof of the question, which Ahab's own conscience might have answered; and the king answered angrily, "How many times shall I adjure thee that thou tell me nothing but that which is true in the name of the Lord?"[1]

[1] 1 Kings xxii. 15, 16.

In this case there was no admixture of sympathy; there was, in fact, no opening for it. The guilty monarch, upon whom the long-suffering of God had had no effect, was beyond the reach of that loving reproof which leads to repentance and amendment. He might be startled by indignation, but he could not be won by tenderness.

And when this point is reached in the history of any individual entrusted to our charge, we shall do well to consider whether the task of education may not better be entrusted to another.

Satire, employed for the purpose of rebuking serious offences, implies deep-seated contempt; and the exhibition of this feeling is so antagonistic to love and sympathy, it creates so deep a wound, that when it has once been used, it is next to impossible to touch the gentler feelings, and so to win the heart. It is, in fact, not so much a reproof as a judicial punishment. We may deem it right to inflict it, but when we have done so, we must be prepared for alienation of the heart from ourselves as its result.

But there is a light satire, free from all bitterness, and appealing to the sense of the ridiculous in the person addressed, which is useful as well as justifiable, in those cases in which the fault attacked does not, upon the surface, appear a sin, but only an excusable yielding to custom, human infirmity, or some generally admitted maxim of the world.

There is no fault, indeed, which is not, strictly speaking, a sin; no weakness, or folly, which is not, in some degree, sinful; and nothing is more difficult than to attempt to draw a strict line between follies and sins. But to refuse to recognize the distinction is simply to repeat the mistake of Draco when he endeavoured to punish all offences equally, and ended by punishing none. We shall often find, also, that in speaking gravely of follies which have custom or sophistry to support them, we raise up a host of excuses and counter arguments, which we are unable, at the moment, to combat; and which will effectually bar the way against the deeper reasoning by

which we know that, upon consideration, we should be able to support our own view.

Instances of petty exclusiveness, absurd following of fashion in dress, affectation and pretence, may all be classed under the category of folly, and all are open to an ironical reproof. Not that such reproof will be instantly effective. It will, indeed, most likely be rejected at the moment, and the individual attacked by it may retreat without having apparently yielded; but it will not be forgotten, neither will it willingly be encountered again. And to be ashamed of these things is a great point gained towards their uprooting. We must often have met with persons really Christian in feeling, and anxious to do right, who are victims to some of the follies above alluded to; and we may have wondered how it was that such aberrations of principle and taste should exist in connection with good sense and good feeling upon other points. What has been wanting in the formation of these characters has, most likely, been a little good-natured irony in youth. Lectures upon worldliness may have probably been given, but the words have been too serious for the examples to which they were to be applied, and so have failed to make an impression. A grave discourse upon the vanity and selfishness of some peculiar kind of dress, or a sermon upon pride, applied to the customary etiquettes of precedence in fashionable society, strikes the hearer with a sense of the ludicrous. Yet the grave discourse may have a foundation in truth; and there is no doubt that the assertion of precedence is often associated with pride. It requires, however, thought and reasoning power to discover the sin which is hidden under such folly; and young people think and reason but little, and so they do not pay attention to what is said, for they consider it exaggerated. If folly can be knocked on the head by good-humoured irony, even before principle has time to exert itself, a great deal of apparent inconsistency will be avoided. It cannot, however, be too carefully borne in mind, that this method of rebuke, when used by a superior to an inferior, can never be safely exercised, except

where there is a strong feeling of affection on one side, and of respect on the other. Where anything like coldness or distrust exists, it is fatal to real influence. The arrows of satire, and even of irony, are always, more or less, steeped in poison, and in aiming at the fault, the greatest care is needed, lest we should miss the mark, and only inflict a deadly wound upon charity. Another mistake in reproving lesser defects is one which has been alluded to before, that of generalizing. A child is told, "You are so affected, or so stupid," or "so blundering;" and the mind is cast down by a vague sense of faultiness, which clouds it all over, like a mist on a November day. No special instance of the fault has been given, and, therefore, no special effort can be made to overcome it. But tell her that she drawls her words, or puts her head to one side, and she knows what she has to watch against. Show her that she does not take care to move things out of her way, and, in consequence, knocks them down, and she can improve. These defects are, indeed, only symptoms, and, no doubt, the root of the disease is that which we have really to guard against; but it is, unfortunately, the case with defects of manner, that, from habit, they remain, and entail painful consequences, even when the wrong principle, which was their root, has been, in a great measure, eradicated. An affected girl will, most likely, be an apparently affected woman; an awkward girl, an awkward woman; and the harsh-judging world will condemn what it dislikes, and will never take the trouble to inquire from what source the defect springs. Untidy dress is, also, a most fertile subject for these lighter kinds of reproof; in fact, many of the jars of family life, in the nursery and school-room, arise from it. Some children have a kind of talent for dress. Everything they put on fits them. With others it is just the reverse. Yet it is common to treat the latter case as if it arose from a moral fault. Children are scolded as if they were really bent upon looking their worst; and yet, perhaps, they have spent double the time that others have in endeavouring to make themselves appear as their friends wish. There is no want of will, but

there is an actual want of power. They are near-sighted, and do not see what is amiss, or they cannot use their fingers rapidly and well. They want careful, patient teaching; instead of it, they get irritable reproof; and the consequence is, that they grow nervous, and dress just as badly as before, and will probably continue to do so all their lives, to their own great annoyance and that of their friends. Real untidiness from carelessness is quite a different thing; but even here, we shall find that it is no use to give a lecture upon it as if it were a mortal sin. Children do not feel that it is so, and they will never accept what they consider an exaggerated censure. They will own that their conduct is naughty, vexatious, tiresome, but it is no use to call it sinful, for they cannot perceive its sinfulness. Constant small penalties, exacted according to definite rules, and, therefore, having the effect of natural laws, will, in this case, be more efficacious, and certainly less fretting than lectures. Unpleasant, awkward tricks, also, must, no doubt, be reproved, and that very sharply; but, as in the case of carelessness, we can never make a young girl own that it is sinful to be constantly putting her hand to her mouth, or resting upon one foot. What is required in these cases, is patience and temper. No doubt it is most wearisome to be always recalling the attention to the same thing. It must give cause to suppose that no effort is made to improve; and yet, very likely, there is a real effort, only habit is so strong. We might, perhaps, under such a trial strengthen our patience by thinking of our own habits in God's sight. How many things there are which He has all our lives been warning us not to do, and yet which we still persist in doing! And we might help the child we are educating by showing why these apparently slight things are of such importance. Tricks are like little tormenting insects constantly buzzing about us. We try to overlook them, but they will thrust themselves before us; and when the annoyance is felt every day, and all day long, it becomes almost unbearable. Even a very strong affection will scarcely stand the ordeal of a perpetual, disagreeable, or even

a merely fidgety trick. Say this to a child, and she will recognize the necessity of watchfulness, and endeavour to correct her bad habits; but without such explanation, the moral virtue of standing straight, and keeping her fingers quiet, is beyond her comprehension; and although she certainly ought to strive to do what she is told, as a matter of obedience, yet, after all, human independence is strong, and human beings, even children, will ask, "Why?" when they find that great stress is laid upon seeming trifles.

Unpunctuality, again, is a most vexatious fault, which must be constantly noticed, because of its fatal consequences, and which yet can scarcely be called a sin. Practical reproof is desirable in this case. If a child cannot be ready in time for a walk, she may be left behind. If she is not dressed for a party, she may stay at home. If she cannot get up in the morning, so as to appear at the breakfast table, she may be compelled to lie in bed. This kind of reproof is but forestalling the discipline of society, which punishes unpunctuality most effectually; and if deliberately carried out it will probably have some effect, though not all that we hope or imagine; for persons often reach middle life before they open their eyes to the moral evil of unpunctuality. To these practical remedies may be added, from time to time, an earnest appeal to a child's right feeling and good sense. She may be made to see the consequences of unpunctuality, and so her better principles may be roused to make a strenuous effort against it. To this may be added with great effect one definite rule: to take first that which *must* be done; and afterwards that which *may* be done. If it is a question between writing a note, and preparing to join a party for a walk at a certain hour—dress for the walk first, and write the note afterwards. If it is necessary to be ready for an early journey, let the carpet-bag be packed, and then sit down to read. It is but a simple rule, but if it can once be thoroughly rooted in the mind, it will be the means of avoiding innumerable trials of temper. And in this, as in so many other cases, what young people want is to be shown how

they may do right, to have something distinct, marked, put before them. Every one feels personally the annoyance of unpunctuality. The delinquents are nearly as much provoked with themselves as their friends are with them; but every time the temptation arises some excuse presents itself, and without a definite rule by which to guide themselves they almost inevitably give way to it.

One more remark may be made upon the subject of reproof, addressed to those who cannot bring themselves to reprove at all. This is not a very uncommon case with mothers, and to them nothing can be said except that they are abdicating a solemn duty, and that upon no sin does the punishment of God more surely follow. As it was in the days of Eli, so it is now. Because his sons made themselves vile, and he restrained them not, therefore God swore unto the house of Eli, that the iniquity of Eli's house should not be purged with sacrifice nor offering for ever.[1]

And yet Eli expostulated, which is more than many persons can bring themselves to do; but because he was not zealous for God's honour, therefore the curse fell upon him.

And is not this sin of parents more or less the temptation of all who are called upon to educate? We speak when we are angry, we reprove when our attention is particularly drawn to any special fault, but indolence interferes with our quickness in perceiving what is wrong, and want of moral courage prevents us from rebuking it when we do perceive it.

The father continually puts off the unpleasant task of reproving upon the mother, and the mother is very glad to devolve it upon the governess, who, perhaps, doubting the extent of her own influence, thinks it better not to attempt it.

It is easy to scold a little child, but it is by no means so easy to find fault with a girl of fifteen or sixteen, and excuses for not doing so are always ready. "It will do more harm than good; it will only irritate. Girls of that age are wilful, and very jealous of interference." These things are easily

[1] 1 Sam. iii. 13, 14.

said, and readily believed by a self-deceiving heart. And moral cowardice is so common, and conceals itself under so many garbs, that we scarcely recognize it as being wrong.

But if we have not learnt how to give pain when necessary, if we cannot bring ourselves to utter an unpleasant truth, we may as well relinquish the task of education altogether; it may almost be said we may as well relinqnish the attempt to do good under any form.

Truth is the foundation of respect, and unless we have the respect of the young, we shall never have their love. There are things most unpleasant to be said, for which there seems no fitting opportunity, which are repugnant to our taste or our reserve; but if it is right to say them, they must be said; and if we do not say them, we are educating upon a falsity, and we shall hereafter reap the consequence. The most humiliating rebuke which can be uttered is more palatable to the young mind than the tenderest sympathy of language or manner, when it is felt that beneath this tenderness there is a shrinking from expressing what is really thought.

Truth, as the basis of reproof—truth, uttered gently, softened by sympathy, but pure and unalloyed! It is the burden which God lays upon every individual soul to which he has entrusted the charge of another. We may flee from our duty as Jonah fled from preaching to the Ninevites, but punishment will assuredly overtake us as it did the prophet; not perhaps now, in the busy rush of the world, but in those lonely hours when our work is well-nigh done, and we fold our hands wearily and look back upon the past, and trace the separate courses of the young lives which we have been permitted to influence, and compare what they have been with what they might have been, if we had only had the courage to reprove when we were bound to reprove, to warn when the heart was open to warning.

CHAPTER IX.

FORGIVENESS.

After reproof comes forgiveness, a subject upon which there would seem but little to be said. Forgiveness, it may be thought, is pardon, the putting away and forgetting the offence. And yet when we come to inquire, we shall find that this is not always the idea formed of it.

A little child is forgiven quickly and readily. It throws its arms around its mother's neck, and she wipes away its tears, and covers it with caresses, and the next moment the mouth is bright with smiles, and the voice is ringing with laughter. But it is not so at a more advanced age. Forgiveness in the mind of a young girl of thirteen or fourteen is often associated with the idea of a homily upon the offence which has been committed, with the addition, perhaps, of a warning against other faults, more or less connected with it. This is by no means an encouraging prospect to a child—proud, probably, and resentful, conscious of having been in the wrong, yet seeing many excuses for herself, and battling by the aid of a will, as yet only half converted to the right, against the strong temptation to stand up for her own cause.

But let us look at some instances of rebuke and forgiveness in the Bible. There is one which will present itself at once to us all; that of Nathan and David. The tale by which the prophet strove to open the eyes of the self-deceived monarch to the extent of his iniquity, was the most cutting reproof that the tongue of man could administer; and when it failed in its

effect, the words, "Thou art the man," were like the arrow aimed at the heart which, it might have been thought, would have destroyed, rather than reawakened its spiritual life.

A hardened sinner would have been more hardened by it; but David was not hardened, and Nathan knew it; and when there is any tenderness in the conscience, it will respond to truth before all things. The prophet followed up the bold assertion, with a yet more bold enumeration of the sins which had been committed, and the punishments which were to follow. "And David said unto Nathan, I have sinned against the Lord. And Nathan said unto David, The Lord also hath put away thy sin; thou shalt not die."[1]

We hear no more of reproof, nothing even of warning, or exhortation. There is, indeed, the declaration that God would, for the sake of others, inflict on David a sorrow which all should know and understand; but, then, "Nathan departed unto his house."

We will turn to other examples of forgiveness in the New Testament. "A woman which was a sinner, when she knew that Jesus sat at meat in the Pharisee's house, brought an alabaster box of ointment, and stood at His Feet behind Him weeping, and began to wash His Feet with tears, and did wipe them with the hairs of her head, and kissed His Feet, and anointed them with the ointment."[2] It was the silent confession of her guilt—the silent entreaty for pardon. Our Lord took occasion from her conduct to reprove the Pharisee in words which, if his proud self-righteousness had not so fenced his heart as to render it impenetrable, must have touched him to the quick. To the woman He only said, "Thy sins are forgiven. Thy faith hath saved thee; go in peace."[3]

That was no solitary case. Have we not all marvelled at the perfect, the free, the unexpected pardon of the woman taken in adultery? Have we not all read the parable of the

[1] 2 Sam. xii. 13.
[2] St. Luke, vii. 37, 38.
[3] St. Luke, vii. 48, 50.

Prodigal Son, with somewhat of a sense of astonishment, that the very first movement of repentance should be received, and the sin apparently overlooked, as if it had never been committed?

God's ways are not as our ways: His thoughts are not as our thoughts. We think that the time of confession and forgiveness is the time for warning and counsel. He knows that it is not so. He sees how sensitive the wounded spirit is at such a moment; how quickly it catches the least tone of lingering anger, and how soon the barely subdued pride rises again. He knows that the heart wants confidence, that it can scarcely at first believe in the fact of forgiveness, and so He gives it rest, that it may learn to understand its new position.

If we forgive, and if we mean our forgiveness to be effective, as was that of our Redeemer, it must stand complete, and alone. When the words, "I am sorry," are spoken, and we know that they are not words of course, we must give an instant, hearty pardon, and let the past fault be buried, until, with the full consent and wish of the offender, it is brought out again to be examined, so that it may be guarded against more carefully for the future.

We may sometimes, especially in cases of deception, have tried the plan of half forgiveness. We may have received a child's confession, and had what is called a serious talk, upon the offence, and we may have ended with saying, "I forgive, but you must remember I cannot look upon you as I did before; you have no right to expect it." And the answer will probably be a murmur of sorrowful acquiescence. And upon this species of agreement we may have separated. But we shall find that we cannot keep to it. There is no such thing as half forgiveness. Pardon is like truth. It is one, indivisible. A half truth is a whole falsehood. A half forgiveness is a whole enmity and punishment. We shall feel it ourselves, and the child will feel it also. We shall be restless under it, and a further explanation must speedily follow; at least, when there is a real desire for mutual good understanding—for improve-

ment on the one side, and sympathy on the other. There are, indeed, many cases in which acknowledgment of error is superficial; there is no real sense of wrong, and the words of contrition are mere worhs of course. But even then it is better to say at once, "I cannot thoroughly forgive, I do not trust you," than to use the sacred words of pardon with anything like a double meaning. It will have more effect upon the child's mind. If she has been told that she is forgiven, she will feel herself justified in putting the offence away from her memory; but as long as she knows herself to be unforgiven, the fault will burden her conscience, and she may possibly feel compelled to exert herself to get rid of it by amendment and sincerity of purpose. This retaining of anger is, however, a very doubtful measure. It can only be safely resorted to after long experience of unreality and carelessness. God's method of pardon is surely our safest example. "Seest thou how Ahab humbleth himself before Me? because he humbleth himself before Me, I will not bring the evil in his days: but in his son's days will I bring the evil upon his house."[1]

And yet God at that very moment knew that Ahab would die in the battle unrepentant and under a curse.

But it may be said, this full pardon, where repentance is doubtful, will encourage indifference to transgression. If a child is perfectly sure that she will be forgiven as soon and as often as she owns her fault, she will become careless as to committing it. This would, no doubt, be true, if forgiveness and escape from punishment were one and the same thing. But we do not find that they are so in God's moral government, either in nature or revelation. The spendthrift owns his sin, and through the Atonement of Christ it is blotted out as if it had never been; but he does not therefore escape the punishment of poverty. When Nathan pronounced the pardon of David, he did not therefore revoke the sentence of family misery, which was to be his curse for the remainder of his life; and because a public sin required a public retribution, further

[1] 1 Kings xxi. 29.

punishment was added. "Because by this deed thou hast given great occasion to the enemies of the Lord to blaspheme, the child also that is born unto thee shall surely die."[1]

Now, if we look into these punishments, we shall see that the first were what may be termed natural; that is, following in the natural course of events, as cause and effect; whilst the second was judicial, that is to say, a special suffering was inflicted for a special sin.

That the first punishments were natural will be evident to any person who studies the sequence of events which followed David's fall; the respect of his people lost, and the way thus opened for Absalom's conspiracy; that conspiracy strengthened by the assistance of Ahithophel (the grandfather of Bathsheba), by whose direct counsel the punishment prophesied by Nathan was carried into effect; and—perhaps the most striking natural punishment of all—when Absalom's rebellion was crushed, the miserable subjection of the repentant monarch to the imperious will of Joab, his confidant and the instrument of Uriah's murder.[2]

As these events followed each other, David's memory, and David's heart, must have recognized in them those seemingly inevitable consequences of human action, which take from them the idea of their being instances of God's present wrath, and suffer the conscience still to find repose in the thought of being forgiven. God had pardoned, but He would not interpose to alter the fixed laws by which one event succeeds another, and therefore David suffered. He was, as it were, his own executioner. But in the case of the death of the little infant, it was different. There was no fixed law, at least none which the human mind could recognize, according to which the child must die. The affliction appeared in the light of a direct punishment from God, and therefore, as it would seem,

[1] 2 Sam. xii. 14.

[2] The whole of this argument, as to the consequences of David's sin, is taken from Professor Blunt's "Scriptural Coincidences," Part II. chap. xi.

the severity of its announcement was tempered by a merciful explanation of the reason for which it was sent.

David was forgiven. He was to look upon God as his merciful and loving Father, and although a special judicial punishment was to be borne, it was to be for the sake of others, and not for his own. He was repentant already; he needed nothing to make him more so. He might have been set free, and no distinct punishment exacted; but "because the enemies of God might blaspheme," when they saw an instance of, what might be called, prosperous guilt in the case of a king who professed to be God's servant, therefore his child must die.

The distinction between the two kinds of punishment inflicted upon David will perhaps give us some clue as to the mode in which the difficult but often necessary task of combining punishment with forgiveness, may be carried out in education.

We have already spoken of natural punishment, that is to say, fixed rules according to which certain penalties are affixed to certain actions. These are analogous to the natural laws, according to which the moral government of the world is directed; and, as in the instance of the Jewish monarch, there is no call upon us to interpose so as to prevent their being carried into effect against an offender, although forgiveness may have been complete, without even a memory of the past remaining. No one who is really penitent ever expects or even wishes for such an interposition, and therefore to say, "I forgive, but you must still submit to the punishment you have incurred," excites no resentment, and raises no doubt as to the sincerity of the pardon. But if we feel it necessary to inflict any extra punishment, we must give our full reason, and we must be careful that this reason shall be such as will carry with it the accordance of the person who is to suffer.

David, indeed, prayed for the remission of the sentence passed upon him. The feelings of the parent were too strong to admit of his acquiescing without an entreaty that his child

might be spared to him; but when he knew that the decree was irrevocable, the fact did not lessen his consciousness that God's favour was restored to him. He could still say, humbly and trustingly, "Restore unto me the joy of Thy salvation; and uphold me with Thy free spirit:" and with that recognition for God's outraged honour, which was the reason given for the infliction of his own chastisement, he could add, "Then will I teach transgressors Thy ways; and sinners shall be converted unto Thee. Deliver me from bloodguiltiness, O God, Thou God of my salvation: and my tongue shall sing aloud of Thy righteousness. O Lord, open thou my lips; and my mouth shall shew forth Thy praise."[1]

And this same perfect acquiescence in punishment, when used as a means to correct a fault, or for the sake of warning to others, will be found in children. They will see instantly that such punishment has no unkindness in it, for their recognition of what is right and just, and in accordance with reason and common sense, is clearer than that of the generality of persons more advanced in age.

If they rebel against what is demanded of them, from passion or resentment, they do not attempt to disguise the fact. Let any one watch the sophistries of his own heart, or observe those which reach him every day from the false reasonings of men, and contrast them with the simple free acknowledgment of sin, and acceptance of sin's consequences, from the lips of a child of twelve or thirteen, who is really sorry for having done wrong, and really anxious to do right, and he will at once own that the intellect of the head and the intellect of the heart (if such an expression may be admitted) by no means correspond. The child perceives at once the truth which the man or the woman sees, only indistinctly, through a mist of proud and sophistical argument. We too often confuse the idea of suffering with that of atonement, and suppose that by suffering, we in some way make amends for our sin. The child sees the distinction between the two,

[1] Psalm li. 12–15.

and accepts forgiveness as a free gift, and punishment, when justly inflicted, as the inevitable result of its own misconduct, or as the needful warning for others. Children are wilful and unreasoning, but we shall often find that they, in their simplicity, are nearer to God than we in the strength of our human reason. "Except ye be converted, and become as little children, ye shall not enter the kingdom of heaven."

We look upon these words as allegorical. It may be that we should be more successful in the task of education if we accepted them literally; if, whilst educating the young, we also educated ourselves; confessing even as a child confesses; receiving forgiveness, even as a child receives it; and acknowledging the necessity of chastisement, even as a child acknowledges it, when it receives and returns the kiss of pardon, and then leaves us to bear the penalty of its fault, with a brave heart, and a loving spirit, which converts the chastisement for sin into the blessed instrument of restoration and amendment.

CHAPTER X.

ADVICE.

It has been implied in what has previously been said, that anything like a repetition of reproof should never accompany forgiveness; but advice is not reproof, and it will very often happen that, after forgiveness, advice will be both needed and requested. The mode in which it may best be offered is a very important subject for consideration; but before we reach this point, we must inquire into the nature of the materials with which and upon which we are required to operate.

Evil, we must always bear in mind, is not a distinct principle in itself, but a perversion of good. That this is so will be evident, when we bring before ourselves the doctrine involved in the contrary statement. If evil is a principle in itself, then it must either be distinct from God, in which case it would be eternal, self-existing, and we should arrive at the Manichæan idea of two deities—one good, and the other evil; or it must have been created by God, in which case it would belong to the Nature of God, and He would cease to be good.

Both these doctrines will at once be rejected with abhorrence; but if rejected, we must accept the only other alternative, and admit that evil is distorted or exaggerated good.

We recognize this truth, indeed, in the very words which we use in speaking of evil. We say that man's nature is fallen—that is, its proportions have been destroyed, but the fragments of which it was composed remain. We say this is a ruined world; that is, a world the order of which has been

disturbed, although the materials with which it was built are still visible. The analogy holds good in other cases. The ingredients of medicine and poison are the same; the natural difference existing between them is a difference of proportion. Fire and water are in their elementary properties alike, whether they nourish or destroy.

But it must not be supposed that the magnitude of evil is lessened by the fact that, instead of being a principle in itself, it exists only in the form of distorted good. On the contrary, it is increased. That all good things become the worst in their perversion is a proverb. God teaches us this in nature, by the instances already brought forward, namely, the destructiveness of the very elements which, when used in their right proportion, are indispensable to man's life and health; and He teaches it also in morals, by the facts which are continually brought before us in our dealings with each other. The most cruel of all creatures is a cruel woman, because by nature she is the most gentle and merciful. The most fierce of all wars is a religious war, because the principle of religion is in its nature the principle of peace.

But if the elements of man's nature require only reconstruction, it would seem that the task is in our own power. The Bible, however, tells us differently. It speaks of regeneration—renewal. It warns us that without the infusion of a new Spirit, the Image of God—that Image in which man was created—can never be restored.

This statement can also, in a measure, be verified by analogy. We cut a branch from a tree, and, left in that state, it will die. We graft it into another, and the living sap circulates in it again, and it lives: the great distinction in this case between natural and spiritual revivification being, that in the former case, even whilst separated from the source of life, the principle of life is still existing in the branch, though it must sooner or later die; whilst in the latter, life is entirely lost, and can only be recovered by actual regeneration.

But, though the nature of man is indeed fallen and ruined,

and only the indwelling Spirit of God, and the principle of love to God, can really restore it to its pristine form, it must not be thought that we have nothing to do as regards arranging and preparing the elements of which it is composed. "Work out your own salvation with fear and trembling, for it is God which worketh in you,"[1] is a command as applicable to education as to self-discipline. God alone can make the children we love holy, but we can assist in removing the obstacles to holiness; and having this object in view, we must examine well the materials of character which come under our influence, and endeavour so to correct and arrange them that we may not, in striving to destroy a fault, overlook the virtue of which it is the indication.

An impulsive, rash, self-confident character is also active and energetic. A selfish, over-careful disposition contains the germs of prudence. An indolent character is usually gentle, and unwilling to accept provocation. A jealous temper is an affectionate one. An irritable temper is sensitive, quick in perception. Vanity is the exaggeration of an amiable desire to please. And the reason why so much good advice, or advice which is meant to be good, is received so badly by those to whom it is offered, very often is, that in touching the fault, the virtue is touched also; and then the natural instinct of self-defence exhibits itself in the form of an excuse.

Now, if we wish to give advice which will be palatable as well as true, we must show sympathy with whatever is natural and innocent in the feeling which has been aroused, before we give a caution against exaggeration. A child we will suppose requires advice as to the control of its temper, a warning upon the sin of giving way to passion, and the frightful consequences which may result from it. Let us begin with sympathy. "Life in all its forms is very trying—our fellow-creatures are doubtless very provoking, and passion comes upon us suddenly: we are not all born with that quiet temperament which can patiently submit to injury, real or imagi-

[1] Philip. ii. 12, 13.

nary, and if we were, many evils would be tolerated which now are overcome. But passion is sinful, there is no doubt upon that point; and as passionate persons have naturally more energy than those who are by nature meek, so they have greater power of self-control, if they only choose to exercise it. The spirit which urges us to compel another to yield to us our right, may also be exercised in compelling ourselves to give way. We must do battle with something; then let it be with our own evil temper: let us, through God's help, master that." When the better feelings have thus been appealed to, more definite advice for special occasions may be given, with every hope of its being well received. So, again, with vanity. It is of no use to tell young persons—any persons, indeed—not to care what is thought of them. They cannot help it. The opinion of others is very important to us all. This truth may at once be admitted; and in admitting it, we show sympathy which touches the youthful heart, and wins its confidence. It feels that it is understood. It will enter, then, into the distinction between a desire for the approbation of those whom we respect, and a desire for the admiration of the world; and it will also understand the difference between wishing to please, and wishing to give pleasure; wishing to please being a refined form of selfishness, and wishing to give pleasure, on the contrary, a form of unselfishness. Advice, however strict, given in this way, will be listened to cheerfully without irritation, and so it will be effective. The principle is the encouragement of good rather than the condemnation of evil, and the former is far more powerful than the latter.

It may, perhaps, be objected that this mode of dealing with faults is irrespective of religious principle; that we shall do better by teaching a passionate child to think of the meekness of Christ, and a vain child to seek for the approbation of God; thus appealing directly to the highest of all motives of action.

In answer to this, it must be said, that the one principle does by no means exclude the other. Because you rouse a

passionate child's energy by reminding her that God has given her a natural strength of character, and that this strength is intended to be used for self-discipline, it does not at all follow that you are to omit the lesson to be drawn from the meekness of Christ; or, because you tell a vain child to seek for approbation rather in giving pleasure than in personal pleasing, it does not follow that you should omit to direct her thoughts to the highest approbation of all—the approbation of God. But it must be remembered that all children and young persons are not equally open to these highest motives. Religious feeling is a plant of slow growth, and passion and vanity are plants of quick growth. Before the former can be applied as an efficacious remedy, it is often needful to do our utmost to uproot the latter. And religious feeling is also delicate and sensitive; if we attempt to force it we shall kill it. It does but jar and irritate the young mind to suppose that it can be influenced by motives which it is conscious it does not rightly appreciate. Some children are early touched by religious motives—they will respond to them at once; but others shrink from them, and turn away when an endeavour is made to thrust them upon them. The greatest possible care is needed with regard to this question of religion, and its direct inculcation as a motive of conduct. The subject must be reserved for another occasion, but it cannot too strongly be stated, that in striving to suggest the mode, or rather perhaps the order, in which advice should be given—namely, that of sympathising with and encouraging what is good before attacking what is bad—it is not for a moment intended to put aside religion as a motive, but rather to dispose the heart to receive it when it can fitly be suggested.

A sanction for this recognition of good in that which, in the form under which it presents itself, is evil, may be found in some of our Blessed Lord's warnings to His disciples. The sons of Zebedee desired to sit, the one on His Right Hand, and the other on His Left Hand, in the Kingdom of glory. Ambition and self-confidence were in the request; but love—a

desire to be with Christ—was contained in it also. Our Lord represented to them the difficulties which must prepare the way for such a reward. Could they drink of His cup, and be baptized with His baptism? Love answered yes; and the answer was sincere. Then came the answer to love, the promise that they should be like Him, that they should be the sharers in His sufferings; and after it followed the gentle reproof, "To sit on My Right Hand and on My Left Hand is not Mine to give; but it shall be given to them for whom it is prepared."[1] So, again, on a similar occasion, there was a strife among the disciples "which of them should be accounted the greatest." In that form the feeling was earthly; but the desire to be great and glorious in the Kingdom of Heaven was a desire which our Lord Himself had inculcated. The earthly wish, therefore, was checked by Him, but the natural and innocent longing was acknowledged and encouraged: "Ye are they which have continued with Me in My temptations; and I appoint unto you a Kingdom, as My Father hath appointed unto Me." Once more, the Apostles rejoiced in their power over the spirits of evil. Our Lord promised them a continuance and increase of that power, and then came the warning. "Rather rejoice, because your names are written in Heaven."[3] And if we would give advice efficaciously, we must also take care that we look at the character with which we are dealing as a *whole*. Every one who knows his own heart at all, knows how easily he may be misjudged by those who take but one phase of his disposition and overlook others. This is, in fact, the root of all prejudice and injustice; and it need scarcely be said that advice to be useful must be fair, and unbiassed. And this general outside view of a character will be peculiarly helpful and supporting to a child, or a young person, because it is so difficult for them to attain it for themselves. Children accept the characters given of them without examination; and if vanity, or obstinacy, or ill-temper, or any

[1] Mark x. 40. [2] St. Luke xxii. 28, 29.
[3] St. Luke x. 20.

other disagreeable quality should happen to be very marked, the fact will in all probability have been impressed upon them by nurses, brothers, and sisters, until at length every other quality seems swallowed up in this unamiable characteristic. "Such a child is perverse or conceited," is said, constantly, as if that one trait described the whole disposition.

It is a gain, which cannot be estimated, when, after a general condemnation of this kind, a young girl's eyes are opened to the fact that, naughty though she may be in this respect, or even in a great many others, there is still some good remaining. People are afraid to tell children of their advantages, whether moral or physical, lest it should make them conceited. But conceit does not consist in knowing what we possess, but in over-estimating its value. No one can make a proper use of his powers unless he knows that he has them. The owner of the ten talents must have been quite aware that he possessed them, or he would never have been able to make with them ten talents more. Truth under any form is the very last thing we have to fear. And a child oppressed by the burden of some besetting sin, which, perhaps, she has for months been struggling against unsuccessfully, will enter upon the contest with renewed vigour, when it is pointed out to her that God has given her, in her own heart, principles and feelings which, instead of being hopelessly bad, are really pleasing to Him.

We do not find that our Blessed Lord rejected the good that existed in those who approached Him, because He also perceived the evil, or that He allowed the one to hide the other. The rich young man came to Him with the impulse of warm-hearted devotion, and inquired, "Good Master, what shall I do that I may inherit eternal life?" Our Lord tested him first upon those points on which He knew a good response could be given; and when in reply to the enumeration of the commandments He was told, "Master, all these have I observed from youth," we are expressly informed that "Jesus beholding him loved him"[1]—loved him for that which was good in him, in

[1] St. Mark x. 20, 21.

no way rebuked him because he had said what in his heart he, however erroneously, believed to be true; but only tested him still further, and by that test sent him away grieved, yet with his eyes opened to the fact that his love was not that which he had believed it.

Again—one of the scribes listened to our Lord as he was reasoning with the Sadducees, and "perceiving that he had answered well," ventured, in a spirit very different from that of the lawyer, to question him for his own satisfaction. Our Lord replied fully, and when the scribe exclaimed, "Master, thou hast said the truth," the Redeemer seized, as it were, upon that sudden conviction, openly approved and encouraged it by the words, "Thou art not far from the Kingdom of God."[1] Yet we do not read that the scribe, any more than the rich young man, was so far in earnest as to follow Christ.

But further, if we would give advice effectually, we must be watchful that we do not thrust it forward uncalled for. Every one knows the irritation caused by an acquaintance, or even a friend, who is always advising. Every one must have felt the impulse to reject the advice, let it be never so wise, simply because it was not asked for. Now, children are by no means so unlike grown-up people as we are sometimes apt to imagine. They are extremely alive to the rightful authority of the persons who advise,—they will not listen to the wisdom of Socrates, unless Socrates has a right to counsel them. Mothers who bring up their own children well, are sometimes apt to think that they may lend a helping hand to their friends who are not quite so successful. They take upon themselves to criticize and suggest, sometimes to approve. Possibly, this interference may be endured by the parent; but it will be rejected by the children, and resented as an offence. Whatever is to be said to the young in the way of reproof or guidance, must be said not only in the right way, but by the right person, at the right time. As a matter of prudent counsel, the result of experience, the warning may be given, never, as a

[1] St. Mark xii. 34.

general rule, to find fault or to advise when the duty belongs naturally to another person. The governess, for instance, must reprove for herself, the mother for herself. If the mother receives the complaint of the governess, and undertakes to rebuke or punish an offence of which she is not personally cognizant, she will very frequently find herself in a difficulty. Excuses will be made which she cannot test, and counter complaints will be brought which, if they are listened to, lessen respect, and if they are rejected without a hearing, will awaken the sense of injustice. And so, again, if want of moral courage, or a dislike to saying disagreeable things, should induce a request that in some particular case we would, taking the office of a friend, reprove or advise instead of the person, whether parent or governess, on whom the duty really devolves, we shall do much better to decline. The request could only be made under the idea that we possess influence, and possibly we may. But if we give advice when we are not called upon to do so, we shall almost certainly lose it. If we would only strive to recall the occasions on which we have been led in this way to interfere without an acknowledged right (and who is there that has not, at one time or other, been guilty of this folly?), we should probably see ample cause, from our failure, to own that we were mistaken. Well-intentioned people are often so very eager to satisfy their consciences by giving advice! It is a great pity that they do not try to satisfy their understanding also. For there is such a thing as a morbid, an ill-regulated, even a selfish conscience, or rather that which calls itself conscience. As Dr. South says, "Conscience is no distinct power or faculty from the mind of man, but the mind of man itself applying the general rule of God's law to particular cases and actions." If, therefore, the mind is not enlightened by common sense, conscience must be at fault.

And so, once more, with regard to the right time for offering advice. We might be more anxious to act judiciously in this respect, if we would remember that, probably, more

than half the mistakes from which we have ourselves suffered in life, some of them, perhaps, being fatal as regards temporal advantages, have been owing less to the saying or doing that which is in itself unwise, than to its being said or done at the wrong moment. Impulse, impatience, the desire to get rid of a disagreeable burden, will urge us to express what is uppermost in our thoughts; and this is the common motive for a lecture at the time of forgiveness. The one idea suggests the other, and we say what we have to say without consideration. If we can only govern ourselves, be patient, watchful, tenderhearted, we shall soon find an opening for the words of affectionate guidance which we long to utter; but (if we examine ourselves, we shall scarcely hesitate to acknowledge it) this longing to give vent to advice which we think will be useful, is too often only the longing to vent a little feeling of irritation; it is the excuse for saying that we have been annoyed or provoked; that we are weary or disappointed.

When our Blessed Redeemer met the disciples, after His Resurrection, He waited for many days, and vouchsafed to appear to them often, before we are told that He alluded to St Peter's threefold denial, even by the question, "Simon, son of Jonas, lovest thou me?" That could not have been because He was indifferent, because He had overlooked or forgotten the sin. But He chose His time He was content to wait. It was not of Himself He thought, but of the Apostle. He desired, we may believe, to reassure St. Peter, to give him ease in His Presence, before He would refer to his fall.

There is a lesson for us in that caution and patience; only, in practising it, let us remember that delay must never be omission. One is almost afraid at times to give a warning against a mistake on one side, lest it should be construed into approbation of a fault on the other.

CHAPTER XI.

TRAINING.

But there are many other ways of training and guiding the young, besides giving advice. Perhaps, indeed, advice, taken by itself, is the least efficacious of all the means we are called upon to adopt. There is a daily, hourly training, which goes on almost unconsciously, and certainly indirectly, through the medium of general conversation, arrangements for the employment of time, words dropped without any particular meaning; to say nothing of that most important of all educational influences, example. We are, in fact, all educating one another more or less. It is not a very pleasant thought, though it is a true one. It makes us so responsible. But we shall not teach ourselves to educate rightly by dwelling constantly upon the idea; for if we do, we shall probably be afraid to move, and shall attempt to remain inactive; forgetting that to stand still when the world goes on, is in its results a movement of the most important kind.

Perhaps, one of the most influential principles to be adopted in this daily, and what may be called unconscious, training, is that of seizing upon the good points of a character, whatever they may be, and using them as engines for the extinction of the bad. This is, indeed, only following out in action the same idea which has been already suggested with regard to words. Implant and cherish good, and so, through God's grace, evil will die away.

"Beloved, now are we the sons of God, and it doth not yet appear what we shall be: but we know that, when He shall

appear, we shall be like Him; for we shall see Him as He is. And every man that hath this hope in Him purifieth himself, even as He is pure."[1] When we feel that we are the sons of God, when we are sure of the blessed hope of Heaven, the struggle for purity follows as a thing of course.

But, it may be objected, young people do not feel that they are the sons of God; they cannot realize the hope of Heaven. Theirs is but an intellectual knowledge. Granted, in too many cases; yet the principle may be applied in a different way. They may not be what is called religious, though there is no reason to assume the fact; but supposing, for the sake of argument, that we cannot appeal to direct religious motives, are there no others which we may make use of?

Let us first consider what our estimate of a character usually is. When we are called upon to describe it, what do we say? "Such an one has a most violent temper, she is self-willed, and proud, but then she is very truthful and affectionate." Another is provokingly indolent and forgetful, but she is unselfish and very generous. A third is decidedly selfish, almost stingy; but she has a strong sense of justice, and is very trustworthy. A fourth is vain and irritable, but her conscience is quickly touched, and she is very open and candid.

There is no character which is all evil; none which has not some one or more good qualities to counterbalance those which are faulty. And if we can see the disposition as a *whole*, so as to estimate the good that is in it, then our wisest plan will be to begin the work of training, by nourishing and cherishing it. An appeal to affection and truthfulness may diminish the violence of passion. Unselfishness and generosity will rouse the indolent to exertion. A sense of justice, and conscientiousness as to truth, may open the eyes of the selfish; sincerity and candour may destroy the self-delusion of the vain.

And there is no danger in owning that this counteracting

[1] 1 St. John, iii. 2, 3.

good does exist. On the contrary, it will awaken hope and energy; it will give heart to begin the struggle with the besetting sin; and let that once be commenced in earnest, and all that can be wished for, as regards religious principle, will speedily follow. People talk as if religion always took root and grew up in the heart in a certain necessary order; first, conviction of sin, then sorrow and repentance, then faith, then amendment; and as if nothing could be genuine goodness which did not follow in that order. This does not seem to be God's idea of religious growth; or, at least, there is a very great deal of thought and feeling which there can be no possible doubt that He approves, and yet which does not show itself in that order. Good in every form must come from Him, and if He chooses to touch one heart through the medium of affection, another through natural unselfishness, another through truthfulness, or the sense of responsibility, why are we to look coldly on the work because, according to our notions, it is not the result of genuine religious feeling? Only lead the young to wish to be good; only make them see what their faults are, and induce them, in all earnestness and sincerity, to strive against them, from a desire to please God; and repentance and faith must soon be awakened, and that in a much more simple and enduring form than can result from excitement of feeling.

A striking instance of the manner in which the good points of a character may be used to neutralize and subdue the evil, may be found in our Blessed Lord's treatment of St. Peter.

The defects in St. Peter's character were undoubtedly ambition, impetuosity, weakness, and self-confidence, united with moral cowardice. We see these traits constantly exhibiting themselves. Ambition made him contest, jointly with the other disciples, the place of honour in Christ's Kingdom; it led him to ask the direct question, "Behold, we have forsaken all, and followed Thee; what shall we have therefore?"[1]

[1] St. Matthew xix. 27.

Impetuosity led him to cut off the ear of Malchus in the garden. Self-confidence, after impelling him to assert his willingness to die for his Lord, induced him to thrust himself into the high priest's palace—the place of danger—and moral cowardice then compelled him to the sin of denial.

Now, if we had been called upon to deal with a character like that of St. Peter, our first thought would probably have been that his faults required that he should be checked, kept in the background. We should, above all things, have feared to place him in a position of prominence, or of great responsibility. But it would seem that our Blessed Lord had no such fear. St. Peter was one of the chosen Three who were the witnesses of His glory, and of His humiliation. To him were words specially addressed, which, though afterwards spoken to all the Apostles, and therefore not exclusively his, have yet given him, in the eyes of a large portion of Christendom, a position above all his brethren. To him, also, was the charge "to feed the flock of Christ" repeated three several times, with the evident design of restoring him to the place of confidence which he had lost by his threefold denial; and to him, though the Apostle of the Jews, was granted the privilege of being the first to open the door of hope to the Gentiles.

What was the meaning of this training—for training it certainly was; and what was its result?

We have spoken of St. Peter's impetuosity and ambition, his self-confidence and moral cowardice. Was there nothing more noble, more winning, in his character? Can we forget the intensity of his affection, his eager self-devotion, his simplicity and candour? Nourish these characteristics, by placing the individual in a position in which they will be peculiarly brought forth, and give him the experience of his own weakness, and the sense of a heavy responsibility, and the very exercise of the good will, almost unconsciously, tend to destroy the evil. It would seem to have been thus in St. Peter's case. Placed in a position of prominence, commanded to feed the flock of Christ, he had full scope for the exercise, in its best

form, of his earnest impulsiveness. Love to his risen and forgiving Lord, converted his natural impetuosity into an enduring desire to live and to die for Christ; the desire was strengthened by every opportunity for action; and when he had learnt to desire Christ's glory, he no longer ambitiously sought his own. His simplicity and singleness of character enabled him to direct all his energies to one sole object, and this gave him a spirit of determination which, to a certain extent, must have counteracted his moral cowardice; though it is evident from his conduct, when the controversy respecting circumcision was carried on, that he was still liable to be swayed by the fear of the world's opinion.

His candour, exercised by the continual call to weigh and judge the character of men, and deepened, doubtless, by the recollection of past transgression, checked his self-confidence; and the sense of an overpowering responsibility gave the balance that was wanting to a disposition containing in itself so many elements of inconstancy and inconsistency.

Let any one read St. Peter's epistles, especially the first, by the light of St. Peter's character and life, and he will see how, through God's grace, and His merciful training, evil may be converted into good; the sins of a fallen nature into the virtues which belong to the saints of light.

There is still the evidence of an ardent spirit, rejoicing in temptations, and regarding the trial of faith as the pathway to glory and honour; but that glory is always connected with the thought of the sufferings of the Saviour whom he so dearly loved; and from those sufferings are deduced the lessons of patience and humility, which the Apostle had himself learnt by such a grievous experience. Urging his converts to warfare —for St. Peter's energetic spirit must always have felt the necessity of conflict—he tells them to arm themselves with the Mind of Christ, to clothe themselves with humility, that so they may have the strength of God on their side; to be sober and vigilant, resisting the devil by steadfastness in the faith; and, as if recalled by these words to the consciousness of the un-

stable, uncertain disposition, which even to the end of his earthly career he must, more or less, have had cause to struggle against, he closes his warning with that most solemn prayer, which contains all that the most anxious heart can crave, for those about to enter on the battle of life.

"The God of all grace, who hath called us unto His Eternal Glory by Christ Jesus, after that ye have suffered a while, make you perfect, stablish, strengthen, settle you."[1]

It is the description of St. Peter's own career, the utterance of his own experience of his Redeemer's enlightening, strengthening, establishing love. And if the training which he received may not, as in fact it cannot, be safely adopted in all its particulars by us, it nevertheless gives us a lesson which may be of infinite importance to us, if we will but apply it, by the light of reason, to the education of the young.

In the routine of daily life it is wiser to cheer with approbation than to be frequently finding fault, wiser to trust than to suspect, to appeal to affection than to reprove and reproach.

Such a suggestion as this may be misunderstood. It may be interpreted to sanction weak-minded indulgence. This is the risk that must always attend every general observation, especially one which has reference to education. Yet the rule may hold good notwithstanding the mistakes of those who attempt to apply it. It is not a rule applicable to little children, or children of three or four years old. At that age, there must be a constant, gentle check, a continued reminding of what has been commanded. The mind is so plastic then, that one idea is almost instantly effaced by another; it is only by repetition that we can produce any permanent impression; and to overlook a fault is in part to cherish it. But it is very different as years go on. The character then develops, as it were, of itself. There will be peculiar tastes, tempers, feelings, all which in part constitute what is sometimes called the idiosyncrasy of the individual, over which we have no control. We can no longer mould it; we can but guide it; and if then

[1] 1 St. Peter v. 10.

we are perpetually reproving and punishing—though there may be just ground for our complaints—we shall destroy the very principles on which we must depend for the conquering of those faults. Let us only ask ourselves (if we have forgotten what we felt when we were young), what we should feel now, if we were openly reproved every time we gave way to a besetting temptation, known perhaps only to ourselves. What irritation and almost despair it would cause! Or if, taking a low view of sin, we strive to resist a temptation merely because we are ashamed of yielding to it, and dread the reproaches of conscience if we do yield, how powerless the principle is! But if we think that our Redeemer is watching us, and will be pleased with us if we overcome, the effort ceases to be an effort. And, in like manner, a girl who has been reproved for a bad habit every day for months, and has never apparently made any attempt to subdue it, but has only become sullen by being continually punished for it, will grasp, and battle with, and conquer it of her own accord, if some strong affection is roused, some motive suggested which shall make it appear in the light of love rather than that of stern duty.

It is in this way, in fact, that the religious principle, when once it has taken root in the heart, acts so as to change the whole character in a degree acknowledged to be supernatural.

The man who would have struggled fruitlessly for his whole life against some favourite sin, when only human motives influenced him, will relinquish it at once when the love of God has touched his heart. And, though in a far lower degree, all good principles have somewhat of this same converting power. Let a careless, forgetful, yet conscientious child be placed in a position of responsibility, and the sense of authority and duty will do more than years of warning towards correcting the habitual negligence. Give an extravagant but honest girl an allowance, and the necessity of strictly paying her debts corrects the extravagance. Let an indolent but affectionate girl be placed in a position which makes others dependent upon her for happiness, and she will rouse herself to exertion.

This appears to be the clue to many of those orderings of God's Providence, which at first sight are so strange and unaccountable to us. We see the weak-minded placed in a position which requires strength; the vain surrounded by those who minister to their vanity; the proud permitted to rule; the selfish allowed opportunities for tyranny; the passionate for violence. We say continually, "If such an one had only been differently circumstanced, he would have done well." But this is scarcely justifiable language. Who ordered or permitted those circumstances? If it was God, then surely He knew best. He must have seen, what we could not see, that there were other counterbalancing qualities in the character which, under those same circumstances, might, if the person himself had so willed, have served to counteract the temptation; which might indeed have done so all the more effectually from the very position of trial in which the individual was placed.

This does not, indeed, prove that we, in our ignorance, may venture to do what God does in His perfect knowledge, and voluntarily place the person, about whom we are anxious, in a situation which, we know, is likely to excite the faults against which he has to guard. But it may reconcile us to many events in life, which appear to us untoward; and it may assist us in the decisions we are sometimes forced to make, in which outward circumstances appear to call a person to a certain post, whilst natural qualities appear to render him unfit for it. We are judges of outward circumstances, so far as to be able to see whether there is any claim of duty in them. We are not judges of individual character, so as to foretell what effect those circumstances will have upon it.

And further—as it is more essential to draw out the good points of a character than to set ourselves to uproot the bad, so there is no reason to dread the effect of praise, when such good qualities are exhibited in action. On the contrary, praise, when well deserved, is a most efficacious instrument of improvement.

An idea is entertained by some persons that praise involves

the idea of merit; and as no one can do more than his duty, and, therefore, no one can, strictly speaking, have any merit, it is supposed that to praise encourages a false motive of action.

If it be so, then is man's system of education wiser than God's. Most certainly we never find that God fails to praise; on the contrary, it would seem as though He carefully singled out matter for commendation, even in characters which, to the human eye, would seem full of imperfection. St. Paul, speaking by the Holy Spirit, gives us a list of those who, in the old times, were distinguished for their faith; he makes honourable mention of them, as those that pleased God. We hear of Gideon, Barak, Samson, and Jephthah, not one of whom but exhibited great infirmity of character; as if to make us feel that the Almighty will never overlook what is right in the heart, though there may be much in it also which is very wrong; and if we would seek for instances of praise, given directly to the individual, the Bible is full of them.

Let us think of Abraham listening to the voice of the angel, as he pronounced a blessing upon the patriarch's obedience. "By myself have I sworn, saith the Lord, for because thou hast done this thing, and hast not withheld thy son, thine only son: that in blessing I will bless thee, and in multiplying I will multiply thy seed as the stars of the heaven, and as the sand which is upon the seashore; and thy seed shall possess the gate of his enemies; and in thy seed shall all the nations of the earth be blessed; because thou hast obeyed My Voice."[1]

Must not the promise, vast though it was, have been, at first, almost overlooked in the overpowering joy of such approbation? Or, let us hear Solomon making his request for "an understanding heart," a request which, we are expressly told, "pleased the Lord;" and receiving for answer, "Because thou hast asked this thing, ... behold, I have done according to thy words: . . . . and I have also given thee that which thou hast not asked, both riches, and honour: so that there

[1] Gen. xxii. 16, 17, 18.

shall not be any among the kings like unto thee all thy days."[1] "Solomon awoke, and behold it was a dream;" but it was no dream that he had received the praise of the Almighty, and in thankful delight, "he came to Jerusalem, and stood before the ark of the covenant of the Lord, and offered up burnt offerings, and offered peace offerings, and made a feast to all his servants."[2]

Again, when Josiah, in his youth, dedicated himself to God's service, and yet failed to obtain forgiveness for the people who had so grievously offended, surely the words of praise for his own individual piety, must have been inexpressibly consoling. "Because thine heart was tender, and thou hast humbled thyself before the Lord . . . and hast rent thy clothes, and wept before Me; I also have heard thee, saith the Lord. Behold, therefore, I will gather thee unto thy fathers, and thou shalt be gathered unto thy grave in peace; and thine eyes shall not see all the evil which I will bring upon this place."[3]

Or, if we turn to the New Testament, can we possibly forget the open, decided approbation shown by our Blessed Lord, in so many instances; the praise bestowed upon the faith of the centurion, and the Syro-Phœnician woman; upon the devotedness of Mary, when she sat at His Feet and heard His Word; and upon the penitent love of the woman who was a sinner? Can we put aside the parables, which tell of the talents diligently used and increased, and the wonderful words of acceptance, "Well done, good and faithful servant; thou hast been faithful over a few things, I will make thee ruler over many things: enter thou into the joy of thy Lord"?[4] Or the yet more thrilling, because more distinctly real, prophecy of that glorious praise which awaits the Redeemed—"Come, ye blessed of My Father, inherit the Kingdom prepared for you from the foundation of the world"?[5]

[1] 1 Kings iii. 11, 12, 13.
[2] 1 Kings iii. 15.
[3] 2 Kings xxii. 19, 20.
[4] St. Matt. xxv. 23.
[5] St. Matt. xxv. 34.

It would seem folly to dwell upon the subject of praise, as if it could ever be a matter of doubt that it is allowable, were it not for the misconstruction of persons who, finding it incompatible with their theory of salvation, or with their experience of human imperfection, imagine that there is such danger in its application, that it must either be as much as possible omitted in education, or counteracted by the constant repetition of the fact, that every act of a fallen creature has in it something sinful, and that the best of men can never *merit* praise.

No one could have known that fact more certainly than He who made man. No one could have felt it more keenly than He who died for him. Yet we never find our Redeemer shrinking from giving praise; we never find Him hedging it about, cautioning and warning at every moment when He is bestowing it. Praise, as it comes from His Lips, comes freely, fully; it is the outpouring of His love. He does indeed, on one occasion, remind His disciples that when they have done all, they have only done their duty; but he expressly adds, "Say (that is, say to yourselves), we are unprofitable servants."[1] He does not declare that *it will be said to them;* neither does He say it. Rather, He tells them that even the "cup of cold water" given in His Name will have its reward. It need scarcely be stated that praise, to be valuable, must be given cautiously, cordially, and rarely. Praise given indiscriminately, as a matter of course or of necessity, is really no praise. But, when well deserved, it should never be withheld, even though it may seem likely to minister to vanity. For vanity, like all other faults, is the distortion of a quality in itself good. Love of approbation is inherent in human nature, and without it we could never know the happiness derived from the consciousness of God's favour; and though in the false liberality and gentleness of the day, a great deal of sinful vanity is fostered under the title of love of approbation, yet the wrong application of an epithet does not interfere with the

[1] St. Luke xvii. 10.

fact that it may be applied rightly. That which is well done —done from a right motive, and in a right way—does deserve commendation; and if from a dread of consequences we withhold the legitimate reward, we shall but foster in another shape the very evil we dread. Mortified vanity, when joined with a sense of injustice or unkindness, is more deteriorating to the character than gratified vanity, because it excites envy and ill-will; and in all cases, by a natural reaction, the fact of not having received the praise which is our due, renders us liable to over-estimate our own deserts.

But there is something more than praise which, in examining the principles of Divine education, we find to be allowable. God's servants were all more or less faulty, and they were reproved and corrected for their faults; but, in so far as they were sincere, their service was acknowledged with tokens of outward respect. The word may seem strange when used in such a connection of ideas, and yet it is not strange. All that is good comes from God, belongs to God, and therefore when He respects and honours it, He respects and honours that which is a portion of His own perfect nature. Enoch, "translated that he should not see death;" Noah, saved with his family when a guilty world perished; Abraham, blessed with the title of "the friend of God;" Job, acknowledged as God's servant at the moment of his deepest humiliation; Moses, bearing on his countenance the reflection of the dazzling glory of the Most High; Daniel, raised to power in the court of Babylon; these, and very many other of the distinguished characters under the Jewish dispensation, were openly recognized as worthy of respect. They were not only supported in the midst of trials, but they were placed in positions in which the world was compelled to own their greatness. And even under the Christian dispensation, when men were to be taught the blessedness of poverty of spirit, and the nobleness of meekness, and this through the medium of the world's contempt and persecutions, it was but in order to the more complete triumph of those virtues. Christianity conquered the world

even outwardly, and it conquers still. God has decreed that it shall be reverenced, and it is reverenced; too often with only an external respect, but even this false homage is the tribute paid to its intrinsic greatness.

It may seem far-fetched to use such an illustration with reference to the education of children in ordinary daily life; but "the child is father of the man," and is open to the same influences. The feeling of being respected by others is a great support to self-respect; and without self-respect the character must be ultimately degraded. A watchful, conscientious child, for instance, is deserving of respect, though there may be very many defects in her character. And it will be good both for herself and others that these qualities should be acknowledged openly; more especially if there should be any deficiency of intellectual power likely to excite ridicule. Respect will help her to bear up against her other shortcomings, and assist her to get the better of them. It will enable her to use the moral capital with which she is to begin her trade. Show a child that she possesses something sterling—something which those to whom she looks up can really value, and she will be encouraged to labour more heartily in other ways. Praise, if given in private, will not be sufficient. There must be a public testimony to moral worth. And this is very different from the praise which ministers to vanity; for it can be given only by those who are judges of what is good, and it will be valued only in so far as it is the result of such sound judgment. Admiration may be offered by the ignorant, and it will be willingly accepted by the vain; but respect necessarily implies the appreciation of the qualities which deserve it, and may therefore be accepted without fear, since none can receive it without being conscious how little—if they were known as God knows them—they would be found to merit it.

CHAPTER XII.

CONFIDENCE AND RESPONSIBILITY.

To show respect for the good qualities which a child may possess, is, it has been said, both useful and important, when we are attempting to educate. But the mode in which this respect should be shown, may not, to all persons, be clear. There are, indeed, many ways of evincing the feeling which will at once suggest themselves, but they seem to belong to a more advanced age; and yet the two which are likely to be the most efficacious may be tried with those who are quite young, and will almost always be found successful as means of strengthening the character and raising the tone of mind. All young people are open to the sense of confidence and responsibility, and these influences being, as they are, of such great importance, it may be desirable to consider them separately, and in detail.

"I tell you this because I trust you," is an appeal to all that is honourable in the heart; and if we would find a sanction for such confidence in God's education of His servants, we shall be at no loss for instances of it in the Bible. Let us turn to that most wonderful interview between the Almighty and the patriarch Abraham before the destruction of the cities of the plain. "And the Lord said, Shall I hide from Abraham that thing which I do; seeing that Abraham shall surely become a great and mighty nation, and all the nations of the earth shall be blessed in him? For I know him, that he will command his children and his household after him, and they shall keep the way of the Lord, to do justice and judgment;

that the Lord may bring upon Abraham that which He hath spoken of him." [1]

It was many years afterwards that Abraham's faith endured its severest trial; but it may surely be thought that the consciousness of the especial confidence placed in him by the Almighty, nerved him, in the hour of fiercest probation, to prove that he was not unmindful of it.

Or, again, consider the case of Daniel;—after three weeks of abstinence and humiliation, a revelation of future events—events which carried his thoughts to the end of Time, and the final establishment of the Kingdom of Christ—was made to him, and the reason is given.

"Fear not, Daniel: for from the first day that thou didst set thine heart to understand, and to chasten thyself before thy God, thy words were heard, and I am come for thy words." [2]

The remarkable point about this revelation is, that unlike the generality of the scripture prophecies which were uttered avowedly for the benefit of a nation, or of future ages, it was given especially for the enlightenment of the prophet himself, and ends with distinct words of consolation addressed to him. "Go thou thy way till the end be; for thou shalt rest, and stand in thy lot at the end of the days." [3]

In this respect it is a striking contrast to the revelation made to Balaam, of which he knew nothing till the moment came when, finding himself compelled to utter it before Balak, he confessed himself the unwilling instrument for foretelling the future greatness of Israel. "Behold, I have received commandment to bless: and He hath blessed, and I cannot reverse it." [4]

Or, once more, let us look to the conduct of our Blessed Lord in this respect, with regard to His disciples. Again and again we are told of His explaining things to them privately, taking them apart, foretelling the sorrows which were coming upon Him. He seems, indeed, to have made it a chief object

[1] Gen. xviii. 17, 18, 19.
[2] Dan. x .12.
[3] Dan. xii. 13.
[4] Num. xxiii. 20.

of His intercourse with them to show that He trusted in them, and to evince this trust by confidence. Almost the last day before His betrayal, as He sat upon the Mount of Olives, we find His disciples gathering round Him with questions respecting the precise fulfilment of the prophecy which He had just before uttered. They came unto Him, we are told, privately, as if assured of a hearing; and the freedom of their inquiry is as remarkable as the fulness with which it was answered. It shows such entire trust in the willingness of their Lord to satisfy them. "Tell us, when shall these things be? and what shall be the sign of Thy coming, and of the end of the world?"[1] Such a question could not have been put unhesitatingly, unless the disciples had, from long experience, known that it would have been received graciously.

And so also yet later, in that marvellous discourse which preceded the Redeemer's agony, there is not only the assurance and the promise of abiding love, but of abiding confidence. "I have yet many things to say unto you, but ye cannot bear them now. Howbeit when He, the Spirit of Truth, is come, He will guide you into all truth: for He shall not speak of himself; but whatsoever He shall hear, that shall He speak: and He will shew you things to come."[2]

Confidence, indeed, is made by our Lord the very test and evidence of love. "Henceforth I call you not servants; for the servant knoweth not what his Lord doeth: but I have called you friends; for all things that I have heard of My Father I have made known unto you."[3]

And the working of the same principle is shown in the formation of the Christian Church. St. Paul, caught up into the third Heaven, and hearing unspeakable words; and St. John receiving a revelation in the Isle of Patmos, were alike instances of men strengthened in positions of peculiar trial and eminence by the encouragement of confidence, as well as the discipline of suffering.

[1] St. Matt. xxiv. 3. [2] St. John xvi. 12, 13.
[3] St. John xv. 15.

Now, it may be thought, that confidence will spring up, as a matter of course, between parents and children; that it is the result of natural affection and mutual interests, and that in consequence there can be no necessity to insist upon it. But upon examination we shall find that such is not necessarily the case. On the contrary, under the present system of education parents and children—mothers and daughters especially—too often enjoy but very little of each other's confidence.

In the first place, their previous lives have, for the most part, been distant. The children have lived in the school-room; the mothers in the drawing-room. This, perhaps, is a necessity, but it does not tend to produce confidence. But the daughters have also advanced beyond their mothers; that is to say, they possess, as a general rule, more showy accomplishments. They can perform more wonderful feats on the piano, and talk French and German with greater facility, if not with greater correctness. They have not yet forgotten the dates of the English kings, and they have caught up the terms of science from attendance upon lectures on all imaginable "ologies." They ride more boldly, and talk more loudly, and dress with greater eccentricity. Their mothers are not their companions, because they do not join in these things. The school-room or the morning room is appropriated exclusively to the "young ladies" of the family; and when their mother enters she is received as a visitor, and finds herself decidedly in the way. This is too often the case even where the daughters have been educated in habits of quiet domestic occupation, and have no desire to be numbered amongst the "fast girls" of the nineteenth century. They are fast in one sense, in spite of themselves; that is to say, they are, in thought and purpose, travelling onwards, whilst their mothers are travelling backwards. All of us who have reached the middle of life, and are descending the hill on the other side, must be more or less conscious of this. How many of us are gaining new ideas, and forming new theories, and striving to carry them into practice as we did when we were young? How many of us

are not rather standing still, gazing around with somewhat of pity and regret, as we watch what we consider the follies of the young enthusiasts of the day? How many of us are not even in a degree retrograding—going back to old established principles, which we once thought we had relinquished for ever, but which experience has proved to be more sound than the theories that once appeared so inviting?

We cannot rush forward with the young, because we see too plainly whither they are going. We cannot hold them back, because they have life and energy on their side; and the law of God's Providence has ordained that they shall be the leaders in life's race. And therefore we stand apart; it may be, carefully performing our own duties—working, according to our own rules, the plans which we have tested and approved; and suffering them to walk at will according to theirs.

The separation between old and young has always existed in a certain degree, and it must continue to exist to the end of Time; the mistake is in permitting it to produce estrangement and want of confidence.

It was the remark of a very shrewd observer of human nature, "Young people *think* that old people are fools; old people *know* that young people are so."

If they know it, then let them make use of their knowledge. Because they are wiser than the young, therefore they are called upon to offer sympathy, encouragement, assistance, so far as they possibly can; to relinquish their prejudices, to endeavour to look at life as the young look at it; to work with them in their way, even though it may not be the most perfect way. The old have once been young, and they can, therefore, in some degree, recall and imagine the feelings of the young. But the young have never been old, and they cannot, therefore, be expected to understand the feelings of the old. All good things, all high, noble, generous wishes, all innocent amusements and pursuits, all efforts at usefulness, however unlike those which we should ourselves have set on foot, demand our sympathy; and if we give it—give it unsparingly—

we shall in time receive our full recompense. Young people delight in the support of their elders, when they feel that it really is support; and they will listen to suggestions, and sometimes even profit by others' experience, so long as they are sure that there is no implied censure underneath the advice offered. They will, in short, give their confidence and share their interests; but in order to this result, one preparatory step is needful—confidence must first be given to them.

And here, in the majority of cases, lies the difficulty, more especially in those instances in which the superiority of talent and energy is to be found on the side of the parent. A clever woman—active in mind and body—accustomed to rule—in the habit of forming plans and carrying them out successfully—is very slow in arriving at the perception that the time is come when others are to be admitted to share her labours; more especially when in that word, others, her children are included. They have been subject to her; she knows all their defects, she has suffered from their deficiencies, she has no confidence in their judgment. What she wishes to do can be done much better by herself. And then they are inclined to differ from her, and she has not been used to be differed from. She does not understand her children being her judges. It seems as if it would be impossible to work with them without mutual frets and jars; and so the mother pursues her duties, and leaves her young daughters to their amusements; not perceiving that by so doing she is really fostering that common self-deceit which leads us all to think that so long as things needful to be done are done, it does not signify who undertakes them. Young people, and elderly people, too, will often entirely neglect certain duties themselves; and yet, because they are attended to by others, never open their eyes to the fact of their own shortcomings. Thus, to perform duties by deputy is the source of some of the most lamentable self-delusions by which the character may be lastingly deteriorated.

Or again, perhaps the mother takes another view of the case. Rule and manage she must. It belongs to her position,

and no one else would, so she thinks, be able to do as well as herself. But her daughters may be made useful, and so she gives them certain things to do. They are to keep accounts, or to visit a school, or to read with a young servant, or to superintend some domestic arrangement, perhaps even to order dinner. They are summoned from their own occupation, and the duties are proposed to them. To the mother's disappointment, the idea is received with coldness. The young ladies prefer their pursuits in the morning room, and do not show any willingness to lighten their mother's labour. She thinks them selfish and ungrateful, and she may not be very far wrong. But there has been a mistake on her side. We, none of us, like duties simply as duties. Those rather cold and selfish girls who devote themselves to what pleases them, and cannot be called to help their mother without showing that they are disinclined to undertake the task, would probably have been the first to assist her with all their hearts, if she had set to work differently. A little confidence with regard to the duties would have caused them to be viewed differently. Accounts are very dull when we have only to add up figures, but they may be very interesting (always supposing we have a capacity for them) when we know what depends upon them. If a girl is told what her father's income is, and what are the claims upon it, she will have an object in watching the expenditure. And so in the care of schools or charities; let young people know what they are working for, and give them a share both in anxiety and in success, and they will put their hearts, as well as their intellects, into the task allotted them. But merely to obey, to do what one is told to do, because one is told, and without being at all enlightened as to the end and object of one's efforts, is to most minds so irksome, that, without a great effort of principle, the duty is too often before long either relinquished, or performed so carelessly, that it might as well be omitted altogether.

There are, indeed, religious systems which teach us to look upon the act of obeying, without the knowledge wherefore we

obey, as the highest of Christian virtues. This is not the place for discussing the question, but one thing is quite clear, that, in the ordinary dealings of God with His creatures, such blind obedience is not required. We might have been so constituted as not to be able to foresee the result of our own actions. We might, for instance, have been as ignorant of the reasons why we are commanded to attend to certain social duties, such as hospitality, courtesy, respect, as Abraham was of the reasons why he was called upon to offer up his son. It is difficult to imagine such a possibility, and yet we shall see, upon consideration, that the moral sense which teaches us that it is our duty to act in a certain way, is quite distinct from the comprehension of the reason why it is good for us to do so. A little child knows when it has done wrong as clearly and as quickly as a grown-up man; but it cannot understand what it is which constitutes what may be called the mischief—the injurious consequence of the wrong. This comprehension is the result of reason; it becomes more and more evident as reason develops; and in thus giving us reason, enabling us to see how, and why, good produces good, and evil produces evil, God has, if it may be said with reverence, given us His confidence. He has taken us into His counsels, given us a share in His intentions, made us, as the Apostle terms us, fellow-workers with Him. If blind obedience were the one end to be obtained by this state of probation, we might have been as children all our lives—gifted, indeed, with moral sense, and placed in positions in which that moral sense would be called into exercise, and the choice of obedience or disobedience be given us—but with no power beyond. But God wills that we should give Him our hearts, and in order to win those hearts He grants us what we must grant to our children, when they are capable of receiving it, a knowledge of the end and object of the duties required, as well as the command for their performance. This confidence, it may be observed, is quite distinct from the indulgence of curiosity respecting others: a fault especially reproved by our Blessed Lord when, in answer to St. Peter's inquiry,

"Lord, and what shall this man do?" He said, "If I will that he tarry till I come, what is that to thee? Follow thou Me."[1] And so it is distinct also from the indulgence of speculations and inquiries respecting subjects which are wisely hidden. Such speculations were embodied in the question, "Lord, are there few that shall be saved?" and were answered by our Lord with the warning, "Strive to enter in at the strait gate: for many, I say unto you, will seek to enter in, and shall not be able."[2]

The confidence which God gives is sufficient to arouse interest, and sustain energy; but it is granted only in that degree which is consistent with His purposes of probation and our own limited faculties. The mystery of evil—including its necessity, and the ultimate object for which it is permitted—is hidden from us; and so, also, is the purpose of our own creation. But the fact that we cannot know all, and that even if we could know we could not understand all, does not prevent God from giving us that amount of information which will enable us to work with a definite aim, and one which He approves, though it cannot be that ultimate one which He himself intends. And so, we may venture to say, parents may give their children a share in their counsels, and explain to them, sufficiently, the objects they have in view, without attempting to bring before them the whole, which they might not be able to understand, or which it might not be fitting that they should. This is peculiarly the case with respect to some works of charity and mercy, in which young girls could not engage if full knowledge of all the circumstances connected with them were required, and yet in which they may be deeply interested, and be made to take a most useful part, by a little judicious confidence.

But it may be said, by thus trusting young people, and giving them a share in works of usefulness, we run the risk of marring those works. Granted: yet, let us ask ourselves in what line of conduct is there not risk? We undertake to do

[1] St. John xxi. 21, 22. [2] St. Luke xiii. 23, 24.

everything ourselves, and a fit of illness comes, and our works fall to the ground—because there are none to carry them on. There is one time of life when our duty is to learn; another, when we are to carry out independently what we have learnt; a third, when we are to hand over our tasks to others, and show how best they may be performed. This third stage is not always agreeable. It tells us too plainly of failing powers. It too evidently bids us look forward to the night that "cometh, in which no man can work." But when we have arrived at this period, it is as much our bounden duty to face the fact, as it is to acknowledge any other of those conditions of our being which set limits to our powers, and direct them into definite channels. To sit by and see our children performing imperfectly what we know we once did easily and well ourselves, is no doubt a trial. But are we unable to bear with that which God bears with? He trusts His work to feeble hands. He waits with patience, whilst, from indolence, or carelessness, we make mistakes, and but slowly learn to correct them. He allows His gracious intentions to be marred, His purposes of mercy to be apparently thwarted—and why? Because He is educating us; and because, for the furtherance of education, responsibility—that second powerful influence to which reference has been made—and with it the risk of failure, is imperatively necessary.

We can, indeed, scarcely over-estimate the importance of responsibility as an instrument in the formation of character. It is seen, perhaps, most strikingly in the career of young men sent early to India, and changed from careless, headstrong, or idle youths, into calm judging, energetic, sensible men. It may be one cause of the fact, so often remarked, that India produces men ready for emergencies. But it may more or less be remarked everywhere, under all circumstances, and its value must be acknowledged, even though we may find cause to deplore the effects of its exaggeration. The children of the poor, the fatherless, and the widow, how strangely old and prudent they are at an age when the children of wealthy parents

are scarcely out of the nursery! The daughter of the labourer, sent out to service at seventeen or eighteen, makes her way safely, through dangers and temptations which the squire would shudder to think his own child could be exposed to; and at two or three and twenty is looked upon as qualified to judge, decide, and act for herself, like a woman of thirty in the upper classes. Or, in the case of persons of a higher grade, let us look at an elder girl left without a mother, and called upon to act as the head of a large family: if she is worth anything, how thoughtful she becomes—how careful and watchful for the little ones—how industrious, how methodical! She has had no training—none at least which can strictly be called training—she has only had responsibility. It is that which has roused her, urged, checked, made her observant, self-controlled, given her sound judgment. Without responsibility, she would probably have been but as other girls; gentle, perhaps, and amiable, and desirous to do right, but not aware of any particular claim for exertion, and, therefore, not thinking it needful to make it.

And it is responsibility which, in the majority of cases, makes the difference between the young married woman and the young girl of the same age. Give a young person a house of her own, and servants to guide, and make the happiness of another dependent upon her, and she must, if she has any good at all in her, acquire habits of thoughtfulness and self-control. But the daughter living in her father's house is, too often, allowed to have no responsibility. Everything is arranged and provided for her without her effort, or if she is expected to undertake any particular duty, it must be performed in a way pointed out for her beforehand; whilst, very frequently, her omissions are corrected by some one more careful, so that she learns at last to think that it does not signify whether she attends to the duty imposed upon her or not.

There is no real responsibility in all this, and consequently no training. If we wish to make use of responsibility as an educational instrument, we must leave free scope for the exer-

cise of individual will, and we must be content to bear the annoyance when that will is wrongly exercised. Once perform a young girl's duties for her, or let others do so, and the idea of training her by responsibility is at an end.

This latter statement will probably be uncontroverted. But the necessity of leaving free scope for the exercise of individual will—what is to be said to that? Is there really any occasion to enforce it?

The fact will probably be disputed. Young ladies of the present day are supposed to have a great deal of will, and, what is more, to exercise it very independently.

No doubt they do, but then they exercise it wrongly, because against their parents' wishes; and that which is now contended for, as being in itself good and desirable, is a sphere in which will may be exercised rightly, because with the parents' consent. To give one very slight, but very common illustration: a girl old enough to be taken into society is old enough to be made responsible for her own expenditure; and in order to do this, she must have an allowance. But she will then choose her own dress, and if she should not quite agree with her mother in taste, there is no reason to charge her with disobedience in following her own will. If, however, the mother should prefer to retain the allowance and the choice of dress in her own hands, then there must, sooner or later, be a clashing of wills. The mother will decide, and will think it wrong in her child not to yield at once to her judgment. The daughter will have the fancies belonging to her age, and may not be sufficiently dutiful to submit without resistance. An unpleasant breach must be the consequence; and both parties will think themselves injured. The mother will say that her daughter ought to be guided by her opinion. The daughter will say that at her age she ought to be allowed to exercise an independent will. The mistake lies in the mother's not having marked out a sphere within which, under certain limitations, will might be exercised. Questions of this kind are springing up daily in private life, too often causing coldness, undutiful-

ness, suspicion, and angry sinful words and feelings, which it is very grievous to watch; they are so entirely opposed to Christian feeling and principle.

Correspondence, friends, the employment of time, of money, the choice of duties, must all, no doubt, have definite limits; but within those limits, why may there not be the free exercise of will? The object of education with us all is to teach us not merely how to obey, but how to exercise our will and to govern. It is this object, recognized in the public schools of England, by a system of delegated responsibility, that makes them what, with all their faults, they unquestionably are—the most important engines for good, apart from direct religion, which we possess. And the value of government is plainly acknowledged in the Bible.

The Apostles, when urged forward by the prospect of future rewards, were told that they were to "sit on thrones judging the twelve tribes of Israel." He who had used his ten talents, so as to gain by them other ten talents, was made ruler over ten cities. To govern well is indeed far higher and nobler than to obey well; and for this reason, that the power of perfect government in finite creatures involves the power of perfect obedience, since, in order to ensure its perfection, it must first be exercised upon self. Self-restraint, self-denial, self-reproof, self-discipline, far stricter than any which we could venture to exercise upon others, are in fact essential for the formation of a really high and noble character; but they are strengthened, if not originally inculcated, by responsibility; and from responsibility, freedom of action is inseparable.

Observations of this kind are undoubtedly open to misconstruction. The tendency of the present day is so greatly to encourage independence, which leads to neglect and irreverence, that a person who ventures to advocate freedom of action in young people is very likely to be accused of encouraging them in their wilfulness and lawlessness. Even at the risk of repetition, it must, therefore, again be stated, that strict disci-

pline, and absolute, instantaneous obedience, at eight years of age, are indispensable preliminaries to freedom at eighteen. The subject under discussion now, is not what is to be done with spoilt children, but how those whose education is just beginning may best be trained. If the advice given should be reversed, or misunderstood, the error will lie with those who apply the counsel wrongly, not with the person who gives it.

And surely we need the less fear granting responsibility to the young, however inferior to ourselves they may be, when we mark the mode in which our Redeemer dealt with His disciples. For three years only was He with them—and yet long before those three years had expired He sent them forth to teach and to preach in His Name; and we hear of no restrictions, no laws, except of the most general kind. They were left to find out for themselves, who, amongst the inhabitants of the cities they visited, were worthy to receive them. They were plainly warned that their position would be that of sheep in the midst of wolves; yet the only caution given them was that they should be "wise as serpents and harmless as doves." And so they went forth, but "when they were returned, they told Him all that they had done." [1]

Here, then, was the check. Certain great principles were impressed upon them, and a definite sphere having been given them, within which they might act freely, they returned to their Lord to tell how they had exercised their own independent judgment, and to receive from Him the further warnings and instructions which might be needful. Such was the training required for those who were afterwards to govern the infant Church; and so we find that when our Lord had finally withdrawn His visible presence from them, they were able to carry out the principles in which they had already been exercised, and to use the experience they had acquired for the benefit of those over whom they were appointed to rule. Very remarkable, indeed, is the freedom upon all minor points which was left to the rulers of the early Christian Church. The great

[1] St. Luke ix. 10.

outlines of government were, we have reason to believe, given definitely—for allusions to them are plainly made in Scripture —but they were filled up as circumstances required, according to the needs of the moment, and the wisdom of the Apostles; guided, indeed, by the Holy Spirit, but yet not so guided as to interfere with free choice and human deliberation. Witness, for instance, the appointment of the seven deacons to undertake the secular business of the little Christian community; the decision of the first Council, upon the question of circumcision; the directions given by St. Paul to the Church of Corinth; in some of which he plainly states that he speaks without immediate guidance from the Spirit of God.

How unlike—how wonderfully different—is all this freedom, to the working of human power! Let us suppose ourselves—if we may be permitted to make such a comparison—called upon to establish a society which should have for its object the reformation of even a small State;—gifted with full powers, moral, mental, and physical—able, in fact, to carry out our will fully, and to foresee and provide against all difficulties. How strict would be our laws—how carefully guarded and checked! How anxious we should be to state precisely the way in which every one was to act under every possible emergency; how disinclined we should be to give even the slightest responsibility to those we felt were our inferiors in intellect and principle! Volumes would not be sufficient to contain our rules, our cautions, and restrictions. This is the instinct of human nature. The power of trust belongs essentially to God. Man cannot trust others, because he distrusts himself. We see this plainly in all cases which involve the foundation of societies, or the working of political schemes: but we see it also even in such personal matters as the making of wills—the entail of property. It seems, indeed, to be so natural to men to wish to hamper their descendants, and take from them responsibility by tying them down to a particular line of action, that in some cases the civil power is actually obliged to interfere to prevent such restrictions being carried into effect.

And when we look at the actual working of societies and institutions in our own day, it is scarcely too much to say that the ruling principle of the majority, when founded for religious objects, is that of concentrated power, rather than delegated responsibility. Absolute authority, minute direction, on the one hand; absolute obedience on the other. The idea of escape from responsibility is, indeed, openly acknowledged, in some cases, to be the temptation to enter such societies. Whether these principles are necessary for the carrying out of the purposes of the institutions in which they are adopted, cannot of course be determined without full knowledge of what those purposes are. But upon consideration it would certainly appear, that action without responsibility, however instrumental it may be for the attainment of certain definite ends, will never be instrumental to the improvement of the individual character; because it is contrary to the training appointed by God in nature, and the principles of education which He has marked out for us in revelation.

Our work is for the future as well as for the present generation. Woe be to us if we forget this!

It was for the worthless favourite of a worthless king to say, "Après moi le deluge." When the one Eternal Future was overlooked, all other futures became indifferent. But it may not be so with us. Even now, as we labour with our whole heart and thought concentrated on some present purpose, Death stands, as it were, on one side of us, and Time on the other. And Time is pointing to the dial-plate on which the hours of our earthly existence are numbered; and Death is watching the hand of Time, as it silently but ceaselessly moves forward; and when Time shall touch the last figure, Death will lift his hand to strike, and our work will cease. But not our influence, not our teaching, not our counsel, and our warning. That will live on in others;—in those who are now the young, the ignorant, the thoughtless, the wilful—who must, perforce, take up our work where we left it—who must carry on what we have left unfinished—who

must, like us, labour in their generation, and for their generation, and for those who are to come after them; or who, if they are unaccustomed to responsibility, will stand gazing in alarm as society—social and political—like the great car of Juggernaut, moves on; until, at length, too timid to move with it, too ignorant to attempt to guide it, they are crushed by its merciless wheels.

It sounds like imagination—unreality. It does not seem as if the conduct of separate individuals, without name or apparent influence, could really be of importance. And the sphere of each is small; the work to be undertaken is, in most cases, local and immediate. Let it be done, so we say to ourselves, in the best way, to suit the needs of to-day; and to-morrow, we may well believe, will provide for itself. True, in one sense; untrue, in another. Our work must, indeed, be done in the best way; but, can that be the best which excludes the coöperation of those who are to take our place when we are gone? If there are no learners, how can there, hereafter, be teachers? If we do not allow the young to practise themselves in independence and responsibility, how can they be fitted to do what we are doing?

And if we will but follow the example set us by our Lord, we need have no fear of the consequences of this independence. The disciples, as we have seen, were exercised in freedom of action and responsibility, whilst their Master was present with them. He did not wait until after His ascension to delegate to them His power; He granted it during His earthly life. All that He required was, that they should be accountable to Him. It is an example for us all. It may be followed in very small matters, but it will have very important results; and most especially in the case of girls called upon to live at home, subject to their parents' authority, at an age when boys are sent out into the world to be, in a great degree, independent.

The same kind of freedom which is necessary for a boy, is, of course, entirely unsuited to a girl. She cannot roam about

by herself, or undertake separate work. She must be kept within limits, which will often appear irksome, and even needless, though, without them, she would be involved in serious evils. The very fact of the necessity of these restraints renders it, however, incumbent on those whose duty it is to insist upon them, to give the sense of freedom within the restricted circle. There can be no interest in home life without it. All that wealth and refinement, and even love, can offer, may be lavished upon the young, but without that freedom of action, which is involved in responsibility, they will still be dissatisfied.

The human mind soon grows weary of amusement; it learns to dislike splendour, and to be sickened by luxury. The one thing of which it never tires is the sense of usefulness; and no person can be thoroughly useful who is not accustomed to responsibility. The girl who is the victim of ennui in the drawing-room, finds time only too short when she is allowed to follow out some plan of usefulness in the school-room or the village; and if this plan is furthered and encouraged by her mother, they must become one in feeling and confidence, and the risk of independence is then over.

The advantage of this early training in responsibility can only be fully perceived by comparing it with the effects of an opposite system.

Work alone—work performed mechanically, simply as an act of obedience—has, it has already been said, but little influence in the formation of character. What we all require to learn is thoughtfulness; and the habit of suffering others to think for us, instead of thinking for ourselves, is very easily gained, but by no means so easily lost. The exceedingly narrow sphere of some persons' duties; the way in which they shut their eyes to the fact that there are claims lying beyond the circle of their own families, is very astonishing to those who are accustomed to realize the fact that no human being can be associated with them, even for ten minutes, without

having some claim upon them for kindness and courtesy, if not for more direct efforts for good. We see persons apparently amiable in disposition, wishing to do right, scrupulous in their religious duties, yet, through it all, living for themselves, working for themselves, studying for themselves, thinking and planning for themselves. We see the possessors of great wealth, both men and women, by no means cold-hearted or avaricious, or wilfully extravagant, attending to the plain duties incumbent upon them as landlords, or heads of households, but spending all their superfluous income upon themselves, doling out their gifts and their charities in a proportion which, when compared with the means that they have in their power, would be ludicrous if it were not so infinitely sad.

We see others, with scarcely any claims upon their time, beating out their scanty occupations like a leaf of gold-beater's skin, in order to make them cover the surface of the day; and yet all the while praising and admiring works of charity and self-denial, taking, indeed, a real interest in them, so far as that can be called interest which shrinks from any actual participation in the work.

What is the secret of this frightful veil of self-deceit, this moral blindness which shuts out from so many the extent of their duties? Merely the want of teaching, of early training, the habit of doing what they have been told to do without exercising independent thought or recollecting their own responsibility. The young girl who goes into a shop and orders what she requires, and has it put down to her mother's account, has not the least idea of the value of money, or the duties which attend its possession. She has no inducement to practise self-denial, because no one, so far as she can see, will be the better for it. The habit of indulging her own wishes without thought for others is in this way acquired, and when at length she has the command of an independent income, she continues the system of self-pleasing simply because it is a habit. And so, again, when the daughters of a family, although performing certain mechanical tasks, concentrate their interests in pursuits

for their own gratification, whilst their mother undertakes to arrange and carry out the social and domestic duties of life; it can be no matter of astonishment if, when they have houses of their own, they are neglectful of the wants of their friends, or unmindful of the needs of the poor. They are but doing what they have been trained to do. The world went on very well without them when they were young, why should it not do so now that they are older? They have no knowledge what poverty, and care, and grief are; how can they search for and sympathize with them? If they had only been practised in thoughtfulness in early life, all this would probably have been different. Responsibility—the consciousness that certain duties were left in their hands to be discharged in their own way, at their own time, but that still discharged they must be, or that others would suffer—would have tended to form a habit of unselfish consideration which might have made them centres of kindness and benevolence in the positions which they were afterwards called upon to occupy.

And it is vain to say that duties are not at hand; that in country places, or amidst the necessary restrictions of a life in London, young people cannot be made useful. The proverb, "Where there is a will there is a way," is never more applicable than in the case of duties. Let us do what comes before us at the moment, in whatever place, under whatever circumstances we may find ourselves, and the performance of this first duty will open the door for a second. If we cannot go out to seek for work, we may find work that can be brought to us. If it cannot be undertaken for a permanence, it may be for a time. Though it be ever so small, ever so apparently unimportant, yet, if it is all we can do at the moment, let it be undertaken. No home affords the materials of true happiness where there is not to be found work for the good of others, in which many may have an interest, and yet in which each may have some separate responsibility.

These are not days in which such work will long be wanting, when there is a real wish to find it. The blessing that

attends it, we shall more truly estimate if we consider what work really is. We often speak of it as belonging to our condition on earth, as part of our punishment, and our probation. We forget that Adam laboured in Paradise, that angels labour for the service of God in Heaven; above all, that the Redeemer himself has said, " My Father worketh hitherto, and I work."

CHAPTER XIII.

HUMAN FAITH.

The advantage of early training in responsibility will perhaps scarcely be disputed when asserted as an abstract proposition, but serious difficulties must arise when an endeavour is made to put the theory into practice.

The human mind is always tempted to exaggeration, and in the present age, especially, the spirit of independence is so powerful, that to strike the happy medium between undue subjection to authority, and undue exertion of separate will, may seem almost impossible.

Yet there are two principles which, if they were only inculcated upon children, from their earliest infancy, would make it comparatively safe to entrust them with independence and responsibility as they grow up. Faith and reverence are the counterbalances to independence in thought, and decision in choice and action.

A child's faith in its parents, and in those set over it, is as essential to its earthly, as faith in God is to its spiritual well-being. Let us, then, consider how faith is to be inculcated.

First of all, what do we mean by faith? The Bible, speaking of religious faith, tells us that it is "the substance of things hoped for, the evidence of things not seen;"[1] and the words may in a lower and more restricted sense be applied to human faith, our faith in each other. A child's faith in its parents includes the belief that all things necessary for its support and

[1] Heb. xi. 1.

happiness will be provided for it, though it cannot tell how; and also the assurance that the commands laid down for its conduct are intended for its good, although the reasons for them may not be seen.

And thus we are accustomed to distinguish between faith and reason; to make faith the foundation of obedience, and reason only the instrument for the confirmation of faith. But is this quite a true statement of the relative positions of faith and reason? Can faith really exist apart from reason? or rather does not the very name of faith involve the idea of reason? Faith is trust—trust in a person. A person, whether human or divine, must have a character, or, in other words, possess moral attributes. Faith, therefore, implies a recognition of these attributes, which cannot be made without the aid of reason. An idiot or a madman cannot exercise faith, except in that modified form of mechanical trust—the result of experience—which is shared in common with the brute creation. Herein lies the distinction between right faith and superstition; between the religion of the Christian and that of the idolater. The faith of the idolater has no foundation in reason; whilst the God of the Christian never demands of His creatures faith which has not reason for its foundation.

For instance, reason teaches us that God *is*, and that He is infinitely just and good. When we have once learnt this truth, then we are called upon to exercise faith, and to believe that all which this Holy God does is absolutely right and just, although we may not be able to understand it. We must obey His commands, though we do not see why they are given. So it is that our Christian faith also rests upon reasonable belief. We have abundant evidence of the truth of our Lord's existence and of His mission; evidence which appeals to our reason. Having this, we are bound to accept all which He tells us. Once own that Christianity is true, and it is as unreasonable to disbelieve any particular doctrine because it does not please us, or does not accord with our preconceived ideas of what God would do, as it would be to reject the truth that God is

the Moral Governor of the world, because in many ways the method of His government is perplexing to us. Reason, in fact, lays the foundation of religion; faith builds the superstructure: let reason intrude into the province of faith, and it ceases to be reason. And the faith which the Christian exercises when, being convinced of the truth of revelation, he submits himself to its doctrines and precepts, is therefore as absolutely reasonable as that which the child exercises in its parents, when it drinks off the medicine given it, though entirely ignorant of the drugs of which it is composed.

It would seem to follow from this, that if man's reason were perfect, his faith would be perfect also.

And we certainly see that when, through wilful self-conceit, or passion, or the temptations or trials of the moment, we become weak and incapable of reasoning soundly—then our faith fails.

Sin is not only sin; it is also folly; and God, who knew this, has most mercifully provided, by His teaching both in nature and revelation, that we should be constantly and practically reminded of the fact. We may sometimes have wondered, as we have watched the career of our friends and acquaintances, or looked back upon our own, why it is that follies, blunders, mistakes, are in this world so severely punished. The bad man—bad in his neglect of God, but wise in his generation—prospers. The good man—good in his desire to serve God, but unwise in his generation—plunges into inextricable difficulties. May not the solution of this problem be found in the supreme importance of sound reason, as a foundation for right faith and true morality? If all the foolish actions of all the good people on earth were allowed to pass unpunished, simply because of their right intention, the cultivation of sound reason would be utterly neglected, and fatal confusion would be the result.

The more earnest a man is, the more devoted to God's service, the greater is his power of influence, and the more needful therefore is it that he should use that influence wisely.

The mistakes of good men are probably more injurious to society than the sins of bad men, and therefore, so it appears, God visits them with a more severe present chastisement.

The paramount importance of reason in the cultivation of all moral goodness or religious belief, and especially as the basis of practical faith, may be seen by examining more minutely into the way in which God has been pleased to reveal Himself to His creatures by evidences which appeal to their reason, before He makes demands upon their faith.

The first question a child is taught to answer, as a foundation for its religious creed, is, "Who made you?" "God." From the fact of its own existence it grasps intuitively the idea of the existence of its Maker. As reason develops, it learns from the wonders of nature the power of the Creator of nature; and from its own moral consciousness it is able to conceive the idea of moral perfection. The child so reasons without knowing that it reasons. It is aware that faith in God is a duty; it does not know that unless God had, through its unconscious reason, enabled it to comprehend the idea of His existence, faith would have been impossible.

This does not, however, mean that mankind, left to themselves, would have been able to reason out fully the idea of God without the aid of revelation. What the power of human reason might have been if man had never fallen, we cannot tell; but certainly our own consciousness, and the experience of former ages, alike tell us that reason, as it now exists in man—liable to be swayed by passion and distorted by inclination—will too often, when left without aid, arrive at the most contradictory and absurd conclusions. Neither is any reasoning in the present day a proof of what reason by itself can do; because we stand upon a vantage ground which we have derived from revelation; and looking to the past days of heathenism, we can only point to one or two instances in which anything like an approximation to the true idea of the Deity was reached. When once that idea was promulgated

by revelation, man's reason, indeed, could not fail to accept it: but the power of examining into and confirming truth is inferior to that of discovering it: and this is a fact which, in extolling the power of reason, we are all too liable to forget; neither do we remember that, even in this modified form, reason can only examine and confirm what lies within its own province; it can only judge rightly of that which it is capable of understanding.

And yet, notwithstanding all these limitations, it is nevertheless clear that it is reason which prepares the way for faith; and so, when we look into the Bible, we shall find that God is continually strengthening His servants' faith by showing them that it has a foundation in reason. Abraham was commanded to offer up his son; but before that greatest effort of faith was required of him, his reason had taught him, by the experience of a watchful Providence, a continual interposition in his favour, a miraculous fulfilment of promise, a condescension unequalled in the history of God's dealings with man, that the Almighty Being whom he worshipped was infinite in His mercy as in His power; and could never demand that which would not ultimately be for the good of those who would obey and trust Him.

Moses was required to undertake a task for which he felt himself unfitted; but before he was sent to Pharaoh, God made an appeal to his reason, by showing him that he would have the power of working miracles conferred upon him. The Jews were required to follow Moses into the desert; but before they set out on their journey they had, in the plagues of Egypt, seen enough to convince them, that in obeying his guidance, they were obeying the voice of God. Gideon was told to save Israel from the Midianites: his faith was weak, and he asked the evidence of a sign—something which should be a pledge to his reason that the promise of success would be fulfilled;—and God vouchsafed to grant him a double sign. Hezekiah was told, that in answer to his prayer he should recover from his sickness; and, in order to strengthen his faith

in the promise, he was allowed to ask for a sign from Heaven; and the shadow of the degrees which had gone down in the sun-dial of Ahaz returned ten degrees backward.

So, again, when our Blessed Lord reproached the Jews for their unbelief, He implied that they did not make use of their reason. "The works which the Father hath given Me to finish, the same works that I do, bear witness of Me, that the Father hath sent Me." [1] And this argument was brought forward as unanswerable by the man who had been born blind, but had been restored to sight: "Since the world began was it not heard that any man opened the eyes of one that was born blind. If this Man were not of God, He could do nothing." [2]

The proofs of the Resurrection—the very foundation stone of Christianity—were reasonable proofs. Our Lord allowed Thomas to thrust his hand into His Side; He ate and drank with His disciples; He was seen of them for forty days; and spake to them of "the things pertaining to the kingdom of God." And when at length He ascended to Heaven, He left with them the power of working miracles, as the appeal to the reason of mankind for the claim which was to be made upon their faith and their obedience. This, then, is God's plan for educating mankind in faith; and we may learn from it that, as nothing can be more erroneous than to insist upon using reason in deciding questions which belong to the province of faith, so nothing can be more unwise than to insist upon faith being exercised, when there is no foundation of reason on which to rest it.

And now to apply this same plan to the education of children.

Faith, as it has been said, is as essential to them in their relation to their parents and teachers, as it is to adults in their relation to God. But there is one vast distinction between the two cases. God may, and often does, insist upon implicit faith in us, because He has taught us, by reason and revelation,

[1] St. John v. 36. [2] St. John ix. 32, 33.

that He is infinitely perfect. But we can never bring forward the same argument to support our claims upon any one, because we are most imperfect. It does not, however, follow that we can make no such claim upon children, or that, according to a theory by no means rare, they are never to be expected to obey, unless they are told the reason why; and are never to be taught anything which they do not understand. There is a claim of authority, based upon the commands of God, which is always a reason for enforcing a child's obedience; and there is a natural superiority of comprehension, and of experience, in the parent, which must always be acknowledged as the reason and groundwork of a child's faith. But when we go beyond this, we must remember that we are likely to meet with difficulties. A child's reason develops with its stature; often, indeed, more quickly than its stature. And as it reasons, so it will instinctively judge, and approve, or condemn. Now, if we find that God, Omniscient, Omnipotent, All-Holy though He is, has such compassion for the weakness of men, that He vouchsafes to enlighten reason in order to strengthen faith, so, surely, we may, in like manner, endeavour to enlighten and strengthen our children.

In infancy and early childhood there can, of course, be no appeal to anything but the principle of obedience. Neither can there be any permission given for disobedience afterwards; but if, when issuing a command, or insisting upon a certain line of conduct, we were to strive, as much as possible, to satisfy children's reason, by telling them, in cases in which explanation is possible, why we so acted, we should find them much more willing to put faith in us in those instances in which it might not be in our power to offer any explanation.

"My mother never gives an order without a good reason," is a thought which will at once still the risings of petulance and wilfulness when a command is not understood. But if we omit to give our reasons when we can do so, the thought will not be suggested.

And this faith in persons older than themselves is needful

for young persons, not only as involves obedience, but as regards the training of their own minds. The reason why freedom and responsibility are dangerous to the young is, that such liberty is likely to inspire them with self-conceit and overweening self-confidence. Faith in the judgment of those who have had more experience, is the natural counterbalance to these faults. But most of us learn this trust in experience only by finding what mistakes we have made in life from the want of it. We can reason now upon the actions of our parents, our guardians, and teachers, and see how wise and right they were, when we thought them absurdly wrong. But we failed, probably, to profit by their experience, when it could really have been of use, because it was never explained to us. We were told what we were to do, and how we were to do it, but the *why* was left to be discovered by ourselves, and, naturally enough, the answer was given wrongly. We attributed motives and purposes which never existed; we thought regulations to be the result of caprice, which were, in reality, the dictates of self-denial and good judgment; we put, in fact, but little faith in our superiors, and so the lesson has been learnt too late to be of use.

The necessity of this education in faith is more especially to be borne in mind as the counterpoise to the education in obedience. The two must never be separated by men, because they are never separated by God.

It will sometimes happen that, from a press of engagements, or from natural abstraction of mind, or simply from habit, parents who are most watchful not to spoil their children fall into the opposite extreme, and treat them as automatons. They expect to be obeyed; and they are obeyed; and because their directions are good and sensible, the children's actions are the same. But with all this obedience in action, there may be a vast amount of disobedience in spirit, and it will show itself as soon as the opportunity for the exercise of freedom and responsibility is granted. Very painful it is to hear it said, "My father, or my mother, brought me up in such

or such a way, and I am resolved that my children shall be brought up precisely in the contrary way." A resolution of this kind is nearly certain to involve very grievous mistakes.

To have no faith in the judgment of those who have been our guides, is to determine to buy our own experience for ourselves; and who, on looking back on his own career, will venture to count up the mistakes, the sorrows, it may be the sins, which have been the price paid for that experience? No one who sets out in life with such a principle can indeed safely be trusted with responsibility. Yet it is the natural result of an education in which the young are not trained to faith through the enlightenment of reason;—in which they obey simply because they are compelled to do so, and seldom or never have the reasons set before them which render such obedience necessary.

CHAPTER XIV.

RESPECT.

THERE is another safeguard against the misuse of freedom, which is closely allied to the principle of faith, and is, in fact, often its embodiment, though it cannot be said to be inseparable from it.

"Honour thy father and thy mother" is the first commandment with promise. What does honour mean?

Any child will reply, "Respect," including in this word all degrees of deference and attention. But suppose a father or mother not to be worthy of respect, what becomes of the commandment then?

We do not find that it alters. It has no exceptions. It does not say honour a wise father, or a good mother; but simply honour them as parents.

There must, then, be a respect which is *always* binding, which concerns itself with the outward form, whatever may be the inward spirit. For the latter may and must be more or less changeable, whilst the command given is unchangeable.

But it may be asked, How can this be? God, we are told, looks at the heart, it is by that He judges. According to the state of the heart each of us will be either acquitted or condemned at the Last Day. If there is no respect in the heart, how is it that God can require or value it in the actions?

In endeavouring to reply to this question, we must examine into the reason of the ordinary proprieties and usages of society, which, in some cases, necessitate the adoption of forms

of civility when the inward feeling of cordiality may be wanting; whilst in others they, in like manner, forbid them, though the inward feeling may exist fully.

We shake hands with a person whom we have known for years, though we feel that he is thoroughly uncongenial to us. We bow distantly to a person to whom we are introduced for the first time, though what we have heard of him may lead us to look upon him almost as a personal friend. The reason of this is, that we are, in fact, testifying by our manner, not our individual feeling, but our recognition of the relative position in which we happen to be placed. When persons overstep this line, and, misunderstanding the meaning of such outward forms, make them, in public, the vehicle of their private sentiments, every one instinctively feels surprised. Whether in general society we see a man refuse to shake hands with a person whom he knows intimately, or a woman fall into her friend's arms and embrace her, we are equally startled.

Respect, courtesy, politeness, are in their several degrees incumbent upon us, apart from the Christian spirit which they are generally supposed to indicate. They have reference to claims distinct from, though consistent with, and even dictated by it; claims which must exist so long as society exists. When they are the result of real feeling, their value is, of course, greatly enhanced in the sight of the persons to whom they are shown; but when there is no such feeling, they still may not be dispensed with, because the absence of feeling does not destroy the fact of the relative position of the individuals.

Persons sometimes speak of the terms used in beginning and ending letters as if they necessarily led to insincerity. They do not see that all which is involved in them is a question of relative position. "Dear" is, in writing, a word of courtesy, adopted by general consent to express that the person to whom we write is, in some degree, known to us, and for certain reasons is, for the time being, recognized as standing on the same social level with ourselves. "Truly," "faithfully," &c., are the same. When we go beyond this, and use

"affectionately", where society only requires "truly," we, of course, take the matter into our own hands, and are then answerable for the sincerity of our words.

The consideration of these forms and proprieties may seem very inapplicable to the respect which a child ought to show to its parents. There can be no formality, or propriety, it may be said, in such a case. Manner ought to be and must be the expression of genuine feeling.

"Must" and "ought" are little words soon uttered, but they have deep meanings. We know very little of what *must* be, and though we may believe that we know a great deal of what *ought* to be, one thing is certain, that we know much more of what *is;* and judging from what we see, there is reason to fear that in many cases children do not really feel respect for their parents. And respect, moreover, is a very comprehensive term: it is not confined to one relation of life. The spirit of the fifth commandment embraces all those distinctions which place men in positions of superiority and inferiority towards others, and respect is, in all such cases, due because of the relative position of the persons, and not because of the feeling which may theoretically be supposed to exist between them.

But in this age the claim of respect is often imagined to have reference to moral qualities alone, and therefore it is supposed that, if we cultivate these qualities, we shall insensibly cultivate respect with them. How mistaken the supposition is, may be perceived by watching the manners and conduct of the young people of the present day. It would be very hard to say that none felt any respect for their parents, or their superiors; on the contrary, we must all know cases in which there is a most sincere and deep-rooted inward respect, joined with an affection of the warmest kind; yet, in the generality of these cases, we shall find that it is the affection alone which is made evident to the world, and that often by means of tones and expressions which savour actually of disrespect. The feeling which exists is in fact independent of the question of

relative position. It is even supposed that the recognition of this difference of position will chill affection, and therefore it is checked instead of being encouraged. Young people who are really fond of their parents are inclined to show their fondness by putting them on an equality with their brothers and sisters. They address them in an off-hand way—rush in and out of a room before them, allow them to wait upon them; strive, in short, to show, as much as possible, that they feel perfectly at their ease with them. And the parents, thirsting for affection, delight in all this ease of manner: mothers allowing their boys to behave almost rudely to them, in their rough caresses and jokes, at the same time petting and fondling them as if the very absence of courteous respect was a sign of genuine affection.

The working of the same ideas may be seen in other relations of life. A young man will show his regard for a person older than himself by talking to him freely, asking questions, expressing his own opinions, as he would to a friend of his own age. This is his notion of civility and attention. A young girl will address or answer the governess whom she likes with a merry good-natured shortness of manner which she imagines to be indicative of the pleasant footing on which they stand towards each other; whilst in the case of ordinary persons, for whom there is no particular feeling, she has simply no manner at all. The little monosyllables of respect which our forefathers used are considered as absurdly chilling; and even deference of tone, which in such a simple, yet courteous way, marks the consciousness of a difference of age, or of social standing, is neglected. We respect each other still; but—we say it openly—we reserve our respect for character or talent, rather than for relative position; and as in the case of social position we do not feel ourselves called upon to show respect in manner, so with regard to age, from habit, we forget to do so, and in the end our respect is altogether laid aside. This is of course a broad statement. There must be many modifications of it, but it will scarcely be denied that it is generally accepted.

There is, however, a very grievous twofold mistake in this neglect of social differences, for it is opposed to the teaching of God, both in nature and Scripture.

Our object in thus making respect depend upon moral rather than social distinctions, is, no doubt, in some degree, a desire that it should be genuine.

Very faulty as the present age is in many respects, and numerous as are the "shams" which meet us at every turn, there is still a prevailing, perhaps we may say, a preponderating desire for truth. Even those who do not feel it are obliged to profess it, and hypocrisy, as it has been well said, is, in all cases, "the homage which vice pays to virtue." Because we desire respect to be based upon a real foundation, we are inclined to restrict its outward expression to those instances in which it is claimed by superiority of talent or of moral conduct. But if superiority of position has also, by nature, a claim upon respect, there must necessarily be a falsity in failing to attend to the claim. To treat a prince like a peasant, is to ignore the true relation in which he stands to his fellow-creatures; and that the claim does exist by nature, no one surely will, upon consideration, venture to deny. When men live together in a society they must, of necessity, institute certain laws for their general government. Those laws must be carried into execution; and some person must be made responsible for their administration. The authority may be delegated, but it still is authority; and being invested with it, the individual claims respect; not from the fact that he is, in himself, superior to all others, for there may be many his equals in talent and goodness, but merely from the relative position in which he is placed with regard to them.

Respect for position is, then, a law of nature; but it is also a law of revelation. This assertion scarcely requires illustration. Besides the numerous positive commands upon this subject contained in the Bible, the whole spirit of the Scriptures, as exemplified in the manners, the conversation, the conduct of the individuals who are brought before us in its

narratives, shows a state of society, the very basis of which is the recognition, with the sanction of God, of distinctions of position.

Titles, gestures, and words of respect and courtesy meet us at the very beginning of the patriarchal life. Who has not been struck with the princely courtesy of Abraham when, bowing "himself to the people of the land, even to the children of Heth,"[1] he entreated to be permitted to purchase a sepulchre wherein to bury his dead? Who has not felt what, in these days, would be called the tone and spirit of a noble-minded gentleman, in the answer of Ephron, when Abraham declined to accept the gift which he had offered: "My lord, hearken unto me: the land is worth four hundred shekels of silver; what is that betwixt me and thee? bury therefore thy dead."[2]

And the same tone is to be traced throughout the whole of the early history of the Jews; and a departure from it is a token of a lowered moral condition. When Joab, after taking Rabbah, sends messengers to David, and, without preface or apology, gives him this order: "Gather the rest of the people together, and encamp against the city, and take it: lest I take the city, and it be called after my name,"[3] we see at once how low David must have fallen in the sight of his own subject, when such a message, couched in such words, could be addressed to him; and pity for the king mingles with indignation at the conduct of the rough, coarse-minded soldier who could take advantage of his knowledge of his sovereign's fallen, though repentant estate, to triumph over him with such proud disrespect.

And in the New Testament, the absence of all respect in the tone and language of the Scribes and Pharisees is most remarkable, as the sign of a degraded state of feeling in the rulers of the people, and, as a natural result, in the people themselves. There appears to have been no medium between worship and equality. Only in the case of a very few persons

[1] Gen. xxiii. 7. [2] Gen. xxiii. 15. [3] 2 Sam. xii. 28.

of social position and thoughtful minds, do we find anything like that outward respect which, even before our Lord's Divinity could be recognized, must have been demanded by the holiness of His Life and the wonderful character of His teaching. Nicodemus begins his inquiries by words of reverence. "Rabbi, we know that Thou art a teacher come from God: for no man can do these miracles that Thou doest, except God be with him."[1] The Galilean nobleman, in his anxiety for his son's life, speaks with eager respect, "Sir, come down, ere my child die."[2] The Roman centurion is so impressed with our Lord's power and dignity, that he confesses himself unworthy to receive Him under his roof: but the Jewish rulers, and the people who flock around our Blessed Lord, address Him on terms of perfect equality; more than equality, of superiority; and, at length, even of contempt.

Let us only look at one short conversation. Our Lord was urging those who were really convinced that His mission was divine, to continue His followers, and warning them that the Jews, although the descendants of Abraham, were not really the followers of Abraham. "I speak that which I have seen with My Father: and ye do that which ye have seen with your father. They answered and said unto Him, Abraham is our father. Jesus saith unto them, If ye were Abraham's children, ye would do the works of Abraham. But now ye seek to kill Me, a man that hath told you the truth, which I have heard of God: this did not Abraham. Ye do the deeds of your father. Then said they to Him, We be not born of fornication; we have one Father, even God. Jesus said unto them, If God were your Father, ye would love Me. . . . He that is of God heareth God's words: ye therefore hear them not, because ye are not of God. Then answered the Jews, and said unto Him, Say we not well that Thou art a Samaritan, and hast a devil? Jesus answered, I have not a devil; but I honour my Father, and ye do dishonour Me. . . . Verily, verily, I say unto you, If a man keep My saying, he shall

[1] St. John iii. 2. [2] St. John iv. 49.

never see death. Then said the Jews unto Him, Now we know that Thou hast a devil. Abraham is dead, and the prophets; and Thou sayest, If a man keep My saying, he shall never taste of death. . . . Jesus answered, Your father Abraham rejoiced to see My day: and he saw it, and was glad. Then said the Jews unto Him, Thou art not yet fifty years old, and hast Thou seen Abraham? Jesus said unto them, Verily, verily, I say unto you, Before Abraham was, I am. Then took they up stones to cast at Him." [1]

This conversation is necessarily abridged, but its *tone* is fully given; and let us ask ourselves whether we do not recognize in it the tone of the present day—cavilling, doubting, critical, captious, refusing to own any power superior to itself, entering upon every inquiry in a spirit of equality, withholding all external signs of respect unless compelled to give them, and even lowering itself at length to insult. Yet we flatter ourselves that we have advanced infinitely beyond the Jews in knowledge, and in that largeness of mind which acknowledges goodness wherever it exists; we are only like them outwardly. As the Jew of our Lord's day could not go back to the ceremonious courtesy of the patriarchal times; so, neither can we go back to the formal civility of our ancestors. It is a question of manner, not of spirit.

But who is to separate the two? More especially, if respect of manner is the natural tribute due to superiority of position, how can we say with any truth that we preserve the spirit of respect, when we refuse to acknowledge by outward signs the existence of such superiority?

In this so-called age of reason, the amount of unreason which we meet with is certainly very singular. Respect, we must all own, can only be testified by outward signs. It is very well to say we feel it, but if we do not show it, it is as if it did not exist. And the perception of relative position is recognized by every one to be the test of good breeding. A duchess who thrusts herself uninvited into the presence of her

[1] St. John viii. 38–59.

Sovereign is felt to be vulgar and ill-bred. No elegance of manner, or of dress, can atone for the ignorance of relative position which such an act indicates; whilst, on the other hand, the peasant girl who pays the respect to the duchess which her superiority of station demands, is well-bred—her cotton dress and her homely language notwithstanding. The rule holds good even in reverse cases. The prince who forgets that he is a prince, and allows the person with whom he associates to take liberties with him, may be liked for his good-nature, but will be considered wanting in perfect gentlemanly feeling. There is no real courtesy in ignoring differences of relative position, because all well-bred persons are desirous of recognizing them; and a lady who refuses to accept the precedence which her rank gives her, makes us just as uncomfortable as one who claims it when it does not belong to her. And so far almost all persons perhaps will agree in allowing that the recognition of relative position is of importance in education; but how few are there who trouble themselves to reason further, so as to perceive that this recognition is a great moral safeguard, a check upon presumption and conceit on the one hand, and a support to rightful self-confidence, and even to the strict performance of duty, on the other.

Society is composed of innumerable wheels, all working simultaneously, but stopped, when necessary, by cogs. Relative position is one of these cogs. Without it, youthful energy, natural talent, physical power—all great engines of movement and progress—would rush on, showing no consideration for other equally important engines, and by going beyond their mark, would, in the end, mar the very work for which they were intended.

It is not dificult, for instance, to imagine the confusion which would ensue if every person who had made a discovery, or formed a scheme likely to be beneficial to society, was able to discuss and thrust it forward at all seasons and in all society; if he might treat his superiors as his equals, show no deference to their opinions, and insist upon being attended to

without consideration for other subjects which might have a claim upon public attention.

A never-ending conflict, a perpetual jar would be the result of such a power; and yet the individual proposing the scheme might have right on his side; that is to say, he might really be able to benefit society, and be perfectly sincere in his wish to do so. People often think it very hard when they find ob stacles put in their way by etiquettes, formalities, proprieties; and no doubt these may be carried to an absurd extent, but the schemes which they have so much at heart would find many more obstacles without them; for, in fact, it is the very existence of these same rules and proprieties which enables any of us to carry out any scheme. And for this reason. The work of the world must be carried on by a variety of agents. No man can do everything that is required for his business or his profession himself: he must trust, in a great degree, to the actions of others. But it is impossible for him to be assured of the fitness of the person he is compelled to employ; on the contrary, he is continually obliged to make use of those whom he knows to be decidedly unfit. If a thorough mental and moral examination could be made of all persons employed in the army, the navy, in lawyers' offices, in domestic service, in any situation, indeed, involving responsibility, and only those were chosen who were found to be fully competent for the duties they were called upon to undertake, in all probability not more than one-tenth of the persons now usefully employed would remain in their present places. But how is it that the work of life is carried on by such inadequate instruments? It is owing in a very great degree to the recognition of relative position. Persons who would naturally be troublesome, self-sufficient, blundering, are kept in their proper place, and taught to perform their part rightly, by the check which is put upon them by the necessity of acknowledging differences of position. Others, on the contrary, who are timid, ignorant, self-distrustful, who have no confidence in their own judgment, and would be afraid to decide the questions which come before

them if left to themselves, yet learn unconsciously what they are to do, and how they are to behave, by the support and guidance afforded through the medium of the same social distinctions. Differences of station, whether arising from birth, civil authority, age, talent, or from whatever cause, are, in fact, constantly educating and training us, so that we may work harmoniously together, not interfering with or encroaching upon each other's privileges. They are the landmarks of society, and if we remove them, society will become a chaos.

So very true all this is. Why should any one take the trouble to repeat it?

Simply because the one place in which this necessary training for social life can be most easily and effectually carried on, is the one place where it is most generally neglected.

God has in His Wisdom cast every man's life into certain different moulds, one mould being intended to fit into the other, like the Indian boxes which we sometimes meet with, each distinct in itself, yet all, together, forming one whole. Home is the innermost of these moulds; it is intended to fit into the mould of social life, and this again is to fit into the mould of national or political life. And for the furtherance of this intention, our home life is so constituted, that in it we may, as children, practise on a small scale those duties which will enable us rightly to act our part, when we are called to enter upon a larger sphere. There is absolute superiority in the parents, a secondary superiority in other relations—in governesses or tutors, or in elder brothers and sisters; and a superiority apart from position and education, arising from delegated authority, and from age, in nurses and servants. And in each of these cases, external signs of respect are naturally due, modified according to the relative position of the parties claiming them.

But do we find upon examination that home life is really thus made use of as a school in which children may be taught the duty and the importance of recognizing relative position?

The idea that respect is due to servants, because of their superiority in age, will probably seem exaggerated; yet St.

Paul places a child only on a level with a servant, for he says: "Now, I say, That the heir, as long as he is a child, differeth nothing from a servant, though he be lord of all."[1]

The courtesy, therefore, of equality at least, is the servant's due. But how do we find that children are allowed to speak to servants? The embryo masters and mistresses issue their commands in a tone of authority, which is as destructive to goodwill as it is offensive to Christian feeling; and this want of respect shown to inferiors is carried upwards through all the relations of life, till it reaches the parents. Or rather it begins with the parents, and then descends. It is their training which gives the first lessons in the impertinence and insolence that society so severely punishes. How few are there who would not think it a severe suggestion, that their children ought never to be allowed to go in or out of a room before them, or sit when they themselves are standing, or interrupt them when they are speaking! How many would be surprised if they were told that they were doing their children a moral injury, by allowing them to ring the bell when they choose, to sit in a lounging attitude, and occupy the most comfortable seat in the room, to appear at the dinner table late without an apology, to help themselves to whatever they like, without thought for their elders. And yet all these things must be attended to, if the children are ever to be fitted for social life. They must then recognize that age and station have claims upon their self-restraint; and if they do not, society—by no means as lenient as a mother—will *taboo* them. Or again, in regard to that most delicate, and yet most intangible test of respect—the tone of the voice—will not the generality of mothers think it a very severe doctrine, that from the earliest infancy, a child should be gently checked when it gives way to an off-hand tone of equality, even though there may be no actual rudeness? It was said by a most wise mother, "Whatever liberties you take with your brothers and sisters, my dear, you will take none with me;" and her son, at forty years of age, paid her

[1] Gal. iv. 1.

the same tender deference which he had learnt when he was a boy of fourteen. This question of voice and manner has become infinitely important to us now, when we have thrown off the ceremonious politeness of our grandfathers and grandmothers, in conversation, and have scarcely any other outward mode of showing our respect. And we are all keenly alive to it. We shrink from what is called the free and easy tone of a colony; we dislike going into a shop where we know that we shall be addressed familiarly; we are provoked with our servants when they answer us shortly; we draw back from a new acquaintance who talks to us in the tone of an old friend. The only case in which we ignore it is with children. They may speak rudely, interrupt incessantly, repeat our words, put themselves in our way, disturb our occupations, and we never think of checking them. And having thus educated them in disrespect in their homes, we are surprised to find that when they enter society, or are placed in situations of responsibility, they make themselves disagreeable, and have so little perception of the deference due to station and age, that they mar their really good intentions by acting without tact; and do what they have to do so awkwardly, that they often give offence where they most desire to please, and are perhaps at last pronounced unfit for their post by the very persons who were most desirous to become their friends.

Good-nature and want of tact are continually found in the same character, and we may sometimes have been pained with ourselves for being so annoyed with the latter, as to be inclined to overlook the former. But we really are not much to blame in this case. Want of tact is, generally speaking, as much a moral fault as the absence of good-nature. It is almost always coupled with a forgetfulness of the claims or the restraints arising from relative position. To thrust kindnesses upon strangers, without any apology for the liberty, may be very good-natured, but it shows great want of tact, because it disregards the fact that society does not permit such familiarity. That offensive kind of good-nature, which exhibits

itself under the form of patronage, is of the same character. The person offering it may have the kindest intentions, but by taking it for granted that some superiority of position sets him at liberty to overlook the ordinary etiquettes of society, he shows a want of tact which neutralizes his goodwill, and creates a cause of offence.

We are all more or less inclined to spoil very young children in this special point of education, the knowledge of relative position. It amuses us so much to see the little creatures aping the manners of their elders, that we cannot bring ourselves to correct them. They are our playthings, and we think it hard that we may not amuse ourselves with them. And so the little fellow of four years old is brought forward to talk and repeat verses, and thrust himself upon the attention of visitors, till he becomes, first, the forward schoolboy, and then the "intolerably disagreeable man;" and the sweet little girl is allowed to chatter to gentlemen, who talk about her bright eyes and her glossy curls, and beg her to kiss them, till she becomes the vain, self-conscious, affected girl, and ultimately ends in "that odious flirt" whom no sensible man would venture to marry.

Alas! for human selfishness!

"Manners makyth man."[1] Not *manner*—not mere external polish—but the recognition, by the intellect and the heart, of those duties arising from relative position, which are as much moral obligations as the laws that enforce honesty and purity.

But this outward deference and respect, when insisted upon by parents, is supposed to stand in the way of the free play of natural affection. Children, it is thought, will not love their parents unless they are allowed to be what is called perfectly free with them; or, in other words, unless they are allowed to be rude to them.

If this be so, then the appointments of God in His government of the world are contradictory to each other; for, un-

[1] The Winchester and New College motto.

questionably, there does exist a strong natural affection between parents and children, and unquestionably, also, there does exist a very stringent obligation to pay outward respect to elders and superiors. If the former is the dictate of nature, so is the latter of reason; for, as Bishop Butler remarks, though in reference to another subject, "the relations being known, the obligations to such (reverence) are obligations of reason, arising out of those relations themselves."[1] The idea that absolute ease, by which is understood absolute familiarity, is essential to the perfection of love, is, in fact, one of those delusions by which men are led astray, because they prefer to listen to the voice of their own low and selfish inclinations, rather than to that of reason and experience. Reverence involves restraint; restraint is, in our present condition, disagreeable to us; therefore we persuade ourselves that it is inconsistent with our highest happiness, which is to be found in perfect love.

But let us look into the truth of this assertion. What is love? Where, in its highest degree, is it to be found? There is an answer which will rise at once to our lips: He alone who is Omniscient knows whether it comes also from our hearts. The love of God is the most perfect form of love.

But the feeling of love, when directed towards God, is, it will be said, something totally distinct from the same feeling when directed towards man.

That is strange! There is a History which we all know. It tells of One who, owning Himself to be God, yet dwelt among men, recognizing all the relationships and sympathies of man;—who was obedient to His parents; tender in His care for His mother; who wept at the grave of His dead friend; who suffered His most cherished disciple to lean upon His breast; who looked forward to the time of reunion and of mutual participation in future glory, as one of the bright hopes which was to strengthen Him in His hour of agony.

What was the feeling awakened towards Him? He was

[1] Butler's Analogy, Part II., chap. i.

God. Was He loved with a love totally distinct from the love of man? Or was that love the purest, highest, noblest, most satisfying, most enduring of all affections—a love which, like the Nature of Him to whom it was addressed, did not cease to be human because it was Divine, but blending the sense of perfect sympathy and comprehension with the most exalted reverence, suffered the heart to pour itself forth without check; and to repose, even in the consciousness of its infirmity, knowing that—

"The Lord who dwells on high
Knows all, yet loves us better than He knows"?

Indeed, indeed, we do ourselves a grievous wrong when we acquiesce in the assertion that Divine and human love are not only different in degree, but different in kind. There is no such essential distinction between the love which we feel for our fellow creatures, and that which we are permitted to offer to our Redeemer, as will admit of our giving our whole hearts in one form to a human friend, and in the other form to God. There is but one *highest*, one *all*. And if reverence is an inseparable element in the perfection of Divine love; then must respect, which is only a lower form of reverence, be an essential element in the perfection of human love.

Love without respect, what is it? We must turn to the miserable history of man's selfishness and degradation for the answer. What sins, what cruelties, what heart-sickening wretchedness, what aberrations of reason, may not be laid to the charge of love, under all its forms, when existing (if, indeed, it can truly be said to exist,—if the feeling which claims the name is not rather some mockery and shadow of love) apart from respect!

Love with respect, who may tell its comfort and its rest? As we journey through life, and learn by bitter experience to look for weakness and want of judgment, if not for openly allowed faults, even in the wisest and best of men, we must at times long to return to those blissful days of ignorance, when all persons older than ourselves were supposed to be actuated

by right motives, and to be guided by sound discretion. Even now we linger fondly on the characters of those we love; we speak of their virtues, their struggles, their aims; but there is something wanting even in our praise. We admire them less for what they are than for what they strive to be, and our strongest feeling cannot expend itself upon them. We love them most fondly, most truly, and constantly, but there is a power of love within us which can never be satisfied by any human affection, because the one element of complete reverence is wanting, and without it love can never be perfect.

But it was not so in youth. Then we had had no disappointments; our respect was without misgiving, without alloy; and the love we felt was of the nature of that full confiding affection which must be the joy of the angels in Heaven, and which we pray, hereafter, to be permitted to share.

This highest form of human love is, however, inseparable from respect of manner. God has given to every human being —to the child as well as to the man—an instinctive perception of the claims of relative position; this perception bringing with it the consciousness of moral obligation. The child cannot escape from it. It knows that it ought not to be disrespectful to its parent, just as naturally as it knows that it ought not to steal, or to commit murder; though, unfortunately, this particular form of moral consciousness is, in too many cases, weakened by the education received in infancy. Still, the knowledge remains: it is never entirely eradicated; and when the child, as it grows up, sees and feels that it is not compelled to acknowledge this relation, in its outward behaviour, its respect for its parent is lessened; and, as an unavoidable consequence, its love is lessened also. And yet more—there is in the very act of outward respect, something which, except where it is an actual mockery, engenders the inward feeling;—this feeling being, indeed, not the homage due to moral worth, but that which belongs to relative position; and which, as it has before been said, is a natural and moral claim. The "divinity that doth hedge a king," is not only evidenced to the senses.

but the consciousness of it is increased, by the pomp and pageantry which surround him. And so, the respect which children pay to their parents, not only marks their inward feeling, but actually strengthens it.

This is seen more clearly as years go on. Fathers and sons, mothers and daughters, must by degrees reach an equal level as regards moral and intellectual wealth and power. The sons and daughters may, indeed, surpass, and in fact they very often do surpass, their parents in these respects; and, moreover, rise above them in social position. But the superiority of nature can be affected by no changes. The father is the father still, the mother is the mother; and the child who has been taught to be respectful to his parents in infancy, will continue to be so, though he may have risen to be the titled general, or the world-famous philosopher, and they may have remained in their original obscurity.

It can be no external homage which is given in such a case, for society does not require it. The nobleman or the philosopher may hold his place and practically ignore his parents, and the world will think little the less of him. But God's laws, God's ordinances, are immutable. He has said, "Honour thy father and thy mother." He has instituted a natural connection between the relationship and the respect which He commands; and this connection can never cease to be felt by any person who, from infancy, has been taught to acknowledge it. Love may change with circumstances, because the foundations upon which it is based may change; but the respect consequent upon the habitual recognition of natural superiority of position, must remain as long as the relation itself remains; and being thus unchangeable, it tends to keep alive, to nourish and strengthen, the feeling of love. The man who might almost have forgotten, or at least ceased to regard, his father, if he had been allowed to treat him with unseemly familiarity, is compelled by the very force of habit to consider his opinion of importance, when he has always been accustomed to own that his father stands above him. The young girl who, surrounded

by friends of her own age, and carried away by the whirl of gaiety, might chalk out her own career without consideration for her mother's feelings, turns instinctively to that mother for approbation, and cannot be satisfied without it, when she has been taught from infancy to show her deference.

All forms—forms of respect as well as of religion—are indeed the moulds into which feeling is to be poured. The feeling may, for a time, exist apart from the form; the form may, for a time, exist where there is no feeling. But the voice of nature, and the teaching of God in revelation, alike teach us that, in such cases, the existence both of form and spirit will be short-lived and imperfect. Man's soul and his body may be separated, and the soul may live still, looking forward to the day of resurrection and reunion. But human feelings know no such resurrection, and the spirit apart from the form will fade and die. "What God hath joined together, let no man put asunder."

CHAPTER XV.

TRUTH.

We have been hitherto considering the duties of parents towards their children. The duty of the child towards its parent has been summed up in the virtues of obedience and respect. But children have many other duties towards many other persons, and no education can be perfect which does not teach them to fulfil those duties. How, then, are these lessons to be enforced?

Now, it might naturally be supposed that, in treating a subject of this kind, we should begin with the consideration of that duty to God, as revealed to us in the Bible, which includes all forms and degrees of duty to man; but if we examine the training of God given by nature, we shall probably be led to own that such teaching is not strictly according to His appointment.

The little child of a year and a half old who disobeys its mother, can perfectly comprehend that it has done wrong, but cannot possibly understand the scheme of salvation. Obedience, therefore, must be taught, before definite religious truths can be entered upon. In nature, as well as in grace, the Law must precede the Gospel. This does not by any means imply that instruction in religion must not accompany elementary moral teaching, for without it moral teaching will ultimately fail of its object; but it does mean that the primary ideas of morality are stamped by nature upon the child's mind, and are absolutely perfect at once, whilst the primary ideas of

revealed religion are acquired as the mind develops. No amount of teaching can make the idea of Truth more clear to a child's intellect than it is by nature; but Faith is a complex idea, which can only be received and comprehended by degrees; and therefore, to wait till the child can understand and exercise Faith before we teach it the obligation of Truth, is to put aside God's system of education, and to adopt one of our own. And upon further consideration, we shall find also that education, so far as it is put in man's power, has no means of directly enforcing any of those virtues which belong essentially to revealed religion. We may advise, and warn, and encourage, and punish; but no counsel and no admonition can produce in the child's mind the feelings of faith and love. Those deep principles of human action lie hidden from us. God alone can set them in motion; though He devolves upon us the teaching of the great truths, such as "His love toward us in Christ Jesus," which are calculated to arouse them. Neither can we by any direct effort make a child humble-minded or unselfish—because outward actions, apart from the spirit in which they are performed, do not constitute humility and unselfishness; and it is only over the outward act that we have any immediate control. We may, for instance, compel a child to take an inferior position, or, for the benefit of others, to make a sacrifice of some cherished wish; but if there is a proud feeling in the one case, or a grudging irritation in the other, the actions themselves cease to be either humble or unselfish. It is true, indeed, that we are called upon constantly to enforce such outward acts, apart from the inward spirit, because, if we fail to do so, the sinful habit of mind will be strengthened by indulgence in it; but the good we do can be only negative, and the child will never be really humble and unselfish, until the principles of those graces are, through God's mercy, implanted in its heart. There are, however, some moral actions, which have, as it were, an independent existence, distinct from the spirit which actuates them, and over these we may in education exert a direct power. Such are

acts of obedience, truth, and justice. Obedience cannot be disobedience. Truth cannot be a lie. A just action cannot be unjust. This is evident upon the slightest consideration. If, for instance, we could suppose any individual to be absolutely just in all his actions, and absolutely true in word and deed during the whole course of his life; it would be a contradiction to say that the actions were not just and true, because the spirit in which they were performed was not that of justice and truth. The bad motive, or feeling, could not make the just act unjust, or the truth which was spoken falsehood. The actions in themselves would be good, though the man who committed them might be bad; and *vice versâ*—a lie is a lie, though spoken to save a man's life; and injustice is injustice, though committed from a wish to do a kindness.

It is in these cases that we are permitted, when judging of an act in itself undoubtedly wrong, to separate in a measure the offender from the offence; to condemn the latter, whilst, according to circumstances, we deal, it may be, leniently with the former.

And it is because of this peculiar character of the three virtues just mentioned that they must be considered first in treating of education. We have no power of directly dealing with a child's mind, and if we make the attempt we shall probably only do mischief. He alone who created man in His own Image can restore that Image when it is defaced. But the particular virtues which have been mentioned, having, what has been called, an independent existence, may be enforced less cautiously, since we may be sure that the practice of the outward act is good, whatever may be the condition of the heart. Of obedience we have already spoken; and justice, so far as it can be practised by children, is so inseparably connected with truth, that in cherishing the one we necessarily cherish the other. A perfectly true mind must be a perfectly just mind. What, then, is the best method we may adopt in order to make a child truthful? Before entering upon this question, it will be necessary to examine more particularly into the nature of truth.

Now, it is often asserted that some persons are truthful, others untruthful, by nature; but it may be doubted whether this is a true statement of the case. The sense of the moral obligation of truth is, we know, in certain individuals so strong that the least suspicion of untruthfulness makes them wretched; and if ever under the influence of strong temptation led into a falsehood, they are miserable till they have confessed it. Their word may always be relied upon; they dislike exaggeration; they see very quickly through pretence; they are inclined to look even with uncharitable scorn upon others who are not like themselves blest with the love of truth. Such characters, though not always very agreeable, are by far the most satisfactory to deal with. Whatever may be their natural faults, this truthfulness may always be made use of to correct them. They will, in fact, by God's grace, correct themselves, for when the love of truth exists very strongly, there is as earnest a desire to avoid self-deception as any other kind of deception.

But because there are some in whom the love of truth is strongly developed, it by no means follows that there may or can be others who have a natural love of falsehood. On the contrary, it seems, when we look into the question, that love of truth is part of that original nature which we derived from God; and which, though it may be marred and distorted, cannot be obliterated in any human being. The most false man that lives will disapprove of falsehood in others; and all men, as a general rule, will speak truth when they have no motive for speaking untruth. If we could suppose any man to have a natural love of falsehood, for its own sake, he must have lost all sense of moral fitness, of the relation of one act to another. He would be unable to live with his fellow-creatures, for his theory and his practice would be totally opposed to theirs. What they might think right, he would endeavour to think wrong; what they might know to be a truth, he would strive to disbelieve. And even if such a case could be supposed, yet the very fact of its being an effort to him thus to

differ from other men, would be a proof that the sense of truth still lingered in his heart. If it were no effort to him, then he would be self-deceived. He might believe a falsehood, for we all more or less believe falsehoods, but he himself might still retain the love of truth. The idolater who bows down before his wooden god, believes a falsehood; but it is not a necessary consequence that he himself should be untruthful, or have pleasure in untruthfulness. Men take great delight in fiction, but it is only whilst it confesses itself to be fiction, and therefore ceases to be an untruth. When a book professes to be true, and then is discovered to be fiction, the interest ceases, or at least is only kept up by the truth which it still retains; that is to say, the accordance between what is described, and what we feel must under similar circumstances have taken place. De Foe's "History of the Plague" is a striking exemplification of this statement. Every one who reads it, believing it to be what it professes to be—the statement of an eyewitness of the scenes recorded—must experience a diminution of interest when told that it is not so. But after a while the interest will in a great degree be revived, because the description of what must have happened is seen to be so wonderfully accurate. It is the sense of truth which even in this case gives the pleasure. So it is again with historical novels; and even in works of fiction which lie quite beyond the domain of our present senses, and our present experience—fairy tales, for instance—the appeal to our interest still lies in the perception of truth. Fairies are always represented as human in their passions and their tastes, and because they are thus, as the saying is, "true to nature," we like to follow them in their disguise, and are amused instead of shocked at the new physical powers attributed to them.

And if we look into the Bible we shall find that this innate perception of and desire for truth is the basis of all the appeals made to man's obedience, and all the commands laid down for his guidance. The Lord is the God of truth;[1] it is one of

[1] Jer. x. 10.

His attributes. His counsels of old are faithfulness and truth.[1] His desire for man is, that he should have truth in his inward parts.[2] The promise given to the Jews was that the lip of truth should be established for ever,[3] and it would seem that the complaints made of their falsehood are more numerous than the injunctions given them to observe truth, because the very moral nature which God had bestowed upon them, and the very necessities of their earthly existence, enjoined truth upon them with a power which nothing but madness or blindness could fail to recognize. To prove from the Bible that truth is considered by God the foundation of morality would, indeed, be simply to quote passages from the opening Book of Genesis, to the closing Book of St. John's Revelation.

And yet it may be said that there are, in the Bible, instances of deceit and falsehood upon which no censure is passed. Is it possible that God can have approved of them?

In answer to this, it must be remembered that the Bible is, in the main, a history of facts. Jacob deceived his father: that is a fact. The Bible does not profess to tell us what Jacob ought to have done, but what he did. And God did not interfere to punish the patriarch by any supernatural punishment, any more than He interferes to punish us. He left him to the natural course of His moral government, according to which deceit and falsehood must bring suffering. No one can carefully read the account of Jacob's subsequent life without owning that the sorrowful confession wrung from him at the close of his earthly pilgrimage, "Few and evil have the days of the years of my life been,"[4] may be traced back to the offence which caused him to incur his brother's wrath, and made him an exile from his home for so large a portion of his life.

A few other instances there are of things done and said untruly, but in no one case were they commanded or praised by God because of their untruth. Rahab, by uttering a falsehood,

[1] Isaiah xxv. 1.
[2] Psa. li. 6.
[3] Prov. xii. 19.
[4] Gen. xlvii. 9.

saved the lives of the spies sent by Joshua to view Jericho. In the Epistle to the Hebrews she is mentioned approvingly, but it is on account of her faith; and it must, moreover, be remembered that actions having their origin in the overpowering instinct to save life cannot be judged by ordinary rules. They lead to questions of casuistry, which are most difficult to determine, and cannot at all affect the general statement that God in revelation, as in nature, requires "truth in the inward parts" as the groundwork of all goodness.

If we would yet more thoroughly be convinced of this, let us consider, for one moment, not only the denunciations upon those who are guilty of that most aggravated form of deceit which consists in attempting to deceive God by honouring Him with the lips while the heart is far from Him; but the two cases which stand distinct from all others as instances of falsehood told directly to God.

The name of Cain is handed down to us as that of the first man who dared to answer his Maker with a lie. "The Lord said unto Cain, Where is Abel thy brother? And he said, I know not: am I my brother's keeper?"[1] Cain was cursed —for murder indeed, rather than for a lie; but it was the lie which aggravated and intensified the murder, because it showed that his was no heart in which repentance could be awakened. And Cain's punishment was "greater than he could bear."

That lie immediately followed man's fall. There was another lie of the same character,—told, that is, in direct defiance of God's Omniscience,—which immediately followed man's Redemption. The story of Ananias and Sapphira inspires a most salutary awe in a young mind, yet perhaps few at once grasp the real intensity of the sin, or understand why it received such a fearful punishment.

The moral government of God in this world deals immediately and visibly with the relations between man and man. Offences against our fellow creatures are punished,

[1] Gen. iv. 9.

either directly or indirectly, by them. The punishment follows the offence on the principle of cause and effect; and a lie told to man is followed by the contempt of man. But offences against God are not, as a general rule, thus punished. Absence of faith, or of reverence, or humility, cannot be brought under human jurisdiction. A person may be guilty of such sins, and the world will know nothing of them; or, if it does know, it will not notice them. Unless blotted out for Christ's sake, they are reserved for a more strict tribunal, a more impartial and a more awful Judge. But there is one offence against God which men are compelled to notice,—perjury. If this were overlooked, the sense of truth which keeps society together and enables us to carry on our dealings with each other would soon be obliterated.

The sin of Ananias and Sapphira was an aggravated offence of this character. The Apostles, visibly gifted with the power of the Holy Ghost, were, even in the sight of their fellow creatures, the representatives of God. The lie told to them, was a lie told directly to God. It was an outrage upon one of His essential attributes. The ordinary punishment of a lie would, therefore, have been wholly inadequate to express its guilt, and to vindicate the insulted majesty of the Almighty. Death was its due penalty, and death was inflicted instantly; as in like cases on record, when an appeal has been made to God, and a lie has been spoken, death also has followed. Men at once recognize such a punishment as just, and why? Because truth is the very foundation stone of the attributes of God, and to attempt to make Him the witness to falsehood, is virtually to overlook the existence of that attribute, and thus to deny His very Being.

Now, we have already seen that God has been pleased to educate mankind in the recognition and practice of truth, by the natural penalties which He has attached to falsehood. We have seen also that in certain cases He has interfered supernaturally in order to testify to the supreme majesty of truth. But when we look into revelation we shall find that it is less

by the punishment of falsehood, than by the perpetual recall to truth, that the overwhelming authority of the latter is enforced.

There is no distinction in this respect between the training of Jews and Christians, for difference of mental condition makes no difference in the perception of truth. The little child understands what is meant by truth, as perfectly as the great philosopher. What both alike need is to be taught its imperative authority; and this, not because the human mind would naturally fail to recognize that authority, but because, being a fallen, a distorted nature, it allows itself to be blinded by sophistry and self-interest. Truth is, in fact, in the Bible, the standard to which everything is brought, the test by which it is measured. The commands and the declarations of God are to be obeyed and believed because they are truth. As the Psalmist says: "Thy righteousness is an everlasting righteousness, and Thy law is the truth. Thou art near, O Lord, and all Thy commandments are truth." [1]

And this will give us a very important suggestion with regard to the education of children. No amount of correction or of warning will train a child in truthfulness, unless truth is the recognized standard of morality amongst those with whom it is brought up. We cannot deceive children upon this subject. They know what is true just as well as we do; and so far as we ourselves are untrue in word or deed, so far will the children, who are to be guided, turn a deaf ear to our injunctions. The caution may appear unnecessary. Falsehood and deceit are so universally despised, it would seem that no one really guided by religious principles would be guilty of them. Yet it is scarcely too much to assert, that to be perfectly true is the most difficult task which a Christian can set before himself. It must be, if we only allow ourselves to think for one moment. Perfect truth is one of God's attributes. Who then can attain unto it?

And what is more—children are truer in their instincts and

[1] Psalm cxix 142, 151.

feelings, and even in their words and actions, than their elders. They will, indeed, be guilty of more direct open offences against truth; they will scruple less to tell direct lies; but they do not understand the false reasonings, which tempt men, even by the very keenness of their intellects, to deceive both themselves and others. If we examine the mode in which the Jews are addressed by Moses, and by our Blessed Lord, we shall see at once the advance made in sophistry, by a nation who had passed from the stage of childhood to that of thought and so-called civilization. The Israelites in the wilderness are addressed as disobedient, obstinate, stiff-necked, faithless, but we never hear of them as deceivers. They lived too immediately in the Presence, and before the Majesty of God, to venture to reason away His commands. They might neglect their parents, and dishonour them, but they would not then have dared to do so, as they did in later times, under the pretence that they were making an offering to God. What says our Blessed Lord to the Jews of His day? "Ye are of your father the devil, and the lusts of your father ye will do. . . . When he speaketh a lie, he speaketh of his own: for he is a liar, and the father of it. And because I tell you the truth, ye believe Me not." [1] And the prophecy which foretells the sins of the latter days, especially warns us that "evil men and seducers shall wax worse and worse, deceiving, and being deceived." [2]

It is a matter of very grave thought with us all. For, inasmuch as the professed aim of the men of this age is to search after truth, so we may be sure that there will be very many who seek for it in the ways of falsehood. Truth and error, sincerity and deceit, walk side by side through the world. Wherever the one is to be found, the other will quickly follow; —error wearing the garb of truth—deceit arraying itself in the mantle of sincerity. And how shall we distinguish between them?

Reality before God! His words taken in their natural sense, and acted upon according to their plain meaning. Re-

[1] St. John viii. 44, 45. [2] 2 Tim. iii. 13.

ality with ourselves! No tampering with secret faults; no turning away the eye from a suspected sin. Reality with our fellow creatures! No striving to appear, no wish even to be thought what we are not; nothing done from form, or fashion, or fear of giving offence. It is a hard, hard task, but we may not, we dare not, put it aside. For our soul's sake—for the sake of the Master whom we desire to serve—for the sake of the children whom we would fain train up for His glory—*we must be real.* If we are, then will God lead us into all truth. If we are not, the very lessons of honour and sincerity which we give will rise up against us in condemnation; "our children themselves being our judges."

This, then, is the first desideratum,—the imperative necessity for all those who desire to foster the sense of truth in the young minds entrusted to them. As God is absolutely true Himself, as He appeals to truth, as He insists upon it and enforces it, so in our measure must we be true; so must we insist and enforce truth. And when we have fully acknowledged this necessity, and asked God to enable us to act upon it, we may then proceed to inquire what means may most safely be adopted to check the tendency to deceit and untruthfulness which, from various causes, will more or less exhibit itself in almost all children, at some period of their education.

The expression, "from various causes," has been used advisedly, because, unless we remember that the perception and the instinct of truth are imperishable in the human breast, we shall be likely to make as grievous mistakes in correcting a child who tells us a falsehood, as a physician does who treats the symptoms of the disease for the disease itself. If the love of truth abstractedly exists in every one, without exception, then the child who tells falsehoods does so from some hidden motive, or feeling; and, until we have discovered what this hidden motive power is, we shall never cure the evil habit.

One very common source of untruthfulness in children is want of moral courage. We will suppose that from this cause a child tells us a falsehood. There are two ways in which we may deal with the case.

We may say, "You have committed a great sin, and have acted most dishonourably; I cannot again put confidence in your word; I am extremely angry with you, and I shall punish you severely." And the child will go from our presence, humbled and possibly repentant, but also extremely frightened; and the next time she is required to exercise moral courage, she will find it even more difficult than before, because her fear of us is increased. In her alarm she will, perhaps, be again tempted to lie, and the reproof and the punishment will be yet sterner. The fear will become greater; the sin will be repeated. The child will be gradually acquiring the character of an habitual liar; and in all probability will be sent away from home, to some person who it is hoped may exercise over her an influence for good. But her character precedes her. She enters upon her new sphere with the reputation of untruthfulness, and of course her word is distrusted. She knows this, and her moral energies are weakened. She is depressed and unhappy, and, as an inevitable result, naughty. Then she is scolded, then frightened. Then she tells a falsehood to save herself from punishment; and so it goes on. What is the hope of strengthening the love of truth under such a system?

But suppose, having discovered, or even only suspecting, that the falsehood is the result of moral cowardice, we take a different course; suppose we speak very gravely—we cannot speak too gravely—of the sin of lying; suppose we show how it aggravates all other sins—how it tends to destroy confidence, and how heinous it is in God's sight; and then, instead of saying, "I am extremely angry," say, "I am extremely pained; I must punish the offence more than I should any other, because it is in itself so grievous—and you may be sure that I always shall punish it; therefore, if you wish to avoid punishment you must be perfectly open and true. Confess what you have done that is wrong, and you will find me always ready to forgive, and help you to do better: try to hide it by a falsehood, and I shall be obliged to punish you double. And now, having given you this warning, I feel confident that the offence

will not he repeated, and I shall trust to your word, because I do not think you will pain me by trying to deceive me a second time."

There will be humiliation, and probably repentance, in this case as in the former; but the child's feelings will he softened and hopeful. There may be punishment to bear, but her mind will acquiesce in it as just. Having learnt what it was which tempted her to offend, she will be the better able to guard against it. And if, whenever occasion offers, she is encouraged and assisted to speak truth, whatever may be the consequence, she will by degrees find her moral courage strengthened; whilst the dread of a lie will become so keen, that at length it will be a greater effort to tell a falsehood and escape punishment, than to speak truth and bear it.

For it may be remarked that pain is by the very instinct of nature attached to falsehood. A child may give way to pride, vanity, passion, selfishness, injustice, and may be sorry and ashamed of the sin when it is pointed out; but there is no such instinctive perception of guilt as there is in the case of falsehood. Some children, indeed, have this perception in a more marked degree than others; but all have it more or less; and it is by working upon it that we may hope so to strengthen the love of truth, as to make it an absolute necessity of the child's nature both to speak and act truly under all circumstances.

And when this necessity is created, we shall have paved the way for another most important phase of truth—that of seeing and owning it. Moral cowardice, for the most part, takes one form in childhood, another in mature age. A child knows what is true, but is afraid to say it. The grown-up man fears what is true, and is afraid to see it. Volumes might be written on the consequences of this weakness—volumes full of the history of personal self-deceit, family distrust, and that unhappy expediency, which, ultimately, bring ruin. The world calls these things by harsh names, because it suffers by them. It may be well that it should do so; for, if it looked upon them leniently, society could not long hold together. But God,

we may hope and believe, judges them more mercifully, and sees in them, not wilful, deliberate sin, but the infirmity of moral cowardice. Only, as the children whom we educate must live in the world, and be judged and punished by it, before they receive their sentence from God; it will be a work of charity in us to endeavour to save them from that which may, one day, prove so terrible a snare.

Never let us be afraid to tell children the truth. This is the general rule; the exceptions can be but few. If they are to take medicine, let them know that it is medicine. If they are to suffer pain, say so. If they are to be deprived of some anticipated pleasure, do not let them delude themselves, up to the last moment, by expecting it. And, if sorrow is coming upon the family—illness, poverty, separation—do not let us attempt to dress up the trial in any false garb. Own it to be what it is; and then teach those who are to bear it to encounter it with the strength which God will give. We must all have experienced, more or less, the confidence—the sense of power and resolution—which results from having looked an evil bravely in the face; having dared it, as it were, to its worst. That done, every slight alleviation is a real gain. We may not disturb ourselves about a trial which, in the Providence of God, may be prevented; but, having reason to expect it, we may calmly prepare ourselves to meet it, and leave the future in God's Hands. This courage of truthfulness in those who have the care of children, operates most beneficially in the way of example, besides giving the young mind rest. Young people are so quick in perceiving when something is amiss, that they are scarcely ever to be deceived upon this point, though their imaginations will continually outrun reality. It is possible to grow up, even from childhood, with a sense of insecurity, in the midst of apparent peace and prosperity; and, with this feeling, there must always be somewhat of distrust of those who try to throw a veil over the truth. There can be no rest with such a feeling. If the child has any force of character, there will be a determined search till truth

is discovered and faced; if not, example will do its fatal work, and the parent, who deceived himself, will unconsciously educate his child upon the same principle; till the heirloom of moral cowardice, handed down from generation to generation, has brought the punishment which must inevitably be its consequence; and then the confession is made—alas! too late—"If I had but been told the truth, and taught to face it in childhood, the whole course of my life would have been different. Now I have sown delusion, and reaped disappointment. Then, I should have worked my way, in the face of difficulties, and, in the end, have conquered."

People little think of all this, when they bring up their children with the one idea of saving them pain and making life happy. They say,—and that rightly,—that childhood and youth are the seasons for enjoyment; that trouble will come soon enough; that it is wrong to forecast evils ourselves. Most true—most worthy of attention; only, if things are based on a falsity, they will, ultimately, bring sorrow. Once give a young person, or even a child, the consciousness of having been wilfully misled, taught to build upon an unreal foundation, to expect what there was no reason to expect, and enjoyment is at an end. By one stroke, the charms of a home of happiness become the mere trickery of the scene painter; and the friends who made its delight, are the actors, who strangely represent reality, but have, in themselves, no affinity with the characters they portray. To give pain, to bear pain, to see painful facts, to look at painful sights, to put painful truths into plain words, are lessons which, if we do not learn in childhood from our parents and friends, God will inevitably teach us by the discipline of life.

They need but two cautions, though these are very needful. One is, not to confound the necessity of truth with coldness, or want of sympathy, or harsh judgment; and the other, to guard it from exaggeration.

The most painful things may be said and borne well if softened by kindness. We may not hesitate to disappoint a

child, or to speak of a trial which must be borne, but we must at the same time express our sorrow for the suffering we are inflicting.

And we must not confound truth with the exaggerations of temper, and suppose that we are giving needful warning or reproof when we are, in fact, merely giving way to our own hasty feelings. Faults and failings must be called by right names, but these may not always be such as we choose to apply to them. A child makes a mistake, and says unintentionally what is not true. Certainly, an untruth is a falsehood, and a person who tells a falsehood is a liar. But to call the child a liar is an exaggeration of terms which, if the matter were less grave, would border on the ludicrous. The reason of this is that "liar," in the sense in which it is generally used, implies the intention as well as the act of lying. We choose to separate the two, and therefore, though literally true in our statement, we are actually untrue. No one has a right to affix to words a meaning which is not generally accepted, any more than he has a right to call a, b,—or b, c,—and then to be angry because his friends cannot understand him when he attempts to talk.

Wilful exaggerations of this character are most mischievous in the education of children. They are discovered at once, and resented as injustice, and then there is no hope of repentance and amendment.

But there are many other temptations besides moral cowardice which lead, in one form or another, to the violation of truth.

A vast number of persons are untruthful from vanity. They like to say things which will attract attention; they are fond of making themselves heroes and heroines. They dress up the world in which they live in a fancy dress, and try to see both others and themselves in a point of view which will create interest. So it is that, instead of repeating a statement simply, as it is made, they think it no harm to put "a hat on its head, and a stick in its hand," and send it into the world in

a more attractive garb. Such persons will tell falsehoods, and persist in them with what appears the most deliberate effrontery, but they are not quite as wilfully untruthful as they seem to be. They half believe what they say. The fact of having said it gives it a kind of reality; and then they are obliged to defend themselves, and to repeat it, and that strengthens their belief, until at length they do quite think that it is true. And so they tell lies in perfect good faith, and are scarcely at all confounded when the truth and the statement are put side by side, and shown to be inconsistent with each other. "They do not know how it is," they say, "but certainly they heard it. The person who told them may have been mistaken. It is strange how apt we all are to make mistakes. But certainly they heard it."

And some cases there are in which there is no such actual blindness; cases in which some personal feeling has led to exaggeration—to a distortion of words, a wilful misconception of meaning. Pride and temper are the incentives to falsehood; and even when the untruth is plainly brought home to the guilty person, pride and temper will frequently cause a persistence in it, even to absurdity. So, again, little meannesses, and petty jealousies, will lead to lies, and when they are discovered, the same spirit will tempt to petty evasions, by which the meaning of what has been asserted may be altered and evaded, and thus the shame of having been untrue escaped.

Prejudice is another, and perhaps the most fruitful of all incentives to falsehood; but it is the sin of mature years rather than of childhood. Grown-up persons tell lies from prejudice, just as children do from want of moral courage. They attribute motives, and the very instant they do this the probability is that they will assert what is not true. But children also have the tendency; we may hear them say, they are sure such a person did or said so and so, because he or she liked or disliked, or felt, or wished something which it is impossible the child should know anything about.

And so also envy and revenge will lead to falsehood, and such instances, though they are more rare, are more flagrantly sinful; but in all these cases—setting aside the absence of moral courage—we shall find the sin of untruthfulness more strongly developed in grown-up persons than in children.

Vanity, pride, temper, meanness, prejudice, when they exist unchecked in the human heart, are stronger at thirty than at thirteen; and the falsehoods which proceed from them are therefore more glaring. Those which arise from the absence of moral courage would be more glaring also, if it were not that the stern discipline of the world converts the very weakness of man's nature into a source of strength; and the contempt which is poured upon untruthfulness makes him afraid to tell a lie.

Now, in order to guard against these manifold temptations to falsehood, it will be necessary always to bear in mind the guilt which attaches to the offence itself, apart from the motive which gave rise to it. We must, indeed, look narrowly into those motives, so that the temptation may be avoided for the future; and we must be just, as well as severe, in our judgment, and not pass the same sentence of condemnation on the child who tells a falsehood from fear, as on one who commits the same offence from envy or spite. But a lie is a lie still; and that which must be impressed upon the child is, that it is a sin unlike almost all other sins, inasmuch as it has a guilt of its own, apart from the motive which led to it, and therefore is to be abhorred, and consequently punished, for its own sake. We may feel very sorry for the timid child who has been led into an untruth; we may think and speak leniently of the proud child who could not bring herself to make a true confession; but—we are not punishing timidity or pride, but a lie, and the punishment of the offence must be proportionably severe, even whilst we show the child that we can fully understand and make allowance for the feelings which led to it. Perhaps the strongest weapon to be used against untruthfulness—including in that word not only direct falsehood, but de-

ceit and equivocation—is contempt; for it is the weapon which God uses in nature. Contempt is the first feeling which springs up in the heart, when we are brought face to face with a lie. It is intuitive. We are conscious of it before we can reason upon it. The person who tells the lie, unless entirely hardened, is conscious of it himself, and self-contempt, as it is a natural, so it is a much more severe punishment than the contempt of others.

We must, then, always speak of falsehood abstractedly, as something utterly despicable; and we may safely use the same tone when the offence is immediately brought before our notice. Only in that case we must take care to mark the distinction between the offence and the offender; otherwise we run the risk of crushing a child's spirit, by rousing a sense of degradation which destroys the energy necessary for amendment. A really honourable child may, from some very strong temptation, be led into falsehood or deceit, and the sense of humiliation following upon the discovery will then be so keen, that if the personal contempt of others is added to its own self-reproach, the feeling will become that agony of a "wounded spirit," which "who can bear?"

One rule, however, we may safely make, for it scarcely admits of an exception. A falsehood is never to go unpunished, whatever may have been the temptation which led to it, or however sincere may be the repentance which follows it. The sin exists as a sin in itself, and we may wisely say to a child, "I never overlook a lie." Of course, this does not include cases in which the falsehood is voluntarily confessed. The honourable act of confession must then be considered as neutralizing to a great extent the dishonourable act of untruthfulness.

In dealing with habitual falsehood the treatment must, of necessity, be different, and more severe, than when the offence is only, as it were, accidental. But even then we must never allow ourselves to speak so contemptuously as to create the idea that we have lost all confidence in the offender. The

moment we do that we lose our influence. A child who knows that she is not trusted, and believed, will never have the heart to strive to make herself worthy of confidence.

And this creates a great difficulty in cases of deception and equivocation, as well as of actual falsehood. To know that a child is likely to deceive, and yet to act as though we gave her credit for sincerity, requires more circumspection and self-control than the generality of persons are capable of. Some are so indignant at the very idea of deception, that they pour down a torrent of wrath and contempt without pausing to inquire how far it is deserved, whilst others are by nature suspicious; and suspicion, more than anything, creates deceit. Young people who are watched and suspected, are driven into it. Their simplest actions may, they know, be misconstrued, and therefore they try to conceal them. This is especially to be observed with regard to correspondence. Parents are naturally and rightfully anxious about their daughters' correspondence, as it may become a matter of much importance, and a common theory (which is as true as most theories!) is, that daughters can have nothing to write which their parents may not see, and that if they have, it must be something wrong. All letters, therefore, are expected to be shown. And they are shown. And if the daughters have good principles, the results may be twofold; they will probably write and receive but few letters—in itself a very good result—and they will beg their young friends to be very careful what they say, and reserve a free correspondence for some time when they happen to be away from home, and know that they can have their letters to themselves. Is this being perfectly open? And yet these young girls may, by nature, abhor deceit.

But supposing the daughters not to be well principled, what is then the effect of this system of suspicion? Will any amount of watching and care prevent a wrong correspondence, if young persons are determined to carry it on? We need only appeal to general experience to prove the contrary. Or suppose that we can by such means check correspondence, can we also check

the evil in the heart which gave rise to it, and which will surely work itself out in some other way?

Suspicion, we may be assured, never yet nourished truth in those already true, or checked it in those already untrue. Confidence, trust, the appeal to the sense of honour which God has implanted in the hearts of all;—these are the means by which we may hope so to guard our children, by making them guard themselves, that our own watchfulness will be unnecessary.

When a daughter can go to her mother and say, "I have a letter, or part of a letter, which I do not wish to show," the mother need have no fear of the contents of the letter. The same honourable feeling which led to the acknowledgment, will be a sufficient safeguard against any abuse of the confidence. Girls of twelve and thirteen must indeed be kept within strict limits in this matter, because they have not judgment enough to see the desirableness or undesirableness of the friendships they desire to cultivate. Their letters are for the most part a waste of time; but even with them—if we wish to make them thoroughly truthful—we must content ourselves with knowing to whom they write, and not be rigid in insisting upon always superintending the correspondence. They may have their little plans and schemes, perfectly innocent, but requiring some temporary secrecy, and if they cannot depend upon their elders to trust them, and not to inquire curiously into their small affairs, they will, unless singularly straightforward, be tempted to use deceptions which are very injurious to the character. But when young people have reached the age of seventeen or eighteen, even the force of circumstances points out that in this matter of letter-writing they must be left free. If they are worth anything, we may be quite sure they will not keep up any correspondence which they know their parents would disapprove; and if they are not, the commands of parents will be of no more avail than their wishes.

With this subject of letters, that of conversation is intimately connected. Young people write to their friends, and of

course they talk to them; and we must make up our minds that, in perfect innocence, they will occasionally say or wish to say things which they do not desire their parents, or persons set over them, to hear. This is a broad statement. It requires explanation. There is a great distinction—one which must never be overlooked—between words and acts which we should be ashamed for those whom we respect to know, and words and acts which we do not wish them to know.

If young people, when trusted together, say or do things which they would be ashamed to own, those things cannot be innocent. But there may be many little confidences and subjects of interest, even matters of mutual confession and advice, of real value, which would at once be put a stop to by the interference or cognizance of a third person. We all can understand this. Two persons not on terms of particular friendship are, we will suppose, talking freely to each other, and really enjoying the conversation; a third person enters, who is perhaps the intimate friend of one of them. The conversation ceases. There were no secrets going on. There may perhaps have been no reason why the new comer should not have heard what was said, and joined in it; but somehow it is impossible to continue. A new element has been introduced, a fresh combination must be formed. To be jealous and suspicious under such circumstances would be wrong and absurd; and yet it is not unusual for elder persons to be fretted when they enter a room in which two young persons are talking, and find that the conversation suddenly stops. So, again, we can, in certain states of feeling, and under certain circumstances, say things to one person which we should be wholly unable to say to others. This is especially the case with the young. They can and do talk to those of their own age with an amount of freedom which it is almost impossible for them to enjoy with persons who stand above them. They do not love their young companions more, they do not respect them as much. They would on no account be guided by their advice in preference to that of their elders, but they are more

free with them; and so they say things to them which they could not say to their mother or their governess.

And if we love them—desire their confidence—wish for their respect—and look forward to their being one day our own cherished friends, they must be permitted to enjoy this freedom. Assist them in the choice of their friends we must (this is a subject to be reserved for future consideration), but when the friendship is formed with our sanction and concurrence, we must not act the spy upon it, still less suspect it.

It is with conversation as with letters, we cannot check it; therefore let us put upon it the restraint of honour. It is the only restraint which will be of any avail. And if we show this loving confidence, we shall very soon know all that we wish to know. When once girls feel that they are trusted, they will continually, of their own accord, come to the mother, or the friend whom they respect, and repeat the very things which they have said to each other, and which they fancied were secrets reserved for their own breasts. They have a natural wish for guidance and help; and they will seek it if it is not forced upon them. Or it may be said (the case has actually occurred)—"I have a secret, something which I should like to tell you, but I must not. I should be glad to ask your advice, but I am not at liberty to do so; but the secret makes me uncomfortable, and therefore I could not help telling you that I have it." Such an instance is an exhibition of perfect confidence on both sides. The young girl knows that her secret will not be inquired into; the mother or the friend feels that it cannot be, on her part, a wrong secret. In due time it will certainly be known. Till then the young girl is learning a most valuable lesson, that of using her own judgment, and trying to act conscientiously under difficult circumstances, yet without any exercise of self-will. And similar confidence should be shown by ourselves. To say—"My dear, you must go away because I have something to talk about which I do not wish you to hear," is an open avowal accepted without in-

quiry. To make a pretence for getting the child out of the room excites suspicion and wrong curiosity.

But we shall often meet with cases in which, although there is no actual deceit, yet from timidity, or vanity, or from some other cause, there is a want of openness, or an attempt at equivocation. Children—little children especially—will say one thing, meaning another. They will ask favours for others, intending them all the time for their own benefit. This species of deceit is irritating from its meanness. It may be met with the calm statement, "What you really want is so and so. Now repeat your request again." A child is startled by this apparent knowledge of its thoughts, and ashamed of having been found out; and the next time it will be afraid to be thus double.

So, again, with regard to exaggeration. No one can overestimate the grievous consequences of this fault, and, therefore, no pains should be spared to root it out. It is especially the sin of later years—of persons who are otherwise amiable and agreeable; who are flattered by society, admired by their acquaintances, grieved over by their friends, and—too often—despised by their relations. For it is only those intimately connected with the offender who, as a general rule, really understand the fatal consequences of this form of falsehood. The careless exaggeration told in society passes by unheeded, or if remembered, it is difficult to fix the stigma upon the right person. Reports, it is known, are always exaggerated, and what is every one's sin is no one's sin. But amongst relations, the heartburnings and discords, the misunderstandings and uncharitableness, caused by exaggeration, would be a history to fill volumes.

Surely the first germs of such a fault should be watched and uprooted! A child comes to us with some made-up story founded upon a fact which has actually happened. We laugh at its powers of imagination, perhaps we may think the story a proof of cleverness. Or if we consider it our duty to reprove, we do so with such ill-concealed amusement, that the child

instantly sees through our assumed anger, and is encouraged to be a little more imaginative on the next occasion which may offer.

There are even cases in which this imaginative faculty is so strong, that stories which have not the slightest foundation are invented and repeated with the most circumstantial details, and apparently without object; and when this is the case, the seeming innocence of evil on the part of the offender is a strong inducement to overlook the fault altogether. But to do this is to commit a fatal mistake. Fact is fact; fiction is fiction. To confound the two is falsehood. This is the lesson to be enforced for life. Quietly and deliberately, therefore, we may in such cases question and cross-question, till we have forced the conviction of untruthfulness upon the child's mind; and then the fault must be punished with more or less severity as a lie. The absence of motive or wrong intention must not be accepted as an excuse.

Exaggeration, which is a much more common form of this imaginative untruthfulness, requires to be treated in a somewhat similar way. A girl who habitually exaggerates is probably not aware of the extent of her offence, neither is she likely to be so for a long time. Some persons, especially great talkers, who pique themselves upon being agreeable in conversation, and therefore dress up their stories in order to be entertaining, go through life without perceiving the sin of exaggeration. But in educating the young, it is our duty to reprove most sharply those faults which are least likely to be noticed by conscience.

We must, therefore, rouse ourselves to some trouble in this matter. As in the case of direct invention, a little questioning and examination will make the child convict herself of her own fault. It will compel her to disentangle the fact from the fiction. She will not like the process, it will be humiliating, but very salutary; and when the fact comes out in its plain garb, she should be made to repeat it, to put it side by side with her own statement, and then be compelled to own that the

discrepancy is a thing to be ashamed of. And the correction of the habit should be constant; no instance of it should be allowed to remain unchecked. It is one of those cases in which it is far less dangerous to err on the side of strictness than on that of leniency. Exaggeration is a weed which grows much more rapidly than we can pluck it up; and if it is once suffered to become a habit, it will mar all that is really valuable in the character. To catch up a person's words, to bring him to task, are expressions which have a very unpleasant sound; and grown-up people so greatly resent the attempt to carry them out in action, that in the world exaggerations are allowed to run their course, to multiply and enlarge, until the careless report becomes the accepted slander, and characters are ruined, and prospects blasted, without any intention of saying what is false, but because no one will take the trouble to be quite sure that he is speaking truth. But children will bear what their elders will not. Though the check may annoy them for the moment, they will not resent it afterwards, and the habit of watchful accuracy thus acquired will be an invaluable blessing to them through life. For with this habit of strict truth, strict justice is inseparably connected. Perhaps there is no one who has not at some time or other in his life suffered from the injustice consequent upon misrepresentation, or who has not found himself tempted to be guilty of it. We make a certain statement, using certain words. The person to whom the statement is made repeats it with, perhaps, the change of one word for another, which he professes to think bears the same meaning. To us the two words have totally distinct meanings. We advisedly used the one, we would on no account have used the other. Upon this statement so altered an accusation is based and circulated; we defend ourselves by repeating the statement as we originally made it. But it is too late. The lie has gone forth into the world, and truth, be it never so swift-footed, will fail to overtake it.

And so with regard to ourselves, more especially in argument. That man must be very singularly true and just who

has never been induced to take up his opponent's words, and twist them to suit his own meaning; and that knowingly, from the eager desire to prove himself in the right. Arguments would be conducted in a very different spirit, if every one would take the trouble to ascertain precisely what his adversary means before he attempts to refute him. Till this is done, the argument must be untruthful, because based upon false premises, and the conclusions deduced from them must be unjust.

There are, indeed, times, when it seems as if the whole world was like Don Quixote, occupying itself in fighting with windmills, believing them to be giants; and in the act of fighting doing mischief which can never be repaired. We may, perhaps, ourselves be dimly conscious of having some special little windmill, against which we have kept up a contest so long, and upon which we have wasted so much time and energy, that the information which should open our eyes to the fact that, after all, it was a windmill and no giant, would be by no means acceptable to us. But, however this may be, at least let us try to save our children from a mistake so reprehensible in its origin, and so sad in its consequences. Let us teach them the meaning and the power of words; show them the difference between what they say and what they wish to say; check them when they give way to exaggerated expressions themselves, or put a wrong construction upon those used by others; and, above all, let us never accept the excuse that the words they use do not in their mouths mean what they do in those of others. The ordinary, natural interpretation of words is their true interpretation. We have no more right to give them a meaning different from that of the world than we have to call sixpence a shilling, and endeavour to pass it as such. Words are the current coin of the common reason; and reason puts her own valuation upon them, and stamps them with her sovereign mark. The value may alter with time, custom, and circumstances, but the power which effects this alteration must still be the same; and the individual who chooses to assume the privilege to himself must be content to be scoffed at

for his folly, and in the end severely punished for his presumption.

These are grave matters, worthy of all attention, small though they may to some appear. We wish our children to be blessings in their generation, as well as a comfort to ourselves. It is the dream of every parent who thinks seriously upon the position in which man is placed in this world of probation, and faces without shrinking the tremendous interests involved in it.

Then, above all things, let us educate them in truth; for without truth there can be no justice, and without justice earth would become a Pandemonium.

CHAPTER XVI.

EDUCATION IN JUSTICE AS THE ANTIDOTE TO SELFISHNESS.

AND thus we arrive at the duty of educating children in justice, or truth in act. Probably we have not often thought what this involves. The ordinary idea of justice is that of deciding fairly between two claimants. Such a task is seldom imposed upon children, and we may therefore naturally think that the duty of justice may be left to be enforced by reason when the age of discretion and responsibility shall have arrived.

But looking upon justice as being, what it is in fact, practical truth, we shall find that it enters into every question of morals, and is in reality the great instrument by which the errors consequent upon weakness and passion are, through God's help, to be rectified. Sin in any form is the result of falsehood. It is based upon a false belief concerning God; a false estimate of present happiness; and false expectations of it for the future. This same falsity, carried out in our actions, produces injustice towards our fellow-creatures, which is in reality nothing but an untrue estimate of the relations in which we stand to them, leading us to acts which are the necessary and inevitable consequence of that belief. Thus, disregard of the true relation between parents and children exhibits itself in undutifulness; and a similar forgetfulness of true social relations produces pride. If we could suppose a child to be educated perfectly in the recognition of every family, social, and political relation,—so long as it carried out the principles of

its education, it could never be proud or selfish, much less mean, or unkind, or ungrateful. But, alas! we have first to educate ourselves; and too many of us do not even know what self-education means; whilst the few who do comprehend it, have probably begun to learn their lesson so late in life, or have from circumstances found such difficulty in perfecting it, that even whilst preaching justice they act injustice, and example being more powerful than exhortation, their words fail to produce any lasting effect.

If, however, the principle of justice is so important, it cannot but be useful to examine into its practical working, as the corrective of two of the most stubborn ingrained faults of human nature—selfishness and pride;—faults into which so many others may be resolved, that in checking them we should check a host of minor offences, which are commonly considered to require distinct treatment.

For in this, as in many other instances, inquiry brings us back to a very few original principles, which if we can once thoroughly engraft in our minds, we shall solve many questions of moral and educational difficulty.

And first with regard to selfishness. What is selfishness? The answer will be suggested at once: an undue regard for self. We may mark that word *undue*, or as it might be more strictly called *untrue* or unjust; for it points to the fact which selfish persons constantly bring forward as their excuse, that there is such a thing as due or lawful self-love, a quality which, as Bishop Butler says, "seems inseparable from all sensible creatures, who can reflect upon themselves, and their own interest or happiness, so as to have that interest an object to their minds." [1]

Self-love comes to us by nature, and is in itself innocent; we have, therefore, no occasion to cultivate, only to regulate it. Even in those very rare instances in which there appears to be an exaggerated unselfishness, leading to folly and weakness, self-love is not extinct, though it takes a form in which

[1] Butler's Sermon "Upon the Love of our Neighbour."

it may be difficult to recognize it. That which is sinful is inordinate self-love, a love which does not rightly appreciate the claims of others; and we shall find, if we have to deal with a candid and true mind, that this perception of truth, acting as an incentive to practice, will be our most powerful assistant in counteracting selfishness.

For it is useless to appeal to feeling as an antidote to self ishness. There may be no real hardness of heart, or absence of benevolence in general, but in the particular case in which selfishness is exhibited, the claims of self-love are felt so strongly, that they overpower benevolence. Treat the question calmly, dispassionately, make a plain statement of the claims on both sides; then leave it to be considered, and even if the victory should be gained by selfishness, it will be accompanied by such a pang of self-reproach, suggested by truth and justice, that the power of the evil principle will at least be checked, and the consciousness of having been guilty of the fault will produce a most salutary sense of shame.

This mode of dealing with selfishness should be constantly put in practice. True claims should be always truly stated, and then left without any appeal to feeling.

And if in any case truth and justice are to be found on the side of the ordinarily selfish claimant, by all means let them be attended to. It is not because in nine cases we have ourselves been unfair, that in the tenth others may be unfair to us. We shall but irritate by compelling a child to a sacrifice which cannot rightly be required of it; and we shall weaken the power of the one great instrument, by which we hope to counteract the power of selfishness—perfect justice.

This cold justice is, indeed, very far removed from what is called unselfishness, which consists in yielding what may fairly be claimed; and not only so, but showing that the sacrifice is a pleasure. But in education we must be content to work with the materials which are given us. To feel pleasure in self-sacrifice is not in itself an exercise of virtue. It is only a

gift or attainment which makes virtue easy. A person who does a kind act willingly, is more agreeable than one who does it unwillingly; but so long as both actions are the result of right principle, both are good. And if we can once succeed in establishing justice as a habit of mind, there will be a pleasure in its exercise which will exhibit itself in a cheerful readiness of manner, producing in its turn gratitude on the part of the person who is benefited. Gratitude will soften the hardness of cold justice, and the result will be that glad forgetfulness of self, which is unselfishness in its best form.

And it is very important to bear in mind that selfishness is not corrected, as some persons are apt to think, by the example of what is commonly called unselfishness—often the contrary.

Unselfish mothers make selfish children. This is a startling assertion, but it will unquestionably be borne out by experience. What is the cause?

An unselfish mother—according to the world's definition—is one who gives up time, thought, comfort, pleasure, often even health, for what she considers her children's good, and yet more—for their gratification. She not only guides and instructs them, but she waits upon them, and works for them. So long as they are comfortable, it matters not that she is uncomfortable; so long as they are enjoying themselves, it is of no consequence if she is slaving for them.

But is this right? Is it the recognition of the true relation between the parent and child—between old and young? The same principle which requires a child to be respectful in manner, and obedient to her mother, requires also that she should be called upon to spare her trouble, to consider her wishes, to sacrifice little personal gratifications for her. But the so-called unselfish mother allows her daughter to forget this. She places herself in an untrue relation, and then supposes that she can work out a right result. If we desire to make children unselfish, we must show them their true duties, and then leave them to be performed.

And again: benevolent parents fall into a similar mistake. The true relation in which the man who possesses wealth, or even a competence, stands to the poor and needy, is that of God's steward. This is, in fact, the relation in which we all stand. We have no property, rightly so called. We are simply entrusted with a portion from the treasury of God, which we are to dispense according to certain laws. For our own share we are to take that which is *necessary* for the maintenance of the station of life in which God has placed us. To go beyond this is, in reality, to be guilty of injustice—to use for ourselves that which lawfully belongs to others.

But one of the first lessons which many really good parents give their children is that of practically denying this truth. Recognizing it themselves, they yet teach their children the contrary, by deliberately pursuing a system which must lead to this wrong result. They lavish upon them every luxury; they give them whatever they ask for; they never allow them to think that money is of any importance, still less do they associate its possession with duty and self-denial; and, more than all, they allow them to be benevolent by proxy. The poor, it may be, are fed; the naked clothed; the ignorant instructed; but it is with no effort on the part of the children of the household. They are brought up on a system of delusion. If they see a case of distress, and their feelings are touched, they run to their parents and ask for money; and it is given them. And in the act of relieving the distress, the instinct of benevolence is satisfied, and a very comfortable self-complacency follows. But personal self-denial, personal self-sacrifice?—They know nothing of it. Their only idea of the extent of the claim to which they are liable is, that they must give what they do not want themselves; and as every passing fancy has from infancy been gratified, of course their personal needs are by no means small.

The effects of such training are painfully visible in after life. The subject is a very large and a very important one, and is forced upon our attention year by year, as public statis-

tics and private observation bring before us the frightful rapidity with which poverty and suffering, with their attendant vice, are increasing, so as to make it seemingly hopeless in any degree to overtake them.

England boasts of her benevolence; her charities are reckoned by thousands. Alas! her poor, and degraded, and ignorant are reckoned by millions!

And these thousands—from whom are they collected? Where are the princely gifts of those on whom God has bestowed the wealth of princes? Never may we forget the few who have, in our own days, come forward to show how riches may be used, so that they may become a treasure in Heaven! But setting aside these noble exceptions, is it not an acknowledged fact, that, with regard to both public and private charities, by far the larger portion of the funds is contributed by those who have only moderate or even small incomes? Are not the clergy—many of them possessing incomes which a nobleman would scarcely consider sufficient for his upper servant—compelled to support by their yearly mites schemes for good, which one effort of real self-denial, on the part of a millionnaire, might establish permanently at once?

Yes, England is benevolent, as the world reckons benevolence! The columns of the *Times* carry the record of our good deeds to the farthest end of the earth, and nations wonder and applaud. But the columns of the *Times* are not the record which is to be produced at the Great Day of account; and when God shall demand of each individual, now revelling in luxury, the principle on which his charities were regulated, there is but one answer which will be accepted. It is embodied in the words of David to Araunah—"Neither will I offer burnt offerings unto the Lord my God of that which doth cost me nothing."[1]

And these rich men—these millionnaires—these possessors of splendid fortunes, or even only of very ample means—are, then, utterly selfish, totally insensible to the needs of their fellow-creatures!

[1] 2 Sam. xxiv. 24.

By no means. They are, for the most part, kind-hearted, estimable, irreproachable in their family relations. They are merely, like Dives, ignorant of the nature and extent of their social relations. They see untruly—that is all. They are quite willing that Lazarus should lie at their gate, and eat of their crumbs; some, perhaps, will even take the trouble to send him out a portion from their well-spread table. What they do not see is, that the sufferer has a claim to more—that he is to be tended, and watched, and nourished; that personal self-denial, for his benefit, is required of them; that wealth is an excrescence which hardens around the heart, and that it must be cut away before that heart can be really touched.

To give, and give, and give, until the self-denial of giving is *felt*—that is the test of whether we have given enough.

And so to be a weak fool—or an enthusiast! Nay, far from it. Once more recur to the law of true relation, the principle of justice, and this vexed question of giving will be made clearer. The relations in which we stand to our fellow-creatures are many. That of wealth to poverty is but one. Royalty, rank, political office, have their claims as well as beggary and ignorance. The encouragement of art, literature, science, the support of national honour, the duties of hospitable and social intercourse, are no more to be neglected than the foundation and support of hospitals and reformatories. The station in which God has placed us by birth it is incumbent upon us to maintain. The fact that God has annexed pleasure and ease to it does not make it wrong in us to keep it up. So long as we guard against any self-deceit in this matter, we are at liberty to enjoy thankfully the comforts which He has bestowed upon us; only—the greater are the necessities of luxury which surround us, the greater should be the unostentatious self-denial which we practise. Doubtless many difficult questions will from time to time suggest themselves as to the extent of the claims of birth and station, but an honest heart will seek God's aid, and so be enabled to an-

swer them upon the whole rightly; more especially if education upon this point has begun early.

Persons accustomed from childhood to recognize claims of every kind will never, indeed, succeed in reconciling them perfectly, for to do this is to exercise absolute justice; but the habit of considering them will give a largeness and clearness of comprehension, which will be a safer guide through life than the most disinterested intentions, taken apart from experience and judgment.

This is more especially seen with regard to personal expenditure. The sooner a young person can be trusted with an allowance the better. Such responsibility will teach real self-denial and economy, and prove the test of true generosity. Nothing is so easy as to give away that which belongs to another; and a child brought up in this habit becomes both selfish and extravagant unconsciously. In all cases, the allowance should be measured by the child's future prospects. It is as great a mistake to give a small allowance to a rich heiress, as it is to give a large sum to a child who may have to work for her own livelihood. What is needed in both instances is the knowledge of the true relation between the individual and her fellow-creatures; and it is as important for the rich to be taught to spend money generously, as it is for the poor to spend it carefully.

For it must be remembered, that people give at thirty according to the rate at which they were taught to give at ten or twelve. If the gifts of the latter age were necessarily limited to a twentieth part of the small allowance, then the gifts of the former will usually be in the same proportion to the whole fortune. Treble the allowance, and the charities and kindnesses may be trebled, for the personal expenses will remain the same; and the habit of distributing these charities wisely will be a lesson to be practised through life.

And, after all, this duty of giving is mainly habit, except in persons of great benevolence. It is astonishing how quickly we accustom ourselves to enlarge our charities or our kindnesses

when once our eyes are open to perceive the duty. Wealthy persons, who give five pounds a year to a charity, might often just as easily give twenty, thirty, or even fifty, if they did but think about it. But this they have never been accustomed to do. Having never felt any need themselves, they have no idea what need is. And in the same way, and much more frequently, they have no perception of the claims of those who are not, strictly speaking, poor, but who are hampered by small incomes or large families. They cannot understand that what is so practicable to themselves is quite out of the power of their friends. Like the princess who in the time of great scarcity wondered that the poor did not eat cake, if they were unable to procure bread, they cannot see where the real pressure lies; and so it never enters into their minds to relieve it, as they often and often might do, by some thoughtful kindness, which, without bringing with it an unpleasant sense of obligation, would really give the aid required. Now all this is a question of early habits, of a perception of true claims—in other words, of justice. That is a hard, cold word; it has no such pleasant sound as benevolence, or generosity; but it is the foundation of both, and without it benevolence is weakness, and generosity but another form of selfishness; since it is the recognition of the claim which we like, in preference to that to which we are indifferent.

Be just before you are generous. Pay your debts before you make presents. What a host of sorrows and disappointments would be spared if these common maxims could only be thoroughly implanted in young minds! And they never can be, unless there is a sense of possession, and with it of responsibility and limitation. So long as a young girl can go to a father or mother for everything she needs, she will have no knowledge of what debt means, no motive for self-denial, no pleasure in giving—and, in consequence, no thought for others. Possessing nothing which she can strictly call her own, she is not called upon to recognize social and charitable claims, and so unconsciously she becomes selfish.

And this strict justice is a most valuable safeguard against self-deceit. There is scarcely anything about which people delude themselves and others so much as generosity. It is such a very dazzling, conspicuous virtue—so extremely pleasant in its exercise, and it produces such immediate results! It comes forth, as it were, full blown; whereas justice is buried in the ground, and when it does exhibit itself, does so often under a guise which is far from pleasing. Probably it appears to be want of sympathy, and niggardliness. It is only as time goes on, and we see the full working of the two principles, that we perceive the true nature of justice, and are compelled to own that without it real generosity cannot exist. When a man who owes another five hundred pounds, offers his creditor a present of fifty, and expects to be thanked for his generosity, the world cries scorn upon his folly; but the same absurdity is carried out continually, on a small scale, in private relations, and the beginning of it may in almost all instances be traced to some wrong training in youth.

Justice may be accepted in lieu of generosity, but generosity can never be received in lieu of justice. And for this reason, that it is not generosity at all. A generous person does what is just, and something beyond. A person who overlooks justice—takes away from A in order to give to B—and then entertains the delusion that he has made a sacrifice of something which was his own—this is simple falsity; an untruth.

CHAPTER XVII.

EDUCATION IN JUSTICE AS THE ANTIDOTE TO PREJUDICE AND ILLIBERALITY.

But truth working itself out in justice is not only the counteracting principle to selfishness, but to narrowness of mind, uncharitableness, want of sympathy. The assertion is almost self-evident, and yet we are apt to make mistakes upon the subject. What many of us are tempted to do is to choose the duties which we like, and neglect those which we dislike; or, even if it is no question of preference, to choose one or two which we think important, and to put others aside: so we become narrow and unsympathetic.

Now, this certainly is not in accordance with the example given us by our Blessed Lord, or with the teaching of His Apostles. Our Lord taught publicly, but He also taught privately. He spent whole nights in prayer, but in the daytime He mingled with crowds in cittes. He lived apart with His disciples, but He was present at the marriage feast, and dined at the table of the Pharisee. And, in like manner, in the directions given by the Apostles to their converts, we find a careful inculcation of the duties following upon all the relations in which mankind stand to each other. Sovereign and rulers, friends, children, inferiors, the rich, the poor, all are mentioned; all have true claims, and, therefore, all must, in their degree, be noticed.

It is this kind of education which alone can make young people large-minded. We sometimes find persons giving up

all social intercourse because they desire to devote themselves more entirely to the good of their families :—a most excellent object, and if the world was peopled with the members of their own household, a most laudable resolution. But as it happens that there are other persons to be considered, and other claims to be attended to, it will generally be found that the effect of such conduct is to create a spirit of narrow-mindedness, unable to undersiand or sympathize with anything beyond its own little sphere of thought and action. So, again, people give themselves up to one kind of occupation, perhaps to some benevolent work ; they devote all their thoughts to it, but they make great blunders, and the work proves a failure. Why? They have taken a one-sided view. They have shut themselves out from the opinions and sympathies of the ordinary world, and, in consequence, are deficient in sound judgment.

This may seem to contradict what has been previously said as to being guided in education by the peculiar talents and idiosyncrasies of the individual. But it does not really do so. No doubt it is right that persons, whether young or old, should, if possible, devote themselves to the work for which they seem specially fitted, but it is also needful that some attention should, at the same time, be paid to other duties in order to keep up a right balance, both of the mental and moral powers.

We occasionally hear of some very small rent paid for a piece of ground, merely as a recognition of true ownership. So should it be with the duties arising from mutual relations. God claims them all from us in greater or less degree. If circumstances compel us to give the larger portion of our time to one claim, then what remains must be divided amongst those which are less imperative. But some notice must be taken of each. The shilling must be paid, though it may be impossible for us to offer the pound. The rule can less easily be carried out with children than by grown-up persons, because the sphere of employment of the young must, to a certain extent, be limited ; but even with them it should never be forgotten. Study must not preclude some thought for the poor. Lessons must

not be so engrossing as utterly to prevent an attention to active home duties and social relations. But in all these things it is the *tone* of a house which educates, and one-sided or narrow-minded parents will make one-sided or narrow-minded children, let tutors or governesses do what they may to counteract the evil. A high standard, a large view, a recognition of all claims, even though it may be impossible to give them more than a slight attention,—this it is which keeps the heart sympathetic and the hand open, and more especially makes the judgment sound. A right view of the relations of life, and truth, and sound judgment, are inseparable.

And, once more, truth and justice are the only support of true—the only safeguard against false—liberality. This principle, taken in the abstract, is the idol of the present day, and its prevalent worship leads many to suppose that it is inconsistent with the maintenance of truth. Undoubtedly, in a number of cases, it is so. Liberality that admits everything to be true, which every one thinks true, does, in fact, deny the existence of truth altogether. But the world would not be so eager in its support of liberality if there were no admixture of good in it. Foolish and wicked as mankind are, they are not idiots or demons; they do not admire folly for folly's sake, nor sin for sin's sake. They may make grievous mistakes as to what is good, but it is because they believe that what they uphold really is good that they value it.

And true liberality is good, because it is based upon truth and justice. Without negativing truth, it recognizes the fact that it may be viewed differently by different persons. We look at a landscape through an ordinary glass, and declare that the grass is green. Another person, without being aware of what he is doing, looks at it through a red glass, and says that it is red. We are bound to uphold the truth, that the hue of the grass is what we know it to be. It would be an absurd liberality to profess to doubt the fact, because of the opposite assertion; but so it would be an injustice not to own that our opponent has a reason for his statement. As he looks at the

grass, it is not green. His fault is not in stating what he sees, but in maintaining the statement without referring to the testimony of other witnesses, and of his own experience, which would convince him that he is under a delusion.

Truth and justice imperatively demand that, in all contested cases, we should place ourselves in the position of the person opposed to us, and, before we begin to argue—much more to find fault—do our very utmost to see with his eyes, and view the subject according to his prejudices. This, we must remember, is not for a moment admitting that the truth which we are regarding has no independent existence apart from our idea of it (which is the false liberality so justly dreaded); it is only putting on another pair of spectacles through which to look at it.

Children may be taught to do this just as much as their elders. But they will not readily acquire the lesson. Perhaps, in the ordering of God's wisdom, it may be better that it should be rather a difficulty; otherwise, with the tendency to exaggeration and misconception common to their age, they would be very likely to imbibe the idea that truth is nothing in itself, and that it does not signify whether what we believe is true, so long as we think it to be true. An error of this kind may, as we learn from the analogy of nature, produce grave consequences. The man who grasps a knife believing it to be a stick, does not escape injury because his imagination deceived him; and false doctrine will lead to wrong practice, and, in consequence, to sorrow and suffering. But though it may be, and indeed is, most necessary to insist upon this objective existence of truth, especially in early years, yet we shall find that, as young people grow up, it is equally necessary to accustom them to consider it subjectively, or according to the view taken of it by different minds. And still more is this habit of viewing a question on all sides, and understanding all the facts connected with it, needful in the affairs of common life.

Hasty judgments, unkind imputations, angry words—all

have their source in prejudice; prejudgment—or judgment formed before the facts of a case are known, and the view taken of it by others is thoroughly considered. We are quite safe in enforcing the exercise of such considerations—or, in other words, of justice—in all childish or youthful quarrels or discussions, because we can never make young people too forbearing, or too patient and just, and unprejudiced, where their own personal interests, or their likings and dislikings, are concerned. If we can teach them to pause before they pronounce a judgment until they have heard what is to be said on the other side, we shall give them an invaluable lesson for life. There will be no fear, in such cases, of their denying the existence of right, because they are compelled to see that there is right, or —more probably—wrong, on both sides. Moral truth is in this unlike revealed truth, that it has a witness in our own breasts which cannot be gainsaid. Two persons may dispute upon the doctrines of the Trinity or the Incarnation, and false liberality, judging between them, may say that each holds truth because each believes himself to do so. But suppose it to be a question of whether it was right, under certain circumstances, to kill a man, the bystander called upon to decide would not for a moment doubt that the act of murder was wrong, though he might be doubtful whether, in the special instance under consideration, the act could be called murder.

And if we can bring ourselves to recognize the duty of true liberality, its extent and its limitations, we shall have gained a valuable antidote to anxiety in our education of the young. Persons who form theories, and act upon systems with their children, are often greatly disturbed by finding them suddenly upset by the events of life. Wishing to be wiser than Providence, they mark out for themselves a plan of life, which is (little though they think it) to be independent of Providence. They settle themselves, perhaps, in a certain locality, because they wish their children to be brought up in Church principles, and believe that the religious teaching will be sound and the society congenial. And so for a time it is,

and the children never hear of erroneous doctrine, except as of something monstrous from which they must be guarded, and are never allowed to associate with any persons but those who agree with them. But unexpectedly the clergyman dies, the society changes, and the parents are in despair. All their plans are set at naught; they must either move to some other place, which perhaps is out of their power, or they must expose their children to instruction and social intercourse which may unsettle their minds. What is to be done?

Surely, to own that God's teaching is wiser than man's, and to submit to it. Let the children go to church, and hear what is said, and then show them at home why, and how, it is unsound. They will learn in this way to distinguish truth in itself, from truth as it is represented under distorted forms, and their convictions will be far firmer than if they had never known the existence of error. And so also let them mix in the society which has gathered around them, hear differences of opinion, see differences of manner, feel by experience the power and earnestness of minds nurtured in an atmosphere quite unlike their own. Some cherished prejudices may be shaken, some narrow views enlarged, and possibly—for there is no doubt a risk of such an evil—opinions which have been held sacred may become in their eyes less important than they really are. But if such teaching and intercourse are sent in the ordering of God's Providence, without effort or fault of our own (in which case it would be unquestionably wrong), we may not fear it. In the end it will work for good, much greater good than any system of ours, though the latter may be carefully considered and effectually carried out. "L'homme propose, mais Dieu dispose." And how shall man's plans be wiser than God's orderings?

There are dangers to which we may not dare to expose children voluntarily, but which, if placed in their path by God, must be intended for their good.

To hold certain principles because some particular person holds them, and we have always been taught to believe that

what he says is right, may serve us very well so long as we are under the influence of this individual, and so long also as he himself keeps in the right track. But experience teaches us that no human being, good and clever though he may be, is safe from fatal error; and our Blessed Lord especially warns us to call "no one our Master upon earth; because One is our Master which is in heaven."

That conviction of truth alone is to be prized which can stand, though angels tempt it to its fall.

> "So spake the seraph Abdiel, faithful found
> Among the faithless—faithful only he
> Among innumerable false; unmoved,
> Unshaken, unseduced, unterrified,
> His loyalty he kept—his love—his zeal:
> Nor number, nor example, with him wrought
> To swerve from truth, or change his constant mind,
> Though single."

CHAPTER XVIII.

PRIDE.

THERE is another fault as common as Selfishness, and perhaps even more dangerous, which will also find its corrective in the principle of truth.

Who of us has not at times felt tempted to be proud of Pride? And to be proud of a fault is to cherish an insurmountable obstacle to its subdual.

Here, again, the mistake lies in a confusion of ideas. Self-love is innocent. Selfishness is not. We confound the two, and bring ourselves into perplexity and error. In like manner, self-respect is good; pride is evil. We do not trouble ourselves to distinguish between them, and cherish a vice whilst we think we are upholding a virtue.

But it may be said, the distinction is so subtle, it can scarcely be perceived.

Not so. The distinction is evident, if we will only try the two classes of feeling by the right test. Truth is the spear of Ithuriel, which will compel pride to show itself in its deformity.

This, however, requires illustration and explanation.

A person who is accused of acting from a wrong motive, when he knows that his only wish was to do right, may justly maintain his innocence, at least as regards intention. It is his treasure, a fact which, being true, he is called upon to assert. And he may also be indignant at having a wrong motive imputed to him, for the feeling thus excited is not pride at all, it is simply self-respect.

But a person who is conscious of this wrong motive, has no

such treasure of innocence to guard. His sole remaining dignity is the acknowledgment of having done wrong, for such acknowledgment is truth. When, therefore, he refuses to own his fault, his feeling is pride, and pride is a sin and degradation. The rule holds good in all cases where acknowledgment of a fault or a misdeed is required. As soon as conscience whispers that we have done wrong, or in any way been mistaken, it matters not whether we are more or less in fault than others—the refusal to own the fact is pride.

Very difficult it is to make children see this, and if pride has been allowed to grow up unchecked, it will strengthen with years, till at length it becomes almost impossible to eradicate it. Men and women will continually show by silent action, that they are aware of having been in the wrong, but perhaps not more than one in a hundred possesses the true nobleness of mind which leads to the acknowledgment in words. It is strange that it should be so, for we must all be aware of the effect which honourable confession of having been in error, or mistaken, produces. We all know how, in an instant, it changes the current of angry feelings, how it blots out past unkindness, and induces us to throw a veil over any lingering weakness; more than this, how unconsciously it engenders a feeling of respect.

We are aware of all this, indeed, with others, but we cannot believe it to be so with ourselves; or rather, Satan tempts us with his own special favourite sin, and, blinding our eyes, prevents us from seeing that the recognition of truth must, in itself, be honourable, even though it may humble us to the dust; whilst the refusal to recognize it must be despicable, though it may seem to maintain us in a position of superiority.

And herein lies the secret of true humility. It is sometimes supposed that, to be really humble, it is necessary to view our faults in an extreme, exaggerated light. It is no such thing. Humility is truth, nothing more nor less. If it were otherwise, could it be required by the God of Truth? It is because of our intense blindness, and ignorance, and self-de-

ceit, that we are ever anything but humble; and if we will only aim at seeing ourselves perfectly truly, owning what is good in ourselves, just as thoroughly as we do what is bad, we shall have made the first and most important step towards humility, because we shall have made it in the way of truth. The miserable nothingness of our best actions, the paltry weakness which mingles with, or follows them, the infinite distance between our goodness and God's perfection—it is very helpful, very salutary, to realize all this; but, in order to do it, we must see all our actions in their rightful proportions. It is "distance which lends enchantment to the view" which we take of ourselves. Look more closely, and the enchantment will cease. If we can, therefore, teach children from infancy to value truth above all things, we shall find that we have engaged the support of a most powerful weapon against the pride which refuses to own itself in the wrong, and though it may submit in action, cannot bring itself to acknowledgment in words. The lesson is to be inculcated less by compulsion than by the respect shown to candour and humility. If a child refuses to own that she has been in fault, it is in vain to insist upon her doing so. A sullen acknowledgment, extorted by the dread of punishment, is valueless. Under such circumstances, we have nothing to do but to show by our manner that our esteem is lessened. Quiet coldness and indifference will often be efficacious, when exhortation and reproof will fail. But we must never be tempted to accept the acknowledgment shown by action in lieu of that of words. It is often an easy mode of escaping a difficulty, but it will be fatal to the child's future good. Heartburnings, rancour, bitter memories, will all be laid up in store for the after years of those who have never learnt to say in open, honest, honourable words, "I was wrong." The practical atonement of a life will never have the effect of that one short sentence.

"And David said unto Nathan, I have sinned against the Lord. And Nathan said unto David, The Lord also hath put away thy sin." [1]

[1] 2 Sam. xii. 13.

And this acknowledgment, it must be remembered, cannot be allowed to be comparative. Two children quarrel—the dispute is brought before the mother; one will perhaps own herself to have been in fault, but she cannot be induced to come forward and make an apology, because the provocation was greater on the other side. This kind of excuse must at once be stopped. In so far as she was wrong, the acknowledgment is demanded. The amount of offence on the other side does not affect her duty. This is the way to carry out the apostolic command, "If it be possible, as much as lieth in you, live peaceably with all men."[1]

But there are other forms of pride besides that which exhibits itself in the refusal to acknowledge a fault. Pride of family and station, and pride of talent, or conceit, are equally common, though perhaps less generally condemned. The former, indeed, is looked upon as a kind of natural weakness; the world may scoff at it behind its back, but it does homage before its face. We often find it even considered as an heirloom, a family inheritance, which, like some peculiarity of form or feature, though not in itself to be admired, is still worthy of respect from its antiquity. The names of particular individuals are associated with it, and they are spoken of as excellent, delightful, admirable, and with only the one pardonable weakness belonging to the family—pride.

When this pride exists in the elders of a family, it is almost hopeless to attempt to root it out in the children, or even to lessen it, by any other means than that one great counteractive to all folly—truth.

It is perfectly true that God has implanted in us a regard for social distinction, even independent of moral worth. It is equally true that this distinction can be handed down from parents to children, and that the longer it has lasted the more valuable in the eyes of the world it becomes. This fact is recognized in Scripture. God chose not Abraham alone, but Abraham and his posterity. The priesthood was confined to

[1] Rom. xii. 18.

the family of Levi. The tribe of Judah was the royal tribe. But these were outward and social, not personal, distinctions; —meaning by personal, belonging to the individual inward being. The fact that Eli's sons were priests increased, rather than lessened, their degradation. The fact that Judah was the royal tribe did not save individual members of the tribe from the punishment of sin. The folly of family pride begins when this idea of social is confounded with that of personal superiority; when one man looks down upon another, and places himself above him in his own secret estimation, because his acquaintance, though equally well educated, and well bred, cannot reckon back the same number of noble or gentle ancestors.

Now in this, as in every other case, we shall fail if we endeavour to cure a fault by a falsehood. We can never make the child of a nobleman humble, by denying that there is any social superiority attached to nobility, because the moment intercourse with the world begins, our lessons will be practicably confuted. What is required is, that this social distinction should be valued for what it is worth, and no more. As regards this world, it is worth a great deal, for there are many privileges attached to it. It ensures the possessor outward respect, it gains him admittance to palaces, and to the houses of the wealthy and luxurious. It will secure for him deference on public occasions. He will walk first in processions; his society will be courted, and in difficult circumstances his claims will probably be first attended to. In some instances he will probably be more mercifully judged than his less distinguished fellow-creatures. As it will be supposed that he has greater temptations, so, if he should give way to them, there will be more excuses made for him, and if he should escape them he will be more admired and respected. These are pleasant things, and by no means unimportant, therefore let them be acknowledged. And even if there should be no nobility, yet the fact of belonging to a family which has for years held an honourable position will procure nearly the same priv-

ileges. When men and women meet in the world, they cannot all go first; and so far as it is a satisfaction to be amongst the number of those who are put foremost and treated with deference, so far it is an advantage to belong to an old family.

And doubtless also there is something better than this in inherited dignity. It is the type of that only true dignity which is ours as the children of God; and when social superiority is acknowledged, as bringing with it a special moral responsibility, it can do us no harm to recognize it. For then we shall try our fellow-creatures by the same standard as we try ourselves, and family pride will disappear, whilst family respect will remain. God's standard will be ours. What He reckons of importance will be of importance to us; and every worldly honour tested by the touchstone of that which must be its end—even Death—will dwindle to its true proportion.

All this cannot be taught to children by words. We may exhort, and lecture; we may exclaim with Wolsey, "Vain pomp and glory of this world, I hate ye;" but if we do not practise what we preach, in this instance more perhaps than in any other, our words will be utterly without effect. For the education of children upon this point is carried on, for the most part, without our being aware of it. Passing observations made in their presence rest in their minds. Discussions as to whose society may be cultivated and whose may not, are listened to by them with the utmost interest. Little practical neglects or slights shown to persons not quite in the same grade are noticed. The fact that they are allowed to be intimate with people of a certain rank, though they may be neither estimable nor agreeable, whilst the society of others who have far more intrinsic worth is avoided, must excite inquiry as to the cause. And these are the things which educate. Young persons may read their Bibles regularly, they may learn texts upon humility, and be told that God "resisteth the proud, and giveth grace to the humble;" they may even have the example of their lowly Saviour pointed out to them, and listen to elo-

quent exhortations upon His life; and, more than all, they may be taught to show great kindness to the poor, with whom there is no question of competition; and yet the exclusiveness which they daily see practised as regards those whose social position approximates to their own, will counteract all these lessons, and they will grow up proud, in the midst of what is supposed to be an atmosphere of humility.

The task of uprooting family pride is, it need scarcely be said, most difficult. Yet to minds bent upon serving God it cannot be impossible. The tendency to this weakness—to call it by no harsher name—is so universal, that we can scarcely err in keeping a perpetual check upon it, and constantly reminding ourselves of its folly. The trials of life must, sooner or later, give it rude though salutary shocks, but only principle can ultimately prevail against it. Perhaps negative correction is better upon the whole than positive. Instead of declaiming against pride, let attentions be shown to those who are really worthy of them, without reference to their pedigree. And let these attentions be respectful, not condescending. Show young people that nobility receives honour by intercourse with those whom God values; and never for a moment let rank be allowed to assume the privilege which is by some persons attributed to charity, and "covers a multitude of sins."

By these means we may, through God's help, at length succeed in destroying the overbearing and absurd self-estimation which is known by the name of family pride; and reduce it to that simple regard for social differences which is necessary in order to prevent society, as it is now constituted, from becoming a confused, lawless struggle for personal precedence.

CHAPTER XIX.

PRIDE (*continued*).

But if the world is merciful to family pride, still more leniently does it view intellectual pride. It affects, indeed, to laugh at conceit, but no one who watches the course of events will fail to see that conceit does, in the end, gain the day. The price which a man puts upon himself is in general that which the world, at least in his own generation, puts upon him. Not, indeed, meaning by the world the thinking, sensible portion of the community, but the world in its large sense, including that vast majority who know not what they admire, or why they admire, but applaud simply because others do so.

And even those who profess to be, and really are, thoughtful and reasonable, will often defend the pride of talent, as if it was a very pardonable fault, scarcely, indeed, to be called one, because talent is in itself something worthy of admiration.

No doubt genius and talent, of whatever kind, are gifts from God, the highest which He bestows, independent of that gift of His Holy Spirit, the fruits of which constitute moral and religious worth. But they can in no sense be called our own, for they are bestowed without reference to our will. They are, in fact, treasures lent for a special purpose, in like manner as wealth, or beauty, or social position, or any other advantage. And will has no power over them, except in regard to their exercise. No man can will himself to be a won-

derful composer, or a great poet. Genius cannot increase itself; and for those who have only talent, they can but labour with such earnestness to improve the power originally bestowed, that it may be cultivated to its highest extent. This question of will forms an essential distinction between intellectual and moral gifts. God has, in His great mercy, vouchsafed to establish a connection between the human will and the gift of His grace. The more we will or desire to obtain that grace, the more it will be granted us; and it is this effort of will in the acquirement and practical use of grace which He vouchsafes to call goodness, and promises to reward. And so far as we will or desire to use God's gifts of intellect for His glory, and patiently labour to cultivate and improve them, so far they have in them a moral worth. But this use of intellect is quite independent of its amount. The dull child, who conscientiously plods over her lesson, and needs an hour to acquire it perfectly, exercises a much greater amount of will than the clever child, who reads it over twice, and then repeats it without a fault; and she is therefore the more worthy of respect.

But the world will not see or own this; neither, in the generality of cases, will the child herself. Mental gifts are at first sight so entirely one with the individual to whom they are entrusted, that it requires a real effort of mind to view them apart. And when the world makes an idol of talent, it can scarcely be a matter of marvel that the fortunate owner of the treasure should lend himself to the almost universal delusion, and in the end prostrate himself before what he conceives to be his own image, and become a self-worshipper.

Here, again, truth is the only safeguard. God forbid that we should despise or depreciate intellect or talent! That which comes direct from God must be in itself most precious. Infinitely small as the powers of the highest human intellect must be when compared with the Wisdom of Omniscience, still they are in their nature the same; and we must, we cannot but reverence them.

The sin of intellectual pride does not consist in admiration of intellect; and the folly of conceit is not to be found in the acknowledgment and appreciation of powers which have really been bestowed. It is when intellect is looked upon in the same light as moral goodness, and the extent and importance of talent are over-estimated, that sin and folly creep in.

The worship of intellect is one of the great sins of the present day. We see it in the reverence openly expressed for genius and talent, whatever may be the use to which they are applied. Scarcely any one hesitates to say—"Such a person is delightful: rather good for nothing, possibly unprincipled; but then so clever—he must be forgiven." Hearing such observations sometimes carries the mind onward beyond this little world, with its infinitesimally small amount of knowledge, its far-off approach to truth and wisdom, or even to that which seems peculiarly earthly—wit—the perception of incongruous analogies—and as there is something very overwhelming in the endeavour to grasp, even for one instant, the distance between the earth and the nearest fixed star; so thought, when it looks beyond this world, finds it yet more overwhelming to contemplate the distance between Newton, Shakespeare, or Bacon, and—Omniscience. And if we regard any inferior intellect, it is so diminished by the juxtaposition as to require a mental microscope to discover it.

And then to hear people talk of this wonderful human intellect, this astonishing talent, these marvellous powers—it really verges upon the ludicrous! They are no doubt marvellous, just as a child's powers of motion are marvellous; but the marvel is in kind, not in degree. That we should be able to think at all, to grasp abstract truth, to comprehend scientific principles, is most wonderful; but the degrees of these powers, the amount which one man possesses more than another, require calculations so minute that they can only be of importance on this side the grave.

Pass it—and Sir Isaac Newton and the little infant who

drew but one breath, and then died, must equally stand amazed and confounded before the Omniscience of God.

Worship of intellect as intellect, is, in fact, an earthly delusion. It cannot stand the test of truth, and, therefore, if we desire to check it, we have simply to bring it to that test, by asking not what clever and scientific and so-called wise men can know or do, but what they cannot. The little infant thinks itself wonderful, because it can crawl across the room on its hands and knees. Place it at the foot of Mont Blanc, and then bid it ascend to the summit, and where will be its self-admiration?

These considerations may be further enforced by a fact, which at once places moral power on a higher elevation than mental, even regarding them both intellectually.

Each is alike a gift from God, each is an emanation from His perfection.

But moral powers, in so far as they are perfect, are so absolutely; whilst mental powers can never be anything but indefinitely comparative.

A child who speaks truth, does that which—let it be said with all reverence—cannot, in so far as it is simple truth, be surpassed even by God himself. But the astronomer who calculates the distances of the fixed stars has not approached within the faintest calculable nearness to God's knowledge. Angels in their perfect innocence bear an absolute resemblance to their Maker; but when we inquire as to their wisdom, we are told that God " charges them with folly."

These truths must be seen by ourselves before we can hope to inculcate them upon our children. The generality of persons overlook them, and probably will continue to do so. For the worship of intellect is far too subtle a snare of the tempter ever to be allowed to fall into neglect. No effective rules or hints can be given as regards saving children from the delusion, if we are possessed of it ourselves, for we shall transmit it to them unconsciously. And it will work in their lives, and bring its fatal results of wilfulness, false principles, too often of

grievous sins; but we shall never trace them to their source, because we have never discovered it in ourselves. If, on the other hand, we have been happily saved from it, or are striving against it, we shall view it in its true light, and our first effort will be to show it truly to our children. A few strong words may stamp the lesson upon them for life. For there is that in the heart of the young which cannot fail to respond to us. They know—we all know—that God does not value any human being for his intellectual powers. They know—we all know—that these powers will at the last day rise up to our condemnation if they have not been used for God's service. Both reason and conscience whisper that the gates of Heaven may hereafter be opened to the unlettered but humble peasant, and barred against the world-renowned philosopher, who seeks admittance in his pride; and thinking of these things, and remembering those most awful words, "Unto whomsoever much is given, of him shall be much required,"[1] it may be that the children, thus early warned, will escape the snare of intellect-worship, and make it their primary object not to be celebrated authors or scientific discoverers, "but to do justly, and to love mercy, and to walk humbly with their God."[2]

Place God first, and talent falls into its right place, and harmony and beauty are the result.

Place intellect first, and, hard though it may seem to say, we do but yield to the temptation through which angels fell, and by which, if we give way to it, we must one day fall with them.

But the worship of intellect is, for the most part, the sin of those who possess intellect. There is another form of intellectual pride, less subtle, but even more common—conceit; a false estimate both of the powers which have been bestowed, and of their value in the sight of the world. The discipline of life is often very efficacious in knocking this folly on the head. Children brought up at home under the eyes of admiring parents and friends are very frequently conceited. Moth-

[1] St. Luke xii. 48. [2] Micah vi. 8.

ers often talk to their children seriously about not thinking much of themselves, whilst they exhibit their drawings to visitors, extol their quickness in language, and repeat the praises which are bestowed upon them by their masters; never perceiving that by so doing they are building up with one hand what they are pulling down with the other. It is quite sad, indeed, to see how constantly even very little children are literally educated in conceit by the absurd folly of repeating what are considered their clever sayings and doings before them. Conceit is one of the faults for which, as it has been said in a former chapter, a severe treatment is necessary. A girl who thinks herself well informed may without any circumlocution be told that she is ignorant; or one who considers herself accomplished may be warned that she is but a mere beginner; and if in consequence she should be out of temper no harm will result. The object is to lessen her self-estimation, and when this is done she will cease to be angry with those who made her see the truth. This method of cure is, however, by no means infallible. Conceit, when ingrained, is blind, and the operation of mental couching is as doubtful as that of physical. The imagination luxuriates in a world of its own; quite different from the true world, and peopled with images of self under different guises. This is evident from the absurd exhibitions of conceit, made by persons otherwise sensible and well judging. The varied forms of this fault can, indeed, scarcely fail at times to provoke a smile in any one who looks upon society without taking part in it, so as to be excited or particularly interested by it. The conversation at a dinner table will often show the singularly exaggerated view which particular individuals take of their own peculiar gifts. A person possessed of some special power, whether intellectual or only mechanical, will sometimes engross the conversation as if there was nothing else worth attending to but that which he himself understands. A clever lawyer talks as if the whole world had but one interest, that of getting up cases and settling legal difficulties. A connoisseur in art lays down the law

about painting and sculpture. A musician can talk of nothing but the comparative merits of different composers. It is not merely that such persons are drawn out, and led to converse upon the subject of which they know most, but that they can converse upon nothing else. The particular profession, accomplishment, or study to which they have devoted themselves, and for which they have a special aptitude, is the one thing for the furtherance of which, if one might judge from their conversation, it is to be supposed that the world was created.

Conceit, when thus rooted in a person of mature years, is perhaps scarcely ever eradicated; partly because its indulgence has become a habit, and partly also, and more especially, because, as people advance in life, no one, or scarcely any one, has the courage to tell them of their faults and follies. The more important, therefore, it becomes to check them in youth.

There is a chapter in St. Paul's Epistle to the Corinthians, which, if applied to earthly as well as spiritual gifts, will be found to contain the essence of all the advice that can be given on the subject. The Apostle speaks of the diversities of God's gifts, and the importance of each separately with reference to the good of all. He takes the analogy of the body, and asks, "If the whole body were an eye, where were the hearing? If the whole were hearing, where were the smelling?" He bids us remember that "those members of the body, which seem to be feeble, are necessary;" and that "God hath tempered the body together, having given more abundant honour to that part which lacked." [1]

If these truths could be borne in mind by us all, where would be the place for conceit?

Granted that we are what the world is pleased to call clever, accomplished, scientific, or whatever the gift may be, it is an advantage to be valued truly only by being weighed in the balance with others. It could not even exist without them. Very rare, indeed, is it to find any person who has great intellectual gifts in anything like equal proportions. The first-

[1] 1 Cor. xii. 17, 22, 24.

rate mathematician is frequently an illogical reasoner. The sound reasoner perhaps finds it difficult to master the first problem in Euclid.

It is the same in everything. We have all gifts of some kind. If we have not brains in our head, they are generally found in our fingers; and without the fingers the head would be very badly off. The balance and comparison of these different advantages, as it will tend to inspirit and cheer those who are intellectually dull, will be a most wholesome check upon those who are the reverse.

View a talent relatively, and it may still be estimated highly, as all God's gifts should be, but conceit will be impossible. The most richly endowed mind of the present age, or of any age, is only partially so: others also have gifts, and they have also a claim to respect and consideration.

This is a lesson for the schoolroom—for home life; it must be learnt by means of constant repetition—perpetual reference to the advantages bestowed upon the different members of the same family or household. And should the tendency to conceit exhibit itself in a false estimate of the actual amount, rather than in the comparative value of the intellectual or artistic powers, comparison may still be efficaciously employed to counteract it. Never let clever children compare themselves with their companions, but always place before them the highest possible standard. B. may do better than A., and C. may do better than B. The comparison is easily made, but it may be in a manner neutralized by a plain statement of facts, which puts C. by the side of Z., and calculates the distance between them. But even the perception of relative inferiority will not always destroy conceit. In one of Miss Edgeworth's clever stories, she gives an illustration of low social ambition, by saying that the question lay between being the "first in Cranbourne Alley, or the last in Weymouth Street." In the case to which she referred, Weymouth Street was chosen; but nine-tenths of the conceit which we meet with in the world has no desire to rise above Cranbourne Alley. And so far it

is a wise desire, that it is easily gratified. To be first in the schoolroom—then in the home circle—then in the small coterie; to be admired by inferiors, wondered at by those who are no judges, and to take all this wonder and admiration into our hearts—to cherish it, look at it, dwell upon it, till we forget that there is any other praise worth having—is a pleasure within reach of any person who has even the smallest amount of what is considered talent. And it can be purchased at a sacrifice very slight in the eyes of the world. We have but to reject truth, and consent to receive tribute in falsehood. And the world for the most part lives upon falsehood; and if there were no Death, no Grave, and no Judgment to come, it might continue to do so comfortably enough.

It is only unfortunate that conceit, like everything else belonging to this world, must sooner or later have an end; and that when we awake in another state of existence, our condition for Eternity will be determined not by the praise of men based upon falsehood, but upon the Judgment of God, which has its foundation in truth.

Conceit, then, in all cases, is but miserable weakness and blind folly. Conceit in women—which is almost always intellectual conceit—is, perhaps, the highest degree of folly, because it has the least ground for its pretensions. This is not the place for entering upon the vexed and really absurd question as to the relative mental powers of men and women. Abstract theories may be strong, but facts are stronger. Possibly, women may be capable of doing all that men do; but practically they do not do it. The cause may be physical, social, or educational—it matters not. Since time began it has been found that men have been poets, sculptors, painters, metaphysicians, and natural philosophers, in the first degree, and women in the second. So long as we continue intellect worshippers this consideration will be very humiliating to women's conceit. Whether it will be of much importance when we stand before the Throne of God is quite another question.

But it is a fact to be remembered, more especially in these

days, when women are taking so prominent a part in literature, and in social, scientific, and even political discussions. There are no doubt subjects which women will treat better than men, because they know more about them. A woman understands her own sex more thoroughly than a man does. She knows what will suit them, touch them, help them. She understands more truly the needs of children; she can enter more fully into questions of domestic economy and household management. But women who aspire to equality with men are not content with this superiority in their own particular sphere. They seek to meet men upon some common ground, open to both; and here it is that they become the victims of an absurd delusion. They are able, no doubt, to attain a certain preeminence; that is to say, a very clever woman may, without difficulty, rival an ordinarily clever man. But she forgets that the clever man has others greatly superior above him. First-rate women must be placed side by side with first-rate men, if we wish to form a true estimate of the relative attainments of the two sexes. But for the most part this is not what women desire, because it brings before them the unpleasing fact that in the preëminence which has been accorded them, they have been treated as the skilful chess-player treats his aspiring but inferior antagonist. The game may be won by the latter, but before it began both queen and castle were put aside.

A great deal of the conceit and the paltry ambition which turns the heads of clever young girls, might probably be crushed in the bud, if this true distinction between the literary and scientific fame of men and women were borne in mind. After all, it is nothing so very great to be the first in Cranbourne Alley. Unless there is some outward call, some necessity about which there can be no mistake, it may be better to content oneself with being the last in Weymouth Street; with being a listener and a learner at the feet of our superiors, rather than the oracle and teacher of those whom we know to be our inferiors. A true estimate of women's talents would

probably show that the larger portion exists amongst the per, sons whose names are unknown; who have had the good sense to see that they could do their duty as efficiently to others, and more safely for themselves, as workers, than as teachers. But there is nothing like a practical lesson on this subject. Conceit, and thirst for fame and notoriety, are follies which will never be thoroughly checked by direct advice. A little practical satire is the only sure cure; and we shall not crush talent by it, because, if a young girl really has a power which she ought to use, it will display itself, in spite of the satire. And the consciousness need not then be dreaded. The one object to be aimed at is truth, and we need never fear to view gifts truly, or to own that they exist, for unless this is done, they cannot be turned to good account.

But it will be asked, what is meant by practical satire? and the answer is—a practical exemplification of ignorance and carelessness. For instance, young girls who have any imagination, delight in exercising it by writing. They string incidents together, and call them stories, and revel in the power of summoning up the creatures of their fancy, and making them walk, and talk, as if they were living beings. And so real are they to them, that they have no perception that they are not equally real to others. They look at them, as the child does at the half-dozen strokes forming a dim outline of a creature with long ears, four legs, and a tail, which it immediately pronounces to be a donkey, and forthwith proceeds to invest with all a donkey's attractions.

Now, as it would be useless to try and persuade the child that the rough caricature was not an image of the real animal, because its imagination provides for all deficiencies; so it is equally useless to try and persuade these incipient novel writers that the creations of their brain are merely vague and distorted outlines. To them they are full of life. And so also with regard to the power of writing. To say to them that they know nothing about it is simply to contradict what appears to be the evidence of their senses. They can understand

their own sentences, and they cannot believe that any difficulty exists with others. Only one thing will bring them to a conviction of the truth. If they must write, let them do it, but give them an abstract of history as an exercise; make them condense facts, and seize upon those which are really important. Insist upon the necessity of agreement between nominative cases and verbs, between relatives and their antecedents; show them how easily, by the misplacement of a word, the meaning of a sentence may be left open to misconstruction. Such a practical exemplification of their incapacity will tell upon them in the end more than any direct criticism. And it will have the advantage of being silent, and not exciting resentment. The lesson will be taken to heart quietly, and acted upon. If there is any real talent, the practice of careful composition will be most useful; and if there is not, there will be a self-conviction which will ultimately crush the foolish conceit and ambition.

And now, at the close of this inquiry as to the nature and the various exhibitions of pride, we come back to the conclusion that truth is the foundation stone of humility, the guardian of self-respect. It may be well to enforce what reason teaches by an illustration drawn from Scripture, and in no instance is it so clearly set forth as in the character of the Apostle whom, more than all others, it has pleased God to bring before us in his social life, in the trials which accompanied it, and in the inward struggles which were their necessary result.

Perhaps there are few who, when reading St. Paul's defence of himself, both in his public speeches and in his writings, have not, at times, been inclined to pause, and ask, Is all this self-appreciation consistent with the humility of a Christian?

"Men and brethren, I have lived in all good conscience before God until this day."[1] "Herein do I exercise myself, to have always a conscience void of offence toward God, and toward men."[2] "Neither against the law of the Jews, neither

[1] Acts xxiii. 1. [2] Acts xxiv. 16.

against the temple, nor yet against Cæsar, have I offended any thing at all." [1]

These are the Apostle's bold public declarations of his moral, religious, and political innocence.

And still more strongly in writing to the Corinthians he says: "Our rejoicing is this, the testimony of our conscience, that in simplicity and godly sincerity, not with fleshly wisdom, but by the grace of God, we have had our conversation in the world;" [2] and, again, we "have renounced the hidden things of dishonesty, not walking in craftiness, nor handling the word of God deceitfully; but by manifestation of the truth commending ourselves to every man's conscience in the sight of God." [3]

And when the question is raised as to the extent of his authority compared with that of others, St. Paul places himself at once on a par "with the very chiefest apostles." He enumerates his labours and sufferings for Christ's sake with a minuteness, which seems to awaken a sense of unfitness even in his own mind; and at length goaded, as it were, by the consciousness of unjust depreciation, to reveal an honour which, up to this time, had been secret between himself and his God; he concludes by relating in words which, if possible, he would fain save from personal application, his mysterious assumption into the third Heaven, and the hearing of those "unspeakable words which it is not lawful for man to utter." [4]

And why? What could induce one who was avowedly a most earnest, if not *the* most earnest disciple of the lowly Redeemer of the world, to make this boast of his authority, of his work, and its reward?

Simply the necessity of truth.

"I am become a fool in glorying; ye have compelled me: for I ought to have been commended of you: for in nothing am I behind the very chiefest apostles, though I be nothing." [5]

Those last words speak the real mind of St Paul. Yes,

[1] Acts xxv. 8. [2] 2 Cor. i. 12. [3] 2 Cor. iv. 2.
[4] 2 Cor. xii. 4. [5] 2 Cor. xii. 11.

he could bear to look all fully in the face ;—his natural powers, his supernatural gifts, his position in the Church, his energy and endurance, his self-denial and courage. He shrank from the acknowledgment of none of these things.

For he stood before the world as the child of a peasant might stand when elected to a throne ; dressed in the robes of royalty, and receiving the homage due to the position in which he had been placed ; but never for one moment forgetting that in himself,—his birth, his power, his qualifications, his own strength and ability, he was—what he had always been—nothing.

Let us love truth as St. Paul loved it, and we also shall look without shrinking at our virtues, our talents, or our social preëminence, because, like him, we shall own that glorying is folly.

CHAPTER XX.

VANITY.

SELFISHNESS and pride are undoubtedly the two faults to counteract which truth may be most effectively employed. It is sometimes supposed that vanity may be reached by the same means; but this idea seems to have arisen from the common mistake of confusing it with conceit. Vanity is an inordinate love of admiration, conceit is inordinate self-esteem.

Conceit may be, and often is, accompanied by vanity, but there is no necessary connection between them. A person may have an overweening estimate of his own powers, and yet, from the very fact, be rendered comparatively indifferent to what is said of him. Whilst, on the contrary, a vain person may be quite aware that his talents are small, and yet be continually looking out for, and thirsting for praise.

And because vanity is not so open to correction by truth as pride is, therefore, as it would seem, it is more difficult to eradicate it. We often hear it said, "Intercourse with others will knock the conceit out of such a person," and the remark describes a very wholesome discipline, which, probably, we have all, more or less, undergone at some period of our lives. But vanity was never yet *knocked* out of any one. It has a clinging, creeping nature, which defies rough blows; and its vitality is marvellous. Cut it down in one form, and it will spring up in another; attempt to destroy it by destroying the conceit on which it fed, and it will give up conceit, and take the garb of humility. If it cannot attract attention by dis-

playing virtues, it will by confessing faults; the one thing it cannot endure is to be unnoticed.

Now, any one who thinks at all upon the subject will see at once that the endeavour to uproot a fault like this by any external process is simply hopeless. The more we work at it, the more it will grow. And the attempt is made even more difficult by the fact that the germ of vanity, love of approbation, is innocent and involuntary. Not to feel pleasure in approbation, supposing it to be deserved, is impossible. Of course, when there is a consciousness that if the true facts were known, it would be seen to be unmerited, a very true mind will regret it, and feel pain at receiving it. But in ordinary cases, as, for instance, when praise is bestowed by a parent upon a child who has been diligent or obedient, the pleasure is not only permissible, but if it were not felt, the character would be imperfect. Here, however, we must distinguish between approbation and admiration. To be approved implies that we have set some standard before us, and have in a measure succeeded in attaining it; the praise which is accorded us is therefore based upon moral grounds, and is not absolute, but comparative. A parent approves a child for being attentive at her lessons, but it does not follow that the child is a marvel of genius. And approval also implies that the person who approves is in a condition to form a judgment; the approbation of one who is really ignorant or prejudiced cannot really be a gratification.

So far, then, love of approbation is consistent with thoroughly earnest and religious principle. But we may go yet further, and acknowledge that even when this love of approbation takes, as it so continually does, the form of love of admiration, or the praise which is given to any gift or quality for its own sake, apart from the attempt to reach a higher standard of perfection; yet in its first motions it is innocent, because it is involuntary, and it is only the consent of the will which makes any feeling sinful or the reverse. A person who pos-

sesses some gift of beauty or talent cannot, as a general rule, avoid feeling pleasure in words of admiration.

But here the innocent love of admiration stops, and vanity steps in. For vanity is a reflex act of the mind. It takes the pleasure excited by the consciousness of admiration, and endeavours to retain it by thinking of and dwelling upon the praise received. This excites a morbid, exaggerated desire for a renewal of the admiration, and various methods are in consequence resorted to, in order to attain it. Again, the enjoyment is prolonged and increased by reflection, and a fresh stimulus is given to the thirst for it; and so vanity becomes a habit of mind.

Now, there are a few general rules to be given as regards this fault, most difficult to put in practice, but the least relaxation of which will probably be fatal to improvement.

We cannot hope merely to check vanity, we must actually uproot it. It must be dealt with in the same way as those noxious spreading weeds which we tear out of the ground, not venturing to leave a fibre behind, lest the plant should grow again.

Very few there are probably who will accept this teaching. It demands an effort which can only be made in God's strength, and with a full sincerity of will. And with the majority will is weak. Better it seems to fight with a foe feebly, for years, sometimes victorious, oftener subdued, but trusting in the end to be conquerors, than by one vigorous—surely we may call it superhuman—effort, to grapple with and destroy him at once. Vanity is a great fault we think, but there is so much in it that is involuntary, we can scarcely call it a sin. We see it in such really good people;—people who are charitable, and self-denying, and deeply devotional,—so much better in many ways than others who do not appear vain.

Granted—all except the assertion that it is not a sin. It is a sin, for it loves the praise of men rather than the praise of God; and because of this love in its most exaggerated form, the Pharisees, we are told, rejected our Lord. And no one,

probably, who has earnestly set himself to the task of self-improvement, and is conscious of being naturally vain, will hesitate to confess that it is the fault which, from its extreme insidiousness, has given him more trouble than any other; that it has marred his best inclinations, and destroyed the happiness of his holiest moments; that it has, in fact, pursued him like a deadly enemy through life, appearing under the most unlooked-for circumstances, and concealing itself under forms in which nothing but a most strict examination could detect it.

And if this is the confession of those who struggle earnestly, what must be the history of those who fight feebly; who have allowed vanity to grow, and spread, till it has actually covered the whole surface of the character, and eaten into it—corroded it, till there is not a single good feeling untainted by it?

The truth is that we cannot be too severe, either with ourselves or with others, when we are dealing with vanity; or, in other words, the pleasure derived from the reflex act of the mind upon admiration which has been offered us. The few definite rules already referred to will, therefore, it may be hoped, assist young people in their struggle with it, even though they may be inclined to call them, at first sight, hopelessly strict.

We may advise them, in the first place, never to ask what any person thinks of them, or has said about them.

Secondly. If they are told—never to repeat the same to their companions, whether the remarks imply praise or blame.

Thirdly. Never, if they can avoid it, to look at any letter or writing in which they know that admiration has been expressed of anything they have said or done.

Fourthly. When they have been admired for anything which they have said or done, or for their personal appearance, never to repeat such admiration to themselves over again. The very instant the memory of it recurs it should be checked, even as a profane or impure thought. This will be the greatest difficulty of all at first, and yet, in the end, it

will become easy, from the working of that law of association which is the basis of what we call habit. When the thought of admiration is recognized as a temptation, conscience will give the warning, and at last, almost without effort, it will, from habit, be instantly crushed.

Exceptions to these rules may, perhaps, be thought necessary as regards the praise of parents and persons set in authority. But, in fact, such praise is of a different character from that of which we have been speaking. It is *approbation*, not *admiration;* and pleasure derived from approbation, or the consciousness that we have tried to do right or well, and that our efforts are acknowledged, is quite permissible. God vouchsafes to approve us, but He can never admire us. When, however, home approval takes the form of admiration, as it not unfrequently does, it is the most dangerous kind of incentive to vanity, and must be crushed as mercilessly as any other temptation.

A child may make a clever copy of a drawing and be praised for it, and may justly feel pleased at the approbation, and even think of it again with a sense of encouragement; but if she is told that she is a wonderful artist, and dwells upon the thought, she must become vain.

Closely connected with this ruminating faculty, by which we feed upon admiration for weeks or months after it has been received, is that of day-dreams, the most common enjoyment of young people with any imagination, and perhaps the most dangerous.

Here, again, the rule seems so rigid that one is tempted to relax it. But it would be false kindness. The mischief of day-dreams is that, in some form or other, they make self the centre. It is a very singular power which we possess, that of separating ourselves, as it were, into two persons, one in imagination acting and talking, and the other actually admiring and praising; though, as will generally be the case, under some disguise which, for the moment, conceals the fact that it is only, after all, self-admiration.

We are not called upon now to enter into a metaphysical disquisition as to the mode in which these powers act, nor the purposes for which they were given us; what we are at present concerned with is, the use which is so commonly made of them for the gratification of vanity. Young people deceive themselves grievously upon this matter. They suppose that because in imagination they act nobly and virtuously, therefore their thoughts are not evil, but, on the contrary, lead to the encouragement of good. But they have only to ask themselves in what the pleasure of the indulgence in these virtuous day-dreams consists. Certainly not in the contemplation of the virtue in itself, for it is comparatively little pleasure to them to think of noble actions performed by other persons. It is the act of reflecting upon self, or in other words, the gratification of vanity, which is so agreeable. And this falsity, this reflecting upon actions which have no existence, except in imagination, will bear the necessary and fatal fruit of all falsity. It will, unless checked, in the end make the whole inward character false, though the outward actions may, for the time, and perhaps always, in some degree, continue true. A person inwardly devoured by vanity may never be so degraded as to tell actual falsehoods, but the self-deceit which vanity engenders will inevitably lead to many things approaching to it.

And for these reasons—the consideration of the present evil and future results of day-dreams—the only advice which can safely be given to young persons, or, indeed, to any person, is to crush them.

It may be well, however, to add, that there is a safe, legitimate use of imagination, with which self has nothing to do. We see it in the works of literature and art, and in the enjoyment which such works give, even to those who cannot produce them themselves. There is no evil, or comparatively none, in dwelling with delight upon the scenes and characters of fiction, so long as they are worthy of admiration. The danger in that case is lest we mistake virtuous emotions for virtu-

ous actions; and because we can sympathize with what is good, may be led to suppose that we are good ourselves. But it is not till we become the heroes and heroines of our own novels that vanity enters, and imagination leads to sin.

Again, it may be owned that the rules which have been laid down upon the subject of vanity are very rigid; but they have one great advantage—they are plain; they can be understood and grasped. Young people work at their own minds, and examine, and analyze, and perplex themselves, and cannot, after all, make out what is right or what is wrong, where good ends and evil begins; whereas, if they can only be told to *do* something—act, or not act—speak, or not speak—exercise self-discipline in some form over which they have a distinct control, they will eventually find that the mind has, if one may so speak, come right of itself. In all cases it is the will which is in fault. The will put into action, either physical or mental, gains strength, and as the will is rectified all the different complex qualities which make up human nature fall into right order and proportion.

Connected with this subject of vanity is the question as to the legitimate use of emulation. St. Paul appears to consider it permissible when he says, "Know ye not that they which run in a race run all, but one receiveth the prize? So run, that ye may obtain."[1] But, on the other hand, the Heavenly rewards to which he points are many, and within reach of all. The truth seems to be that emulation, when it desires to obtain the highest prize, is justifiable; when it desires to surpass others, is not so. If, therefore, we have recourse to the stimulus, we must say, not "the one or two who stand first in the list shall be rewarded because they are first;" but "every one who attains a certain standard shall have a certain reward." This will direct ambition solely to the attainment of the prize, and the question of surpassing others will become unimportant.

But vanity, especially with girls, is most frequently per-

[1] 1 Cor. ix. 24.

sonal. Yet young people must be taught to dress well, or they become disagreeable to their friends, and if they are pretty they will naturally expect admiration. This creates a difficulty. Some very excellent moralists, perplexed upon this point, seek to cut the Gordian knot by forbidding the use of a looking-glass, so that beauty may not be able to see itself. Others institute a species of crusade against dress, and object to everything bright in colour, or fashionable in make. The greater number, however, content themselves with lectures and warnings, and finding these for the most part useless, quietly give up the attempt to stem the evil, and say "all girls are vain of beauty and have a taste for dress, and one can but hope that some day or other they will see the folly of it." But here again we must go back to the first principle of all things —truth.

If beauty really is beautiful, if God has made it a thing to be delighted in, and if the loveliness of a woman is, as almost all persons allow, the most attractive object upon which the eye can rest, then to attempt to deny or conceal that beauty is worthy of admiration, is, simply, to contradict nature.

And so, also, with regard to dress. The appreciation of it, as something important, is an instinct, and is recognized even in Scripture. The dress of the Jewish High Priest, and of the Priests generally, was, indeed, a subject for minute legislation; whilst under the Christian dispensation our Blessed Lord, in the parable of the Prodigal Son, mentions the "best robe" as the especial outward mark of a parent's forgiveness and restored love. No one, therefore, can presume to say that dress is a matter of no consequence—to be attended to or neglected at will.

Beauty is, then, to be admired, and dress is of consequence. Having arrived at these conclusions, we may safely proceed further, and say that it is as wrong to attempt to bring up children upon a falsity on this subject, as it is upon any other. If a child is to learn to be useful, she must learn to dress herself; if she is to do this properly, she must look in a glass;

and if she looks in a glass, she must see herself as she is. Therefore to endeavour to deceive her upon this point is silly.

But there is a vast distinction between the consciousness that we possess a gift and the value which we put upon it. And it is here that, probably with truth, it may be said that nine-tenths of the well-intentioned mothers, or aunts, or friends, who have the care of children in their infancy, practically educate them in vanity.

When a woman marries—supposing her heart to be really in her home with her husband and children—the vanity which she originally possessed, be it great or small, very frequently leaves the obnoxious form of a desire for personal admiration- and takes that of delight in seeing her children admired. Such a feeling can scarcely be called vanity. There is so little of self in it that it often becomes most touching and winning; but it is not, therefore, safe if indulged without caution. A mother with a lovely child longs, very naturally, to have its picture. The picture is brought home, and instead of being kept for the mother's eye, or for those of her friends, it is shown to the little original as its likeness. No one supposes that the tiny creature who can scarcely speak plain has any perception of beauty, or can tell the meaning of the word pretty. But it is a great mistake; the child has eyes, and is subject to the laws of association just as much as its mother. It has already learnt that "pretty dog," and "pretty cat," are creatures to be petted, and made much of; and so when it hears a picture called pretty, and is told that it is itself, it of course learns that the self is, in like manner, to be admired and delighted in for its beauty.

This is the first lesson in vanity. The child sees that its parents think a great deal of beauty, and of course she learns to estimate it herself in the same degree.

But it may be said: even if parents are sensible upon these points, friends and acquaintances are not.

How is it possible to guard against the foolish, incautious

admiration which every child is exposed to, and which is frequently exaggerated, simply to please the parents?

It is not possible to guard against it. We may as well acknowledge that fact at once. Children will hear beauty talked about, and so learn its importance, and if they possess it themselves they will receive thoughtless admiration. But it is the home flattery which does the mischief. Home is a child's world, and if beauty is not considered a matter of great consequence there, the danger of the world's admiration will be materially lessened.

If we wish children not to think about beauty, our best plan is not to think about it ourselves; or if we do think, not to talk; or if we must talk, to speak truth. To tell a pretty child that she is plain, though we may do so with the best intentions, is to sin by speaking falsely, and to prepare the way for an exaggerated satisfaction when the real state of the case is discovered. A little girl, in her simplicity, asks: "Mamma, am I pretty? Mrs. So-and-So says that I am." And the answer may be: "Yes, my dear; I think that you are rather nice looking." And there the conversation may be dropped; and this quiet indifference will check the rising vanity far more than a lecture upon the folly of valuing beauty, which will probably only have the effect of impressing upon the mind that a fact which requires so many cautionary words must be of considerable consequence.

The language of Scripture seems in a measure to confirm this advice. We are frequently told of beauty. Sarah, we know, was "very fair;" so also were Rebekah and Rachel, and the daughters of Job: and throughout the Bible beauty is always mentioned as an advantage, as something to be valued; but it is never dwelt upon. It takes its place as a passing good, and then the attention is directed to something else. And this is really the place which it holds in the world. For a time it has great power, but only for a time. In a vast number of cases its influence is neutralized by the want of other charms; and even if combined with talent and good-

ness, it must soon fade. Young people will not see or understand this, but if they find that it is the opinion of the persons to whom they look up, they will insensibly adopt the same view of it.

The love of dress is another of those follies which children are for the most part systematically educated in from childhood, and for which it is considered a duty to censure them in youth. So long as parents spend large sums in dressing up their little ones in handsome ribbons, and elaborate embroidery, and send them down to the drawing-room to be admired by visitors, who tell them to show their pretty sashes and bright shoes—so long children will like dress, and think a great deal about it. It is really not their fault, it is simply a case of cause and effect, sowing and reaping. People attach such an overweening value to words, and such a very insufficient value to acts. A right principled mother would on no account bring up her daughter to think much of dress, but she is proud of her, and wishes her to equal others in appearance; so, without saying anything direct upon the subject, she, perhaps, makes a great point of procuring some pretty, or possibly handsome, dress for her, the colour and texture of which are talked of *con amore*. The interview with the dressmaker is one of the great events of the week; the question as to the trimming is a topic of conversation for days; the dress, when finished, is tried on, and the young lady is turned and twisted about, perhaps for an hour, till even her vanity can scarcely bear the ordeal. Then she is told that the dress looks very well, that it is very becoming, and, as a reward for her patience, she is permitted to take one look at herself in the glass; and bears away with her the impression of a very elegant, fashionable looking creature, who will form an enchanting heroine for her next day-dream.

This ceremony is repeated, though with much greater attention, and consequent excitement, when the dress is actually to be exhibited in public; but when at length the adjusting and improving are at an end, and the daughter is allowed to depart, the

mother wakes up to the perception of a certain air of self-consciousness and stiffness, if not of actual affectation; and conscience whispering something about vanity and its danger, she exclaims: "Now, my dear, you have looked at yourself enough! The dress does very well; go away, and don't think about yourself. After all, you know it is of much more consequence how you behave than how you look!" Or, as Mrs. Primrose admirably condensed the maternal warning, "Handsome is that handsome does. Hold up your heads, my dears!"

But the home lesson of vanity is not over. The party takes place, and the next day forms a topic of conversation. Still dress is the most engrossing subject. The mother does not actually talk to her child about her own appearance, but she criticizes that of every one else, and of course the daughter does the same. There may be nothing ill-natured in what is said, possibly quite the reverse. Amiable, imaginative persons take pleasure in viewing their friends picturesquely; and to the young girl it is almost as pleasant as a novel to recall the bright party, and to picture to herself in detail the lovely silks, and the rich lace, and the splendid ornaments, which are all brought before her again in such minute and glowing detail.

Half the pleasure of a party, as every one knows, is in talking it over the next day. And the mother feels that she ought to enter into her daughter's pleasure, and is quite certain that she desires to see her simple and unworldly; and she herself devotes so much time to duties of religion and charity, and gives so many warnings against vanity; no wonder she is quite deluded by her own good intentions, and when the conversation ends is not in the least aware that she has been just as sedulously employed for the last hour in cultivating a taste for dress in her daughter, as she would have been if she had deliberately given her a lecture upon its extreme importance, and urged her to devote all her thoughts to it.

Now, if the mother had openly said at the beginning, "My dear, I like you to look well, and to be dressed like other peo-

ple, and so I have bought the prettiest dress I could find, and intend to have it made fashionably," there would have been an open straightforward avowal of a natural object, which would have checked any personal excitement upon the subject. The dress might have been tried and fitted as a matter of business; worn, as a matter of course; and then laid aside, not to be thought of till the next occasion. And if the young lady had thus been taught to trouble herself but little about her own dress, she would naturally have cared but little about that of her friends. It is the unconscious comparison which is the stimulating ingredient in all these topics. Put self aside, and we shall think but very little of them.

It must be remembered, also, that attention to dress may be a duty, and inattention to it a real fault. The latter is sometimes a form of indolence, or selfishness, or love of singularity, or possibly vanity in another shape. And there are also many young people to whom dress is a trouble and difficulty. They like to see themselves look well; but they do not, in the least, know how to attain their object. And so, perhaps, they give up the attempt, and acquiesce in slovenliness and untidiness. There is no virtue in this. To dress neatly and well—that is, in good taste—is a social duty. We have no right to offend our friends by looking ugly when, by a little trouble, we can avoid it. And in the numerous cases in which inaptitude for dress exists, it would be a real kindness on the part of mothers, and nurses, and elder sisters, to take a little trouble and give a few lessons, instead of—what is so often tried unsuccessfully—scolding and reproof. An awkward or near-sighted girl spends perhaps half-an-hour before her glass, endeavouring to make her hair look nice; but it is all in vain, and when she appears at the breakfast table she is received with stern looks, and told to go upstairs and put her hair tidy. But what is the use of the command? She cannot try more than she has tried, and her temper is irritated, and a storm ensues. A little instruction—which is quite as necessary for the hands as the head—would have shown her how it was she

failed, and all the worry and temper would have been avoided. Some girls would be morally much the better for a few lessons from a hairdresser or a lady's maid. It would save them from self-consciousness, and in the end make them think far less about dress. What we know we do badly, and yet are expected to do well, must become a burden to us; and young people often dwell upon their own appearance for a whole evening, when they have a bow or a brooch awry; not in the least because they care for the fact in itself, but merely from the uncomfortable feeling that they will be noticed.

To be particular about dress may, therefore, become a matter of self-discipline, just as much as to endeavour to think little of it. But in this, as in every case, we shall find that the true statement of a definite object is a great moral safeguard. Whether we desire young people to dress well, or in any other way to follow the customs of the world, if we only compel ourselves to state our wishes in plain words, we shall do but little harm, because we shall be forced to give our reasons for them. On the surface they certainly do not bear a very exalted appearance. Dress, for instance, essentially belongs to this life, but it is not in itself sinful. We may rightly wish a young girl to wear a handsome dress because she is invited to a party, where it will be expected of her. We may very naturally desire her to look well, because the sight is pleasant to us. But let there be no pretence about the matter—let us own our true object. If we shrink from doing so—if conscience whispers that we have really a hidden motive of social ambition, or a desire to surpass others—we shall do well to pause before we carry out our wishes. We may make a fair show, and even succeed in shutting our eyes to our own doubleness, but we may be certain that our children will be more clear-sighted, and in this way we shall unconsciously educate them in worldliness and insincerity.

This word worldliness describes a tone of mind with which vanity is intimately connected, and which, like it, is fostered in almost perfect unconsciousness.

Love of excitement, the craving for amusement, considered to be especially the fault and temptation of youth, are in many cases taught in childhood, almost, one may say, in infancy. Instead of making little children self-dependent as regards amusement, the moment they appear in the drawing-room some one is expected to amuse and play with them, and the mother, or sister, or aunt, must give up all her attention to them. Instead of being taught self-restraint and consideration, by being forced to be quiet while others are employed, they are allowed to interfere with every occupation. The exciting companionship of their elders becomes a daily necessity instead of an occasional treat; and after this early training in what is to them dissipation, parents are surprised that their children cannot be satisfied with only common pursuits, but always require some amusement to be found for them. Little do they think that one of the greatest blessings which can be conferred on any one is that of being contented with small pleasures; and that the child of the peasant, who can play happily with a piece of wood, has a possession which the little heir of thousands, surrounded by his splendid toys, might envy.

Few playthings, few companions, few story books. Upon these children may be educated simply and thoroughly. Give them many, and we create artificial necessities, which can only be satisfied by artificial means. And with these necessities there must creep in that wretched spirit of worldliness which is the hidden worm eating away all that is good and noble in a character. The child with her perpetual longing for new tales, her listlessness when she is not actually engaged in study, her constant desire for little fineries, her craving for amusement—some one to play with, or to visit—some young party at home or abroad—is but rehearsing on a small scale what her elders enact on a large one.

She is practising discontent, learning to find duty and usefulness uninteresting, to live for pleasure, to care only for what

may excite, And it is this spirit which, when carried out, ultimately becomes worldliness.

"Lovers of pleasure more than lovers of God." [1] We want no other definition of worldliness. It is impossible to draw true distinctions between one amusement and another; to say that a dinner party is lawful, and a dance unlawful; for greediness and excess may as possibly be associated with the one, as vanity and folly may be with the other; and display may be shared equally by both. When we attempt to define in these ways, we are almost certain to be uncharitable and Pharisaical; but we cannot be wrong in saying, that when amusement and excitement are necessities, the spirit is worldly, and therefore when we teach children to crave them, we are educating them in worldliness.

This will not to many seem a very great danger. Worldliness is an unobtrusive fault. It is cold and repelling, indeed, when we approach it closely, but it is perhaps rather graceful and refined at a distance. And it will never offend our taste, and seldom jar upon us. We may live comfortably with it, so long as we do not come in its way. Cross it, and it will turn against us with a tiger's fierceness; but leave it to itself, and it will never trouble us. On the contrary, indeed, if we only keep our religious peculiarities within certain limits, it will walk by our side, and do us the honour of offering its approval.

There is but one great evil attached to it. It absorbs the mind, and entirely prevents it from forcing itself upon the things which belong to the invisible world. It cannot therefore enter Heaven. Whatever then assists in training children in worldliness, must at the same time be training them for some place which is not Heaven.

That is a grave matter. Perhaps when we are next inclined to indulge ourselves and our children by a round of excitement, whether on a small or a large scale, we may pause and think of it.

[1] 2 Tim. iii. 4.

CHAPTER XXI.

TEMPER.

THE faults which we have last been considering are, as it will have been evident, only partially under external guidance. We may check and discourage them; but we cannot, as in the case of disobedience, exercise any direct control over them. They can only be eradicated by religious principle.

And the same may be said of temper. The question is sometimes asked, "How is it possible to cure such a child of a passionate, or obstinate, or sullen temper?" The true answer is, "It is not possible." The child must, humanly speaking, cure itself. We may avoid the occasions which arouse the temper, and when it is aroused we may deal with it wisely; but the tendency will remain as it was before. We see this in a most disappointing way in the case of children who are very good-tempered with some persons, and very ill-tempered with others. A cross nurse makes a fractious child; an irritating manner in the governess excites irritability in the pupil; a severe reproof from a mother will awaken a spirit of sullenness in the daughter. And in the generality of these cases, it is usual to lay the blame on the individual who arouses the temper; as if the fact that a person is good-tempered when not thwarted, is an evidence of an amiable disposition and wholesome self-restraint.

This mode of speaking greatly misleads both young and old. We should all be very much more ashamed of ill-temper than we are, if we did not "lay the flattering unction to our souls,"

that it is excusable to be angry when provoked. But herein lies the self-deception: to feel angry is excusable, to give way to anger is not so; and whatever may be the provocation it is a sin.

The Apostle indeed says, "Be ye angry, and sin not."[1] But it would seem that he speaks in the first place of the impulse of anger, which, as being involuntary, is not, in the strict sense of the word, sinful; and in the second place, of that indignation at wrong doing, which can in no way be called giving way to anger, because it is a feeling excited by a just cause; and when watched, as it ought to be, is never allowed to exceed the limits of truth and justice. The indulgence of anger, the yielding to wrathful emotions, without making any attempt to check them, is very different from this. It is a great sin, and a great disgrace.

We are all aware of the fact in our own hearts, even though the world in its judgment may deal gently with us.

No man gives way to passion without feeling, in his cooler moments, contempt for his own weakness;—a contempt which is indeed so unendurable, that it compels him, as it were, to cast the odium upon another, by saying, "I was provoked. Such an one said so-and-so, or did so-and-so; it was impossible to help being angry." The amount of injustice, untruthfulness, and self-delusion, which is to be traced to this source, would probably startle us.

The very word which we use in excuse for ourselves is a falsehood. Impossible! no, it is never impossible to keep the temper in order, to subdue the rising of passion, and to speak the "soft answer which turneth away wrath."[2] The task does indeed appear impossible after years of indulgence in passion;—it is the only supposition by which we can account for the astounding fact that men of undoubted religious principle (religious, that is, to a certain extent), and keenly sensible to their position and influence amongst their fellow-men, are known as "excellent fellows—only with such very bad tem-

[1] Ephes. iv. [2] Prov. xv. 1.

pers ; "—but it is no more really impossible than it is to overcome a habit of drinking.

A continued notorious bad temper necessarily implies both a weak religious principle and a weak will. The sooner we make young people understand this, and own that violent temper—with its apparent force and energy, its noise and bluster, and (that which is often accorded to it) its influence of fear—is really a disgrace to a rational being, as well as an offence to God, the greater is our hope of rousing them to the conflict needed to subdue it.

When this conflict is begun early, the victory is as easy as it is sure. For violent temper is something perfectly tangible ; there can be no mistake about it. We have a giant to fight with, but the very fact that he is a giant enables us to see him distinctly, and so prevents our fighting at random.

And children and young people do not generally, like their elders, deceive themselves on the subject of temper. They really are ashamed of it, and it does not give them power by arousing fear, it only makes them disagreeable. If they have anything like religious principle, and possibly even if they have not, they very earnestly desire to get rid of it.

Now, there is a verse in the Book of Proverbs, always quoted on behalf of the government of the temper, which seems to recognize this earnest wish, and to encourage it by an appeal to that remarkable principle of man's nature, which leads him to delight in battle, and which phrenologists call combativeness—" He that is slow to anger is better than the mighty ; and he that ruleth his spirit than he that taketh a city."[1]

Ruling, in this place, cannot mean merely guiding or governing, for the act is compared with a siege and victory. Contest must therefore be included in both. And a violent temper is necessarily accompanied by a tendency to combativeness. We continually see the exaggeration of the latter ending in crime, as the frequent and natural consequence of the

[1] Prov. xvi. 32.

indulgence of the former. Here, then, we have an instinct or tendency that may ultimately become a power, which, if only seized upon at the right moment, and directed in the right way, may prove the very instrument needed to subdue a violent temper.

For temper, it is to be remembered, must be controlled before religious principle can, generally speaking, be expected to act upon it. There is no doubt that the latter will do the work much more efficaciously, and far more easily; but we must not wait for it. From a child's earliest days it must be taught that the battle with passion, the conquest of violent temper, is one of the great objects to which this love of conflict and victory is to be directed.

This is not speaking allegorically or mystically. The satisfaction arising from self-control, self-restraint, self-discipline, is just as truly a satisfaction arising from the exercise of power, as that which is derived from government of any other kind. No person, who is conscious that he is master of himself, that he can trust himself—check himself—be, in fact, the lord of his own passions and inclinations, is insensible to it. It constitutes, in fact, to many minds, the great charm of asceticism; and though it is a feeling that may easily be carried to excess, and is only safe when united with that sincerity of heart which leads us to place ourselves by our Saviour's side, and compare our self-conquest with His endurance; yet it would seem, even from the testimony of Scripture, to be perfectly lawful.

Allowing it to be so, then we can at once make an appeal to a feeling in the human heart, to which it will scarcely fail to respond.

The giant stands before us—Passion. It must be conquered, through God's grace, and with His help, but also by the exertion of the individual will. How soon? How completely shall the victory be gained? We may give a certain time, according to circumstances, for the campaign. By the end of that time, passionate temper must be so overcome that

even keen provocation shall not be able to arouse it beyond the moment. That is a definite object to set before a child, and with it there must be definite rules. Perhaps one only will suffice. When inwardly quivering and trembling with anger, stand perfectly still, and do not speak for the space of one minute. The rush of the whirlwind will be over then, and the consciousness of self-mastery will have invigorated the whole moral being; and even if self-restraint should subsequently be lost, there will still be the feeling of partial victory. Continue this, and soon—much sooner than we could possibly imagine—by the laws of association which form a habit, the instant the giant is aroused, the will which is to overcome him will be aroused also. Of course the real difficulty lies with the will, and here it is that religious principle acts so powerfully; but it may again be repeated, that violent temper is one of those faults which must be stopped in its *very earliest stages*, or it will so get the upper hand, that even a really earnest spirit will not entirely subdue it; and the man who is possessed by it—for in its effects, as well as in the suddenness of its attack, it often appears a species of possession—will remain an inconsistent Christian all his days.

And when this self-mastery is acquired, the impulse of temper, as well as its stormy ebullition, will be arrested, and by degrees the violent temper will really become gentle. Men are most frequently passionate because they do not give themselves time to listen or think. They misconstrue, misunderstand; they call up a phantom, and then, brandishing their clubs, rush violently to attack it. The habit of pausing, considering, striving to be sympathetic, to hear and see as others do, is a most effectual check upon this folly: it will at length become a habit; and habit, we must remember, is as efficacious for good as it is for evil.

Most terrible as the effects of violent temper have been, and may be, yet, of all the faults to which our fallen nature is liable, there is probably not one which can be so entirely overcome, or which, in the effort to conquer it, leaves such lasting

marks of good upon the character; since the force of will which it demands and cultivates, is a power to be exerted against every other fault or temptation.

All this may be said to a child as soon as it is able to understand reason; and if we add the sense of God's approbation of such efforts, and the desire to please Him, the victory is nearly certain. But for the child, we must remember—not for the man. By the time the age of fourteen is reached, if not sooner, the giant must become a slave, or it will in all likelihood be a tyrant for life.

But there are many other forms of bad temper besides that of passion; and they are so much the more difficult to deal with because they do not assume so palpable a form. Obstinacy, perverseness, irritability, fretfulness, sullenness, are really greater trials than the temptation to violent bursts of passion, for they meet us at every turn, and require continued watchfulness quite as much as an energetic will. And of these it may, perhaps, be said, that they will scarcely ever be thoroughly eradicated on this side the grave, because they belong more or less to physical temperament. Religious principle, and nothing else, will in any degree successfully attack them. What we have chiefly to guard against in education is strengthening them by want of tact, and bad management. Children, indeed, should never be allowed to call such faults by gentle names, or to make excuses for them; yet a little care may often ward off their outbursts.

If a little child has a fit of obstinacy, we shall only strengthen the evil by insisting upon carrying out our will. A simpler and more efficacious mode of dealing with the case is to say: "Very well, my dear; as you don't choose to do what I tell you, I will not allow you to do it. You were told to pick up that book, and you refused; now I forbid your doing it; but instead, you shall sit upon that chair for the next quarter of an hour and look at it." Put the child upon the chair, and leave it. The obstinacy will have vanished, merely because it finds that there is no longer a law against which it can hold out.

Perverseness may be dealt with in the same way. Some children—and a great many grown-up persons—have an intuitive desire to object to whatever is proposed, and especially if it is thought that it will give them pleasure. Nothing can be more trying to those they live with, and nothing is so likely to cure them as to take them at their word. A child is told that she is to go into the garden for some pleasant amusement, and being in a perverse mood says, in a complaining tone, that "she does not want to go." Instead of trying to persuade her that she will like it, take her at her word, and say, "Certainly, then you shall not go, as you dislike it." The next time she will be afraid to be perverse. The same kind of spirit shows itself in raising difficulties. There are innumerable cases in life in which it is impossible to avoid a difficulty. Instead of acting upon the wise maxim, "Of two evils choose the least," perverse people, whether men, women, or children, are constantly jumping from one to the other; so that you can never grasp them and bring them to reason. If you say, "Suppose we do so and so," the answer is, "Oh, no; that can't be, because of such or such consequences." If you then turn round, and say, "Well! then let us do so and so," you are met with, "Oh, no; that is quite impossible," because of some other consequence. And yet one of the two alternatives must be chosen. No argument will be of any avail in such a case. You may have the lever in your hand with which to move the world, but you have no fulcrum on which to rest it. A much shorter way of settling the matter is to say, "Well, then, decide for yourself; what do you think may or ought to be done?" When driven up into a corner by this question, the folly of the perversity is seen, and the choice of difficulties is made.

These peculiarities of disposition require very careful watching and guiding, whilst children are young, for otherwise they take root insensibly, and develop most unpleasantly in after years, when perhaps they are scarcely acknowledged as faults, and therefore not struggled against. And when persons have

to live and act together, especially in the case of large families, where the interests and happiness of many are affected by individual peculiarities, they become of vast importance to the comfort of daily life, even though they may not, upon a cursory view, appear to mar the real worth of the character.

Irritability is perhaps less easily checked by efforts external to the person who gives way to it, than any of the other developments of temper of which mention has been made, for it is very often the result of physical weakness, or nervousness. We see this in the case of children in infancy, or, indeed, at any age, when an illness is coming on, or when the process of recovery has commenced; and in such instances we must be particularly careful to avoid exciting it. But when we are attempting to educate, though we must always ourselves bear the extenuating circumstances in mind, we must take care that the children, whom we are training, do not seize upon them as an excuse. This is a general rule. There may and must be exceptions. If we have ever watched by a sick bed, which must soon become the bed of death, and heard the sorrowful confession of irritability from one who is too weak to exercise self-command, and whose brain is scarcely in its natural state, so as to be able to realize the force of religious truth, we shall have found ourselves compelled to say, "Do not think irritability a sin. It is only a weakness. God will look mercifully upon it." But this is by no means the language which can rightly be used in any case except that of illness, and for this reason: irritability is not so much a disease in itself, as the symptom of some other disease—it may be physical, it may be moral. With a person in ordinary good health susceptibility of the nerves is no excuse for an irritable temper. It may make gentleness more difficult, but it does not render its attainment impossible. The nerves are excited by some outward object; irritability, therefore, depends, for the most part, upon the view which we take of those objects.

Selfishness is one most frequent source of irritability.

We think of ourselves, care for ourselves, seek our own comfort, and so are irritable with every person and every thing which interferes with self. Vanity also will render us irritable, by awakening a desire for notice, and a consequent fretfulness when it is diverted from us to others. Self-conceit—love of power—will act in the same way; and even when irritability is caused by actions and movements which offend our taste, or jar upon our peculiar mood, it can always be checked by the thought that there is no intention of annoying us; that we may be quite as much in fault in indulging these particular fancies, as the person we complain of is in giving way to the habits we dislike. Or, should we be really justified in calling them disagreeable, still there is the duty of self-control, and sympathy with infirmity. When we think of sensitiveness and susceptibility as connected with the human frame, we shall scarcely err in believing that no mortal body could ever have been so nervously alive to all that would jar upon and pain it, as that of our Blessed Redeemer; but the idea of irritability as connected with Him, we feel at once to be blasphemous.

In dealing, therefore, with irritable children, we have first to take care that they are kept in good health; and when we are satisfied about that point, we must watch the cause which gives rise to the irritability, and by attacking the origin of the disease, and teaching them how to attack it, we may hope, by degrees, to get rid of the symptom.

And in this case, as in that of violent temper, our best safeguard is to begin early. Irritability, indulged, grows into a confirmed habit; indeed, it is one of those faults which will spring up in advancing years, even when it has but slightly shown itself before. The only thorough preservative against it, at any age, is that "answer of a good conscience," which gives us inward peace, by filling us with the blessed consciousness that we are walking in God's ways, and in His favour. A half will, a weak struggle, and a keen conscience, will make any one irritable. It is not the question whether, our past

sins being forgiven, we have a blessed hope of final salvation; we may have that, and yet be restless and irritable, because we know that God having done so much for us, we are not doing our utmost for Him. This is the consciousness which makes us dissatisfied with ourselves, and, as a necessary consequence, inclined to be dissatisfied with others. The "peace which passeth understanding" cannot coexist with anything but the offering of a whole heart, a steadfast will; and there is no other peace which can really soothe the susceptibilities of an irritable temper.

With sullenness or moodiness we are perhaps dealing most wisely when we leave it to itself, and take no notice of it. A very large proportion of this wrong temper will probably be found to arise from morbid self-consciousness. Children, young people, and a great many who are not young, like to know that others are thinking of and watching them, even when they are out of humour. They are not aware of being affected, and there is no actual pretence of feeling, but there is an unconscious exaggeration, proceeding from the desire to attract notice, Leave them to themselves, and this will die away. They will be tired of making themselves disagreeable for no purpose, and will by degrees recover their usual tone. When the mood has passed, it will be well to speak seriously about it, and show how inconsistent it is with Christian principle; but, at the time, such exhortations will only serve to increase the self-consciousness, and so to strengthen the mood. But after all, nothing can be done to cure, or even really to check, a sullen, moody temper, until, through God's grace, it is conquered from within. The feelings which give rise to it are too secret and complicated for us to reach. We may, indeed, observe the circumstances which seem to bring on the mood, and frame our own words and conduct so as to avoid arousing it unnecessarily; but even this is very difficult; for children and young people must be reproved, and yet it is reproof which most often makes them sullen. A few words on the fault which is to be noticed, spoken gently, but decidedly, will, with such dispo-

sitions, be found better than an endeavour to touch the feelings. And especially we must guard against any irritating preambles, such as, "Now, my dear, I know you don't like to be spoken to, but I must tell you so and so." Dragging secondary faults to light in this way is irritating to the temper, and the reproof or the advice which may follow will in consequence be taken amiss.

There is one more form of evil temper which we may very likely be called upon to combat with, but which must be encountered with very different weapons from those employed in other cases. We have all, no doubt, met with some instance of a jealous temper—a most miserable thing for its possessor, and a source of unnumbered evils to those who have to deal with it. And yet, strange though the advice may seem, probably our only way of gaining influence over it for good is to begin by sympathizing with it. It is such intense pain, and it so shrouds itself in the garb of love; we shall only repel and make the wounded heart shut itself up with its own misery, if we begin at once to speak of it as a sin. Feel with it, pity it, gain its confidence, and soothe it; and then say, "This is natural, but it is wrong, and there is but one cure for it—to make a sacrifice for the happiness of the person of whom you are jealous. That being done, there will be the sense of God's loving approbation, and 'when He giveth quietness, who then can make trouble?'"[1] There is, however, another kind of jealousy, which does not pretend to be based upon love; jealousy of power, of admiration, of influence. This is really nothing but selfishness, and it should be treated as such, called by its true name, and shown to be despicable. But the idea of punishing jealousy in any form is absurd. We can but place it in its true light, and then leave it to God, through the working of His Holy Spirit upon the conscience, to correct it.

We are, indeed, apt generally to deceive ourselves as to the power we possess of controlling children's tempers. Bad temper of any kind is so very trying, it destroys so completely

[1] Job xxxiv. 29.

anything like domestic happiness, that we constantly find ourselves having recourse to any expedient which may suggest itself in order to keep off its outbursts; and when we have succeeded we boast of our success, and flatter ourselves that the temper is cured. But to pet and humour a bad temper is really only to encourage it. Be it passionate, or moody, or irritable, it becomes in this way the tyrant of a household; no one has the courage to oppose it. It is very curious, indeed, to watch the effect which it produces. Except in very exaggerated cases, we know that it will exhibit itself in nothing worse than words and manner, and these cannot really injure us; yet there are probably very few persons who would not as soon go through the ordeal of sitting down in a dentist's chair, unknowing what pain may be in store for them, as deliberately encounter an outburst of violent temper, or suffer from irritability and moodiness. And thus it is that we run away from temper, speak smooth words to it, do anything rather than provoke it. And, unless duty calls upon us to confront it, this is a wise course to adopt. But if we treat children in a similar way, we are doing them an irreparable injury. The little tyrant of the nursery becomes the bully of the school, and the imperious lord of a household; and so the evil nature is fostered and strengthened, until it has become so confirmed a habit that it is not looked upon as a sin; and the man goes down to his grave with the burden of violent, uncharitable words and deeds upon his conscience, and wakes in another world to find himself in the presence of Him who has numbered "hatred, wrath, and strife" as amongst the "works of the flesh," and bids us remember that "the fruit of the Spirit is love, joy, peace, long-suffering, gentleness, goodness, faith, meekness, temperance: against such there is no law." [1] Surely, then, it is incumbent upon us to take warning in time, and allow neither ourselves nor our children to be in the slightest degree self-deceived upon this question of ill-temper.

The caution is most important for girls as well as boys.

[1] Gal. v. 22, 23.

A woman's temper is seldom perhaps as violent as a man's, but when once excited it is more ungovernable. And irritability and sullenness are, it must be remembered, just as much offences in God's sight as passion; and how many homes are made miserable, how many hearts are saddened, and how much love is checked, and in the end extinguished, by the indulgence of what is called a disagreeable or an irritable temper, in the gentle-mannered, soft-voiced, perhaps attractive girl, who in society is the object of universal admiration!

CHAPTER XXII.

PURITY.

Side by side with Truth surely we must place Purity; or rather, may we not look upon truth as the guardian—the protector of purity? For it can only be through the instrumentality of sophistry, self-deceit, and false imaginings, that any woman ceases to be, in however slight a degree, modest and refined in word and deed. The instinct which tells her that the reverse of this character is wrong, is as innate as the perception of truth; and nothing but falsehood—though a falsehood to which her own will consents—can lead her to think the contrary.

And it is to this instinct, this inborn sense of what is pure, that we are all accustomed to trust, for the most part implicitly, in the education of young girls. Time was, indeed, when it was thought necessary to use plain words and strong language—to call vice by direct names. Those were days which we look upon as evil—we could not bear them now. We cannot read the literature of those times unless in expurgated editions. We know that we should be unable to tolerate the manners and the conversation which then were thought perfectly admissible.

We have adopted another theory; we say, coarse words bring coarse ideas: we feel that God has mercifully left a remnant of the innocence of Paradise in the natural purity of a young girl's mind, and we believe that woe will be to us if, through any imprudent anxiety, or over caution, we should

give rise to a thought of evil which, left to itself, the mind would never have suggested. And, acting upon this theory, we leave—or at least we think that we leave—young girls to themselves; taking, perhaps, one precaution, that the books they read should be, on the whole, unobjectionable. If we are very strict, we reject novels altogether; and if we are not, we admit, at the age of seventeen or eighteen, a few—the very best; but at any rate we keep a watch over girls' reading, and we are careful that they should not form what we consider to be injurious friendships; and then we trust them—to nature.

And what is the result? Most highly satisfactory! Are not our English girls the very models of all that is refined, delicate, and modest? Is it not a delight to watch them wherever they are congregated together? Have they not beauty, freshness, grace, freedom of tone without familiarity—ease of manner without forwardness?

There is a rumour, indeed, that they are becoming "fast"; that they are beginning to like to make themselves conspicuous; that they wish not only to look like men, but to talk and act like them. It is even asserted that they are more acquainted than a few years since would have been thought credible with the evil which abounds in the world, and are more tolerant of it. But all this we choose to consider a mere question of fashion. It is, we say, a wave of folly which will sweep over the surface of society and retire, leaving it very much what it was before. English girls are modest and pure-minded: they must be so. It is a scandal and offence to suppose it possible that they can be the contrary. And so again we smile at such young follies, and fold our hands, and perhaps sigh; and then leave our girls—to nature! It is too sad to disturb such a pleasant dream—too cruel to suggest suspicions—to speak of the need of warning, the necessity of watchfulness. If the Eye of God were as the eye of man, and Heaven could be won by fair appearances, one might almost say that we have good reason to be satisfied.

Almost! But there is another side to the picture—a side to which we seldom turn—which we dare not let the pure young minds of our children think upon—which we scarcely venture to think upon ourselves. It comes to us in the form of penitentiaries, refuges, reformatories; intended—so we think—for the lower classes; for those who have no such safeguards, no such examples, as our children have. The inmates of those moral hospitals are the lowest of the low now; they must, we suppose, have been so always.

True—they are the lowest of the low; none but themselves can tell how low. In the "lowest deep" a "lower deep" has opened for them, and they have sunk into it. True also, that, except in some most sad cases, they have not generally belonged to what are exclusively called the upper classes. Those who, in the upper classes, sin like them, have money, and rank, and friends, and flatterers, to shield them. They can brave the world even as they brave their God; and the world will suffer them to go their way, and even bow down itself before them. Yet these mournful harbours for the all-but lost do too often include amongst their inmates English girls, brought up in quiet homes, under seemingly good influences, without any apparently great temptations—girls left to the teachings and warnings of nature; and who, in outward manners, have been just as modest, just as retiring, though they may not have been just as elegant and cultivated, as their sisters of the higher ranks. When we boast of the purity and delicacy of English girls and English women, we may not take the happy majority who have been saved from open transgression, and put aside the miserable minority who have fallen into it. God looks down equally upon all.

Can the condition of England in this respect be well pleasing in His sight?

Yet still further. Let us ask ourselves what purity means—what it really is. Purity before God. No thought, no wish, no feeling, which may not be brought into His presence, and there welcomed and blessed!

It is the inheritance of Angels; and whilst still dwelling in this body of sin and death, we may think that we cannot hope for it. But can we be contented with less for ourselves? Can we seek for less in others? Will any right-minded mother, any true friend, endure for an instant the idea that the child whom she loves is to sit down satisfied without it? We bear with imperfect temper, with lingering selfishness, with unsubdued pride—we can love and cherish all that is good in the character, even whilst we recognize the existence of these qualities of evil; but we cannot so bear with what is not pure. To admit the possibility of it in children involves the destruction of an ideal; and because this is painful to us, we close our eyes to what we do not like to see, and say, "God has given the instinct of purity to a young girl, and nature will guard it. We need not trouble ourselves with it, except so far as to be careful that nothing shall approach to mar it."

And even while the words are uttered, there must be some from the depths of whose hearts a voice arises telling them they speak foolishly. The ideal child has not—they are but too truly aware of it—in their case expanded into the ideal girl and woman. They know that they were once thought to be what they were not; and, because of that involuntary deception, they know also that they have had to work out for themselves a bitter experience of their own weakness, from which a word of warning might have saved them. And yet they continue the like dream with regard to others; they will not believe what they know, but what they wish; and so they in their turn form an ideal of purity, and simplicity, and modesty, and call it their child; and then thank God for giving it them, and consider that their work is done.

In thus acting, persons follow a principle directly opposite to that which has been proved to be necessary in other cases. We all know the revolution which the principle of reasoning from induction has effected in natural science. Both sceptics and believers are, at the present moment, clamorous that it should be applied to the study of revelation. Why, then, is

it to be discarded in morals? We may say, because it is not needed; because the truth of the present theory is proved by its results. We cannot wish our young girls to be different from what they are, and therefore we are content with the system which has trained them.

A most satisfactory and wise answer, if only it were founded upon true premises. We cannot wish our young girls to be different from what they are! How do we know what they are? If purity be, as surely it is, that perfect spotlessness of deed, and word, and thought, which God can look upon and bless, then we may be quite sure that these young people—simple-minded, innocent as they appear, and as in a certain sense, no doubt, they are—are not pure. And if any, looking into their own hearts now, and recalling the memories of their childhood, can see occasion for bitter regret and humiliation before God, though there may be no shadow of reproach in the sight of man; surely, by the most evident reasoning from analogy, there is cause to fear—more than to fear—to believe, that the same dangers are lying in wait for the children of the present day; and it is our imperative necessity, our bounden duty, so far as it lies in our power, to shield them from them.

The real secret of all this wilful delusion is, that although theoretically we desire purity both for ourselves and our children, yet practically we content ourselves with a standard short of that which God requires.

"Blessed are the pure in heart: for they shall see God."[1]

The immediate Presence, the visible Majesty and Holiness of the Almighty, and our own hearts! Can we bear even the juxtaposition of the two ideas?

And yet it is to the pure in heart alone that the promise is given. However unattainable such purity may appear, we are nevertheless commanded to strive after it. And though the merits of our Redeemer form the only title of admission to Heaven, yet it is that same Redeemer who says, "Be ye therefore perfect, even as your Father which is in Heaven is perfect."[2]

[1] St. Matt. v. 8. [2] St. Matt. v. 48.

To place anything short of purity of *heart* before us as our aim, is to fall short of God's command, to risk being of the number of those who shall never "see God."

How is it, then, with us? What is it we look for in these young girls, so innocent, that they may be left without fear to the guidance of nature? We reply, they are irreproachable before man, society cannot frown upon them, envy will not sneer at them, scandal dares not whisper against them; and we are satisfied. We wish for nothing more. The world's standard is our standard, and we have succeeded in attaining it. True, there are rumours of hidden evil, which at times reach our ears, but it is not pleasant to listen to them. True, we are at times startled by some terrible catastrophe which wrecks the happiness of quiet homes; but those are rare exceptions. They are not to be taken as the ground of reasoning and action. True, also, that the dress of these modest English girls is a subject for sarcasm to all other nations; but the world, society, custom, sanction it; we should be ridiculed if we attempted to alter it. We need not ask what God says upon these subjects, it is sufficient if man approves. The young daughters of England are what we wish them to be, what we are determined they shall be. "Blessed are the pure"—as man reckons purity;—we may not doubt that they shall one day "see God!"[1]

Now let us turn to the Bible.

It is a very startling—one may even say a very uncomfortable—book. It does not in the least recognize this innate purity, this perfect simplicity and innocence which we so fondly dwell upon. The facts of the Bible and the facts of the world harmonize exactly; but the theory of the Bible and the theory of the world do not harmonize in the least. The Bible has a code of laws for men and women, for boys and girls alike. The world says they are not needed for the last, because nature herself is their law. And this difference makes the Bible, as it has been said, a startling book. No doubt

[1] St. Matt. v. 8.

there are portions of it which, though absolutely necessary as parts of legislation, were never intended for general use; but putting aside these, the Bible certainly does take it for granted that purity of heart and life is a thing to be prayed for, striven for, watched for, by all alike. It uses very plain language upon these subjects, which of course, being in the Bible, is right and necessary. But we could not possibly use such language ourselves! What effect it has upon the young girls who listen to it we do not know, and we would rather not inquire. So we leave it. It is the only thing to be done in all these matters—we leave it. Nature, time, common sense, will bring it all right.

Let it be so. Since we trust so much to this education of nature, it will do us no harm to inquire what it is likely to be.

We will look into a nursery. The education of nature begins there. There are two or three rooms, closely adjoining,—a day nursery, and night nurseries. Four or five children are congregated in them—boys and girls—varying probably in age from seven years old, downwards. The youngest is a baby, scarcely looked upon as a human being, and treated accordingly. There are nurses—one or two, as the case may be—who have been brought up in country villages, accustomed, probably, to the use of one bedroom for a family, and looking upon two as a complete luxury of decency. To them, it is quite a thing of course, that boys and girls, at that early age, should be herded together indiscriminately. The children have not yet arrived at the dignity of *he* and *she*, they are simply *its*, and so they play, and romp, and dress, and undress, and the little doll baby is tossed about, and nursery questions are discussed, and arrangements made, and the idea of paying attention to the ordinary decorums and proprieties of grown-up persons is totally set aside. The children live a life in public, and, as a natural result, they do not wish for anything else. They have no idea what privacy means. The theory of nature, however, says that it is not needed, for that

little girls have an instinctive delicacy, which is, in fact, their most precious gift. Poets rave about it, and fathers and mothers dream about it. The little creatures, when dressed in their best clothes and taken down into the drawing-room, are looked upon as angels of modesty. But—it is strange—they are not quite the same in the nursery. There, they are often rude, and unrefined, and wanting in delicacy. The nurses are obliged to caution them before they go into the drawing-room, and sometimes, in spite of the caution, they will do and say very unpleasant things. But it is all simplicity—nature! The mother leaves them to nature. They know no harm. How, then, can they be capable of it?

But the time arrives when some change must be made. The boys go to school, the girls have a governess at home. They leave the nursery, and they have bedrooms of their own; two, possibly three, occupying the same apartment. Very comfortable, pleasant rooms they are—delightful for the public life to which the children have been accustomed; but privacy—still there is none. What need is there of it? The little girls who have always been together, who have not a thought concealed from one another, who are absolutely one in taste, and feeling, and sympathy, cannot require, or even wish for the arrangements which would be essential with grown-up persons and strangers. And there is nothing in the outward behaviour of the children to lead any one to suspect that this unrestrained, unguarded familiarity is doing them the least harm. The little improprieties of the nursery have all passed away. In society they are retiring; to their parents they are obedient. If there was a tendency to rudeness and indecorum when they were very little, it was mere simplicity. Now, they have arrived at the age of shyness and modesty, and nature is still more delightful in its training. It must guide them aright!

There are, however, a few circumstances which are not quite satisfactory. The governess says that she has occasionally heard a few words of conversation pass between these

children upon subjects which it was not fitting they should discuss; and she has seen smiles and side glances, which give her an idea that the children know some things which it would be better they should not know; she doubts if they are quite as simple-minded as they appear. But the mother is incredulous. "What evil can her girls have learnt? So carefully as they have been guarded from all objectionable companionship, kept entirely under her own eye, and at such a very early age! At seventeen or eighteen, of course, young people will be silly, and talk of love and romance; but little girls of ten, eleven, and twelve, who have been well brought up, can know nothing and say nothing which the whole world might not hear." An appeal is made to the nurse. She also is incredulous and even indignant. "The young ladies have never learnt any harm from any one to her knowledge. Now and then they have asked odd questions, but she has always told them they were not to trouble themselves about things which did not concern them. They would know all about it when they grew up, but it was no matter to them whilst they were children."

An answer, of course, consummate in its wisdom! Not in the least stimulating to a child's curiosity! At any rate, the mother is satisfied. The governess, however, is not so, and she is all the more uncomfortable at her suspicions, because, as she says, "she has always been so extremely careful to keep the children's minds innocent. Awkward passages are met with in history, and, indeed, in the Bible. There are some things even in the Catechism which are not pleasant; but she has always passed them over as rapidly as possible. She has never allowed the least comment upon them. If the children have asked for explanations of things which could not be explained, she has said very much what the nurse said: that those subjects did not concern little girls, and they had better not think about them."

The state of the little girls' minds cannot, however, be ascertained, because the very fact of examination would create the evil which is dreaded. Before any person can tell

whether he or she has committed a fault, it must first be understood what the fault is.

No. There is nothing to be done but to be still more particular, and to fall back upon nature for comfort. The children were born pure-minded; they have heard and seen nothing to make them the reverse; therefore they are pure-minded! And in this full confidence in nature and simplicity, the children are left more and more to themselves, and allowed free intercourse with the young friends who have been chosen to be their companions. As occasion arises, they share the same room with them, and are on terms of the same entire familiarity as with their sisters. No one suspects the slightest evil. They do, indeed, sit up too late, and gossip together over the fireside; but all girls will do this; and they are so young, it is impossible that any harm can arise, except, perhaps, to their health; and they do not meet often enough for this to be really injured by late hours!

They are so young! There lies the fallacy. If these girls were some years older, there would be comparatively little danger. They would then have acquired the habits of outward delicacy and refinement which society gives; and they would not choose to lower themselves by conversation of which they ought to be ashamed. But at twelve, thirteen, and fourteen, this shyness does not exist. If young girls are then herded together without care, and if they have had their first delicacy of feeling blunted by neglect in the nursery, they will do and say whatever suggests itself at the moment, with all the more zest, because they are conscious, though they know not why, that it is forbidden. And thus it is that hundreds of young minds are contaminated. And how deep that contamination in some cases is, we should probably be very much shocked if we could know. But whatever the amount of the mischief may be in man's judgment, it must be great in the sight of God; for it is the first mark laid upon that modesty of nature, which is His most precious gift to woman; and which, under no circumstances, can be injured without the consent of her

own will. Neither can we forget, that when a girl of fourteen or fifteen ventures to speak to another girl of her own age, upon subjects which she would shrink from mentioning to a person whom she respects, she has opened the door to very grave evil. Possibly it may not enter; but possibly also—very possibly, it may.

It is not because sin is hidden that it does not exist. There are many who, through God's mercy, pass through life actually ignorant of the terrible dangers which beset the paths of others. They shrink from the knowledge of evil; and who shall blame them? But unless they face the fact that this evil does exist, although they may never have been brought into personal contact with it, they act but like the ostrich, "which leaveth her eggs in the earth, and warmeth them in dust, and forgetteth that the foot may crush them, or that the wild beast may break them. She is hardened against her young ones, as though they were not hers: her labour is in vain without fear; because God hath deprived her of wisdom, neither hath He imparted to her understanding." [1]

No one becomes wholly wicked at once. The sin which shocks us in its development in mature age, had its germ in childhood and youth; and in the case under discussion that germ is unquestionably to be found in the tainted mind which, in the indulgence of a morbid curiosity, tampered with subjects deadly to those who approach them without sanction, though perfectly harmless when met with in the path of duty.

Society, indeed, does not utterly discountenance anything but declared vice. But even that must have had a beginning. When the thoughts are pure, the words will be pure; and when the words are pure, so also will be the deeds. But let thoughts and words once be tainted, and it is only God's merciful interposing Providence which keeps any human being from open shame.

And is there no disgrace, even public disgrace, short of that which is absolute ruin? Is it not disgrace to overstep the

[1] Job xxxix. 14, 17.

modesty of a woman's nature? to be bold in tone and language? to stand upon the brink of sin, and give rise to the suspicion that we may have plunged into it? Is it not disgrace when young girls do and say things which make their brothers blush for them? when they find amusement and satisfaction in books in which the fundamental principles of morality are utterly set aside?

How could fashion overcome nature, and convert the shy retiring girl into the fast young lady, if the mind had not first lost its delicacy? There may be a fashion in the shape of a bonnet, or the trimming of a dress, and it may vary with the variations of fancy, and leave no trace behind it. But the change from modesty to immodesty is no question of fashion. It cannot take place without a corresponding change in the inward being; and if the manners of English girls are becoming, what is popularly termed "fast," it is because the minds of English girls are losing their native purity. And the disgrace of that loss, who may estimate?

It seems a very hard thing to say;—so many there are who do as others do without thought, and so many cases there may be in which young girls are led into a style of behaviour in itself objectionable, merely because they have not the courage to stand aloof and confess their inward shrinking from it. So also in many cases the motto, "Honi soit qui mal y pense," is perfectly true and applicable; and yet excuse, argue as we may, the main fact remains. Things are done and said which are unrefined, indelicate, immodest, and they cannot proceed from a pure source.

And if they do not,—if a girl's mind is not pure,—if her own instincts are so blunted that she cannot *feel* evil before she can explain it,—if she cannot shrink from it without knowing why she does so,—may God help her! for the wisest safeguards which the best of friends may provide for her will never be sufficient to secure her from danger.

We have looked at the worst consequences of this early initiation into the knowledge of evil; but there is a brighter

side to the subject. No one, however strict, would for a moment assert that these early offences are so ineffaceable, that the mind, once tainted, can never be restored to purity. God's grace, and an earnest will, and an incessant watchfulness, will work marvels in the way of such restoration; but even then it will never be anything but restoration. The scars will always remain; visible to the inward eye, though unseen by man, and, as we may humbly trust, blotted out by God. And they will not only be seen as scars, disfigurements, but they will be felt as wounds; they will give the pain of wounds; an ever increasing pain as the spirit longs more and more intensely for that purity of heart bestowed upon them who shall hereafter "see God."

And we, by our ignorance, our absence of watchfulness in infancy and childhood, have been, perhaps, the authors of that pain! We have left a stain upon our children's memories; a thought of sorrowful reproach. "Oh that I had been warned! that I had not been left to the workings of my own mind! that I had learnt in infancy to be ashamed of those things which I felt to be evil, though I knew not why! But I was left without a word of caution, and now I can but struggle to forget, what with that caution I might never have learnt."

Is not such a thought sufficient to rouse us to watchfulness? If we long for our children's happiness, is it possible we can be indifferent to the pang arising from that deep humiliation to a mind striving after purity—the consciousness of evil thoughts, the result of evil knowledge wilfully acquired?—a consciousness which may haunt those who are exposed to it through life, and never leave them until the gracious sentence of final acceptance is passed; and renewed, re-made in the Image of Christ, they are once more pure, even as He is pure.

And this, let it be remembered, is the best—the very best—that we can hope for any one who has wilfully tampered with the knowledge of evil; who has wilfully marred that blessed simplicity which is indeed, as mothers so delight to

think, the inheritance of their young daughters, and which, if only guarded in childhood and youth, would never be lost, whatever might be their lot in after life.

"Unto the pure, all things are pure."[1] The deep meaning of that saying perhaps nothing but the experience of years can teach us. We begin life shrinking from words and facts; we end by acknowledging that words and facts have no power to hurt us. Evil is that which is contrary to God's law. Whatever therefore is in accordance with God's law is not evil; and it is only evil which we have any cause to dread. There are women, in our own day, who are brought into immediate contact with all that is most repulsive and degraded in the sight of purity; and we look upon them as doing the work of saints. We see others tending the sick, performing the lowest, most menial, and even loathsome offices, and we say that they are following in the footsteps of ministering angels. Given the sense of duty, necessity, labour for the good of others, and there is nothing which may not be done, or spoken, or endured. The facts which taint the mind ineffaceably when learnt through the indulgence of a wrong curiosity, leave no taint when they come before us in the path of duty, or in the course of nature. And the mind which is the most simple, which has the least affinity with evil, will be found by experience to be the bravest in confronting it. We dread that which contaminates us; but the sense of contamination arises from something in our own hearts. God looks upon sin, and in the power of His Omnipresence dwells in the midst of it. But He is not affected by it. If we were Angels, we should not dread contact with any evil; and therefore if we would serve God as the Angels serve Him, we must seek for that purity of heart which will enable us to be fearless like them.

It is from thus unconsciously despising the teaching of God, that mothers will sometimes forbid their daughters to go amongst the cottages of the poor, lest they should hear or see things which may shock their delicacy; whilst they allow them

[1] Titus i. 15.

to sit half the day in easy chairs, reading doubtful novels; not perceiving that they are thus fostering in them habits of indolent self-indulgence, which in themselves have seeds of far deeper evil, of the very nature they dread, than any they may think to shelter them from.

The rule which has been mentioned holds good universally. In the ordinary affairs of life, the moral courage, the perfect simplicity, the good sense which can face what is wrong, and grapple with and overcome it, will almost always be found existing in exact proportion to real purity of heart. There are evils in the world which we all more or less know, which we all more or less deplore, but which we all unite in ignoring, because we shrink from acknowledging them. We put a varnish over everything. We refine our language till the condemnation which God pronounces against sin is felt to be unreadable. We make use of periphrastic expressions, and think that by so doing we do away with unpleasant facts. We picture to ourselves an ideal world, filled with ideal people, and imagine that in this way we make the real world more pure. But vice does not lose its evil when it loses its coarseness. Sin is not the less sin, because we dress it in silk and satin, and call it fashion; and purity is not the more pure, because, in dread, it turns away its face from defilement, and will not own its existence. On the contrary, real purity is essentially allied with truth. And when it is through God's grace ours, we shall be able to confront life as it is, we shall not fear to see it in its true colours, *so far as that knowledge is needful for God's service, though not one degree beyond;* and we shall turn away in greater disgust from the shams and pretences of virtue than from the most openly acknowledged vice.

If there is one proof stronger than another of the unreality of the so-called refinement of the present day, it is to be found in the literature which can be tolerated, and even admired. Shakespeare is felt to be, in many parts, unreadable. The Bible itself makes us uncomfortable; but we can take up a

novel—English or French, as it may happen—there is often very little to choose between them—and dwell with satisfactory excitement upon the most insidious and highly coloured pictures of the approaches to vice, if not of vice itself, so long as the unpleasant names which belong to it are avoided. If we were to meet with them, we should be compelled at once to put the volume aside. It does not signify what the evil may be which is suggested; if it is not called evil, it is supposed to do no harm. And why? Because society allows it. Because society has its own standard of purity, and if a book does not fall short of this, it may be admitted into the drawing-room, and even find a place in the young lady's boudoir. Names—names are the things we fear! Not thoughts, not feelings, too often not even deeds—only names! Save us from these, and we give up all else, as merely a question of fashion, and the manners of the times.

Is this an exaggeration? Our own consciences must answer.

And now, what is the remedy? If the dream of natural purity is destroyed; if evil really works insidiously, and, when it has entered the heart, hides itself from our view, how is it possible to guard against it?

We must go back again to the nursery, and seek for the answer in the analogy of nature, and physical purity. Those little infants whom we watch so unweariedly, require to be tended with the greatest care, simply in order that they may be kept now, and learn by degrees to keep themselves, in that condition of cleanliness which is essential for their bodily well-being. If we do not thus accustom them to external purity, they will become insensible to it. Why this should be, is a problem, which, it would seem, can only be solved by recognizing the condition of a fallen nature. Faces and hands, for instance, require very frequent washing. In themselves, as God made them, they are clean; but, though dirt is repulsive and disgusting, there is nothing more difficult than to make a child keep itself as God made it. We are therefore very

particular in enforcing nursery habits of cleanliness. We do not trust to nature—to the fact that God has given the child a perception of cleanliness, and an appreciation of it; but we think it necessary to cultivate and educate that perception, till it becomes a habit. And so, as time goes on, we find the results of this education. The children themselves shrink from anything which is not clean. They guard themselves in a measure, though it is long before they can be entirely entrusted to do so. As they grow up, and are thrown more upon their own guidance, and placed in new positions, they necessarily learn more of the existence of the many painful, loathsome spectacles that are to be seen in the world. Poverty, illness, ignorance, vice, force it upon them. They learn to think of it, talk of it, reason about it. They are compelled to do so. It is their duty. And this must be the case not only with men, but with women. But there is no real contamination in consequence. Even if they are brought into temporary contact with it, it does not adhere to them. When called upon to discuss it, they are enabled to do so by the means of technical phrases, which present the abstract idea of what is meant, but give no distinct image of it to the eye. It is indeed this power of seizing upon abstract ideas, and conveying them to one another, which enables us in the least to carry on the necessary business of every-day life. Without it, we should all rush from one another into the wilderness and the desert, shrinking from the view of the infirmities of our common nature. And so it happens that although this world is a very dirty world, yet men and women can contrive to live in it satisfactorily, with a fair amount of cleanliness and comfort; and even more than this, with real physical enjoyment from freshness and purity. They do so, be it observed, not by ignoring the fact that dirt exists, still less by closely examining it, but simply by recognizing and guarding against it.

And from the analogy of these simple facts we may learn how to deal with the question of moral purity.

Children are in one sense pure, even as in one sense they

are clean; that is to say, they have no knowledge of actual evil; but they bear about with them a fallen nature, and if left to themselvcs that nature will speedily develop itself. The first thing to be done, then, is to guard against such development. God has very mercifully aided us in this task, by making it part of a woman's nature to shrink from anything which is wanting in delicacy and modesty: but this instinct is very much stronger in youth than it is in infancy and childhood. At first it is scarcely perceptible, and it requires to be fostered just as much as the sense of truth, or the habit of obedience. We punish a child severely for telling us a falsehood; why do we not punish it just as severely for saying or doing anything which is not refined or modest? We should be shocked at the idea of placing our little ones in positions which would lead them naturally to want of truthfulness: does it never strike us that their nursery habits must lead them naturally to want of delicacy? It may be difficult to know how to manage with them; but the fact that it is more easy to herd them together as little animals, than to treat them as beings born for Heaven, does not make it right to do so. Thought, good sense, care, and watchfulness, will do wonders. It is the principle which is needed, and it can always be enforced by a few rigid rules. Grown-up persons are often thrown together in what would be very uncomfortable familiarity if they did not consult each other's convenience and feelings: why may not children be taught to do the same?

Mothers are extremely strict in maintaining the nursery regulations which they think concern their children's health; it would be very little increase of difficulty if they would take the trouble to make and to maintain a few regulations which concern their delicacy and purity. And when once established, the latter would be much more easily kept than the former, because nature then would become the assistant. The refinement of feeling which was scarcely perceptible at the beginning would strengthen day by day with habit; and at length the children themselves would shrink from doing or saying any-

thing which was not in accordance with modesty. And any offence against these regulations should be punished sharply and instantly. It is said that when Benvenuto Cellini was a boy, his father thought he saw a salamander come out of the fire, and pointing out the marvel to his child, he gave him a box on the ears, that he might remember all his life that he had seen the creature. A similar box on the ears would be a very great help in teaching a child to remember when it has been guilty of any offence against delicacy. Warnings, grave reproofs, and good advice, are worse than thrown away in such cases, for the child no more understands the nature of its misdeeds than Benvenuto Cellini understood the nature of the salamander. What is wanted is not comprehension, but obedience; only, in order to obey, there must be commands—definite and rendered practicable—which shall be based upon those common rules of decorum that must be observed in after years, and which should be enforced on the nurse as well as the children.

It must be confessed that this enforcement will be no easy task. Education begins in the nursery, and yet it is there that parents must trust a great deal to persons who too often are very unfitted for the charge they undertake.

Good nurses are rare, and bad ones may do incalculable mischief. And if children live entirely in the nursery, or apart from their mother's superintendence, it is no marvel that they acquire habits which may be their ruin. So also persons who have small houses and small incomes cannot make the same comfortable arrangements for their children as those who are more fortunately circumstanced. The very best theoretical laws may be laid down with regard to nursery habits and discipline, but it may be next to impossible to carry them out efficiently, either because the nurse is incompetent, or the nursery is inconvenient. No system of nursery training of any kind can indeed be suggested which is certain to work satisfactorily. The very fact that it is a system is against it. What is wanted is principle, and for this the mother is responsible.

She must form her rules according to the capabilities of her household. But when the right principle is once firmly established in her own mind, there can be no doubt that God's blessing will rest upon her efforts to enforce it in act. If children cannot have entire privacy, at least they may have it partially. If boys and girls cannot be completely separated, at least precaution may be taken to avoid their being thrown together without care. Arrangements may be made with regard to time. Habits may be strictly watched. The nurse may be taught that neglect upon these points will never be overlooked. Only teach the little creatures, who have as yet but a dormant sense of right and wrong with regard to these subjects, that they are to take no liberties, to practise no rudenesses in the nursery which would not be allowed in the drawing-room, and then the instinct of modesty, delicacy, purity, which is God's precious gift, will, through His blessing, be retained uninjured. The teaching will be still that of nature, but it will be nature as it came from the Hands of God, not as it has been corrupted and defiled by fallen man. And when the lesson of modesty and refinement is learnt in the nursery, the task of instilling it as a principle to be acted upon, when children are left to themselves, is well-nigh completed. The little girls may perfectly well share the same room. They will only require arrangements for privacy such as they have always been accustomed to. And as they have learnt to be modest in deed, so they will be modest in words. That blessed, hallowed instinct, which God has given them, and which has never been blunted, will be their safeguard into whatever companionship they may be thrown ; and though they will not be entirely free from danger, it will be danger infinitely lessened.

Only one point will then require special warning and watchfulness. As the absence of sensitiveness is the source of evil in the case of a little child, so curiosity is the source of evil in youth. It grows with the growth of the intellect, and to stop its working is next to impossible. We may check and reprove, and it will hide itself from us, but it will work still.

Here again, for the sake of society, for the sake of the souls of our children, for our own sake, let us not delude ourselves by dreams, or think, by refusing to look at a difficulty, to escape it! We have seen how nurses and governesses, for the most part, meet the queries put to them. They defer the answer to some future time, upon which the child's mind of course rests, with eager expectation, as the period when all things mysterious are to be made known. But God deals with these questions in a very different way. From its infancy, the child is made to perceive two facts which, in its own mind, unconsciously stand to each other, though in a vague way, in the relation of cause and effect;—one is, that the habits of married life are different from those of single life; and the other that the birth of a little brother or sister is connected with its mother's suffering and illness.

Nature, which is God's Voice, never told a child that babies grow in beanfields, or are brought as presents by the doctor! But nurses talk this kind of nonsense, no one reproving them for it; and then of course there arises a mystery and perplexity in the child's mind. Nature and the nurse are at variance. Curiosity is awakened, and in time, in spite of all our care, it will be gratified unlawfully, to the injury, in every way, of the moral sense. And that, because we choose to make ourselves wiser than our Creator, and to suppose that it is possible for the mind to be tainted by following the guidance of nature and common sense; and kept pure by ignoring what must be known as soon as reason begins to work; if it be only through the plain words of the Bible, and the services of the Church.

Again, mothers and governesses meet with awkward passages in history—and histories are unquestionably very often most wrongly and unnecessarily coarse—and they slur them over, they hurry by them. Probably they imagine that because the children ask for no explanation, therefore they seek for none. They are very grievously mistaken. Those little minds are working in secret, and will by no means rest satis-

fied with having words and facts slurred over. If curiosity is stronger than principle, the children will seek to be enlightened by books,—forbidden books,—dictionaries, and such like. If they have, in the slightest degree, lost their delicacy, and blunted their natural instinct, they will talk upon these subjects amongst themselves—with companions—not impossibly with brothers; for brothers, unless very carefully warned, will injure their little sisters' minds, in some cases irretrievably. And how has such mischief arisen? Simply because, instead of listening to nature, reason, and the Bible, those who have had the care of the children have taken the mock proprieties of the world to be their guide, and have followed the impulse of moral cowardice, and averted their faces from a difficulty instead of confronting it.

If there is one thing more patent than another to the apprehension of the whole world, including children as well as men and women, it is the sacredness of the marriage vow—the allegiance due from a wife to her husband—from a husband to his wife. When a wife forsakes her husband, or a husband forsakes his wife, and cleaves to another, it is a breach of the Seventh Commandment. Thus far any child can understand, and thus far surely any parent or teacher can explain. It is the explanation which St. Paul gives in the seventh chapter of the Epistle to the Romans; and if, *forestalling questions*, we would give it of our own accord, the little mind would, for a considerable time, rest satisfied.

And this same kind of matter-of-fact explanation is ready for us in many other cases of similar difficulty. Marriages are events of great ceremony. Religion and the law of the land are alike required to sanction them. If persons despise this necessity, and choose to live together as husband and wife without having made, solemnly and publicly, the vows required, their children are not acknowledged as legitimate; and they, themselves, are stigmatized by certain names, commonly met with in history and in the Bible.

It is really necessary to give these illustrations, because

the wonderful want of common sense, the wrong mystery frequently exhibited in connection with these subjects, does more irreparable injury than any one without experience and knowledge of facts could possibly imagine. We come back, again and again, to the same truth. No knowledge which God gives by nature, or which comes to us in the way of duty and necessity, can do us harm; but the knowledge which we seek for ourselves, to gratify an evil curiosity, will leave a wound which, on this side the grave, may never be entirely healed.

Before a child's strength of principle can be trusted, the temptation of curiosity must, then, as far as possible, be forestalled. When the occasion presents itself naturally, tell what must be known, and tell it simply, without comment, or caution, or haste; above all, without any show of mystery, but as a mere question of fact. In speaking in this way we are, as in the other cases alluded to, following the guidance both of nature and of the Bible. Every woman feels that if disagreeable subjects must be discussed, she can bear the ordeal perfectly well so long as what is said is put in a dry, business-like form. The subject then passes from the mind, and is forgotten. But the moment there is any apology made, or any hesitation or shyness evinced, she shrinks back pained, and, probably, disgusted; and the unpleasant impression of the conversation remains, perhaps for years. From the same instinct a woman will pardon a coarse word which may shock her refinement, whilst a *double entendre* is felt to be unpardonable. And is not this one amongst many reasons why the facts and the warnings of the Bible produce such a different effect from any others of a like kind? There are no hints or suggestions in the Word of God; for He who inspired it is the Author of human nature; and He knows what that nature will bear, and how it may most wisely be addressed. When the Bible speaks of evil, it does so directly and simply, without provoking curiosity, but as a repulsive matter of fact; and viewed in this light, the purest mind will not shrink from confronting it.

But even supposing all needful information to have been given, and that in the best form, there will arrive a time when it will not be sufficient, when the mind will work further. And then comes the appeal to principle. We are afraid, perhaps, of awakening a thought of evil in a young girl's mind. We shall not escape the danger by refusing to recognize that there is such a thing as evil. What we may not choose to talk of she will think of, and that often without at all knowing what injury she is doing herself. There are, therefore, certain plain cautions which it is our bounden duty to give. They may, indeed, excite the suspicion of hidden evil; but if they do, it will be only that it may be guarded against, in the spirit of obedience and truth. If, in any case, curiosity should be dangerously aroused, and indulged in consequence, we may be quite sure that it would have been awakened just the same whether we had given the warning or not.

Some minds, indeed, appear to have a natural morbid craving for everything forbidden, of every kind. They must be dealt with separately. We cannot lay down general laws for them. But no child of ordinary refinement and right feeling will be injured by being told that there are many things which it is very undesirable she should know, and many forms of evil which it is misery and shame to come in contact with, or even to hear of; that to seek for knowledge upon these subjects is a sin, for it is yielding to the temptation which overcame Eve, when she ate the fruit of the tree of knowledge of good and evil. It cannot be amiss to say to her, that whatever question she desires, from mere curiosity, to have answered, should be put to some person whom she respects; and that if she shrinks from this, she may be sure it is better to remain in ignorance. Neither can it do her any harm to insist, again and again, upon the *absolute necessity* of listening to the slightest misgiving of conscience with regard to anything unrefined, or unmaidenly, or wanting in delicacy, which when alone, or with others, she is tempted to say or do, at any time, under any circumstances. If this sense of the paramount claim which

such instinctive feelings possess can only be fully impressed upon her, it will save her, through God's mercy, from almost all perils. God never leaves us without warning. We must all, in looking back upon our young days, remember things from which we shrank, without knowing why; words which we dared not use, though we could not have explained them. It may be—we may well thank God if it should be so—that this instinct of ignorance remains with us still. There is no fear now of our acting against it. We know how blessed it is; for it brings back to us somewhat of the freshness and innocence of childhood. Except when duty requires the contrary, we desire nothing better than to have the knowledge of evil kept from us. And we judge the feelings of the young by our own. The things which are hateful and disgusting to us will, we take it for granted, be so to them. There lies our mistake. They have the same instincts, but they have contrary feelings warring against them. Knowledge of any kind, especially that which verges upon the hidden or the forbidden, is a temptation. Excitement of feeling, romance, imagination, can dress up things, in themselves utterly loathsome, till their true nature is entirely concealed. And even where there is very little excitement or romance, Satan can make use of sophistical reasoning, and whisper, that because it is not clear to them why what they desire to do is wrong, therefore it is permissible.

Here, perhaps, is the greatest peril of all, and it is at this point that a premonitory caution would prove such an invaluable safeguard. When we urge upon children, in the very strongest possible manner, the necessity of listening to God's warning, given them through conscience, we strengthen that warning, we make its voice louder. It may seem to us that our words will have but little effect, yet we must utter them. God guides the young in this way, and so must we. He does not give them a full knowledge of the evil they are to avoid, because by it their minds would be tainted; but He gives them a check, the sense of a wound or pain, whenever they come

within reach of it; and so He bids them draw back. And if we will only work with God, they will draw back. In some happy cases, indeed, they will do so, whether we do our part or not; but this is not the rule of God's government. It is the exception, and we must not reckon upon it. If God gives warning, Satan offers temptations; and God has willed that it shall, for the most part, depend upon education whether the warning or the temptation be the stronger. It is impossible, indeed, for us to begin *too soon* to warn children against the sin of saying or doing what they would be ashamed for their elders to know, because *we can never tell how early evil may be suggested to them.* If, from want of moral courage, we neglect to do this, then the guilt of thoughts, and words, and of deeds, should such be committed, may rest upon our heads as well as theirs. On the other hand, if we only take precaution in time, the necessity for watchfulness will soon cease; and pass but a very few years, and the thoughtless girl of thirteen or fourteen, ready to plunge into any danger, to grapple with any question, so that she may but have the amusement and excitement of gratified curiosity, will have become the modest, self-controlled woman, who, in her dignity and simplicity, shrinks from the unnecessary knowledge of evil as from its contact, and needs no protector but God; no guide but the instincts which He has given her.

One more caution may, perhaps, not unnecessarily be given. If we desire wise and safe counsel upon these questions to be given to young girls, we must take care that their advisers are women.

To many persons such a caution will appear wholly uncalled for. Nature itself would seem to warn us that there are subjects which a man was never intended to name to a young girl. But experience tells us that this warning of nature is not sufficient. Cases occur in which young girls trust themselves, or are trusted by others, to the direction of men, probably most excellent and pure minded, and from these causes, as well as from their sacred office, worthy of all respect; but

wanting in one most essential qualification for the guidance of a girl—knowledge of a woman's nature. When men have to advise upon these points, they necessarily take for their assistance one of two theories. Either they suppose that a girl's mind is so innocent that she requires scarcely any warning; or, reasoning from their own knowledge of human nature, they imagine that, with certain reservations, they may safely give her the same directions and cautions which they would give to a boy. Now, neither of these theories is strictly true. Girls do require a great deal of warning, but it is in order that evil may be kept from approaching them, not that they may actually see it, and be roused to do battle with it. They will sometimes say and do things which might, under certain circumstances, lead to most fatal consequences; and a man, looking at such words or actions, and knowing how likely the consequences would be to follow in the case of a boy, gives warning and directions with a view to them. The result is that the young mind is bewildered and disturbed. There is a vague sense of some terrible evil of which nothing is really known. The conscience is burdened, and self-respect is lost. With this there must also be lost the energy and hopefulness which are needed before improvement can be hoped for. A woman dealing with such a case would simply put aside the thought of consequences,—certainly would not suggest their possibility; she would merely insist most strongly upon the necessity of caution on the score of delicacy, refinement, modesty, which are what a girl thoroughly understands; and thus, whilst the evil would be averted, the conscience would be left unburdened, and the brightness and simplicity of the character would remain undisturbed.

It is a very grievous thing to distress a young girl's mind with the fear of sins which may never approach her. She has not yet the moral strength to bear it. Anger may lead to murder, and grown-up people do well to remember it; but to place such a consequence before the eyes of a sensitive girl, and to give her directions as if she was in danger of commit-

ting it, would be just sending her forth on the road to a lunatic asylum. It is the same with other sins. God does not teach her to dread them; He only closes up the avenues which may lead to them. When shall we learn to study His ways instead of our own theories?

CHAPTER XXIII.

LOVE.

But the education of young girls can scarcely be said to end when they have attained to womanhood. They cannot be thrown upon the world like men; and it will, probably, be found, upon inquiry, that the parents who have trusted most confidently to the teaching of nature in the nursery, are often the most rigid in placing restraints upon their children in society. They act as they find it necessary; though, perhaps, if they had only reversed their education, and begun with restraint in the nursery, they would have found that all which was needed in society was advice.

The instinctive delicacy of a girl's mind would then be her own restraint, and we should no longer hear the rumours of the worse than follies of fashionable life, which make those whose paths are marked out for them, in more quiet spheres, shrink from the thought of its temptations and its risks, as from the possible contamination of open vice.

There is indeed a great natural difference in girls as regards simplicity. Some are flirts and coquettes almost from their cradles. Others, though certainly these are exceptions, never really understand what flirting and coquetting mean. But, whatever may be the natural character, there can be no doubt that the little incipient flirt, if brought up in an atmosphere of purity and refinement, may be converted into a lively, agreeable, sensible woman; whereas, if her training is the reverse, she may become all that it is most grievous to contem-

plate. This every one will acknowledge. But what is meant by an atmosphere of purity and refinement? The words sound well, but what do they mean?

They have many meanings. The world translates them into propriety. Propriety is easy of acquirement; purity difficult. And in these days we like royal roads from which all the stones have been removed. So we make our children *proper.*

To speak of love is improper, that is to say it is improper so long as a girl is in the schoolroom. Up to Midsummer or Christmas, in such a year, it is a subject *tabooed* even in thought, because the young lady is not "come out;" but after that time it is quite natural.

So again—novels must on no account be read whilst French, German, and Italian, music and drawing are the occupations of the day; but the moment these sensible pursuits are laid aside, then they are matters of course—needful for conversation; no one can get on in society without knowing something about them.

Here again, our "wishes are the fathers to our thoughts." The children do not talk of love, therefore they do not think of it!

But what is it that makes us so certain of the fact? It does not appear that God has drawn any such veil over the subject. On the contrary, children can have lived but a very few years in this world without discovering that there is such a thing as falling in love, and that a very common result of it is marriage. And certainly we shall not prevent their thinking of it, by making any mystery about it; for the love of mystery is innate in all children. Still less shall we keep them from it by shutting them up in the schoolroom, and not allowing them the society of any but persons of their own sex, for all things which are kept from us are invested with a double interest. Neither is it, perhaps, such a very grievous offence that children should think of love and marriage, and even talk of them. Free ventilation may be the best safeguard against moral as

well as physical ills. It may be that a girl who looks at love through a grating may be more excited by the contemplation than one who is allowed to walk abroad, and view it as it really is. At any rate, there is one very essential difference between love looked at through the grating, and love as it actually exists, which it is most desirable should be learnt early; and yet which never will be so learnt unless a certain freedom of observation and discussion is permitted.

Seen through the grating, marriage is the one end and object—the *ultima thule*—of a woman's life. Seen as it really is, it is simply the most important accident of life. It is this distinction which creates the difference between romance and reality.

Romance says, "And so they were married, and lived happily ever after."

Reality says, "And so they were married, and entered upon new duties and new cares."

The child looking through the grating sees nothing but the wedding day. Neither is she told of anything beyond. She sees, indeed, that the sister or the cousin who is married is an angel then, and an ordinary prosaic human being a year or two afterwards; but the illusion is too strong for her youthful imagination. As it is difficult to separate the actor from the person whom he has represented—as Mrs. Siddons must always have retained more or less the form of Lady Macbeth to those who had once seen her personate the character—so the "lovely bride" of the newspapers is still the object of envy and admiration to the child, even when she knows that she has since become a worn, anxious wife and mother; expected to wait upon her husband, instead of being waited upon by him; and occupied in home duties, instead of the excitements of society.

And so marriage becomes the one dream of the secluded child's imagination; or rather, not marriage with its solemn responsibilities, its imperative duties, its great happiness, but also its very serious risk—but, the white silk dress, and the

Brussels veil, the myrtle wreath and orange flowers, the wedding cake and the favours. And of course she believes that the moment she is emancipated from the schoolroom these joys are awaiting her; and as the preliminary to them must be falling in love, therefore every gentleman who approaches her must be viewed in reference to this important end. Will he admire her, or will he not? Does he pay her attentions, or does he neglect her for some one else? The time is come when she ought to be married—when she must be married. How is it that she is not? And so years go on, and possibly—very possibly, in these days—they fail to bring with them the long looked-for event. Slowly, most unwillingly, the truth forces itself upon her: she is amongst those whose destiny has in some unforeseen way been thwarted.

It was always meant that women should marry, but she is not married. And what is to become of her? What is she to live for? What has life to offer? It had but one prize, and that prize has been missed. What then remains? Nothing.

Now, all this is very sad, very grievous; all the more sad and grievous because it is a sorrow perfectly unnecessary, brought upon the sufferer simply by the false way in which she has been accustomed to look at life.

Women were meant to marry. Marriage is very important. A happy marriage is the most happy of all happy events. But it is not the purpose and object of life, the final cause of woman's creation. It seems almost absurd to suggest the possibility of such an idea, and yet so-called rational human beings talk and act as if it was; and fiction, being only the counterpart of the world's facts, recognizes it as such, and thus presents it to the imagination. Girls are so wrongly taught from childhood that they are led to stake their all upon this one cast. No marvel, therefore, that when they lose it, they sink in repining or despair. And the delusion begins in the schoolroom, in the mystery and excitement which the very fact of a forbidden subject creates. Love and marriage as they are, are realities involving risks, responsibilities, duties. Would it injure a

child's mind to hear them spoken of as such, and to be allowed freely to express her thoughts, her hopes, and anticipations? The real mischief of all such conversation lies in the gossiping secrecy which usually accompanies it. When girls chatter among themselves in their bedrooms, they do themselves untold harm. When they talk openly in the drawing-room, to persons they respect, they are safe. If these subjects interest them, and naturally and rightly they do interest them extremely, they ought to be allowed to say so. Their ideas may be very foolish, their anticipations greatly exaggerated, but so long as they can be expressed plainly and simply, they themselves will be simple-minded. And it is only in this way that the true view of life can be put before them—that which faces the fact that very possibly they never may marry; and that if they do not —instead of being condemned to a life of desolate repining— they will have to undertake another set of duties, to throw themselves into a different sphere of interests, tending, even as the duties of married life, to the training of the immortal spirit for Heaven, and its preparation for the full enjoyment of that Love which embraces all other love, and in which is to be found the perfection of happiness for which their young hearts are thirsting.

It sounds like an ideal—an imagination. It is so wholly unlike the world's theory, as regards the vocation of women. And facts and experience, it may be said, are against it. From the beginning of time women have always set marriage before them as the highest joy, the completion of their being. To the end of time they will continue to do so. What is the use of bringing before them the dreams of hermits and mystics, which not one in a hundred will ever be able to understand, and which if understood might unfit them for the duties they are called upon to fulfil?

Simply, because if this view of life, which makes marriage an accident instead of an end, is not true, then, with all reverence be it said, God has created a vast number of immortal beings without a purpose. He has given them feelings, affec-

tions, aspirations, power of enjoyment, but there is no object to satisfy these cravings. If the inhabitants of the earth could at this moment be paired, and each man could take his wife, there would still be a surplus of women. What were they made for? Why are they sentient, suffering beings? Far better were it to be stocks and stones, or even as the beasts that perish. Created for an object which is unattainable. Created merely to live and breathe—to eat and drink—to joy and grieve—to dream of a happiness which is never to be theirs—and then to die!

The very thought is blasphemy. The great Creator of the universe, the Author of all good, has not thus erred in His foresight. He has not thus failed in His calculations. If even a sparrow falls not to the ground without His permission, if there is a purpose in the creation of the tiniest insect that breathes out its life in an hour, then there must be an end and object for the creation of those many women, who, whether shut up in cloisters, or free to find their homes in the world at large, pass the term of their earthly probation without having met with a heart which shall answer to theirs; or who, having met with it, have not been able to enjoy the happiness of married life.

And that end and object must lie beyond the grave. There is "one event which happeneth alike to all," and when we wake up after it, it will be to find ourselves in a world where there is "neither marrying, nor giving in marriage." The destiny which awaits us *there*, is the destiny for which we are created, for which we are now preparing; a destiny independent of earthly happiness, untouched by the accident of marriage. And when a woman looks forward to this, when she makes this her object, the home for her thoughts, and the dream of her aspirations, her needs are satisfied. God has given her the knowledge of reality—the one awful, immutable, eternal, ever-blessed reality—life in His presence—in the consciousness of His love; and she is content to leave the "changes and chances" of this mortal existence in His hands; satisfied

that, whether married or unmarried, whether in the enjoyment of the highest human love, or of that which is only secondary, she will equally find the pathway to Him in whom alone is rest.

And then she is simple-minded.

It is a great grace—simplicity. The most worldly admire it, the most ardent followers of fashion strive after it; but none but the simple in heart attain it.

Simplicity is singleness, oneness of purpose and desire. That which mars simplicity is the fact of having two objects. If a woman, a young girl—for it is of such we are now speaking—desires but one thing, to fit herself, through God's grace, for Heaven, her whole life becomes simplified. Everything that happens is viewed with reference to this end, and judged accordingly. It may be love, it may be marriage, it may be a life without either; but in any case she has no wish except to place herself in God's Hands, to see His Will, and do it now, as she hopes one day to do it in Heaven. And with this simplicity of heart must naturally come simplicity of manner. Manner is only the mould into which the inner being casts itself. Quiet ease, freedom from affectation, absence of restraint in conversation, the natural expression of thoughts which are really thought—all so rare, but so indescribably winning to us when we see them united with the freshness and beauty of youth, are the natural result of a simple mind; a mind which has but one object. We sometimes perceive in persons both young and old, who are pleasing, graceful, courteous, and perhaps really amiable, and in a measure religious, the presence of something, not exactly put on, not exactly unreal, but which gives the impression of unreality, and which repels us. We are apt to call it worldliness; and perhaps we are right; but we might better grasp what we mean, if we called it two-mindedness. It is distinct from double-mindedness, for it is not the blending of two objects in one, but the endeavour to hold both together, to serve God and mammon. Such persons are never simple, and it is the want of simplicity which jars upon us.

It is quite true, indeed, that persons may be simple without being necessarily religious. Devotion to any one occupation or study, to the exclusion of all others, will tend to render the manners simple; but it will be an eccentric—probably, an uncourteous, awkward, simplicity—certainly not such as would be pleasing in the young. And the simplicity of which we are now especially speaking is that which regards a young girl's manners in society, and especially in her intercourse with men. Let her have two objects in view—one to do her duty to God, and be happy in Heaven; and the other to get married, and be happy on earth; and she will be in a perpetual state of effort to harmonize the two. She will be full of fears, and proprieties, and perplexities, thinking whether this is allowable, or that will be noticed; whether she has talked too loud or too fast; whether she has been agreeable or dull; whether she has expressed herself correctly or incorrectly. It may be all very sincere and real; but it will not be in the least simple, and, as a natural consequence, it will be far from pleasing. But let her sole object be to accept life as it is given her by God, and use it in the best way she can for His glory, and all this anxiety about propriety and effect will be at an end. Her womanly instinct will tell her what she may or what she may not do; there will be no self-consciousness or self-retrospection; and if she should by any accident transgress the precise limits which society has fixed for a young girl's behaviour, the mistake will be one which the most severe critic will hesitate to criticise. For there is a charm in *real* simplicity which it is quite impossible to withstand. We find it, in fact, so universally admitted, that every species of vanity and worldliness will endeavour to take its form, in order to render itself more attractive. The simple young lady in novels can never see or understand when a man is falling in love with her, though she draws him on by saying and doing things which would be absolutely impossible for true simplicity; since *that* never loses its common sense or its keenness of feminine instinct. So, again, the fast young lady in real life apes simplicity when she sets aside the re-

straints of society, and dresses, talks, and acts just as vanity or the spirit of bravado may suggest. But no one who has the slightest insight into character can really be deceived by any of these counterfeits. True simplicity is something so pure, so beautiful, so unearthly, that when once seen, nothing else can ever be mistaken for it. There is that in it which is *felt*, which cannot but be felt. It is, through God's blessing upon it, its own safeguard, and vice dares not approach it.

Persons sometimes ask, Is simplicity a gift? If not born with us, is it possible to attain it? It is, indeed, a gift, inasmuch as all good things come from God; but it is not a gift in the same sense as beauty or talent. If we will only live to God solely and heartily, it may become ours; for when we do thus live, the question what is to be our lot during the period of our probation becomes so secondary, that it ceases to disturb the mind, except when the question of some present interest is brought before it.

Again, all this will doubtless be thought imaginative, but facts do not become imagination because it is the custom to call them so. There is one touchstone which we may apply without difficulty to this, as to every other question that has respect to our earthly condition, and which we desire to see in its true light—the thought of death.

If marriage is the one object which the world makes it, then what becomes of that object at death?

It is essential for English girls, perhaps, above all others, to be taught to view this matter rightly. Common observation teaches us that the number of these who remain unmarried is increasing. It is useless here to pause and inquire why this should be; we are only called upon to accept the fact. The young girls whom we cherish and educate with such care and tenderness may very possibly, even very probably, not marry. It will be both wise and kind in us to prepare them for such a possibility, and to teach them to be happy and useful under it. And this can only be done by the tone of our con-

versation respecting life in general,—taking in love and marriage as its most important accidents.

Free sensible conversation of a general character does much more than lectures and advice in training a young mind. We may preach, with the wisdom of a philosopher and the earnestness of a saint, against the folly of thinking and dreaming of love; and the children will listen to us with ill-concealed impatience, and run back to their story books, and their fairy tales, and revel in visions of handsome young princes and beautiful princesses; act over again in their own minds all the scenes of romance and excitement; and count the days till they themselves are to be emancipated, and permitted to share in similar delights. Nature is much too strong to be controlled by lectures and advice. As a general rule, men and women were intended to marry, and therefore young people will always think about it. But truth, observation, experience, act as a counterpoise to the promptings of nature. If children are accustomed early to hear life spoken of as it really is, they will by degrees learn to look at it in a true way. Marriage, in fiction, is the end; in truth, it is the beginning of what may be called a woman's career. An unmarried life is, in fiction, a lot of sober sadness and regret, with no object and few duties, and which nothing but the spirit of resignation can make endurable. An unmarried life, in truth, may be (if people choose to make it so) a life of great usefulness, great interest, bringing to the mind a pleasant sense of independence and freedom, blessed with much inward peace, the very brightest hope, and the possession of a Love, the faintest breath of which is enough to make this troubled earth a paradise.

Still, girls will dream of love; and if their dreams are realized, their lives will indeed be blest. But to look upon marriage as so essential, that it is needful to rush into it, in order to avoid the supposed dreariness of a single life, is a mistake as fatal to goodness as it is to happiness.

What, however, will tend more than anything else to coun-

teract fiction, and to give a young girl a right view of the proportion which marriage really bears to the other events of life, is to bring her early into contact with men of a superior stamp, a good deal older than herself, who will take no notice of her, and only allow her to listen to their conversation. Elder brothers are a very great assistance in this matter. Doubtless, they will be likely to flirt and fall in love—probably they may marry; but matrimony is not the exclusive subject of their thoughts, as it too often is in the case of girls. Professional affairs, politics, local interests, all share, and, at times, engross their attention. Love is a good deal to them, but it is by no means everything. And not only brothers, but all men who have good sense, and pursuits or professions which interest them, will teach the same lesson. A girl who is thrown into the society of men at an early age, is much less likely to grow romantic and sentimental than one who is shut up in the schoolroom. She sees what it is which really occupies their thoughts; she learns to discriminate their characters; she perceives their faults, and hears their dispositions discussed, and so is the less likely to be led away by an ideal. Nothing is more dangerous than to bring up a young girl in perfect retirement, and then to throw her constantly into the society of any one man. Let him be who or what he may, she is nearly certain, in time, to make a romance about him. "Propinquity"—as Miss Edgeworth says in her novel of "The Absentee"—"Propinquity"—that is the danger. Throw people together exclusively, and they must fall in love. It may be a case of Beauty and the Beast, but the Beast is sure to gain the victory. But bring a girl of fifteen or sixteen into the society of a number of gentlemen, and she is so occupied and amused in thinking about them all, that she has not leisure to fix her thoughts exclusively upon any one. And seeing them together, she will judge of them truly. They will talk to each other as they would not talk if separated and thrown singly into the society of women. When men meet one another, the pretty nothings which turn a young girl's head are, for the

most part, forgotten. They become interested in other things. They prefer business to play, and the young lady is put in the background. It is rather an unpleasant experience for youthful vanity, but it is a very useful one; and if it can be given early, it will not really be mortifying. At fifteen it is natural to be overlooked; and when a young girl has learnt that half the gentlemen she sees think nothing about her, and of the other half not above one in fifty is likely to fall in love with her, she moves about amongst them with a simple ease and freedom from vanity and affectation, which saves her from unnumbered vexations, and is in itself a grace that no effort could acquire.

Where there is great beauty, this ease and simplicity no doubt become more difficult of attainment, because beauty is in itself so attractive that even grave politicians and philosophers are more or less fascinated with it. But great beauty is very rare. The vainest persons are those who have only a moderate share, and have set their hearts upon making the most of it. A little wholesome neglect is for them most beneficial. Where there is real beauty—beauty which cannot be questioned—it is perhaps better, as has previously been said, to acknowledge the fact, just as riches or talent may be acknowledged, and then estimate the gift at its real value. After all, what a woman really cares for, if she is worth anything, is genuine affection for herself. As she loathes the man who worships her for her riches, and grows weary of him who cares only for her talent; so she despises him who is the slave of her beauty. There may be an intoxicating excitement in the first adulation of the world, but it is very transient, and the heart sickens when it is over, and in the dreariness of reaction a most salutary lesson is learnt. Regular beauty is in fact by no means so great a snare as that insensible fascination, which in some cases is exercised over all persons; and which makes its possessor the flattered pet of her friends and companions, as well as the idol of society.

But all this endeavour to keep girls simple, and to make

them take a true view of life, its happiness, and its temptations, must, it may be thought, be neutralized by the teaching they receive from books. It is under this idea that novels are in general carefully excluded from the schoolroom; and the exclusion is, up to a certain point, very desirable. But to suppose that a tale of love will do more harm at thirteen or fourteen than it does at eighteen, appears upon examination to be a mistake.

In what does the harm of novels consist?

First—above all, in the untrue view which they afford of life, giving it but one object, one prize, and staking the whole of a woman's happiness upon this.

That is a harm which is certainly likely to be felt more at the age of eighteen than at thirteen, for the immediate interests of a girl of thirteen lie before her, in the schoolroom, amongst her young companions. She gazes into the future, as men and women gaze into Eternity; and lives for it, even as men and women live for Eternity; owning its existence, dreaming of it, thinking themselves influenced by it, and then turning away to seize upon some passing joy, and find an absorbing interest in hopes which wither as they are grasped.

But, secondly, the harm of novels is to be found in the excitement of the imagination; so that not only life as a whole is viewed untruly, but the present position and circumstances of the reader are, in her own eyes, idealized. She becomes her own heroine, acts her own scenes, in her own home; converts the persons about her into characters of romance; and by so doing blinds herself to the real world, its homely duties, and demands for self-sacrifice and self-restraint. But here, again, the danger is greater for eighteen than for thirteen. The child of thirteen has lessons and regular work to do; she is compelled to attend to them, and there is nothing in French and German exercises to encourage day-dreams. But the young lady of eighteen is emancipated from all this routine; her time is at her own disposal, and everything about her tends to foster instead of to check her imagination. There are per-

sons standing near ready to be invested with imaginary charms. There are incidents daily occurring, which may be the germs of the event which is to change the current of her life. The child of thirteen knows that to fall in love is an absurdity; the young lady of eighteen thinks that it is her special privilege—almost her duty. And if novels have been kept from her up to this precise moment; and then, emancipated from the school-room, she is allowed to enjoy them for the first time, at the very season when she is able to convert them into realities; can we wonder if the excitement should be too great for her good sense, and she should plunge into a course of novel reading, throw up every attempt at continuing her studies, and so lose, in vanity and nothingness, the most valuable portion of her life?

The question is not whether novels are, in themselves, desirable for the mind. We cannot exclude them from the literature of the day; and if we could do so, we should effect no good; for imagination is a faculty bestowed upon us by God, and it requires to be fed, just as much as any other faculty. Novels are not what they ought to be; but so, no literature, be it poetry, history, philosophy, or science, is, in all things, what it ought to be. We must, in this world, accept that which is given us, and make the best choice we can from it. Novels will be written, and they will be read. The point for us to decide is, at what age, and under what limitations, such reading shall be permitted.

Now, it will probably startle many persons to hear it said that a girl of twelve or thirteen may not only with comparative safety read a novel judiciously chosen; but, further, that novels, generally, will do less harm than they otherwise would, if the mind is accustomed to them early.

The assertion is made with hesitation, and is to be received with much caution. But the previous observations may, it is hoped, have tended to show what is meant. A child reads a novel as she reads a fairy tale. The world described is an unreality, so are the persons described in it. They all live in

imagination. They are not brought down to inhabit her own earth; and it is only when they are thus transplanted that they can really affect her moral nature. And when she has once become accustomed to the excitement of fiction, that excitement lessens. The interest in a measure palls, and instead of looking forward to being permitted to read novels as the greatest delight in store for her, she begins to feel that there may be a pleasure higher and more lasting in truth. If this conviction can be attained before the age when the imagination is likely to be excited by society and the temptations of the world, it is certainly a great gain.

On the other hand, there is, no doubt, a serious risk. If novels are allowed too early, the taste may be so vitiated that there may be no appetite for any food less stimulating. This is the reason why such books are looked upon with suspicion.

But the exaggeration of a truth does not neutralize the truth itself. The danger here alluded to will be found to attend *all* works of fiction. If read constantly, to the exclusion of every other kind of literature, they will all equally vitiate the taste. But it is not the admission of the element of love which does the mischief. There is a fashion in all these matters. People adopt certain codes of laws,—without taking the trouble to inquire why,—merely because others adopt them. It is supposed that a book which treats of young people may be safely read by young people, though there may be precisely the same ingredients in it as those written expressly for their elders. A book which describes little girls and boys as flirting is still a "young book," and therefore admitted into the schoolroom; but a book which describes the devotion of the heart, belonging to more advanced years, is not safe, and must be excluded. So again, half the children in England would be permitted to read such books as "The Wide, Wide World," and "Queechy," in which fascinatingly simple little girls of ten or twelve are petted and caressed by respectable gentlemen of five-and-twenty or thirty, who afterwards take the form of

lovers, and marry them. No one calls these books novels, and yet they are novels, just as strictly as the most exciting love story to be procured from a circulating library. And what is more, they are much more likely to do injury to a child's mind. To suggest to a little girl that the kind friend who is petting her, perhaps for her parents' sake, may some day turn out a hero of romance, and ask her to be his wife, is certainly more injurious to her simplicity than to put before her a picture of what may occur at some far-off day between herself and an individual absolutely unknown. And in like manner, to interrupt the unconscious freedom of intercourse between young boys and girls of fifteen and sixteen by thoughts of incipient rivalry and jealousy, has a much worse effect upon their minds than to let them know that such temptations may meet them in after years:—to say nothing of the untruthfulness of these representations, since, as a general rule, girls of sixteen cordially dislike boys of their own age; and boys of sixteen, if they have any hearts to lose, part with them to women of five-and-twenty.

It cannot then, strictly speaking, be the introduction of love into works of fiction, which we dread, for, if so, we must weed our schoolroom libraries of half their favourite authors. Neither can it be fiction altogether; for then we must deny the existence of the imaginative faculty, and the duty of providing food for it. The fact, perhaps, is, that we really do not know what we dread, or why we dread it. We have bought our opinions ready made, and they serve our purpose, we think, just as well as if we had formed them for ourselves. But there is a curious tendency in society to work itself out of these ready-made opinions; or, at least, to test them, and throw aside those which are really valueless. It may be seen, with regard to the present subject, in the common exception to the ban placed upon novels, in the case of Sir Walter Scott's writings. Almost all children are allowed to read the Waverley novels, and it may perhaps safely be asserted that no child was ever the worse for that reading.

Why is this? They are highly imaginative, intensely exciting, not always refined in the language put into the mouths of the different characters, and the plot of the story always turns upon love. Nearly all the objections brought against novels in general, might, in fact, be brought against Sir Walter Scott's. Nearly all—but not all. There is one great exception. They are true—true to nature. They represent life as it is, or as it has been, or may be. They place the interest of life in those things which really do form its interest; love being one ingredient, a very important one, but by no means to the exclusion of others. What is commonly said of Sir Walter Scott, that he always makes his heroes and heroines secondary, constitutes in fact the great charm of his books, because, in it, is to be found their truth. And it is this element of truth which renders them safe; it is this which we feel unconsciously; and, as a general rule, it may be said that any book in which the same element is found, may, without hesitation, be placed in the hands of a child, whether the plot of the story turns upon the little excitements of the schoolroom, or the great excitements of love and marriage.

For where there is such a love of truth, such a perception of it, there will also be a nobleness and purity in the mind of the author, which must tell upon that of his readers. Vice is only alluring when seen through a veil. No one who desires to look at it as it is, can make it attractive in description. Whatever Sir Walter Scott touches, into whatever scenes he introduces his readers, the purity of the author's mind is felt throughout. It is with him, as with Shakespeare: the expressions which may be found fault with are merely characteristic words—not vehicles for the writer's thoughts and feelings; and it is these alone which have an influence for evil.

But Sir Walter Scott's tales are not the only books of the kind which may be used with the view of accustoming children's minds to novels, without injuring their taste, or corrupting their principles. Historical stories, as a rule, are safer than others, because the interest is divided between love, and

stirring events which have really taken place. But even amongst regular novels, there are some—such for instance as Mrs. Gaskell's "North and South," or "Sylvia's Lovers"—which will be found to be equally innocuous. In the former, the interest of the love is entirely subservient to the development of character, and to the marked peculiarities of the people of the manufacturing districts; and in the other, it is carried on beyond marriage, and shown in its effects upon the whole course of life. The mind and taste of a girl of thirteen will be raised to a higher standard by reading books of this stamp, when she does read fiction, than by spending her time upon the first efforts at composition of girls but a few years older than herself, although the incidents they relate may be of the most perfectly harmless description. And when the mind has once learnt to appreciate a good novel, it will turn with dislike from anything that is bad; not merely bad in the sense of being wrong, but bad in style and taste; and this is a great safeguard. So few novels are really worth anything, that if a correct and pure taste has been early formed, it will be impossible for the mind, when left to its own choice, to find its whole satisfaction in the contents of a circulating library.

But perhaps the greatest of all checks to the dangers of exciting fiction will be found in reading it aloud. An inferior novel will not bear this test; but to read a good novel—"Ivanhoe," or "Kenilworth," for instance—to a party of children is delightful. And there is no danger, then, of their becoming engrossed by it to the exclusion of study; or being tempted to deceit in the enjoyment of a forbidden pleasure. And, after all, these are some of the greatest evils which an early acquaintance with novels is likely to bring with it. Everything done or said against the warnings of conscience (supposing, of course, that conscience is not morbid) becomes a sin, though in itself the act or the word may be innocent. As St. Paul tells us, "He that doubteth is condemned, ... for whatsoever is not of faith is sin." [1]

[1] Rom. xiv. 23.

A story read aloud is also a test of the characters of those who listen to it. More insight into children's dispositions may be gained in seasons of recreation, by the knowledge of their favourite heroes and heroines, and the criticisms passed upon their conduct, than by the most careful observation made during the hours of study. And it is, besides—and this is very important—a bond of sympathy between the reader and the listeners. There are comparatively few pleasures in which the old and young can fully sympathize; and it is most important, therefore, to seize upon the enjoyment of reading, and to connect with it all that pleasant interchange of thought, and unity of feeling, which tends so strongly to bind human hearts together.

Reading aloud has another advantage. It gives the power of weeding the book of passages which are objectionable—a process of some difficulty, but which requires no concealment. Children are quite prepared for it, and if they have the slightest sense of honour, they will never look into a book afterwards to see what has been omitted—so long, that is, as they are plainly told that, as a general rule, there will be omissions. It is only what they suspect that they are tempted to search into. There are many portions of Dickens's works which may be read in this way, and, indeed, this is probably the best opportunity for becoming acquainted with them. At the rate at which the literature of the present day is proceeding, no writer of fiction can expect his works to be universally read for more than four or five years. At the expiration of that period his first productions will be considered in a measure obsolete.

But even if good novels cannot be read aloud, they should always be read openly, and discussed freely. There may be portions, as in the case of the Waverley novels, which it may be necessary to omit when reading aloud; but children, in reading to themselves, are so carried on by the interest of the tale that they do not pause to dwell upon particular passages; and even incidents which we should dislike to bring before them ourselves, will be passed over with only a half-comprehension;

and if there is no mystery made about them in conversation, they will cease to dwell upon their minds.

Mystery, hints, whispers—those are the things which mar a child's simplicity; for mystery implies that what is attempted to be hidden is, in fact, partially revealed; and when a part is seen, the wish to discover the whole is awakened. Whatever is read through, or spoken of without hesitation, does comparatively little mischief; and if, in reading aloud, awkward passages are stumbled upon unexpectedly, it is far better to go through them boldly, than to show the least aversion to them.

What has now been said is, of course, open to much misconstruction. It may be interpreted to mean that novels are recommended as desirable in general for children of thirteen and fourteen; that they need not necessarily be unobjectionable; and that it is better to treat the evil contained in them boldly, than to attempt to shun it. These assertions would possess a fair semblance of truth, and, as a general rule, it is a vain and hopeless task to attempt to guard against misconstruction. The most carefully guarded expressions—the most exact words—will not save writers from it; and it is wise, therefore, to be indifferent to it, or at least to accept it as part of life's discipline. But the present subject is one of such importance, that, at the risk of tediousness, it may be well to repeat more clearly, and condense into few words, the opinion which has really here been expressed.

Novels are *not* recommended as general reading for very young persons; but it is thought that a good novel—good in style and pure in principle, and in which the interest is not wholly concentrated on love—may *occasionally* be read aloud to children quite safely, and with advantage, as accustoming them to a class of books which would be injuriously exciting if they were first given to them at the period of their introduction to the amusements and freedom of after-life. It is also thought that children may safely be allowed, from time to time, to read novels of this superior kind to themselves, so long as they are encouraged to talk about them freely.

It is a short conclusion, arrived at after many words. But the theory and the practice of education are upon these points so greatly at variance, that it has been necessary to enter fully into the subject, in order to see how the difference has arisen; and, if possible, to discover its cause, and the mode by which such theory and practice may be made to agree. Parents and governesses inveigh against novels, and yet children read them: and in this there is a great evil; much greater to both parties than would naturally result from the actual fact. If we believe that we are doing an injury to children by allowing them to read a novel, then, at whatever cost, we are bound to forbid the enjoyment. We can never justify ourselves to our consciences, or to God, by saying that "we do not know how to prevent it; it is a kind of fashion, and the children would be dissatisfied if they were forbidden to do what their companions do."

There is in this case, as in so many others, a difficulty. We slur it over, and think that by so doing we have escaped it. But there is no way of escaping a difficulty except by facing it. If, in doing so, we are compelled to give up part or a whole of some favourite and generally received theory, we shall still be wiser, happier, and better, than by admitting it, in order to agree in words with the serious, thinking portion of our fellow-creatures; and acting against it, in order to make ourselves friends with those who laugh all such caution to scorn. It will be well for us, then, to ponder the question carefully, to make our rules with reference to the characters of the children whom we have in charge, and to keep to them; especially bearing in mind that the selection of books is most important, and that it is essential to accustom children early to restrictions with regard to them; whilst, in reference to one style of literature—if it may be dignified by the name—*newspapers*, we are only safe by actually forbidding them. Extracts may be read aloud often very usefully; but if the paper itself is put into a girl's hands, she is almost certain to

stumble upon scenes and facts which taint the purity of the mind, and excite a morbid and evil curiosity.

And now, it may be thought, having considered the preliminaries—the stepping stones—which lead to that point at which a young girl may be likely to be thrown into general society—to fall in love, and to marry—it may be thought that the next subject would naturally be the circumstances and conditions under which an engagement may be formed. But the idea of offering an opinion upon such a subject as this is really absurd. The course of a comet may be predicted; but the course of love can no more be foreseen, than its cause can be assigned. If we are true, disinterested, and bent upon seeking God's will, we shall act rightly in these matters; and if we are not, no counsel will be of any use to us. And if children have been brought up in habits of purity, simplicity, candour, obedience, and reverence for all that is good and noble, they will, as women, judge better for themselves, in all questions in which their affections are concerned, than any one can judge for them.

We may lay down the wisest, or apparently the wisest, laws for ourselves, making the strongest resolutions against some particular course of action which seems to us undesirable; but we shall almost certainly find that sooner or later we are compelled to adopt it. It seems to be God's constant lesson to us, not to attempt to be our own Providence, or take the direction of our own lives, or the lives of others, into our own hands; but simply to accept it, as it is marked out by Him, and to do with it that which is most in accordance with His law.

In France, parents arrange marriages for their children themselves. We cry out against the custom, for we suppose that a *mariage de convenance* can never be a *mariage d'amour*. This, however, does not seem to be a necessary, though it may be a frequent sequence; and if the results of the system appear to us unsatisfactory, yet the system itself has at least this advantage, that it is a perfectly open and acknowledged mode

of proceeding. The most honourable and conscientious persons adopt it.

In England, the same thing is often done surreptitiously, under false pretences, because it is supposed that marriage ought always to be a question of free choice; and the effect is degradation of character and principle to all concerned in it. Here, again, we have a theory of one kind and a practice of another, and in consequence deceit and unreality. Upon the natural theory—that theory which supposes that children in a nursery are angels of modesty, that little girls are models of simplicity, and young ladies perfect in refinement and delicacy—it is also presumed that no heart is ever won unsought; and that no young girl ever thinks that an offer is going to be made her until it is made. This is the easiest theory possible; it leaves everything to take its course without any anxiety, any forethought. Parents have nothing to do but to enjoy their children's society as long as they can, to invite to their house whomsoever they like, to let young people be together just as circumstances may point out. Everything is certain to go right. A well brought up English girl can never oppose her parents' wishes. If an offer should be made her by some one considered ineligible, it will be sufficient to say that he is not approved, and she will of course reject him. She cannot love him—for upon the natural theory that is not proper!

And so it is that hearts are sacrificed—that the happiness of life is wrecked.

French parents expect their daughter to marry a man whom, perhaps, she does not actually love, but whose character, circumstances, and position are, they believe, likely eventually to ensure her happiness. English parents throw their child into daily association with a man who, from poverty, or ill-health, or from other causes, cannot give her the prospect of a happy home; and then, when she has become attached to him, and an offer of marriage is made, turn round and express their extreme surprise, possibly their indignation, and pronounce the sentence of separation for ever.

Surely a theory which produces such results as these, must be wrong! It may be—it is—utterly odious to plan and manœuvre for a wealthy marriage, or one of rank, or, in fact, for any marriage at all; but to say that we are therefore at liberty to risk a young girl's happiness, by never taking thought about marriage, is far worse than foolish—it is cruel.

If she is penniless, and we dread her marrying a poor man, we are bound not to encourage the visits and the attentions of those that are poor. If we know the secret history of any individual, and feel sure that his character is objectionable, we are bound to keep him at a distance. If we see symptoms of an incipient attachment, we are bound at once to make inquiries, and to assure ourselves that should it come to a question of an offer of marriage, there would be no reason to withhold our consent.

These precautions are simply the dictates of kindness and common sense. We may stop affection in the germ, and do no harm; but in attempting to destroy it, when it has once taken root in the heart, we risk the destruction of the hopes of a life.

But if, negatively, we may so far interfere in questions of marriage; positively, we must not. French customs in these matters are sometimes adduced as in a measure sanctioning, or at least affording a parallel to the manœuvring of fashionable mothers in England; but no one who has ever known what the arrangements for a good French marriage really are, would ever think of making such a comparison. It is one thing for parents and friends to consult together beforehand, and, with the gentleman's consent, to agree to give the parties concerned an opportunity for knowing each other, and becoming really attached, which is the French custom; and quite another to act without any such arrangement, and merely from worldly ambition, to throw a young girl into a position in which, it is true, she may attract the person it is wished she should marry, but, on the other hand, in which she very probable may not. The one is a *bonâ fide*, open agreement, in

which the wishes of the parties principally concerned are consulted; the other is a mean, degrading speculation, involving the almost certain loss of happiness—and on the lady's side, the violation of every feeling of dignity and self-respect.

And even where there is no personal interest concerned, to meddle in questions of marriage by bringing persons together, and striving to give them favourable impressions of each other, is a most dangerous playing with edged tools.

Supposing that by our efforts we can on one side awaken affection, yet there is the risk that obstacles to marriage may be interposed; and then the misery which will follow must be laid at our door. Marriages, the proverb says, are made in Heaven. People smile, and ask, whether this can be so, since so many are unhappy? But that an event is ordered by God, which is the graver meaning of the saying, does not necessarily imply that it is made for present happiness.

The events of life, among which marriage holds the foremost place, are not only sources of joy, but also of probation and discipline. And when a young girl marries, God takes her education out of our hands, and places it in those of another. To Him we must leave the choice who that other shall be. We have but a negative voice allowed us; and even that only up to a certain point.

If we allow foolish intimacies which end in a foolish marriage, we are answerable for the misery of that marriage, because we could have foreseen, and ought to have prevented it. If, on the other hand, we try to bring about a marriage, we are equally answerable for its results, or for the unhappiness which disappointment may cause.

All that we can do is to give young girls a high standard for their judgment of men; to introduce them, as early as possible, into the society of those who are really superior; to guard them from constant intercourse with any whom we know it would be unwise or impossible for them to marry;—and then to leave the event to God.

CHAPTER XXIV.

FRIENDSHIP.

BUT suppose a young girl does not marry; suppose—which is by no means so rare a case as some persons imagine—that she does not make marriage her ideal of happiness; that she is contented with a happy home, and useful occupations, and is not always dreaming of her wedding day, or thinking that every gentleman who speaks to her is going to fall in love with her; is she, therefore, likely to escape the sorrows, trials, and disappointments connected with the exercise of the affections? Is friendship perfectly safe, whilst love is proverbially unsafe? The home history of half the families in England would probably compel an answer in the negative.

Who has not known more or less of the evils of an exaggerated or unwise friendship? evils which crept on so stealthily, the germs of which were so slight, that it might have seemed almost impossible to discover or check them. Jealousies, suspicions, unwarrantable influence, neglect of home duties, perhaps ultimate estrangement from home relations—all to be traced to some unfortunate friendship!

And looking at these things, mothers dread their children's friendships with cause; and yet, if young people have no friendships and do not marry, their lives will be desolate.

It is the mother's dream that she is to be sufficient for her children's happiness. She forgets that they are not sufficient for hers. What we all need is companionship of our own age, whatever that age may be. The child, living amongst grown-

up persons, pines for the society of children; the parent or the governess, living amongst children, pines for the comprehension and sympathy of those of her own standing. And therefore the mother's dream, based upon an expectation contrary to nature, is constantly doomed to disappointment; and, what is far more important, it acts, as all unfounded expectations must act, injuriously upon both the parties concerned. It makes the mother unreasonable and exacting, and the child ungrateful and irritable.

When a mother parts with her daughter in marriage, she is, to a certain degree, prepared for and resigned to the knowledge that she must thenceforth hold but a secondary place in her affections. It is the law of nature, and she receives somewhat of an equivalent for the sacrifice she makes, in the sense of having secured a safe position and protection for her child for life. But when she awakens to the fact that, without any such claim from nature, and without having any such equivalent, her daughter's affections are withdrawn from her, and that the confidence and sympathy, which have hitherto been hers, are bestowed upon some female friend, perhaps a recent acquaintance, perhaps personally distasteful, there does arise a very strong sense of ingratitude—a very strong inclination to look at the friendship in the worst light, and at once to interfere and put a stop to it. She may try to conceal the feeling, but it will show itself; and the moment it is discovered, the daughter becomes restrained in manner, probably in words; the mother is more annoyed, and shows her annoyance; the daughter resents the irritation, and is irritable herself; and so, by mntual reaction, the breach widens, until it can never be healed. If the daughter gives up her friend, in her secret heart she accuses the mother of having made her wretched; and if she does not give her up, the jars, and jealousies, and suspicions which are engendered, make life a torment.

Now, all this might often be avoided if mothers would only, at the very outset, recognize the fact, which must sooner or later be forced upon them, that there is a period in the lives of

all young people when their strongest affections will have a tendency to centre themselves on some one out of the family circle.

The romance of almost every young girl's nature is first drawn forth by some companion or friend; and in these cases a little play of excitement and sorrow, jealousy and exactingness, often goes on, which is, for the time being, as absorbing to the parties concerned, and as provoking to the bystanders, as any of the true lovers' quarrels, which are commonly accepted as only making love more precious.

Some girls, who have no great depth of character, have a succession of these romances: others are true to one. But there are many of a graver character, who expend their feelings upon some persons older than themselves, whom they invest with all imaginary virtues, and from whom they seek advice upon subjects—especially those connected with religion—which they have never had the courage to mention to any one else. This latter phase of romantic friendship is often more trying to a mother than any other, because it trenches especially upon her own peculiar province. She considers herself, and very naturally, her child's best adviser; and it is extremely hard to see her counsel set aside for that of a new friend, or followed only in compliance with this friend's request. There is nothing to be said about all this, except that it is human nature; and as we cannot alter nature, we shall do wisely in adapting ourselves to it.

The love of relations is one form of natural affection, the love of friends another. The Bible recognizes both, and puts each in its true place, so that they may not interfere with one another. The tie of choice is the more exciting: the love of Jonathan for David "was wonderful, passing the love of women;" [1] but the tie of nature is the more enduring. Joseph's love for Benjamin survived long years of separation and exile. To say that a brother or a sister is a friend, is to state what is considered a thing of course. To say that a friend is as a

[1] 2 Sam. i. 26.

brother or a sister, is to describe friendship of the most lasting character. When our Blessed Redeemer called His disciples His friends, He exalted them to the dignity and the privilege of angels. When He said, "Go to My brethren, and say unto them, I ascend unto My Father and your Father,"[1] He raised them above angels, for He acknowledged them as partakers of His own Nature.

That the ties of relationship are very frequently severed, and that when severed they are more difficult to reunite than any others, does not, in the least, militate against their being intended by nature to be the strongest of all. The tendency of nature is never to be judged by its failures; and the very fact that "a brother offended is harder to be won than a strong city,"[2] shows how strong must have been that original principle of union which, when once lost, it is so almost impossible to restore. And, if we would only have faith in the strength of these natural ties, these bonds which God himself has formed, we should be less suspicious of those which seem the result of choice. Being less suspicious, we should be more sympathizing, and with the presence of sympathy in relations, a large portion of the dangers of friendship would be avoided.

Jealousy is the very cankerworm of love in every form, and no mother need be jealous of her child's love, if she will only act wisely. When a daughter can go to her mother, and speak openly of the affection she feels for another person, be that person young or old, there is little to be feared from the friendship. And young girls will do this most willingly if they are sure that their confidence will meet with encouragement. It is the perception of jealousy which causes reserve. And though the excitement and romance of affection will go to the friend for a time; yet in such a case, almost certainly it will revert to the mother afterwards. The fact of finding in her mother a person who can understand young feelings and young pleasures touches a daughter's heart deeply; whilst good sense and experience must ultimately teach her what the value

[1] St. John xx. 17. [2] Prov. xviii. 19.

of that love is, which is independent of her own faults, or of the accidents of life; and she will then look to her mother as her friend all the more trustingly, because, under her sanction, she has tried another friendship, and known its trials and its precariousness.

And this necessity of sympathy with friendship as a safeguard against its risks, is applicable equally to those trying cases in which young persons turn from their own natural advisers, and desire to be guided by some person out of their own family. There is no question that such extraneous influence may be injurious; but if, foreseeing the possibility of it, we have allowed it to grow up without check, we are bound to be merciful to it. Romantic and overweening friendships between governesses and pupils are often found to be objectionable; but instead of checking them at the outset, when the task would be easy, they are frequently allowed to go on, because there seems nothing tangible to complain of; and when the mischief has reached its height, some sudden severance is effected. But it is too late then to repair the evil. The influence has done its work; and it may, perhaps, take years before it can be undone. Undue influence and exaggerated friendship are things to be watched and guarded against carefully, but they can only be uprooted in their germ. When once they have been established, our wisest plan is to recognize them, and try to neutralize them by sympathy.

And if, as will frequently happen, the influence exerted should be that of a really kind and wise friend—one who sincerely wishes to give safe counsel—then, however greatly it may jar upon our self-love, or disappoint our dreams of exclusive affection, we cannot do better than to suffer it to take its course, and, even more, to encourage it. By encouraging, we make the influence, as it were, our own. The daughter who leans upon her mother's friend, does in fact lean upon the mother herself, and by degrees she will see this; and then the natural tie will be felt to strengthen and hallow the friendship, and so by degrees influence will return to its natural channel.

Show anything like jealousy, and such a possibility is at an end.

But it will perhaps be said, all these things are questions of feeling. We cannot frame laws for affection. Persons will love each other according to their own fancies, and not according to relationship. And after all, what is the need of laying so much stress upon natural ties? Why may not a friend be dearer than a brother or a sister? Why may not a guide out of one's own family be more reverenced than one in it? Now, this is misstating the case. We cannot frame laws for affection. Nothing is more true. We may love a friend more than a sister, and reverence some person out of our family more than any one in it. And if friendship never went beyond the expression of this feeling, we might have cause to lament it, but no cause to blame. Even when young persons, or persons of any age, belonging to different families, have formed so devoted a friendship that they cannot be happy apart, it is still only a misfortune. Circumstances do not generally allow of individuals separating themselves from their relations, and forming a home apart; and because of this, such exclusive affection awakens, in most cases, a tantalizing, dissatisfied feeling, and is likely to produce more unhappiness than happiness; and therefore it is to be guarded against, though it may not be condemned. But when romantic friendship puts itself forward as having a claim above those ties which God has formed by nature, it becomes the source of untold misery to all who are connected with it.

And this is, of course, its tendency. Overpowering feeling of any kind naturally claims to be its own law, in opposition to the definite laws of God. It is the Dictator to which for the time all must submit. And in the case of affection, this assumption cuts the Gordian knot of so many difficulties, that it is not unfrequently adopted by friendship, as well as by love; and persons will neglect the plainest, most paramount duties of their homes, for the sake of some self-chosen friend, and think themselves justified, because the feeling on both sides is so

strong that it would be cruel to expect a different course of action. Now, such a delusion as this cannot, without great difficulty, be mastered, when feeling has long been allowed to hold dominion over reason and principle. And because, in some form or other, more or less exaggerated, it is likely to meet us continually in life, it may be well to inquire more closely into the mental training which is required so to keep affection in its proper place, that it may never claim an unlawful authority. For it is mental, quite as much as moral, training which is needed. The error alluded to is owing to a confusion of ideas as to the relative claims of natural and self-chosen relationship—taking that word in its extended sense, as including the relations into which we enter with all persons in the intercourse of life. These claims, like those of law, are binding in different degrees; but the first paramount claim of all is intended by God to be that of blood. In order to confirm this assertion, we need only remark the fact that civil law, which is based upon natural law, is not at liberty to recognize any other claim. If two persons were to go into a court of justice, and one were to rest his title to an estate upon distant kinship, whilst the plea of the other was that of devoted friendship, the latter would be considered a madman. And society recognizes the same imperative claim. The first question which is asked when a man leaves his money to a friend is: Had he any relations? And if it should be proved that he had, although the relations may be distant and unknown, and the friend very dear, yet there will always arise a certain sense of injustice; possibly not well founded, for the claims of blood may be diminished till they become scarcely recognizable; and the claims of friendship, on the other hand, may be of a very overwhelming character;—but the mere fact that it is possible to argue upon the question, whether a man who leaves his fortune to his dear friend, ought not rather to have chosen as his heir his third or fourth cousin, whom he has never seen, shows what the feeling of society, founded upon the laws of nature, is, as to the permanent claim of ties of blood.

And if we look to the Bible, we shall find this claim of blood everywhere clearly acknowledged and displayed. Abram's appeal to Lot is, "Let there be no strife, I pray thee, between me and thee, and between my herdmen and thy herdmen; for we be brethren."[1] Joseph forgives his brethren with a freedom from reproach which would have been almost impossible if they had been only friends. Very grievous as was the wrong which had been done to him, yet the yearning for the restoration of the tie of blood was so great, that it overcame the sense of injury; and every one in reading the story accepts this feeling as natural.

The laws which Moses framed for the Jews under the sanction of God, are all founded upon the recognition of the same tie. The instances are too numerous to require quotation. So also David, after the rebellion of Absalom, reproaches his relations, his brethren of the house of Judah, that they had overlooked this tie: "Ye are my brethren, ye are my bones and my flesh: wherefore then are ye the last to bring back the king?"[2] And, inspired by the Holy Spirit, he devotes a special psalm to the description of the blessings which rest upon brethren who observe it, and who "dwell together in unity."[3]

And when we turn to the New Testament, we shall find that the family relationship is considered so sacred, that it is adopted as the exclusive symbol of the more solemn and lasting tie which exists between those who are admitted into the family of Christ. "Brethren" is the one title applied to Christians viewed in their relation to each other. "Brother goeth to law with brother,"[4] is the stern reproof of St. Paul. And the duties of brethren include the exercise of a forbearance, courtesy, and sympathy, to be exhibited at all times, and under all circumstances; and leaving no room for questions of choice or varying feeling, such as might arise in the case of friends. Brothers are brothers always, and so also are Christians.

[1] Gen. xiii. 8. [2] 2 Sam. xix. 12.
[3] Psa. cxxxiii. [4] 1 Cor. vi. 6.

And why should all this be said? No one will dispute it.

Very true. But almost every one will, when the occasion offers itself, act against it.

In fact, we make the very strength of the claim a plea for disregarding it. Because we know that the tie between brothers and sisters cannot, in one sense, be broken; too often we venture to play with it and weaken it. Children are allowed to do this in the nursery. They tease each other as they would never tease their playfellows. They are rude to each other when they would be ashamed of being so to strangers. Boys tyrannize over girls, and girls are fretful and aggravating with boys; and no one thinks it of much consequence. Brothers and sisters, it is said, always quarrel, and things will come right by and by, when the children are older! Perhaps it may be so. There is a very wonderful tenacity of existence in these family ties. It would seem sometimes as if no rough usage could really destroy them; but the "threefold cord," which cannot be violently broken, may be untwisted; and the hand which untwists will often unknowingly be that of a friend. When the gentleness, consideration, and unselfishness, which are rightfully the due of a brother or sister, are bestowed upon a friend, there springs up a sense of injustice. Upon this will follow unkind thoughts and reproachful words, and then will come alienation of heart. And if children are not taught from their infancy to recognize the fact that these family ties have a paramount claim, they will almost necessarily fail to perceive its truth; or if they do perceive it, they will almost as certainly reason themselves out of it. Personal feeling, similarity of tastes, the mere romance of friendship, are all so many apparent counterbalancing claims to those of family relationship. And the self-denial which is required to act in opposition to them is great, and few will attempt to practise it. Doubtless, it is the fact of the estrangement of the affections from home relations, which is the real grievance in the case of exaggerated friendship; but this estrangement is almost always accompanied by little neglects,

forgetfulnesses, want of accustomed sympathy, trifling acts of selfishness, which awaken and aggravate the incipient jealousy; and which would have been guarded against if a due consideration for home ties had been enforced from infancy.

People so little imagine the mischief they are doing—the seeds of future discord which they are sowing—by allowing their children to behave uncourteously to one another. Family life, in its great unreserve and familiarity, must always be a trial to the infirmity of human nature. Politeness, deference, and mutual respect, which constitute the police of society, and, upon the whole, manage to keep the peace well, are equally required in private life. And the family, it must be remembered, is the training school for the world. The brother who is taught to be courteous to his little sister in the nursery, will be considerate to her when he is a man. The sister who habitually regards her sister's feelings in childhood, will not disregard them in later years.

Family feeling may, indeed, like everything else, be exaggerated. It may become prejudice and exclusiveness, but its fundamental principle is a right one; and as it is unquestionably one of the great safeguards of social order, so it will always be found to be the mainspring of right action in private life.

In many cases the claim of relationship is, indeed, the only guide we have in the perplexity of conflicting duties. God has stamped the seal of His approval on it. He has made an offence against a brother far more deadly than an offence against a friend. Nature, society, declare it to be so; and the Bible proclaims it in every page. The sin which may and must separate friends, because it destroys the respect and affection which formed the bond of friendship, may not separate the members of a family. It must be acknowledged and lamented, but it does not justify alienation. And the personal offence which we should rightfully resent in the one case, must be overlooked in the other. It is almost impossible to overstate the importance of inculcating this primary principle upon children; for the events of life will try its strength to the very

utmost. The most fatal of all heirlooms is the inheritance of a family quarrel; and yet no one can avoid the differences of opinion which may lead to it; and nothing but the deepest sense of the sacredness of the ties of blood will, in the hour of trial, save us from becoming a party to it.

And, after all, watch as we will, warn as we will, friendship and family ties will continually come into collision, and we cannot prevent it. It is an imperfection belonging to our present state of being, and we have nothing to do but to accept it. Yet we may, in some measure, guard against it. Even when children are very little, we shall do well to watch their companionships. When they are rather older, we shall be wise in checking altogether anything approaching to extreme and exclusive intimacy. Girls of twelve or thirteen are much better without anything of the kind. The charm of such intimacy generally consists of secrets and confidences which are exceedingly injurious; and as it is difficult to prevent these without showing suspicion, it is safe to keep the children, if possible, out of the way of temptation. But beyond this age, when the mind and the deeper feelings of the heart begin to develop, we shall probably do more harm than good by interfering with friendship. If we can share it, we may render it safe. If we insist upon the observance of all family claims as a first duty, we may lessen the risk of its interfering with family happiness, but we can do nothing more.

Human affections are in the hands of God. He only can direct them. And ignorant as we are of the events which lie before us, it is not for us to say what will or will not be best for our children's happiness. We interfere roughly with a girl's friendship, and we erect a barrier which prevents her from ever again clinging to us in confidence. We think that we are saving her from undue influence, and we leave her to desolateness of heart. Far rather may we trust these things to God. Where there is no actual right or wrong in the case, where there is no moral reason for interfering to stop a friendship altogether, the question of its degree is one which it is

best to leave. We can never make young people care for each other less by telling them that their love is foolish. If we will but wait patiently, time and the changes of life will work for us in many ways which we could little have anticipated. And after all, friendship is part of the discipline of life. It is intended to have a certain influence in the formation of character, and God, through its means, is effecting that formation. We are apt to think that we can do so much in developing character. We talk as if human hearts were in our own hands to mould just as we will; that we may make the young what we choose by placing them in safe positions, giving them good associations, surrounding them by wise friends. It is all a mistake, founded upon the supposition that we know what is safe, and good, and wise. We have only to watch the trees and flowers: the children we love so anxiously are just like them. What can we do for them? Plant, water, prune, train—it sounds like positive work: but look into it narrowly, and it is only negative. Rain and sunshine, dews and frosts, must be sent in the proportion which God sees fit, or our plant will not flourish; and if, attempting to take the work out of His Hands, we remove it from its natural soil, and place it under shelter, and watch over it exclusively ourselves, it will die.

CHAPTER XXV.

THE PRINCIPLE OF RELIGION.

MANY subjects have now been discussed in connection with Education—Law, and Obedience, Reverence, Truth, Justice, Selfishness, Pride, Vanity, Purity, Love, Friendship; and the principle which is the basis of all law, that without which every other principle must fail of its completeness, has been omitted. Nothing has been said definitely of education in Religion.

The omission has, perhaps, appeared strange, but it has had a purpose. We are sometimes told that before receiving any other instruction children should be instructed in religion. Now, what do people mean when they say this? What is the popular idea of religion?

The answer will probably be, Christian doctrine—the Love of God, founded upon the revelation which He has made of Himself, in Jesus Christ.

Undoubtedly, this is one phase of religion—its most important phase. But religion cannot mean only this, because, if so, what do we understand by natural religion—that religion of which Bishop Butler speaks, when he says, that "the general system of religion is, that the government of the world is uniform, and one, and moral; that virtue and right shall finally have the advantage, and prevail over fraud and lawless force, over the deceits as well as the violence of wickedness, under the conduct of one Supreme Governor"?[1] Surely this refers to a religion distinct from Christian doctrine.

[1] Butler's Analogy, Part I. chap. iii.

No, it may be replied, it does not refer to religion, but to morality. But what is morality? How is it to be distinguished from religion? If it implies obedience to the moral laws of our nature, who impressed upon us those moral laws? Was it not God? And must not everything which has reference to Him be religious? Can truth and justice exist apart from Him? And when we educate children in truth and justice, are we not, so far, educating them religiously?

It may appear an abstract question, of no very great moment, and yet upon the answer must depend the whole system of religious education.

If religion and morality are entirely distinct, then certainly we are required to explain clearly to a little child, from the first dawn of reason, what religion means. We must point out wherein it differs from morality, and insist upon the superiority of those duties which have reference immediately to God, over those which are connected only with man. But if, on the other hand, morality is and always must be more or less religious, then we may be happy in the consciousness that every time we instruct a child in its moral duties, and teach it to be truthful, obedient, reverent, and unselfish, we are actually instructing it in religion; and we may choose that mode of inculcating religious duty which the child can most easily comprehend; taking the course which God appears to point out in nature, and leading it upwards from the laws of its own moral consciousness, which it perceives intuitively, to Him who is the Author of those laws.

Under this view, we shall recognize, as a child's first religious act, the obedience which the little infant pays to its mother, before it can even comprehend the fact of the Being of a God; and every successive act of obedience, or, indeed, any exhibition of moral goodness, may then be regarded as an act of religion. It is not required that the child shall clearly understand the obligation of these moral laws; it must obey long before it can understand them; but the principle of subjection to them is the same principle which must afterwards be

more fully developed when it is capable of understanding the moral obligations which are involved in man's relations to God, not only as his Creator, but also as his Redeemer and Sanctifier.[1]

The man who can understand these relations, and fails in the duties of gratitude, devotion, and obedience which are rightly consequent upon them, is irreligious; but the child who cannot understand them, and therefore fails to fulfil them, is not irreligious, so long as he does fulfil those obligations which are open to his comprehension.

A mistake upon this point is the source of very fatal errors in education. Earnestly religious parents, desiring above all things that their children should grow up in the love of God, and acknowledging nothing as worthy the name of a religious act, but that which proceeds from the definite motive of devotion to Him, strive to awaken in their children that same deep sense of Christian doctrine which they find so infinitely influential in themselves. They imagine that by constantly quoting the Bible—especially those portions which refer to man's sinfulness and our Blessed Lord's Atonement—and by appealing to the children's feelings of love and gratitude, they shall arouse interest, and quicken affection. When they find that they fail —that the children become cold and constrained, and shrink from these subjects—they say that it is an evidence of the corruption of a fallen nature—the result of the natural alienation of the human heart from God. Perhaps they redouble their efforts—most certainly they pray for the children's conversion; or, as they term it—with a singular disregard of the distinct meaning of the two words—their regeneration. But through it all, they feel it is a case in which man is so entirely helpless, that he can but bide God's time; submitting to His Will, whilst mourning over the hardness of heart of the children in every other respect so amiable.

But suppose the truth to be that the children are not really averse from religion, but that they shrink from the peculiar

[1] Butler's Analogy, Part II. chap. i.

form in which it is presented to them; that they cannot understand it, and that, from some cause or other, it jars upon them. This is quite possible; in fact, if we examine the question carefully, we shall find that it is very probable.

The foundation of Christian doctrine is the sense of sin, the deep consciousness of the need of a Saviour. The man who, after a life of alienation from God, wakes up to the perception of God's just hatred of sin, and his own danger in consequence, feels this need intensely. The Atonement of Christ, and his own consequent pardon, are to him the very foundation of peace and unutterable thankfulness. He rests upon that one thought, and it becomes to him the mainspring of a new life. So also the man whose heart is already devoted to God, who strives to serve Him with a perfect service, feels more and more, day by day, the infinite imperfection of his service, and the absolute necessity of some other plea than his own righteousness, if he is ever to hope for acceptance with an All-Holy God. With him also the Atonement of Christ is the one thought of rest, and the one influential motive of action.

But when we speak to a child of this deep sense of sin, this overpowering need of atonement, we speak to it of what it can only partially understand.

The conviction of sinfulness cannot possibly be overwhelming in the heart of a child, for it is only learning by degrees what sin is. It is in the effort to be obedient, truthful, reverent, loving, that it perceives its own weakness. The more a child longs to do right, the more it will grieve because it does wrong. The "law is its schoolmaster to bring it unto Christ."[1] If we expect to bring it to Christ without the law, we shall fail. For this order of religious training is that adopted by God in His dealings both with the world in general, and with the Jews in particular. The history of the heathen before the coming of our Lord, is the history of fallen man's vain and fruitless efforts to find out God, and to please Him. As St. Paul said to the Athenians, God "hath

[1] Gal. iii. 24.

made of one blood all nations of men for to dwell on all the face of the earth, and hath determined the times before appointed, and the bounds of their habitation; that they should seek the Lord, if haply they might feel after Him, and find Him."[1] Mankind failed in this search. Some few amongst the heathens, indeed, recognized the law of God in their own moral nature, and set themselves to obey it; but they were powerless to convert their fellow-creatures; and when at length this powerlessness had been fully shown, the great principle of renewal—faith in Him who had atoned for sin—was revealed, and the weary heart of man accepted it, and the world became Christian.

So also it was, in a measure, with the Jews. They were in the position of children, and the mode by which God taught them to know Himself, is that which we must employ, if we would teach our children to know Him. The Jews had a perfect law given them in the Decalogue, which was the republication of the natural law written upon their hearts. They had also many positive laws, based upon this natural law. It was said to them, "Keep these laws and ye shall live." But they did not keep them; and because God knew that they could not, therefore He gave them also sacrificial rites, shadowing forth the One Great Sacrifice which was eventually to be made for the sins of the whole world. It was in the midst of their shortcomings, and by the means of them, that He led them to look to something out of themselves, as the plea for their acceptance with Him. The principle of obedience led them on to the principle of faith. When they knew that they had disobeyed, they knew that a sacrifice must be offered. They connected the idea of atonement with that of sin. They learnt the need of it through the obligation of law. If the Jews had been left without definite laws, or without having them enforced upon their observance, they would never have appreciated the mercy which appointed the means of pardon; and if called upon to be thankful for those means, their

[1] Acts xvii. 26, 27.

hearts would have refused to respond to the appeal. And the obligation of law, and the need of atonement, were, it must be remembered, the lessons of every-day existence. The minuteness of the Jewish laws brought religion into the daily life of the Jewish people. An undisciplined race, fresh from the servitude and degradation of Egyptian bondage, they could never have worked out for themselves the necessity of absolute obedience to God in small things as well as great. The perfect law of the Decalogue, so broad and deep as to embrace the whole compass of man's duty, would have failed to influence them, because, in its vastness, it would have been misunderstood. It requires the thoughtful mind of the philosopher to reason out the truth that negative commands imply positive duties; and that the omission of the latter is a breach of the law, as really as the neglect of the former. The Jews were taught their own sinfulness and weakness by secondary rather than by primary laws. And in this respect children are precisely like them. The very necessity we are under of bringing them up upon rules—though rules based upon principles—points out the mode by which insensibly and involuntarily we educate them in the comprehension of the nature and the extent of sin. The first consciousness of evil in the mind of a little child is not that of vanity or worldliness, or indifference to God; but of some trifling act of disobedience towards its parents; the infringement of some temporary law; and the first sense of sin against God is awakened by the fact of having sinned against man.

But we must observe further, that this sense of sinfulness, developed by the transgression of laws which are not in themselves obligatory, but which derive their authority from the person who enforces them, will never produce the same keen sense of guilt, as the transgression of the eternal laws which are part of man's moral nature.

The Jews must have felt this, and they were permitted to feel it. It is true that all their laws came immediately from God, and were all therefore binding to an extent which can

belong to no law proceeding from human authority; but the difference between the feeling of repentance for sins against secondary laws, and that of repentance for sins against primary and eternal laws, is clearly shown in the one instance in David's life, in which we are told of his especially offending God.

The Almighty had commanded sacrifices to be offered for the sins of the Jewish people. He had given minute directions concerning them, and David had been a devout observer of these directions during the whole course of his life. But when he sinned in the matter of Uriah the Hittite, we read nothing of a desire for such ritual atonement. The offence was too grievous, the conscience was too deeply wounded, to be soothed by anything short of the direct pardon of God; and in the sorrow of his heart David exclaims, "Thou desirest not sacrifice; else would I give it: Thou delightest not in burnt offering. The sacrifices of God are a broken spirit: a broken and a contrite heart, O God, Thou wilt not despise."[1]

This is the repentance of the *man* as distinct from the repentance of the child. The latter is the prelude to the former, but it is not and cannot be the same; and therefore when we appeal to a child's sense of guilt, speak to it of the wrath of God, the necessity of punishment, the abounding mercy of our Redeemer's Atonement, and the unutterable gratitude which is due from us in consequence of it, we are appealing to a sense which, though it exists in the germ, is not yet fully developed; and as a necessary consequence the heart is cold.

Now, if we attribute this coldness to the natural alienation of the child from God, we shall of course be unhappy, and perplexed. The child will be to us a little heathen, and we shall be inclined to treat it as a heathen, to lament, and expostulate, and entreat, and argue; and—worst of all—to exhibit our own feeling, to express ourselves enthusiastically; and the result of it all will probably be that the child will become more and more cold, more and more averse

[1] Psa. li. 16, 17.

from our society, and why? Simply because we are talking to it of what it does not yet understand, and of feelings which it cannot as yet recognize as real: and the mind of a child shrinks, as instinctively, from the slightest touch of unreality, as the sensitive plant does from the touch of the human hand.

But meet a child upon its own ground, speak to it of the faults and feelings which it does comprehend, and all this coldness and deadness will vanish.

It knows perfectly well what to be naughty or wrong means; it has not yet learnt what being wicked means. Then let us take the sense of naughtiness, and touch the feelings through it. We may not complain of the child because it cannot see that all faults are sins; though unquestionably they are so. That knowledge will come by and by, and a very bitter knowledge it will be; and when it does come, the heart will open to God, and repentance, and confession, and prayer, and the need of atonement will follow. But for the present let us be contented with and thankful for what we have. Better far is it that the child should say to its mother in simplicity and sincerity, "I am sorry I have been so naughty; please forgive me;" than that it should adopt the language which it does not feel, and say, "I am a grievous sinner, and I cast myself upon God's mercy in Christ as my only hope."

Cant is very easily learnt—cant of all kinds; whether it takes the form of Scripture texts and peculiar phraseology, or of a vain and morbid self-inspection and confession; and cant is the mortal enemy of true religion.

There will, indeed, be occasions in which more than this human sorrow, if it may be so called, will be felt, and more expressed; when, as in the case of falsehood, the innate instincts of the moral sense have been wounded; and the little heart awakens to the awful consciousness that it has sinned against its Maker. Such instances are, however, comparatively rare, and as a general rule, we must content ourselves

with a repentance which will fall far short of this, and which yet does not in the least betoken hardness of heart, still less indifference to religion itself, especially when it is exhibited in a practical form. Any person who has ever had experience in dealing with children will know that nothing is more easy than to arouse their earnestness and interest upon subjects connected with their moral improvement; so long as they are spoken to simply and unaffectedly, with gentleness, sympathy, and without any direct appeal to their devotional feelings. *That* they cannot endure. If these feelings do not exist, it is irritating to have it supposed that they do. If the contrary, the natural reserve of youth, and the instinctive sense of the sacredness and delicacy of such a subject, make it next to impossible to mention them; and should they be led to do so, it must always be with the risk more or less of unreality, since a child's religious experience is almost necessarily mixed up with vanity and self-consciousness as soon as it is brought to light.

And are we, then, to leave what is peculiarly called religion, entirely? to bring up a child upon the system of heathen philosophy—trusting to time and thought to expand this moral teaching into Christian doctrine?

God forbid! We will look again at the education of the Jews. They were taught their sinfulness by the experience of their inability to keep the laws which were given them; but they were also taught God's willingness to forgive, by the sacrifices which were offered and accepted. These sacrifices were of various kinds; but the morning and evening sacrifices were of daily occurrence. How much they understood of the typical meaning of these rites is uncertain. The comprehension must have varied according to the thoughtfulness and intellect of different individuals; but the solemn mystery which lay hidden under them must have become more clear to the Jews as a nation as years went on, and the prophecies expanded the truths originally shadowed forth in symbols and ceremonies; since we find that when the great Antitype ap-

peared there were those who were "looking for redemption in Israel," and who anticipated the advent of the Messiah as the fulfilment of all which the law had prefigured.

Now, what sacrifice was to the Jews, that the habit of prayer, in the Redeemer's name, is to a child. The sacrifices had a double meaning; they were acts of outward obedience, and types of the Great Atonement. The Jew who looked deeply into their meaning, and assisted in them with real faith, was doubtless more acceptable to God than he who merely participated in them as an act of obedience; but the outward worship was required alike of all; to all it was the daily reminder of sinfulness and atonement. As the mind of the nation developed, the Jews were, indeed, taught more and more clearly how valueless was the external act apart from the inward spirit. The Prophets gave them striking and solemn warnings upon this point: "To what purpose is the multitude of your sacrifices unto Me? saith the Lord: I am full of the burnt offerings of rams, and the fat of fed beasts; and I delight not in the blood of bullocks, or of lambs, or of he goats. . . . When ye spread forth your hands, I will hide Mine Eyes from you: yea, when ye make many prayers, I will not hear: your hands are full of blood."[1] But the laws of the Pentateuch enforce sacrifices with a strictness which appears to show that the act itself was important, apart from the comprehension of the worshipper. When the Jews as a nation were able to feel the meaning of their rites, then that feeling was required of them: but whilst they were in a state of infancy—only learning to know God—the outward act of obedience, so long as it was performed *in the spirit of obedience*, was accepted.

Somewhat of this same character may surely be remarked in the mode by which nature and custom teach us to educate a child in religion—by means of prayer. There may be some who suppose that it is useless to teach a child to pray until it can understand the meaning of the words it uses; but this is not a very common belief. The generality of persons—if they

[1] Isaiah i. 11, 15.

have any religious feeling at all—teach their little ones, as a matter of course, to repeat prayers, morning and evening, as soon as they can begin to lisp the words. They do it, they know not why. They obey what may almost be called an instinct; even as the Jews acknowledged the necessity of the morning and evening sacrifices, with only a distant understanding of what was implied by them. But if persons are very earnest, they probably are not satisfied with this practice; prayer is to them the expression of the inmost soul—they wish it to be so with their child. The little voice utters those all-powerful words—"through Jesus Christ our Lord;" and the mother longs to make the heart unite with it. And quite rightly—quite naturally. But it will not be quite rightly and naturally if she supposes that she can really carry out her wish. She may explain, and the child may listen, and—what is infinitely wonderful—grasp the abstract idea presented to it. But abstract ideas do not touch the heart; they are but the distant glimmer of the Eternal Light which is to be our guide to glory; and the mother will be greatly disappointed, if she imagines that because her child from the very dawn of reason was led to think and speak of God, and of salvation through Christ, therefore it can be led to act from what are peculiarly termed religious motives.

It may be well to look into this more narrowly. That a child's mind can take in the idea of God—comprehending in that idea Infinity, Eternity, Omnipotence, and Omnipresence—is a proof that it was originally made in the Image of Him in whom these attributes centre. That it can recognize moral truths, is a proof that, in the Being from whom its nature is derived, moral perfection is embodied: and so also, it would seem, that the readiness with which the little child receives the two ideas of Incarnation and Atonement is a witness to the abstract truth of these ideas.

But we must all know the difference between recognizing great truths intellectually, and recognizing them morally and practically. It is only when the abstract is presented to us in

the concrete, that the latter effect is produced. The God of the Pantheist and the God of the Christian alike represent Omnipotence and Omnipresence, Eternity and Immutability; but the one is an idea, the other a person, and it is only as a Person that the perfections of the Deity can awaken personal feelings. Love, gratitude, reverence, obedience, are aroused, not by the abstract idea of God, but by the perception of His actual being and His moral attributes.

Now, the abstract is grasped at once. It is felt before it is understood; the idea of truth is grasped, by being felt, though the child cannot explain what truth means. The concrete, on the contrary, is understood only by degrees. And from not appreciating the distinction between these two forms of comprehension, parents are often startled and perplexed in dealing with their children's minds. They find in their little ones most marvellous powers of taking in the very deepest abstract ideas, united with the most infantine absurdity in the mode of exhibiting them. One moment, a child appears a prodigy of intellect and thought; the next, a prodigy of simple ignorance. It will put together the most incongruous ideas, exciting the sense of the ludicrous in connection with the most solemn subjects, and all the while be perfectly insensible to the incongruity. In these cases, it is trying to form a concrete representation of the abstract idea which it has in its infant mind; and because the true representation is not yet realized, it creates for itself that which, it imagines, most nearly approaches it.

Not long ago a little child of two years old said to its mother, "I shall go up to heaven quite alone, but I won't be shy. Only I won't shake hands with God, but I will kiss Jesus Christ, and play with the angels."

Every one will feel that although a smile may rise to the lips when these words are repeated, yet there is no smile in the heart, but rather a tear. For as the child spoke she recognized the spiritual under the material, and touched the fountain springs of that poetry, which is far deeper than philosophy. Unconsciously the little mind had grasped the abstract ideas of

the awful, incomprehensible Nature of God, the Father; the human as well as the Divine Nature in God, the Son; and the finite Nature of the angels. The wisest philosopher could not *know* more than the child *felt*. When she wished to express these abstract ideas she seized upon the first concrete ideas which presented themselves, and under these forms she exhibited them.

The result might, to our blunted perceptions, be ludicrous; but in the sight of God we may not doubt that it was sacred and acceptable.

The working of the same incongruity with similar results may be perceived in the infancy of poetry and art; in the latter especially. The Pre-Raphaelite Madonnas, and Fra Angelico's Angels, at the first careless glance strike us as quaint if not grotesque. Study them more closely, and the purity of the abstract ideas embodied in them comes clearly into view; and the very discrepancy between the majesty of the conception, and the childish simplicity of the execution, touches our hearts to the quick.

Wonderful as a child's unconscious grasp of abstract religious truth unquestionably is, it cannot, however, be depended upon as a motive power, apart from its realization under a true and definite form. Yet in most cases it is the utmost that can be expected either in infancy or for several years afterwards.

Let us look back ourselves. What can we recall as our understanding of the meaning of the Lord's Prayer when we were very young? Or even yet more simple prayers, the first we were ever taught, how vague were the ideas which the words we uttered conveyed to us! To expect deep feeling in connection with those half perceptions would be as unreasonable as to expect that the Jew, who assisted at the offering of sacrifice in the wilderness, and understood that in some way, he knew not how, it shadowed forth an awful sacrifice to come, could feel what the disciples felt when they stood at the foot of the Cross; or what we ourselves may sometimes have felt,

when, burdened by the intolerable sense of sin, we have knelt at our Redeemer's feet with the cry: "O Lamb of God, that takest away the sins of the world, have mercy upon me!"

Pray, children must. It is their one recognition of their immediate duty to God. And be taught the meaning of prayer they must; for as their minds develop God will require the worship of the whole being, and we must gradually prepare them for it. And pray in the name of the Redeemer they must; for however little they may realize what is involved in that Name, it is, and can be, their only plea for acceptance; and, by degrees, God will open the eyes of their mind, and teach them how to rest upon it. But if we attempt to force feeling, if we desire to draw it forth, and gaze upon it, in order to satisfy ourselves of its presence, we shall infallibly destroy it.

There is, indeed, a sorrow for faults committed against man, which a child will express naturally and readily; and very touching, and full of self-reproach it is to the proud spirit of mature years, to hear the simple confession, "I am so very sorry," come forth as it often does from the very depths of the little heart, which is only just beginning to feel its capabilities of sin. The natural impulse of an earnestly religious parent, then, is to lead a child upwards from this feeling to the higher sense of having sinned against God. And it is, no doubt, quite right to bring before it this deeper view of the fault that has been committed. But when we have done this, we shall, in almost all cases, be wise to pause. A very few words said with real earnestness, and without any restrained solemnity of manner, will be sufficient to show our meaning, and then the child is much better left alone to the working of its own conscience, and the influence of God's Spirit. Feeling, if excited, will rarely show itself in our presence. We may kneel down and pray—some persons would think it wrong not to do so—and the child may kneel by our side; but the act of kneeling is not prayer. Left to itself, the young heart, if really moved, would pour itself forth without restraint, and would, perhaps,

learn, for the first time, what prayer really means; but the feelings awakened towards God can at that age be expressed only before God. The slightest shyness causes restraint and coldness; and thus, instead of assisting, we only check the devotional feeling, and the child leaves us, conscious of a jar, and with a fresh sense of sin from finding in itself, as it supposes, a dislike to religion.

This observation is, indeed, open to correction. Children vary, as grown-up people do, in sensitiveness and reserve. The fact that some persons care only for extempore prayers, whilst others find their devotion chilled by them, is a sufficient proof that we cannot lay down rigid laws upon this subject. But it is certainly safe to calculate upon a child's reserve upon sacred subjects; more especially as this will prevent us from yielding to disappointment if we do not discover any indication of religious feeling; or from pursuing that most unwise plan of forcing its expression, in order to convince ourselves that it exists.

But acquiescence in what is apparently a state of dormant religion in children must, of course, be based upon the acknowledgment that they are members of Christ's family; and that their inward development may be safely left to the working of the Holy Spirit in their hearts. If we do not accept this fundamental truth, we shall no doubt be miserable about them, until we see some distinct evidences of their regeneration apart from their obedience to the moral law.

What view those who do not look upon their children as admitted at baptism into the family of Christ take of their condition, it must be left to themselves to explain; but there is probably no person who has accepted this truth as a starting point, and patiently and conscientiously acted upon it, in a course of Christian education, who will not bear witness to the wonderful assistance which it gives in training and developing Christian feeling and principle from the very dawn of reason. It must do so necessarily. The first idea of definite religion which the child grasps is that of the Existence of God. But

this abstract idea requires to be presented in a certain form, before it can influence conduct. Tell the child that God is its Father, and you have the true form at once. The relation of child to parent is the actual relation in which, according to the acknowledgment of all Christians, the true follower of the Redeemer stands to his Almighty Creator. Half the difficulties of our religious life, both in doctrine and in practice, would vanish, if we would only reason upon the feelings and acts of God, according to the analogy of this human relationship. The little child, therefore, who is taught that God is actually its Father, sets out on its Christian course with a clue by which it may learn to disentangle almost all difficulties. From the love of its earthly father, it learns to understand the love of its Heavenly Father; from the sense of dependence in the one relationship, it learns to realize what is meant by dependence in the other; from the tender sympathy of the elder brother, it learns somewhat of the nearness and sympathy of Christ; from the spirit which pervades the family, uniting them in one body, it learns to realize the existence of the one gracious Spirit dwelling alike in every Christian heart. All these lessons depend upon the one primary truth that the child is God's child. Take away this, and the truths derived from it must of necessity be negatived. And in like manner, as it has been before observed, recognize the fact that the child is Christian by virtue of its baptism, and you can afford to wait patiently for the evidence of definite Christian feeling. The little one who is taught that God is its Father, learns to be religious, as it learns to be obedient. Submission to a parent is its first notion of duty, but the abstract idea of a parent is blended in its mind with the abstract idea of God. The two grow and expand together. Obedience to the earthly parent becomes sacred, because the relationship is the same which exists between the child and its God, and thus the little daily acts of submission become insensibly hallowed. The child does not know, consciously, that it is acting from the wish to please God, but it *feels* that the parent embodies the idea of God; and,

blending the two, it increases, even as the infinite Redeemer Himself, "in wisdom and stature, and in favour with God and man."[1]

For there is growth, though it may not be evidenced to us, in the particular form in which we have been led to expect it. The blossom is not the fruit; yet, without the blossom, there would be no fruit; and the blossoms of religion are reverence, obedience, and truth, as its fruits are faith and love. Watch over the former, cherish and nourish them, and, through God's grace, in due time the fruits will appear. Attempt to force the fruit, and we may, perhaps, obtain a few feeble specimens, which we may regard, for the moment, as marvels, and call upon the world to admire; but the plant from which they have been gathered is, in its constitution, sickly, and when the time comes that it must be exposed to the bleak winds of temptation, it will, in all probability, perish.

[1] St. Luke ii. 52.

CHAPTER XXVI.

DEFINITE RELIGIOUS INSTRUCTION.

We have spoken of what may be called the blossoms of religion, as distinct from its fruit. Of these, the one which peculiarly needs cultivation as a preparation for religious feeling is reverence. The moralist, the sceptic, or even the unbeliever, may strive to bring up a child in obedience and truth, but to recognize the primary duty of reverence belongs exclusively to the Christian. For by reverence, in its full sense, is meant not only mental reverence, though based upon the full acknowledgment of the power and goodness of the Almighty; but outward, personal reverence, such as no one can mistake;—reverence evidenced by signs, as clearly as the respect shown to the position of an earthly sovereign, or the dignity of human authority.

To make a little child kneel down quietly, repeat its prayer carefully,[1] rise from its knees slowly, and remain still for a

[1] Prayer, though the most important of a child's religious duties, is that over which we can exercise least direct influence, except with regard to outward reverence.

We may not interfere with it; we can, only in a general way, give hints for its guidance. Forms of prayer are very necessary at first; but we dare not insist upon their being always used. We may, however, as young people begin to take an interest in religious subjects, suggest the desirableness of collecting and arranging prayers, psalms, and hymns for themselves; and if they desire such aid, we may assist them in the work. We may also point out strongly the necessity of constant prayer, and that not confined to the morning and the evening. At special solemn seasons, we shall find that even a very young and thoughtless child will be thankful to be given a short

few seconds before its mind rushes towards other subjects, may seem mere formality to the mother, whose only thought is how to make it feel the words it utters; but it is the only lesson of religion which it is in her power to give, and, in all probability, it is the only one which the child, for some years, will be capable of receiving. Words of repentance put into a little child's mouth, or repeated for it, do not, necessarily, awaken the feeling of repentance, because the child does not as yet understand the nature of sin. But a child's reverent action calls up the spirit of reverence, because there is in the very nature and position of childhood, that which answers to the appeal. Children are born reverent, because they are born to recognize and submit to power. Many things—carelessness, temper, pride, the difficulty of fixing attention—may give rise to irreverent actions, but the spirit of irreverence is not inevitably connected with them. And if we would only, from children's earliest infancy, accustom them to be simply reverent in all things connected with their religious duties, we should do more towards maturing the spirit of religion in their hearts than we could by giving them the fullest doctrinal instruction, or accustoming them to the freest expression of their needs in their daily devotion.

"These ought ye to have done, and not to leave the other undone."[1] Doctrinal instruction, prayer from the heart, are excellent—most excellent—but they belong to a more advanced age. The child of two years old may be made reverent; and when it is old enough to receive instruction, it will listen all the more humbly, and when it pours forth its first conscious petitions, it will be all the more earnest, because,

prayer, to be used in the middle of the day; whilst, as time goes on, the practice may be urged as most important always; for it will tend, more perhaps than any other habit, to deepen and perpetuate religious feelings; and the check upon self-indulgence which it necessitates, will, even apart from the great spiritual blessings to be expected from it, help to keep the young mind real in its religion.

[1] Matthew xxiii. 23.

before it could either understand or pray—in the true sense of prayer—it was made to exhibit in action that first principle of religion—which, as yet, was all it could comprehend—reverence for the Almighty Being who created it.

And surely this is the teaching of the Bible. Reverence was the one great lesson given, first to Moses, and then to the people whom he was to rule—the nation of children.

"Draw not nigh hither: put off thy shoes from off thy feet, for the place whereon thou standest is holy ground. . . . . And Moses hid his face, for he was afraid to look upon God." [1]

"And Mount Sinai was altogether on a smoke, because the Lord descended upon it in fire: and the smoke thereof ascended as the smoke of a furnace, and the whole mount quaked greatly. . . . . And the Lord said unto Moses, Go down, charge the people, lest they break through unto the Lord to gaze, and many of them perish." [2]

And following out this principle, the whole of the Mosaic law was an exemplification of the principle of reverence for God's Name, His sanctuary, His ark, His priests, His worship; a reverence shown in the most minute details, as if it was a point so carefully to be guarded, that without it no other form of obedience could be acceptable. It was the teaching needed for the religious education of childhood. With the deep devotion, the vivid realization of religious truth which belongs to a more advanced period of life, reverence is joined of necessity; it becomes a thing of course. And so it is that we find in the New Testament the external forms of reverence left almost entirely to man's choice, whilst the inward Spirit is insisted upon as the one thing needful.

"God is a Spirit," were the words of our Blessed Lord to the woman of Samaria, "and they that worship Him must worship Him in spirit and in truth." [3]

But this outward reverence should, in the case of children,

[1] Exod. iii. 5, 6. [2] Exod. xix. 18, 21.
[3] St. John iv. 24.

be very simple. To kneel, or stand, or sit perfectly still, and to repeat solemn words slowly, will be quite a sufficient effort for a very little child. And as time goes on the lesson will be more and more frequently inculcated. If the Bible is read there will be a little preparation for it. It may seem a very small thing to move all other books from the table when a party of children gather together for Scripture reading; or to insist that no other book shall be laid upon the Bible; and yet this strictness will recall the attention of the most thoughtless. A prayer, such as the Collect for the second Sunday in Advent, said, as the children stand up before beginning to read, will force upon them that the Bible cannot be studied like any other volume, but that it requires the special aid of God's Spirit if we are to profit by it. And in reading, if, instead of having the sacred words stumbled over by those who can scarcely pronounce them correctly, and certainly cannot appreciate their meaning, the mother or the governess would read them herself, a vast amount of unintentional irreverence might be saved; whilst the risk of inattention may be prevented by careful questioning, and explanation afterwards. This habit of reading the Bible to children, instead of making them read it aloud themselves, is also an advantage, because it admits of a choice of chapters and passages in the Old Testament, which, especially in a mixed company of boys and girls, is both helpful and desirable.[1]

[1] The daily reading of the Bible is a duty which we are all ready to own, but with regard to which we frequently find a difficulty in educating children. Some persons suppose that this daily reading ought necessarily to be always devotional. But this does not appear to be the intention of God in giving us the Bible. The sacred volume is historical, geographical, social, political, poetical, as well as devotional; and under these phases it requires a careful study, without which the strictly devotional portions cannot be perfectly understood.

Why this should be so, it would be presumption in us to attempt fully to decide; but it is evident that if the Scriptures had been, as we are often inclined to wish, thoroughly clear on all points, mankind would never, for such a long series of years, have found in them an engrossing occupation

Reverence in learning and repeating sacred lessons, the Psalms, Collects, Catechism, Hymns, &c., ought, also, to be strictly enforced. It may be permitted to give the sense instead of the words of a lesson in other cases; it cannot be so where the words to be remembered are sacred. This necessity of correctness in repetition will involve more time in learning what is to be repeated; it will make the words seem more important, and will impress that importance upon the young mind. God's Words, or even those words which speak of Him, will not be common, and, therefore, they will be more fully valued.

And so, also, with regard to behaviour in Church. Perfect reverence, involving an absence of all affectation and singularity of gesture (which, indeed, awaken not reverence, but self-consciousness), will be found absolutely essential if we wish our children to grow up in that "fear of God" which will lead them to depart from the "ways of evil." But reverence in Church, we must remember, demands restraint for a much longer time than reverence in private prayer. And a little child cannot bear this restraint, and we must, therefore, be merciful to it.

for the intellect as well as the heart. Even as, in like manner, if the laws of nature had been self-evident, science would never have busied itself to discover them, and the mind of man would have been comparatively unemployed.

And looking at the Scriptures as intended to exercise the mental, as well as to guide the moral, powers, we shall scarcely err in directing children's attention, cautiously and reverently, to all which may throw light on what may be called the temporal aspect of the Bible; the connection of sacred history with profane; the peculiarities of ancient customs, and the difficulties of language. Young people will take a vivid interest in such subjects; and when we have awakened thought in this way, it will not be difficult in a few words, simply and earnestly, as occasion may suggest, to bring forward the deeper and more hidden things of the Word of God. We shall, probably, find this plan more successful than that of making Scripture reading strictly devotional; for on the subject of personal religion, children are apt to be very sensitive; their feelings shrink from human touch, though they will expand freely under the Eye of Heaven.

It is much to be questioned whether the custom, common in our national schools, of collecting together in Church little children of five or six years of age, and making them stand, and kneel, and sit for two hours together, scarcely speaking or moving, is really conducive to reverence. Possibly it might be better if they were spared the ordeal of the sermon, which, undoubtedly, they cannot profit by. But there are great difficulties in the way of such an arrangement, and all that is urged now is for the consideration of those who are at liberty to carry out their own ideas. To them it may be said that Church services will, probably, be more highly estimated if they are regarded as a boon, than if they are insisted upon as a duty.

A baptism is, perhaps, the best service to which a child of three or four years old can first be taken; there is so much interest in it; and the impression left upon the mind is likely to be lasting and very salutary. After this, a short afternoon service—especially if there should be singing, and no sermon—may be tried; then, as the child learns to repeat the Lord's Prayer, a morning service may be chosen, care being taken that the Prayer is repeated whenever it occurs, so that the child may feel that it can bear a part in what is going on. But it would seem better—not only in very early childhood, but for some time afterwards—to hold back certain portions of the Church services. For instance, to go to Church twice in the day, when looked upon as the privilege of elder persons, will be a coveted permission instead of an irksome burden. A week-day service will be a treat, if it marks special *fête* days. If we thus begin gradually teaching our little ones to associate the idea of God's House with rewards and enjoyments, the feeling of liking for it will increase insensibly, and we shall very soon find, if we are only consistent and reverent ourselves, that our children are learning to consider it a hardship when they are debarred from it.

And when this feeling has once been awakened, we may rest satisfied at least for a time. A taste for going to Church

does not, indeed, necessarily imply the existence of religious principle in the heart, but it prepares the way for it. In these days, it must be owned young people often show great interest in Church services, take a prominent part in choral music, and are critical, and even learned, as to ritual observances, and yet are not one whit the less conceited, presumptuous, self-willed, and uncharitable. But the fault lies not in the Church, but the home. If these same young people had been brought up reverently, they would handle sacred things reverently. If they had been taught to watch their own hearts, they would be on their guard against the temptations to which now they yield. No doubt it is worse to be vain and worldly at a daily service than in a ball-room; but it does not, therefore, follow that a ball is better for the mind than a religious service. Outward forms, ceremonies, sacred music, are nothing in themselves; they may be turned to great evil, all the more because they profess to be, and indeed are, the instruments of great good; but we may easily test both ourselves and our children in all these matters. If we do not like to go to Church unless we can worship in a beautiful building, and listen to exquisite music, and hear an eloquent sermon, then we have no *real* liking for religious services at all. What we do like is merely the excitement—that very self-same kind of excitement which meets us at the opera, and which is less dangerous because it is less self-deceiving. But if, on the contrary, we can join heartily in the prayers of the Church, and find rest in them under any circumstances, then the fact that our interest, or our feelings, are excited, or that our taste is gratified by the adjuncts of music and architecture, is nothing to be alarmed at; but rather an indulgence which God, we may believe, has granted to us here, as a foretaste of the pleasures which we are to enjoy hereafter.

Reverence for the Lord's Day is another very important religious lesson to be early inculcated. The term "the Lord's Day" is used advisedly, because it seems to embody the principle by which the occupations of the day should be regulated.

Sunday is a heathen, the Sabbath a Jewish term. We are neither heathens, nor Jews, but Christians; and we desire to keep sacred the first day of the week in a Christian spirit. The first thing to be remembered, then, is that it is the Lord's Day,—a day dedicated in an especial manner to the service of our Redeemer, so that it permits no employment to be undertaken which has not, directly or indirectly, reference to Him. And the second is, that it is a day of joy—a festival. Bearing these two points in mind, we shall find little difficulty in bringing up our children to regard and make use of it rightly.

Now, very little children cannot be made to employ the whole of the Sunday in a definitely religious manner, because they are only learning, by very slow degrees, to comprehend the meaning of religion. But they can be taught, from their earliest infancy, to look upon it as a festival, a pleasant day, one on which they are to enjoy some special treat,—very trifling, perhaps,—merely being allowed to be more with their parents, to join them at dessert, to take a little walk, to gather flowers and make up nosegays,—it matters not what the pleasure is, so long as it is something, quiet and domestic, and reserved for Sunday. The first association with Sunday will then be that of enjoyment.

With this sense of enjoyment the sense of sacredness must undoubtedly be joined; but, still, the effort should be to make sacredness pleasant. Children must have something to occupy them. If we take away their dolls and toys, and give them nothing in return, they will be just as weary, restless, and irritable, as grown-up people who have nothing to do. Neither will they safely bear the excitement of play for a whole day on Sunday, any more than they will on any other day. To begin the day with a very little lesson, perhaps only a verse of a hymn, will be a tonic for all the hours that are to follow; and then there may be the pleasure of something especially put aside for Sunday,—a book of sacred prints, a Noah's ark, which, quaint though it is, has from long association acquired

a *quasi* sacredness,—anything which deepens the idea that Sunday is a peculiar day,—very happy,—but on which it is not right to do precisely the same things that we do on other days. As children grow older and are taken to Church, they have necessarily less unoccupied time. They will be expected to learn Collects and Psalms, and repeat their Catechism, and have it explained; and this will employ a large portion of their leisure. Then there may be Sunday story books, and music, and at a later period some time may be spent in teaching others. All these employments will differ in different families. Some may have more leisure, some less; but the result will be the same in all, if the two great principles of sacredness and pleasantness are kept in view. It will not make children careless if they know that punishments are, as a rule, never carried on over Sunday; and if they are more readily excused any little forgetfulness on that day than on any other. The very fact of knowing that it is a day of jubilee will touch their sense of honour; and they will try to do well on Sunday from the highest of all principles—reverent love, which does not fear punishment, or look for reward.

And there may and ought to be definite religious instruction on the Sunday, but then it should be given orally, more in the form of conversation than as a lesson. Little children will listen with delight to stories told them out of the Bible. Those who are older will take great interest in explanations of the Catechism, if they are given with illustrations, and brought home to their own experience; and older girls will really enjoy discussing subjects connected with Church history and Church government, and will enter into really deep moral questions, if only the mother or the governess who is instructing them, will throw her own heart into the subjects brought forward, and show that she is studying for herself as well as for them.

Sunday lessons should never, strictly speaking, be lessons, because the principle of the day is freedom and enjoyment; freedom in God's presence, enjoyment in the consciousness

that we are devoting our attention to things which, in a special manner, relate to Him. If young people are idle and careless when such subjects are brought before them, they may be quietly sent away, because they are disturbing others; but punishment will better be left for another occasion. That which is a pleasure to their companions is not so to them, therefore it will not be forced upon them; and neglect will, in most cases, prove more efficacious than reproach.

And it is through the means of this general conversation upon the externals of religion, that we shall at length succeed in reaching that which constitutes its reality. It is so in worldly matters. When two strangers are brought together, they do not begin by talking of their private interests, their feelings and affections. They keep upon the surface. They test and try each other, as it were, and then, if they find that they have any mutual subject of interest, they discuss it more intimately, with a certain increasing sense of union and cordiality; and so, at length, they arrive at a knowledge of each other's tastes—perhaps of difficulties, sorrows, and trials. But such unreserve is a result reached only through time and caution. If either of them had plunged at once into the secrets of his own life, and given an account of his feelings, the probability is that he would have repelled his friend instead of attracting him.

But all this is too often forgotten in religion. People suppose that they can awaken children's religious feelings by preaching to them, quoting texts, urging the necessity of spirituality. There is but one way which, through God's grace, will ever naturally and almost necessarily make our children religious, and that is, acting religion before them earnestly, consistently, and, for the most part, with but few words. The Spirit of God, working in the child's heart, makes itself heard in silence, for its voice is "still and small;" and though the religious feeling, when roused, will at certain times, and under certain circumstances, find an utterance, we cannot compel it to make itself known by speaking to it. And when

these moments of unreserve do arise, we shall be wise in still retaining our caution.

The children need loving advice, and our object must be, therefore, to draw them on to tell their difficulties—not, be it remembered, their feelings; or, at least, these are better only alluded to. We do not want to extract confessions of deep sinfulness, or of longing for increased spirituality. These are for the Ear of God, and when we find the young heart burdened by such convictions of guilt and helplessness, which constitute the essence of inward religion, we shall probably do well to use but very few words, pointing to the mercy of the Atonement, and the promised aid of the Holy Spirit, and then leave the hidden mind to be influenced and moulded by Him who made it.

But one most frequent confession of all children—may it not be said of all persons?—is, that they cannot feel;—that they can see the claims of religion, that they can even strive to attend to them, but that their service is mechanical. Enthusiastic representations of God's Love, fervent appeals to the sense of gratitude, will not, under such circumstances, awaken the heart from its state of conscious deadness. But there is a thought, which, when made practical, will seldom fail to touch it. Any action, be it ever so trivial, which is done deliberately with a view to please God, does please Him. Let the next thing that presents itself in the way of duty—no matter what—it may be only writing a note, be performed with the thought that God is looking on, seeing why and how it is done, and approving it, because it is an effort made definitely for Him, an attempt to do His work.

That must be a very cold heart—much colder than a child's heart generally is—which can be insensible to the consciousness of that approval—which does not thrill at the idea of the Redeemer's loving smile. Deepen, enlarge, and perpetuate the thought, and we arrive at the principle of Faith, "the substance of things hoped for, the evidence of things not seen;"[1]

[1] Heb. xi. 1.

and then will come permanent feeling, rising by degrees, as the religious principle intensifies, from the love of a child to its parents, to the love of the redeemed sinner for Him who died for him. A life thus based upon faith, cultivated by the constant recognition of God's presence, rests upon a foundation which nothing can disturb. For with true faith there will ever be joined that full dependence upon God's aid, that simple reliance upon the Gift of His Holy Spirit, which, after all, is the one absolute essential for the formation and growth of the religious spirit.

We have spoken of earthly means, earthly instruments, words, and deeds; because God has pledged Himself to work for us only if we work for ourselves. "Work out your own salvation with fear and trembling. For it is God which worketh in you both to will and to do of His good pleasure."[1] We must educate children wisely if we hope to reap the fruits of wisdom, but the greatest unwisdom of all is dependence on our own strength.

This is a truth which must especially be insisted upon when writing upon education, because the very necessity of dwelling upon human means compels us at times to speak as if human wisdom was everything.

Effort without prayer is simply useless. We have one duty, above all others, connected with the religious education of children; and that is, to put them into God's hands, and to teach them that "His strength is made perfect in their weakness." It is with us all, as many may have felt when a strong hand has been placed behind them to help them up a steep ascent. If the aid is really to be used, they must lean upon it, even whilst they move forwards. There must be the sense of powerlessness accompanying the energy of exertion. Attempt to move without leaning, and the natural weakness is felt painfully; for the aid which might have been so efficacious is of no avail to those who cannot bring themselves to rest upon it.

[1] Phil. ii. 12, 13.

CHAPTER XXVII.

DEFINITE RELIGIOUS INSTRUCTION—(*continued*).

HAVING given the caution contained in the last chapter, a few more remarks may be made upon the right religious teaching which is needed for a child's education. The heart can, as it has been acknowledged, only be touched by the Spirit of God, and all the instruction we may give will by itself utterly fail of attaining the end we have in view. Yet it is nevertheless most necessary, and, without it, fervent devotion, and even sincerity of heart, may ultimately lead only to fatal errors.

God gives the spirit of devotion; but in a certain sense it may be said that it is left to man to determine into what kind of mould that spirit shall be poured. Religious feeling, when strongly excited, adapts itself to the form through the medium of which it has been awakened. The man converted by a Baptist becomes a Baptist, or by a Quaker becomes a Quaker. The emotional impulse is so much stronger than the intellectual, that it is next to impossible for any person who is, for the first time, thoroughly roused to a perception of his immortal interests by one peculiar exhibition of divine truth, to sit down calmly and examine whether this is the most true and well-grounded statement of it which he can hold. His feelings and prejudices are all enlisted in its favour, and he seems to have no alternative but that of accepting the inward witness, which he thenceforward is led to assert to be the only and true witness.

And though sudden conversions are the exceptions rather than the rule in religious experience, yet conversion of some

kind every one who has attained to the conviction that religion is the one, sole, infinitely important object of man's interest upon earth, must have undergone; because this conviction does not belong to the ignorance of a fallen nature. We may have awakened by degrees—we may not be aware of the precise moment at which our eyes were first opened; but awakened we are; and because of this awakening we feel ourselves compelled to act; and action must always be carried on according to some external law, either chosen for ourselves, or presented for our acceptance by others. And therefore, before the devotional spirit is stirred in the mind of a child, before we can even expect to see its faintest movement, we must prepare for it by forming the mould into which we desire it should be cast.

Parents and teachers would do well to consider this. We marvel at the eccentricities of the young in the present day. We learn almost to dread the enthusiasm of devotional feeling. We see that it leads to differences of opinion and of action; that it breaks up the unity of families, and exhibits itself in peculiarities which are offensive to our sober judgment. We are almost inclined to think that the old ways of our forefathers were the best; that if the young in those bygone ages were not so earnest as they are now, yet at least they were not so troublesome.

But who is to blame? We let our children grow up in ignorance. We do not teach them (probably because we do not know ourselves) what are the grounds of their faith; why they believe the Bible; why they belong to one Church rather than another. We think that they will learn these things intuitively. We have a vague idea that the knowledge of them is, in some way, imbibed with the repetition of the Collects, and Psalms, and Catechism. We are perhaps members of the English Church ourselves; our ancestors were so, and we have followed them, and our children, no doubt, will follow us. Or, it may be, we take delight in Church services, and the children like to help us in Church decoration. They under-

stand all about Saints' Days and Festivals; perhaps even they may be learned in Black Letter Saints, and chant the Gregorian tones wonderfully! "Of course," we say to ourselves, "these things will attach them to the Church."

Now, all this is a great folly. Collects and Psalms teach us how to pray, but they do not tell us why we should pray. The Catechism instructs us what we are to believe, but it does not give the grounds of belief; and Church festivals and music are very attractive, but the existence of the Church does not rest upon them. This reckoning upon a foundation where none had been provided is by no means unusual in other cases. There is a peculiar kind of mud, common in some parts of England, and known by the name of "blue slipper," which, when it hardens, is supposed to be as substantial as solid rock. And in consequence of this supposition houses are built upon it, roads rest on it, and, in fact, it is made the foundation of every kind of superstructure, few suspecting that it is not perfectly safe. But the rain moistens it; springs from the hills work themselves into it; it becomes mud again; and, when completely saturated, it begins to slide—at first slowly, with a scarcely perceptible motion—but still it moves, and by its movement the buildings erected upon it totter; and then the mud slips faster, and the buildings totter more alarmingly; until at length, by an accelarated impulse, the blue slipper not only slides, but rushes downwards, and the superstructure becomes a mass of ruins.

There are characters which, in like manner, rest upon moral blue slipper; there are families which are more or less built upon it; more than all, there is a religious faith—alas! is it not the faith of thousands in England at this moment?—which has no better foundation.

Devotional reverence for the Bible or the Church, merely as a matter of feeling, will never save any one from the snares of Rationalism, or the enticements of the varied forms of error. That which we believe in and reverence to-day, we may very probably—such is the infirmity of human nature—disregard

to-morrow. What we have to learn ourselves, and to teach our children, is to give a reason for the faith that is in us; to know why we hold the Bible to be true; why we belong to the Church of which we profess ourselves to be members; and these reasons are to be found first in facts, chiefly historical, and external to our consciousness. But in order to explain this witness to young people, we must understand it ourselves; we must read, and think, and not only feel. Now, reading and thinking are difficult to many persons, whilst feeling is easy. To say, I believe the Bible to be true, because it speaks to my heart, is a ready and all-sufficient argument for the individual who is conscious of the influence which the Bible exerts; but it is not an argument which will stand against the scoff of the unbeliever. Our Blessed Lord, when addressing the Jews, rested the claims of His mission upon external evidence. He appealed to His works, His miracles; and so also the truth of the Bible, and the authority of the Church to which we belong —let it be what Church it may—must be open to proof, drawn from external testimony, of a like kind with that which, in other cases, is constantly appealed to as the witness to fact.

The amount of evidence which we are at liberty to demand is another and a most important consideration; and one which ought specially to be brought before the minds of the young. We may be beyond the reach of sceptical temptations ourselves (though who in these days can venture to make such an assertion?), but they are not. They will, in all probability, soon be induced to plunge into those mines of darkness, miscalled of wisdom, which are filled with the miasma of philosophic doubt. The torch of human reason, which they bear with them as their guide, may, at any moment, enkindle the vapour, and the flames which light up the obscurity will then but the more rapidly hurry them to their destruction. We cannot hinder them from undertaking the venture, but we can provide them with a safety-lamp. We may so guard the torch that it shall never become an incendiary match; whilst we show them how to carry it, so that it may be a guide in the gloom; point-

ing out where they may venture to go, and what they may accept as reality, and what reject as imagination. In other and unmetaphorical words, we may prepare their minds with the arguments of sound thinkers and cautious theologians; and then when we send them forth into the world, instead of listening to every idle phantasy, they will calmly test the difficulties brought before them, and discover their fallacy, though they may not be always able to refute them.

An involuntary sigh arises as this thought is suggested. Who will take the trouble to read and think? Who will go back to the fountain head? Who will study Butler, and Hooker, and Bull, and Nicholson, and Sanderson, mastering intricate arguments, and translating obsolete expressions? Students of theology may, because they are obliged to do it—but women? It is an absurdity to expect it of them. They will read reviews, short essays; they will catch up what is said in conversation, and believe it till they hear something which sounds to them more plausible;—but study for themselves! how is it possible? They cannot get at these books, and if they could, they would not have the time to read them. As children in the schoolroom they were too young to understand them, and, indeed, they never heard their names. As young girls they were busy with music, drawing, history, and the "ologies," French accent and the German declensions. As young women they have balls and picnics, dinner and croquet parties; as married women they have the cares of a household, the claims of society, and the education of their children for this world;—for the same round of lessons and accomplishments, amusements and cares, through which they have themselves passed! How, in the midst of such pressing present pursuits, can leisure be found for laying the foundation of faith?

And yet the task would not prove so difficult if we would only attempt it. We are not called upon to make our children read all these books, or even to read them ourselves. One or two, carefully studied and thought over, would furnish

us with invaluable assistance in conversing with young people, and understanding the perplexities which, we may be morally certain, will, sooner or later, arise in their minds. Butler's Analogy, and—if we wish for condensed information in a modern form—Wordsworth's "Theophilus Anglicanus," would, alone, do more to clear our own minds, and enable us to explain the grounds of our belief, than volumes of controversial pamphlets and newspaper essays. It is the art of reasoning, the power of perceiving fallacies, which young people want; and if we can give them this, with a certain amount of definite historical knowledge, they will hold what they do hold so firmly that we need have very little fear for them. And by degrees, as their intellects strengthen, and their interest in these subjects deepens, we may lead them to study such books for themselves. They will find it rather an effort, but if they have been early accustomed to thought they will not shrink from it. There is a satisfactory sense of security afforded by sound reasoning and deep learning, which is appreciated even by those who cannot thoroughly master the arguments brought forward. Definiteness and authority have a vast power in this uncertain world. In them lies the attraction which leads hundreds to the Church of Rome; and the young, especially, cannot rest without their support. If they are not provided for them, they will seek for them; and in seeking in a wrong direction, possibly in a wrong spirit, in dependence upon their own understanding, and their own judgment, they must, almost necessarily, fall into error. But this support can only be given by forming, early, a mould for the religious spirit, and taking care that it shall be composed of historical facts, and sound, yet humble reasoning; united with the principles of reverence, obedience, and a sincere love of truth. If this mould is provided, then, when, through God's mercy, the *feeling* of religion shall spring up into consciousness—as assuredly under the light of a consistent example it will—we shall find that it will, naturally, and without effort, develop itself in the form prepared for it, and in that form will deepen

and intensify;—silently, without doubt or controversy; and, above all, without any of that bitterness which makes a self-chosen creed, and an adopted Church, too often synonymous with uncharitableness and narrowness.

And this must be the system of our religious education. For it is a system, inasmuch as it deals with definite aims, and works with definite instruments. Members of the English Church will desire to see their children grow up in that Church. It is to them that the advice, proffered by one who is blest in belonging to the same Communion, must necessarily be addressed. But the principle put forward is universal. In order to be firm in the faith ourselves, and to bring up our children in a like stability of religious belief, we must understand the ground upon which we stand; and determine the limits within which human reason may safely be trusted, and an independent judgment be exercised.

It is more important than any knowledge connected with this world. We may be content to leave our children ignorant of geology, and botany, and chemistry; we may even give up the cherished hope of hearing them speak French with a Parisian accent, and discuss the merits of Goethe in his own tongue; but if we leave them ignorant and uncertain as regards the foundation of their religious belief, there may come a day,—possibly it may not be far distant,—when the cry of the human soul as it stands upon the brink of Eternity, and demands why it is to believe what it has heard concerning that Eternity, will startle us with an appeal which will close our ears to the claims of all other knowledge.

If it should ever be our lot to hear such a cry, and to feel that it is too late to attempt to answer it, we shall then learn to estimate the value of the inquiry. If we should ever know what it is to watch a young mind,—strong in its natural powers, eager in its self-confidence, yet subject to the influence of a weakened and agonized body,—looking forth from the bed of death, longing for certainty, but owning no authority except its own reason, no guide except its own feeling, we shall then

own how important,—how infinitely important,—it is, to clear away the mists from the judgment, before that hour of trial shall arrive ;—before the evening shadows close around, and the night cometh in which man cannot think, even as he cannot work.

Still more fully, perhaps, shall we comprehend it, if it has been our privilege to minister to the young and the dying who have never known doubt, because they have always been taught to recognize the true ground of certainty.

We may have been called upon to mark the sudden decay of a young and beautiful life ;—the rapid downward steps of disease, the rush that it makes towards Death ; and we may have trembled in anticipation of the possible suggestions and uncertainties as to Divine truth, which in some hour of weakness may shake the faith that would fain rest wholly on its Saviour. But we have no cause to fear. The heart trusts then, because it has always trusted. It believes, because it knows that it has ground for belief. Its habit has been that of quiet conviction ; the grasp of certain truths to which it may cling, even were the universe crumbling around it ; and the shock of Death cannot now disturb it. Though the bodily frame may be daily weakened, and the affections may at times be troubled, and the brain for a moment confused ; the inward abiding stay remains still untouched. And at the last, when Death is very near, perhaps God will permit us to witness its full power, in a sudden development of spiritual life,—of love, and faith, and hope,—which would seem the foretaste of the great change that shall convert the earthly into the Heavenly, and clothe the mortal with Immortality.

Or again, there may be no sudden change,—only the gradual fading away, the dying out of the old life, and the gradual dawning of the new. There may be little pain, no fear,—but rather, calm hope gradually brightening into joy ; obedience, which uses thankfully the aids offered it, because it has always been taught to value them as means of grace and blessing ; an untroubled imagination, which pictures death as "a sleep from which it shall wake up dazzled ;" and a faith which rests upon

the Redeemer, because the young heart, with all its consciousness of sinfulness, has no thought that it can go to any but Him, and longs that "He, rather than the angels, should come to bear the soul away, because with Him it would feel more safe."

Very beautiful, unutterably comforting, is such a deathbed! —even though there may be bodily suffering and weariness before the spirit is permitted to return to its God. The Lord has been "the shepherd," feeding the soul with His truth, "so that it should not want." He has made the awakening intellect to lie down in "green pastures," even the rest of a firm conviction; and now He calls the young spirit to Himself, that He may "lead it beside the still waters"—the rivers that gladden the Paradise of His Redeemed.

These are no fictions. They are not ideal pictures. They are facts, truths, Eternal Realities. The well-grounded faith of life is the preparation for the calm trust in Death. There is an abiding objective truth; and apart from it, truth which is subjective can never expect to stand against the temptations of a scoffing world. God has united them, and we may not dare to separate them.

And the teaching of this objective truth is put in our power; whilst the implanting and growth of subjective truth is dependent upon the working of God's Spirit. We can instruct children in the evidence upon which faith in their Redeemer is built; but we cannot make them recognize its Divine origin, from the effects which it produces in themselves, until, through God's grace, the principle of faith is awakened in their hearts.

Yet it is necessary to guard these statements from misapprehension. It is not for one moment meant that an acquaintance with the grounds of faith constitutes saving faith, or that salvation depends upon such knowledge. Thousands, we may fully believe, will hereafter enter Heaven who have never even known what is meant by the grounds of faith; thousands who have loved their Saviour, and worshipped in humility, accord-

ing to the fashion of their forefathers, without being able to give any answer to the question,—why they believe the Bible, and why they submit themselves to the Church.

But it is equally true that such inquiries are rife in these days; that they will, in all probability, meet our children in their after life; and that the fact of being unable to answer them may involve danger to the faith by which they are to be saved.

And it is also true, that these subjects, when taken up heartily and thoroughly understood, give a feeling of stability to the whole system of religion which acts upon the moral character; sobers and strengthens it in life; and is, through God's mercy, the means of guarding it against the temptations of Satan in the hour of death.

And for that higher, more spiritual teaching, for which we so earnestly long, we must look to the working of God's Spirit, and His blessing upon our fervent prayers and our consistent example. Young people *feel* earnestness and sincerity more quickly than they feel any other qualities; and they will respond to them involuntarily and unconsciously. People talk as if the minds of children were naturally antagonistic to religion. It is not so. None who have been conversant with the education of children, and have put their hearts into the teaching they have given, will ever make such a statement. If children dislike religion, it is because they are teased with it. It is thrust upon them at unseasonable moments, or presented under a form which strikes them as affected or unreal, or awakens their sense of the ludicrous.

God made the child's heart for Himself, and He will win it, if we will not mar His work by our impatient folly.

What is really wonderful to those who watch the development of a young mind under definite, consistent, religious teaching and example, is not how great a dislike exists to religion, but how readily the heart is awakened to it,—how instinctive the longing for it is,—how soon it acts as a powerful principle. The interest which a child takes in conversation

upon serious subjects—upon matters affecting the conscience and practice, or even what may seem abstruse doctrines—is the deepest reproach to the so-called intellectual man of the world. He is spending his time in searching for pebbles, whilst the littte one whom he despises is gathering diamonds. It is the young in whose minds

> "———those truths do rest,
> Which we are toiling all our lives to find,
> In darkness lost—the darkness of the grave." [1]

The one thing which we have to guard against is the permitting shadows of religion to be mistaken for religion itself.

Feeling is very apt to deceive young people upon this point, and there is a time when they are especially exposed to the temptation—the time of their Confirmation and first Communion. A child brought up carefully and religiously in the English Church is taught, and very rightly, to look forward to this period as a most important one; as giving a fresh starting point; and when it arrives, there is a good deal of excitement mixed up with the solemn duties of preparation. Peculiar earnestness of feeling is likely to be aroused both in those who instruct and those who are taught, and the result is the growth of religious feeling. God forbid that any disparaging words should be uttered of such influences—much more that the benefits of Christ's ordinances, and the vast efficacy of His sacramental grace, should be for an instant doubted. But we shall be grievously disappointed if we suppose that any amount of feeling, awakened under peculiar circumstances, is a sure indication that the heart has been touched abidingly. In conversing with young people at such times, it is necessary to prepare them for the reaction which will almost inevitably follow the luxury of devotional excitement. Steady, even hard reading, and stern, practical tests of principle, require to be enforced at these times more than at any other; and if we see that the character does not stand this test, that there is a shrinking

[1] Wordsworth.

from little hardships and self-denial, though there may be very real compunction for past offences, very true faith, and earnest resolution, we may be perfectly sure that disappointment is in store for us. The mind has not yet grasped the fact that the full meaning of self-dedication is self-crucifixion. The heart has not yet given a *whole will* to God, and the course of the Christian life will probably be, even for years, fluctuating, feeble, uncertain.

We must be very patient, very gentle, with such weakness. It will never do to interfere too much. We shall only give an unreal stimulus by constant reminders, warnings, expostulations. The young soon learn to lean upon false supports. After a grave conversation the heart is softened, and new resolutions are made, and feeling is, as before, unconsciously mistaken for duty. We are all more or less liable to this mistake. Grown-up people are in the habit of bringing themselves up before the tribunal of their own hearts, confessing and sorrowing, and giving themselves absolution upon the strength of their penitence; and then going away and offending again; and when this confession is made by a young person to a tender and sympathizing human friend, the feeling of sorrow is assisted and encouraged, and the sense of the imaginary absolution is intensified; and so at length the mind learns to rest upon these seasons of better feeling, and to make them, as it were, a balance against the faults committed through weakness at other times.

In such cases, what is needed is that the character should be allowed to develop by itself; that the young heart should be left, if it must be so, to err, and to suffer from the error for a time, so that it may fully realize its own instability; and then suddenly be roused by an expostulation which will show plainly how far from the right path it has wandered.

So, again, fashions in religion are most delusive. Young people think themselves religious because they like daily services, accompanied with beautiful music; or because they listen with pleasure to a stirring sermon, or take an interest in

Church matters, and are fond of the village school-children. They do so just as their elders suppose that to enter eagerly into controversy implies a liking for religion; and that to criticize every service which does not come up to their own standard implies reverence. It does not do to be always preaching either to old or young upon these subjects, still less to cry them down, for they are no doubt important, and may be made real tests of right feeling; but it is very needful to show how entirely distinct and apart religion itself is from these adventitious circumstances. And more especially is it essential to watch against that form of feminine romance which Sir James Stephen so happily characterizes as "hieropathy," and which, if allowed to get the upper hand, will convert the solemnities of religion into the incentives to vanity and self-deceit.

And perfect simplicity and earnestness are above all things needful, as the basis of true charity. "Love, joy, peace, long-suffering, gentleness, goodness, faith, meekness, temperance,"[1] these are the things against which "there is no law." They may be found amongst all those who profess and call themselves Christians, and where they exist we are bound to recognize and honour them. Once lay firmly this broad foundation, and then we may, without danger, build upon it the edifice which we believe ourselves to be truth. For to admit that others think themselves to be right, and to honour them for sincerely acting upon their convictions, does not in the least imply that we do not consider them wrong, or that we are willing to yield one iota of the truth which we ourselves hold. We may be as steadfast as we will in supporting the purity of the faith,—and the more steadfast the more acceptable in God's sight,—only, we may not venture to speak harshly of those who differ from us. We condemn their opinions, but themselves we leave to the judgment of our common Master.

This is the most difficult lesson of all to teach young

[1] Galatians v. 22, 23.

people. They cannot see the distinction between conscientious and wilful error, so they are intolerant; and when they do see it, they are in danger of falling into the opposite mistake, and forgetting that we are all answerable for the right regulation of conscience, and therefore if we fail to use all the means in our power for enlightening it, we are guilty of a moral offence, though conscience itself may never raise its voice to warn us of it. Considerations like these are too abstruse for the young. They will never, or very rarely, work them out for themselves. Their warm feelings make them zealous, their ignorance makes them narrow-minded. If they have any religion at all, it is almost always sure to take a sectarian form, meaning by sectarianism that circumscribed view of Christianity which cannot separate truth from the error with which it is mingled, or recognize it under any form but that in which it has been presented to itself. The dogmatic liberality which makes a creed of scepticism, and would scornfully persecute all who decline to accept it, belongs to a more advanced period of life.

But there is no way of enforcing this charitable judgment, combined with the strict maintenance of truth,—there is no way, indeed, of enforcing any Christian practice or virtue,—except by exhibiting it in ourselves. Education is example. It is so in religion even more than in anything else, for religious influence is the action of heart upon heart. It is, indeed, but another word for God's grace. That sacred motive power which urges us forward will, sooner or later, through a blessing upon our instrumentality, urge forward others. All that we have to do is to put no obstacles in the way.

We wonder that our children are not religious, but are we so ourselves? Or if our hearts are really given to God, are we consistent in our practice? Have we always been so? May not the coldness we now deplore in these young creatures, in whom our affections are centred, be the working out of some of our own errors in former days? Even if the latter should be the case, there is no cause for despondency. God is pleased

to work in His Providence according to natural laws. As we sow, so shall we reap; and we are gathering now the fruits of our former folly. But there is no moment in this life in which we may not sow the seed of salvation with one hand, even whilst we are reaping the results of the seed of corruption with the other.

What has been done or left undone is, indeed, beyond recall; but the prayers, the love, the patience, the consistent example of holiness, which are to-day in our power, may be committed to God's keeping, in the full confidence that even if not permitted to gather their reward on earth, in the present conversion of the children we love, it will be ours in the great To-morrow of Eternity, when we shall be permitted to recognize the fulfilment of that enduring promise, "Cast thy bread upon the waters: for thou shalt find it after many days."

CHAPTER XXVIII.

SCHOOLS AND PRIVATE PUPILS.

AND now, alas!—may it not be said?—how unsatisfactory is all this! So many words used, but so little help given!

Principles! the world is weary of principles. What it wants is practice; rules, illustrations, definite landmarks. We all know what right principles are. The necessity of speaking truth and being obedient, is a necessity which dates from the Creation. The difficulties connected with intellectual instruction are the real stumbling-blocks in the way of good education. Who in these days cares for the fact that a little girl has never been known to disobey, or to tell a lie, when she is so dull that she cannot repeat the dates of the French kings, or state when Newfoundland was discovered?

And besides, the advice which has been given has been addressed to mothers; and the young girls of the present age are placed under the care of governesses, at home, or at school, as the case may be. Why is not some help given to these unfortunate foster-parents, who, without any of the happiness, have all the labour, and a great share of the anxiety, of mothers?

This latter complaint is natural, and in one sense just. A great portion of what has previously been said has been uttered under a supposition, which experience proves to be in England untrue, namely, that daughters are brought up by their mothers. But the advantage of principles, as opposed to systems and rules, is, that they are suited for all ages, seasons,

and circumstances. They may be carried out by the governess as well as by the parent; and as we have not yet arrived at the acknowledgment that mothers can lawfully delegate their whole responsibility to others, so we are compelled to address them as if they were in all cases willing to undertake it.

Or, it may also be said, education is distinct from instruction. The former—the training of the heart—belongs to the parent; the latter—the training of the intellect—to the governess. A book which treats upon education must, therefore, necessarily be written for mothers. But there is a fallacy in this assertion.

It is quite true that education and instruction are distinct, the one from the other. Education, is carried on by moral influence, exercised in the various modes which are furnished by the events of life. Instruction, is definite information or teaching, given upon particular subjects. We do not always know when we are educating, but we cannot be doubtful as to when we are instructing. But when we say that education and instruction are so distinct, as to be capable of entire separation, we fall into very serious error. We may, indeed, educate, without attempting to instruct; but it is impossible to instruct, without, at the same time, educating.

Every teacher, every master, admitted into a family, assists in the education of the children. It is a consequence not to be avoided. No lesson, however dry and commonplace, can be given without the exertion of a moral influence. Much more must this influence be exercised, when the lessons are given by some one person daily; and when this same person must be the constant companion, guide, and referee of the young mind committed to her charge.

This is a very grave thought, especially when we consider what, in so many cases, these teachers and governesses are;—how young and inexperienced, even when they are most excellent in their efforts and intentions.

It might, however, be, in a degree, a help to themselves if they would fully face the fact, and prepare themselves for it.

It would make their task much more arduous, but it would also make it infinitely more noble. They cannot be called upon simply to impart so much knowledge of French and History, since they must, in the very act, impart principles of self-command, patience, sympathy, gentleness, or the reverse. For these qualities are necessarily exhibited in the mode in which instruction is carried on; and every exhibition of a moral quality in ourselves, tends to impress it upon the mind with which, at the moment, we are brought into connection. All teachers—more especially those peculiarly termed governesses—have, therefore, very high influential positions in God's world.

But, it is said, they are dependent. They are earning their own bread, and are, in various ways, subject to human caprice.

Very true. Acknowledge it. An unpleasant truth is always less disagreeable when we have grasped it. And when it has been acknowledged, let it be held firmly, and let the world be confronted with it. We need have no fear, the world is a great coward. It will always run away from those who look at it courageously.

"Yes, I am a governess; earning my own livelihood; dependent, in so far that I have certain duties to perform, for which I am paid. But my work is not the less God's work, because I receive payment from man. The Rector of a parish is not the less Christ's Minister, because he receives tithes. God appointed the circumstances of my lot. He ordained that I should have no means of living, except by labour; and in that very Providential arrangement of my life, He showed me what I have to do for Him. It is a great work, and I thank Him for it. My friends think I am lowered in social position, and they are correct. According to the world's estimate, I am lowered, and I am willing to be so. I should be admired if I worked gratuitously. I should be thought a saint and a heroine. But work for God can only be undertaken in the form in which He sees fit to give it. He will not value me the less

because I perform two tasks instead of one; because, whilst working for His little ones, I also provide for my own maintenance, and perhaps help a mother, or a sister who cannot help herself. I accept, therefore, the world's commiseration, with the amount of gratitude which is due to it. It is meant kindly, but I do not need it. I take the materials of my life as God has given them, and do with them the best I can for His service. The prince upon his throne, the statesman in the senate, the philosopher in his closet, can do no more. I am content."

The world would smile were such a speech as this made to it. It would whisper of enthusiasm, romance—perhaps bring forward an accusation of pride; and it would watch for a while, suspiciously; and at last it would turn away in perplexity—but with respect.

And when the world's respect has been won, we can well afford to disregard its wondering smile! There is one pride, and one pride only, which is justifiable, because it is consistent with the deepest humility. To be God's special servant, His instrument for any particular purpose, is the highest dignity to which the human being can attain; and no one undertakes the education of a child without being raised to it.

Only one condition is required. The task must be fulfilled cheerfully, willingly;—not, indeed, always without a struggle, because human nature soon becomes weary, and longs for rest; and the heart is weak, and will at times sigh for the enjoyments of freedom and luxury;—but, nevertheless, with an entire subjugation of these inferior desires, and with a thankful sense of the infinite privilege of working in a definite manner for God.

And, now, what is the real state of the case as regards governesses, whether in private families, or in schools? What is the view which they themselves take of their own position, and which, therefore, they assist to form in the minds of others? For it must be remembered, as a general rule, that the world will place us on that level on which we place ourselves. It will do so often very absurdly. But the fact is true, and

those who watch the course of life cannot fail to remark it. If governesses are looked down upon, it is because they look down upon themselves; because they cannot, in the slightest degree, grasp the greatness of their duties.

They deem themselves victims to misfortune, and regard the world as their enemy. They think a great deal of social position, and are always guarding their dignity. So, they meet the world upon its own ground, and are of course judged by the world's judgment. Directly or indirectly, they are told that the place they wish to take is not that to which they have a right. They turn away offended, and show their annoyance by moodiness and unhappiness. Of course their employment becomes irksome to them; and—what is worse—the children given to their charge are regarded as the instruments of their suffering. But for their pupils, the world would treat them with respect; and the thought causes a fretting irritation, which makes the presence of the pupils a trial, and the very mention of them a source of annoyance.

Now, what is there noble in all this? What is there of the spirit which works for God voluntarily, thankfully? Allowing that it is natural, yet is it not petty and ungrateful? Can we think that God will acknowledge as done for Him that work which is only done because without it we must starve? And does not the world recognize the meanness of the spirit? Do not the children feel it? If the governess works only because she is obliged to do so, and reckons the worth of her services at so much per annum, will they not take her at her own estimation? will they not look upon her instruction merely as so much teaching given in return for value received?

The question is one to be answered by all persons who undertake the duty of education as a profession.

According to the spirit in which we work, so will be the value put upon that work. Labour for the world, and the world will put its own price upon us—history so much, languages so much, accomplishments so much. An accurate valuation to be made in gold—and in nothing more. Labour

for God, and no matter what we receive—be it little or much, according to the capabilities which God has given us for our vocation—there is one talent the value of which is priceless; the influence of a noble, disinterested, religious mind, which accepts its place in the world with indifference because it has a place in the vineyard of God. And we may be assured that, let the world strive as it may to undervalue this talent, it will in the end be compelled to estimate it at its true worth.

It is, indeed, vain to insist upon the necessity of right principles of education—to explain and enforce them—so long as the persons who are to carry them out are themselves devoid of the very elementary principle which forms the foundation of all lasting religious influences. Children are not educated by the *act* of instruction, but by the *spirit* of instruction. If we look upon them merely as so many instruments for gaining money in an unpleasant way, we may talk to them like Angels, and they will receive our lessons and repeat them, and then turn away and do precisely contrary to them.

It is not, indeed, requisite that all persons who undertake to be governesses should delight in the act of teaching, or rejoice in the anxiety inseparable from the charge of young people. A clergyman does not necessarily like visiting the poor, or superintending a Sunday School; but what he does—if he is really in earnest—is to put a noble spirit into his work; to like it, not in itself, but because it is done for God.

And when once this spirit possesses the heart, all worldly considerations—even those which concern that most difficult subject of pecuniary remuneration—will soon assume their right proportion. It may be desirable to enter into this point more particularly. The same Master who appoints the work gives it to us also under certain conditions. In the case under consideration it is to be work done for His glory, but also for an earthly maintenance. Prudence, forethought, a due self-estimation, are therefore as necessary as earnestness and industry. If persons have pupils in their own house, they are

not at liberty to indulge in speculations, and experiments, and lavishness. Supposing they had money at command and could work—voluntarily, as it is called—such things might be allowable; but God has placed them under certain restraints, and they must submit themselves to them. Every one understands this. Children understand it. No child when sent away from home for education expects to find the same luxuries which are to be met with in her father's house; because, as society now exists, the act of taking pupils is a confession of being, in a certain sense, poor. But there are some things which children require, even if they do not expect them—liberality, refinement, propriety, and that amount of care for their physical well-being which shall make them comfortable, and teach them how to observe the niceties and decorums essential for their after life. These things are just as much a part of good education as instruction in moral duties, and far more so than the teaching of languages and accomplishments. Are they cared for as they ought to be by all who receive pupils into their own houses? If they are not, what must be the result?

Whether the effect of crowding young girls together in one bedroom, giving them no means of privacy, stinting them in the time necessary for their toilette, summoning them to hasty ill-appointed meals, and hiring inferior servants to wait upon them—can be compensated for by any amount of first-rate masters, or any quantity of "classes" for imbibing science and history, may be proved by the tone and style usually known as that of a school-girl. It is not the *learning* together which makes girls school-girlish; it is the *living* together; the being herded like animals in one fold;—the sense of sham and pretence, the fact that the decencies of life are disregarded in the bedroom, though there may be damask and ormolu in the drawing-room. No child thinks the less of the governess who says, "My dear, I cannot afford to give you such or such indulgences," but every child despises the effort to conceal economy by false appearances. And this disgust will develop itself into secret contempt. The slightest taint of meanness

or unreality will utterly destroy children's respect. They are very severe judges, and they cannot make the allowances which their elders can. They do not know the pressure of poverty which lies behind the outward show of affluence. They are aware that their parents give a certain sum for their education, and they feel that for this sum they have a right to expect certain comforts. They can tell nothing of the outlay required before a school can be opened; or of the family claims which carry away what might otherwise be profit. If they did, they might be more merciful to shabby economy; or, in other words, economy which is ashamed to confess itself what it is; but they would never respect it: it is not a thing to be respected. Poverty may be honourable; truth must always be so; but pretence is and ever must be despicable. And unless a child respects her governess, she will deceive her. There lies the great evil of inferior schools. Deceit is not taught, but it is imbibed: it exists in the atmosphere; and upon deceit will follow a train of unnumbered, unutterable evils.

School-girl tricks, a school-girl tone, are accepted by many persons as belonging to a certain age, but as being sure to pass away with that age. It is a great mistake. The school-girl tone is low, untrue, irreverent: it is based upon the belief that education is a mere matter of bargaining; and that as the governess desires to make the most for herself in money, so the pupils may make the most for themselves in what they call fun, or, more truly, deceit. And it will last long after the period of school life is over. It will exhibit itself in an outward polish of manner, but no ease; a flimsy show of accomplishments, and very little information; a flippant tone of conceit, and a weak judgment; an intense secret worldliness, combined with the newest fashion in religion. It is not only essentially "of the earth, earthy;" but it implies the lowest kind of earthliness. And let the instruction given in a school be what it may—let the scriptural instruction be orthodox, the precepts of morality pure, the French and German teachers

unwearied, the music master first-rate—this will be the result of school education, so long as the pecuniary profit is the first subject of consideration, and mean economies are practised in order to save money.

And yet pecuniary profit must be a consideration; the very existence of a school implies that it is.

Undoubtedly.—But let it be avowed to the parents, not exhibited to the children.

If young people, not members of the family, are to be brought up in the habits of cultivated society, they must be accustomed to comforts and refinements. If they are to learn what is meant by Christian liberality, thoughtfulness for their equals, consideration for the needy, these virtues must be exhibited before them. And if the governess does not ask a sufficiently large sum to pay the expenses of her household, and to leave a surplus for other claims, she cannot teach them these important lessons; and she is almost inevitably induced to make economy her first object, and the well-being of the children her second. She cannot give them separate rooms, because that involves taking a larger house, and house-rent is ruinous. She cannot even fit up the rooms she has, comfortably, so as to ensure privacy, because this involves buying new furniture, and making other arrangements which cost money. She cannot give them a good dinner, because that necessitates a good cook; and good cooks demand high wages. She cannot have a well-appointed table, with sufficient attendance; because that again requires well-trained servants, who will expect liberal remuneration. And with all her care, her own future needs meet her at every turn. How is she to provide for them?

Numbers. That is the secret. Boys are congregated together by hundreds, and head masters are said to make wonderful fortunes. Why may it not be the same with girls? One thing is certain, that no one ever made money—according to the usual acceptation of the phrase—by taking a few private pupils. It is possible in this way to live, and to live in com-

fort; but to save largely is out of the question. So it is that the cry for cheap schools is followed by the establishment of large schools; and with a large school set up for the purpose of making money, there must necessarily be associated the hateful school-girl tone.

And the remedy? It lies far back, and is very difficult of attainment, for it rests with no less than three parties. First, and most obviously, with the governess. A person who undertakes to educate, cannot conscientiously make money a first object, however much it may be needed. When we have to deal with immortal souls, everything which exercises an influence upon those souls becomes of primary importance. If therefore privacy, refinement, personal comfort—a thing perfectly distinct from luxury—and that general sense of ease and liberality which cannot fail to be associated with a well-ordered household, are means of influence—as undoubtedly they are—then must these things be provided before any attempt is made to save. To ask a small sum from the parents, and to make it go as far as a large one, by stinting the children in regard to those necessaries of life which must tend to form their characters, and give them the habits and tastes of ladies, is deceit of the worst kind.

And still further, if the fact of herding young girls together in numbers—even when liberality is practised—involves any absence of provision for delicacy and modesty; if it renders it impossible for the governess to give them individual attention; and necessitates leaving them to inferior teachers, and indiscriminate companionship, and neglecting the personal superintendence, which is the only means of gaining a real influence over them, then must the idea of making money by numbers be relinquished. It is a question for each person's conscience. The ill effects of congregating girls in numbers may not be evident to all. There may be some who see, or think they see, means by which it may be avoided. It is only the principle which is here insisted upon. Education is a religious task. It must be undertaken in a religious spirit. The fact of being

paid for it, and of needing that payment as a means of subsistence, does not, in the very slightest degree, lessen its responsibility, or release those who undertake it from the obligation of consulting, first, before any private advantage, the moral well-being of their pupils.

But does this mean that large private schools, low terms, and good education for girls, are as a rule incompatible? Perhaps it does. Perhaps it would be better for the community at large if the fact were acknowledged.

Certainly it would be much safer for parents. They would not then be tempted by cheap schools, in which the deficiencies of quality are to be made up by quantity. And it would certainly be happier for the governess, who must often be sorely tried, whilst endeavouring to satisfy her conscience, without giving up her object.

When we have no anticipations, we have no disappointments. It is the "hope deferred" which "maketh the heart sick." We shall do better without any hope, than with one which is exaggerated. To limit the number of pupils, and to give them all which is essential for their education in refined habits, will probably leave only a small surplus for what may be termed profits. And personal claims may be many and heavy; and sickness and age may be looming in the distance; and when men can summon boys together by hundreds, and after a few years' labour retire with a fortune, why—it may be asked—should not women be permitted to do the same with girls; instead of being called upon to labour for many years, and retire with only a bare maintenance?

The answer may be very distasteful. But what are we to do if nature and experience tell us that this gregarious education for girls is injurious?

The aim of education is to fit children for the position in life which they are hereafter to occupy. Boys are to be sent out into the world to buffet with its temptations, to mingle with bad and good, to govern and direct. The school is the type of the life they are hereafter to lead. Girls are to dwell in

quiet homes, amongst a few friends; to exercise a noiseless influence, to be submissive and retiring. There is no connection between the bustling mill-wheel life of a large school and that for which they are supposed to be preparing. This alone is a sufficient reason for supposing, even on a cursory glance, that to educate girls in crowds is to educate them wrongly.

But there are other objections even more important, though perhaps less obvious.

A boy's mind is not so easily sullied as a girl's. Indiscriminate companionship may with the former have an injurious effect for the time, but it does not leave the same lasting stain as with the latter. Undesirable knowledge is not an equal shock to the moral nature. If a girl's natural delicacy and modesty are wounded by intercourse with those who have learnt evil, of which she has hitherto been ignorant, the scars of the wound remain for years, and the conversation of one hour will leave its stamp upon the memory for life. And so also the spirit of independence and determination, the conflict of opinion, the roughnesses even of a large school, are congenial to a boy's nature, they are utterly opposed to that of a girl. There is an element of good in these things, but when applied to girls the evil preponderates. Strong-minded, or, in other words, masculine women, are no doubt useful in their generation; but we may well desire to be delivered from them as a race. And yet further—there is amongst boys, especially at public schools, a recognition of the world's opinion, a traditionary honour which acts as a check to the pettiness, the deceit, and frivolity that too often characterize assemblies of girls. Boys sin more openly, but less meanly than girls; and because their offences are open, they are more easily known and punished, and have less enduring consequences. Girls in a large school may for months carry on a course of deceit which may injure them for life, and no one will be the wiser. These considerations alone may be sufficient to show that the objection to crowding girls together in large schools is founded upon common sense and experience. Many other evils might be

adduced, but public opinion, though in this case often exhibited in the form of prejudice which can give no reason for its decision, is for the most part enlisted on the same side; and therefore the subject does not need to be enforced further. The best that can be said for the opposite view of the question is, that large schools are generally cheaper than those with limited numbers; and that it is hard that women, who have to labour in the arduous vocation of teaching, should not make a full profit by it.

Even so; it is hard, in the worldly sense: but it is not hard in any other sense, because it is in accordance with the dispensations of God. His Providence works by general laws, and according to those laws women are not meant to stand alone, but are made dependent upon men. Exceptions to a law cannot be judged by the same reasoning which is applied to the law itself. They must always press hardly, and therefore it is that women who undertake the task of education require above all things to put their work upon the very highest religious grounds. If they undertake it in the hope of really making money, they will in all probability either be tempted to sacrifice the good of their pupils for the attainment of their purpose, or they will labour in a liberal and conscientious spirit for years, only to sink at last under the disappointment of unfounded expectations.

Surely it is better far to face the truth at once—to look upon education as a profession in which persons are especially appointed to labour for God's service, so long as He gives the power; and by means of which He wills not that they should make a fortune and then live at ease, but simply be provided for when He takes away those powers.

To collect as many children as we can possibly crowd together,—to summon masters and mistresses around us, and with their aid to carry on a whirling dance through the circle of sciences and accomplishments supposed necessary for a finishing education,—and at the end of a few years to pause breathless, and exclaim, "Thank God, it is over; I have made

so many thousand pounds, and now I am free!" may be very natural, but it is certainly not very elevated. And should the dance be continued through many years, and no thousands be forthcoming at the end, then must it be owned to be bitterly disappointing; whilst under any circumstances, if higher considerations are taken into account, the retrospect of such an earthly aim can scarcely fail to produce keen self-reproach.

CHAPTER XXIX.

SCHOOLS AND PRIVATE PUPILS—(*continued*).

We have seen that it is incumbent upon those who receive pupils to look at the facts of life bravely; to make pecuniary advantage a thoroughly secondary object, and to put their work before them in its highest point of view; but assuredly if this be so, parents are no less called upon to regard education as a good for which they must be willing and prepared to make sacrifices.

Many—all, indeed, who have their children's true interest at heart—do so; but they would, perhaps, be more satisfied if they would sometimes, in imagination, change places with those who have the responsibility and expense of education, and ask how they could themselves have managed, if placed in a similar position. Persons at whose call money has always been ready, do not in the least understand what it is to set up a house without money—to begin life with a burden, and to struggle for years, and still to be apparently no nearer the moment of release. It is not the yearly expenditure which presses upon the majority of women who undertake a school, but that which must be incurred before a single pupil can be received. Education is and must be expensive so long as it is carried on as a speculation, though one which is perfectly honourable. If, therefore, parents dread the unavoidable evils which accompany crowding girls together in large numbers, and inuring them to shabby economies; they must not be surprised if they are told that smaller numbers, refinement, and liberality, are incompatible with low terms. They may be vexed to find it so, but they will do wisely to acknowledge it.

As a general rule, no education at all at home is better than that of a large boarding school, where money is a matter of primary importance. And when parents become convinced of this, and refuse to sacrifice their children's highest interests by supporting them, some other means of cheap education will, it cannot be doubted, be found.

We have learnt to despise day schools; they are looked upon as plebeian, and, unquestionably, there are serious disadvantages connected with them. Yet, upon consideration, we may, perhaps, come to the conclusion, that the bad effects of promiscuous association for a few hours in the day, and for a special purpose, are not likely to be as great as an almost equally promiscuous companionship, not only at certain times, for certain purposes, but throughout the whole day—during seasons of recreation, and even by night. Children will not learn good manners at a day school; but will they learn them at a large boarding school? If a governess at home is, for any reason, undesirable,—if careful education, with small numbers, is found too expensive,—it might, possibly, be worth the trial whether a very superior day school, established in a locality which provides good masters, might not be carried on with sufficient pecuniary profit to the governess, and with greater intellectual advantages, and much less risk to the children, than that which attends the present system of herding them together in one house. There would be a good deal of prejudice to contend against at first, and especially the fear of indiscriminate companionship, which is so objectionable to our English feeling. But it must be remembered that we are only considering a question of comparative evils. And such a school as is here intended would not profess to be a cheap school, so as to hold out attractions to persons of really inferior social position. Five-and-twenty pounds a year would be considered very expensive for a day school; but for that sum a thoroughly well educated, clever, and high-principled woman might take the superintendence of twenty children, provide most efficient assistance, live herself in comfort, and make a

yearly provision for the needs of illness and old age. If she had to make a home for them, and were to ask forty instead of five-and-twenty pounds, she would be compelled to take an expensive house, and so to burden herself with debt at the outset; to crowd the children in a way which would be utterly demoralizing; to stint them of everything but bare necessaries; and to obtain the cheapest assistance of whatever kind it might be; and at the end of the year she would, in all probability, find herself not only as far off as ever from a provision for the future, but actually with an increase of debt upon her shoulders.

Really superior women will not take these risks, much less will they sacrifice the good of their pupils for their own profit. Cheap schools, therefore, must fall into the hands of an inferior class. Now, it is for parents to consider which is the best: to give their children the advantage of thoroughly good teaching for a few hours in the day, undertaking themselves the responsibility and expense of their home life; or to give them very inferior teaching, lowering influences, and education in unrefined habits;—only with the comfort of knowing that the children will be entirely off their hands for a certain number of months in the year. The idea here thrown out is merely a suggestion. It may not be found to answer, but the present state of female education in England certainly demands that some change should be made by which persons of small incomes who, from any cause, find it undesirable to educate their daughters at home, may be enabled to give them really good instruction, and not be compelled to have recourse to cheap boarding schools.

Perhaps if some such school were once established and supported, it would draw around it persons with small incomes in the same way as endowed grammar schools do. The daily instruction given at a grammar school will not compare with the training which a boy receives at Eton, Winchester, or Harrow, but it is unquestionably better than that of Dotheboys Hall.

Before, however, such a form of education can be adopted, parents must be prepared to make considerable sacrifices of time and personal comfort. A governess at home is a luxury, because she is always ready to do what the mother does not find it convenient to do. She may be young, inexperienced, ignorant—still she is the governess, and the children can always be left with her. A child at a boarding school is still less of a charge, in fact she is no charge at all; the responsibility has been yielded to another, and, except in the holidays, there is no cause to be anxious about her.

But if young girls are to be absent only a few hours in the day, they must be their mother's companions at other times, or what is to be done with them? This is certainly a serious difficulty; but, upon consideration, it seems to have assumed its present proportions very much in consequence of a huge evil which has, almost unknown to ourselves, crept stealthily into our households, until it is gradually moulding the whole character and tone of the educated classes of the women of England.

Mothers and daughters live still in the same home, but they have ceased to live the same lives. The mother's home is the drawing-room, the child's home is the schoolroom; and when the mother goes into the schoolroom she is decidedly *de trop*, and when the child goes into the drawing-room she puts on her best frock, and assumes her company manners. Such an assertion as this is, indeed, very broad—a vast number of exceptions to it may be brought forward—but, nevertheless, it is most certainly the spirit of the English education of the present day. Mothers do too often devolve their duties upon others, and suffer a loss of affection and interest in consequence; and any kind of education which throws back upon them the daily charge of their young daughters will be likely to be felt as a burden. So long as this is the case, a boarding school, though inferior, will always carry away the palm from a day school, though the instruction given in it may be of a first-rate character.

Parents therefore, as well as governesses, must be ready to

do their part in education, if the training of English girls is to be improved. Those who can give but little for their children's instruction, must be willing to take a larger share of trouble of a different kind. But, beyond and before all this, there is a third mode by which the position of governesses of all kinds would be improved, and the cause of education advanced. It is very obvious—so obvious that the mention of it will, probably, provoke a smile—and yet it is often singularly overlooked.

Why is it that, in England, so many fathers in the professional ranks—from which the majority of governesses are taken—give little or no thought to their daughters' future maintenance, except so far as it may be secured by marriage?

A man, we will suppose, proposes to marry upon a comfortable income, dependent upon his own exertions. He is ready to make some small provision for his wife; perhaps sufficient for herself, but not in the least sufficient for the expenses of a family. The wife's relations are satisfied with this. The wife herself has, probably, no fortune, and, therefore, her prospects are for the present bettered by her marriage; and the husband's good professional income will, it is thought, allow of his saving enough for his children. So the marriage takes place, and for some years all goes well; the household is kept on a liberal scale; no comforts are denied to any one, and social claims are well attended to. The boys are sent to a public school, and from thence to college. The girls are educated at home by a succession of governesses, aided by expensive masters. The father feels that he labours to make money, and thinks he is at liberty to enjoy it. His circumstances are affluent, and he has a right to live with all the luxuries and refinements of affluence. Suddenly he is taken ill; he is on his deathbed; he thinks of the future for his wife and children, and he is satisfied. He made a provision for his wife when he married, and women require but little; his boys are all placed in professions; his daughters will no doubt sooner or later marry. So, in regard to this one point, he dies happy.

But what is the true state of the case? There is a provision for the wife—just enough for her to live upon; but what is there for the daughters? The sum which was barely sufficient for one, how can it meet the expenses of four, or perhaps five? The daughters see this plainly. They cannot be dependent on their mother. There is but one thing to be done. They will take pupils. But this involves a large house—furnishing; the unnumbered expenses of a new establishment. Then comes borrowing, then debts and anxiety, and bitter disappointment. They begin life penniless, and in all probability they will end it penniless.

And this is taking a better case than usual. In very many instances, women of the educated classes, who are forced to labour for themselves, have nothing at all to fall back upon; there is not even a provision for their mother. It is impossible for them, if they receive pupils into their own homes, to make education cheap; for to them it is very dear. They must make the parents of their pupils pay for the claims which burden them, as well as for the outlay demanded by their occupation. If they did not, it would not be the part of prudence to labour in such a vocation at all. But now, suppose the father had exercised a little forethought upon these matters—suppose he had, during the whole course of his married life, kept before him, as a subject of the first importance, the position of his daughters after his death, in case they remained unmarried. What difference would it have made in his actions? First of all, he would certainly have done his utmost to lay by something for them—even though it might have entailed the giving up of all personal luxuries. But it is probable that in many instances, even with the greatest self-denial, to lay by anything would be found impossible. Saving is a very slow process, and family and educational expenses are heavy; and the profession of a gentleman requires, even for its own support, that a man should live as a gentleman. In that case, surely, a man of sense and principle would put this fact before his children, and prepare for it.

Which is the worse for a young girl—to enter upon life perfectly acquainted with her true position, and ready to do a definite work in the best way? or to wake up to the necessity when her nerves are weakened and her heart is oppressed, and both body and soul are bowed down by the weight of an overwhelming affliction?

It is cowardice and cruelty—the words may seem very severe, but they are not the less true—to bring up girls with false expectations; to accustom them to unnecessary luxuries, and to waste the money which would be of inestimable value in the future, in indulging all the useless fancies of the present. True, a father may not be able to leave his daughters enough for their comfortable maintenance after his death; but he may save something which shall be an assistance to them when they are thrown upon their own resources.

A thousand pounds will produce but a very small income; yet it may make all the difference between beginning work with a burden of debt, or in the comfort of independence. And if young people are told what they are to have, and taught beforehand how they are to act, they will lose that sense of helplessness and isolation which crushes a woman's spirit even before she begins to face the struggle of life.

For women are wholly unlike men in this respect. A young man is stirred and stimulated by the consciousness of how much depends upon his own exertions: a young girl is, speaking generally, oppressed by it. She may rise superior to it—hundreds do,—and struggle nobly, and breast the waves which threaten to overwhelm them, and at length reach a secure haven; but it is with the continued sense of something unnatural in their position. There is a strain upon the intellect, a tension of the nerves, which blunts the capacity for enjoyment, and produces premature old age; and this result is almost inevitable: yet it may be infinitely lessened by care and forethought.

A father who loves his daughters, and takes pride in them, cannot bear to think of the future in store for them; and because the subject is painful he puts it from him; but if he would

make that future *present*, he might often lessen its burden a hundred-fold.

They must work eventually—why should they not work now? He is at hand to give them advice and assistance. If they must hereafter support themselves, either entirely or mainly, it will surely be much happier for them to go forth to their labor with a knowledge that they have a shelter to which they may return, and parents who are watching their success, than with the terrible sense of desolation which accompanies the first break-up of a happy home.

The father may find it pleasant to himself to spend his full income in giving his children indulgences; but it will in the end be unspeakably pleasanter for them if he will appropriate his surplus funds to setting them out in the world, through which they will afterwards have to make their way alone.

It is indeed against our English prejudices for persons living in a certain circle of society to come forward and bravely state that they have not the means of maintaining their families in comfort at the present moment, and at the same time providing a sufficient income for the future. But there are a great many English prejudices which are in the process of being broken down; and there are none which may not be ultimately conquered if only some determined minds will exert themselves to combat them. If but a few of the daughters of men living in comfortable homes, and moving in cultivated society, yet having no provision for the future, were bravely to come forward and undertake either to be private governesses, or to receive pupils in their own homes, whilst their fathers are living, they would set an example which would by degrees be followed; the world would be compelled to accord to the profession a higher position, and the prejudice would at length be conquered. With this the whole tone of education would be raised. Children imbibe insensibly the opinions of their parents; and because, in a social point of view, their governesses are considered their inferiors, therefore, without meaning it, they learn to look down upon them; and the reaction upon

their own minds is most injurious. A boy does not feel this towards his tutor. Society recognizes the clergyman who takes pupils as being on a footing with any other gentleman; and even the young nobleman knows that his present master may, at some future day, take his seat in the House of Lords. But there is no such elevation in store for a lady. Her profession is in most cases a descent in the social scale. She cannot bear to acknowledge this in her own immediate neighbourhood; and in consequence, when compelled to provide for herself, she seeks a situation where she is unknown, and where that which she considers humiliation may be less keenly felt.

Yet her work is directly appointed by God. She is employed to train souls for heaven! If the smile of derision could ever cross the face of an angel, might it not be excited by the pride which can think it noble to live at ease, and spend the precious days of a life, on which Eternity depends, in croquet, light literature, and music;—and humiliating to labour with the Lord of the Universe, to be a fellow-worker with the Redeemer of mankind?

But that thought is one which it is in vain to bring before the world. It may be a support to the governess, but it will not act upon society at large. *That* can only be reached by appeals to its own principles. When the sons of gentlemen voluntarily enter any particular profession, that profession is necessarily raised. When the daughters of gentlemen voluntarily do the same, we may expect similar results.

But how would this affect the principles on which school education is carried on, and how would it act upon the question of expense? Probably in this way.

If ladies, not absolutely at the moment obliged to educate, would come forward to undertake the task, they would do so under more favourable circumstances than can possibly be anticipated under the present system of extreme compulsion. They would not have the same pressing family claims, or be called upon to incur a great outlay without being certain of the

means of providing for it. Immediate pecuniary profits would be a less indispensable condition of all these plans. They would be able to make more careful domestic arrangements, and the necessity of numbers would be less felt. And these things would act upon the pupils. They would be a check upon the school-girl spirit, and raise the whole tone of the household. A good school in which there would be no overwhelming numbers, and where the privacy and comfort of the children were perfectly secured, might be carried on for much less if there were not relations in the background to be provided for, and borrowed moneys, demanding a high interest, to be paid off. Still more would this be the case if the work could be recognized as a pleasant and honourable profession, involving no loss of social position; but which might be undertaken in the vigour of life, and be a happy employment for years, in a home neighbourhood, and amongst home friends. Highly educated, superior women, who now undertake schools, begin their task, for the most part, in middle life, when the spring of their energy is destroyed, and they are broken down by sorrow. They know that they have but a few years in which they can work, and therefore they are compelled to set a high price upon their labour. They feel that it has displaced them from their original position, and they find it in consequence unutterably irksome, and their one desire is to shorten the term of their trial. They cannot afford to wait in the hope of gaining their end by slow degrees, for if they do they know that they shall never attain it at all. High terms or none are their only alternatives. If society complains of the expense, and the inferiority of female education, it must make the profession more attractive; it must offer counterbalancing advantages for the sacrifice which it requires. It will never do this of its own accord, yet it may be compelled to do so by outward pressure; and that pressure can be put upon it by persons already holding a position in cultivated society, who bravely and voluntarily enter it, working with the highest of all aims, and not bowed down with the weight of *immediate* pecuniary need.

CHAPTER XXX.

GOVERNESSES IN FAMILIES.

But all this time we have been speaking of that much to be envied class of instructresses who are enabled to carry on their work in their own houses, and who, whatever may be their labour and their responsibility, have at least the luxury of independence, and can make their own arrangements, and dictate their own terms.

But governesses in private families, what is their position? How can it in any way be improved? According to general report, the position of an upper servant in England (they manage these things better abroad) is infinitely preferable to that of a governess. And yet society, as it now exists, cannot get on without governesses. It is, after all, the cheapest kind of education for a family, and most in accordance with our English habits. To send a girl away from home for education is almost always a *pis aller*. It is a plan adopted because nothing better is practicable. How is it, then, that persons so indispensably necessary, are looked down upon and made miserable?

There would seem to be two reasons. First, the social position in which the world places them. Secondly, that in which they place themselves.

The first of these subjects has been partially discussed in the observations already made. Whether a person is a governess in a private family, or undertakes to receive pupils in her own home, she must come before the world with a claim

for pity, when she begins her work, because she is driven to it by great pecuniary necessity; and the world's pity is certainly much more akin to contempt than love.

It is very sad, but we shall never make things better by trying to hide from ourselves the truth. Lessen the compulsion and the pecuniary need, and you lessen the contempt. Parents only can do this. They only can sacrifice their own present gratification for their children's future benefit; and seeing what lies before their daughters, not only prepare them for it, but send them out to their work with the shelter and support of their own name and position. Parents in the lower classes do so. They place their young daughters in situations where they can earn their own livelihood; and the little girl begins her work in the freshness of youth, and earns her small independence; and, if any care is taken of her, is enabled to put by trifling sums which, gradually accumulating, become the nest egg that is to give her the means of marrying should the opportunity offer. Amongst the lower orders, the woman can contribute her share towards the commencement of housekeeping, because she has been permitted to work for it. Amongst the educated classes she pines in silent dejection and hopelessness, because society has thought fit to assert that the woman who works for herself loses her social position; and no one has the courage to brave the assertion, and the daughter is not permitted to labour for herself, whilst the father holds his social rank as heretofore.

But even supposing a young girl to begin life as a governess under the most favourable circumstances—with a parent's sanction and assistance, without any heavy pressure of pecuniary need, and with all the hope and energy of youth—still the position is one of dependence and inferiority. Servants will be disrespectful, visitors will be wanting in courtesy. There must be a sense of humiliation.

Must! That is a word very commonly used, merely because no one will take the trouble to inquire whether any other is more fitting. Humiliation implies the loss of something to

which we have a right; but if we have no right there can be no humiliation. The prince is humbled when he is treated as a subject; but the subject accepts the same treatment with indifference.

And it is a question of serious moment whether the complaints of neglect made by governesses do not very frequently arise more from the false view which they take of their own position, than from any intentional absence of kindness and attention from the persons with whom they live. As a general rule, foreign governesses are much more agreeable inmates of a house than English ones. Something of this may be owing to the interest excited by difference of manner, dress, and tone. Something, also, to the imposing influence of a foreign tongue, which takes no note of difficulties that to ourselves are insurmountable. A good Parisian accent will always command a certain amount of respect. But beyond all is the fact that foreigners are less tenacious of their dignity—they are less suspicious of insult, and therefore less apt to take offence. No doubt this arises in a great measure from their ignorance of English customs. They are ignorant of what ought to be, and therefore they cannot criticize. The result of such happy ignorance is an ease of manner which produces similar ease in the persons with whom they live. They find each other mutually agreeable, kind, helpful; and so are ultimately placed on a footing of cordiality, and often of real friendship.

Now, all this is quite apart from the question of sterling worth. The English governess may be worth tenfold more than the foreign one—looking to moral qualities and real information; but if she is inferior in good-humour and agreeability, she will never be placed on the same comfortable footing.

The real discomfort of a governess's position in a private family arises from the fact that it is undefined. She is not a relation, not a guest, not a mistress, not a servant—but something made up of all. No one knows exactly how to treat her, and therefore she is subject to what appears to

be caprice, though it is often merely awkwardness and ignorance.

This is very unpleasant; but so are a great many other things in life. It rests with the governess to make it less so by recognizing it. She enters the family as a stranger. For the most part its members are quite as much afraid of her as she is of them. If it is their duty to put her at ease with them, it is equally her duty to put them at ease with her; and this can only be done by showing that she knows the place she is called upon to fill, and that she desires to fit herself into it, and make herself comfortable in it. *Comfortable*—not necessarily happy; for happiness must depend upon many circumstances over which strangers have no control. A young girl, for instance, who, having lost her father, has just been thrown penniless upon the world, and knows that those she loves best are enduring heavy trials, cannot be happy; but the persons with whom she is to live as governess are not responsible for her unhappiness, though they are for her comfort. False dignity, however, never can make itself comfortable; it is always on the *qui vive* to take offence, and as a natural consequence it is always giving offence.

A governess not being a relation cannot expect immediately to be treated as such. She cannot enter into all the little family interests, and at first she will often feel herself in the way. Then, surely, it is the part of wisdom to keep out of the way. If a husband can only enjoy his wife's society for a few hours in the evening, he can scarcely help feeling the constant presence of a third person an annoyance. The governess may, as a general rule, expect always to join the family party in the evening, but it may be more considerate at times to keep away from it; or to go to her own room earlier, just to show that she recognizes her position, and is not fretted by it. So, again, she is not a guest. She cannot, therefore, expect the privileges of a guest. The mistress of the house will pay attentions to her friends which she will not pay to her; yet there may not be the slightest intentional neglect. If the gov-

erness will fit herself into this state of things, and instead of standing proudly aside, waiting for notice which never comes, will take advantage of being an inmate of the house, and unobtrusively do her best to make everything pass off pleasantly, she will find both the visitors and the lady of the house much more ready to meet her on a pleasant footing, because they unconsciously feel at ease with her. Once more, she is not the mistress of the house, therefore she must often obey, and always show deference in manners and words, and this is a severe trial to a proud, independent spirit. But the moment a mother feels that the principle of recognition of her own position and her supreme authority is owned, she will be contented; and in return for the acknowledgment on the part of the governess that it is her part to yield, she will be ready to allow that the governess is not a servant, and must, therefore, in her own peculiar province, be permitted to rule.

The relation between a mother and a governess does, indeed, require tact, but it is a tact founded upon self-evident truths. If a governess will not own these truths she must be miserable, but she has only herself to blame. It is not, indeed, for a moment asserted that the life of a governess is not one of great trial, or that the sources of her wretchedness lie wholly in herself; but there is a tendency in the present day to attribute the trial entirely to the position without regard to other circumstances, and thus to make it appear that it is impossible for a person holding such a position ever to be happy.

Now, putting aside the very low view of duty, which this idea involves,—ignoring, as it does, that the consciousness of working for God may be, in itself, a very deep and lasting happiness,—there is little doubt that the view thus commonly taken of a governess's life must act prejudicially on the minds of those young persons who are called upon to enter it. It is painted in such lugubrious colours that they shrink from it as from some inevitable suffering. The energy and hope which would brace them for their duties are taken away before they

can enter upon them. The mother of the family is always to be stiff, the children are to be spoilt and obstinate, the visitors are to be proud, and the poor governess herself is to be intensely lonely.

Certainly these things are too often met with; but, on the other hand, there are instances, not few, in which the governess, by high principle, refinement, tact, has made her way into the hearts of those with whom she has lived, until she has become their dearly valued friend, and has lived with them happily for years. There might be many more if, at the outset, the life were not looked upon with a jaundiced eye. The effect of that mutual ease which arises from a clear perception of relative position, has already been spoken of, and, when once this freedom of feeling has been attained, the situation of a governess will no longer be irksome.

And for the other trials which in all probability will press heavily upon her, it must be remembered that they are not necessarily connected with her office. They belong to the special kind of adversity with which it has pleased God to afflict her. She is poor—but it is not being a governess that makes her so. She is compelled to live away from her relations—but so are a great many other persons in every rank of life. Servants pass their lives amongst strangers, but we do not find that they are always miserable in consequence. She is obliged to work when she is weary and heart-sick. Who amongst the millions that earn their own livelihood is not compelled to do the same? She has no certain provision for sickness and age, but as a governess she has at least a chance of securing something.

But she has lost her social position, she is treated with neglect and disrespect. Yes. There is the trial. There lies the obstacle to happiness, and in so far as it is not the result of a morbid worldliness which would make its owner wretched in any situation, it must be removed by the governess herself.

She must make her own position by defining it for herself instead of leaving it for others to define it for her. What she

is, or may be, if she will—in the sight of God and His Angels—has already been said. It would seem that no earthly honour could add to or take away from the dignity of a fellow-worker with Christ.

What she is in the sight of man must depend upon her own conduct. No pride, however overbearing, can long withstand the quiet self-respect of thorough good breeding, which will always accord to others the place that is their due, and will never thrust itself into a position to which it is not entitled.

But if much of the *happiness* of a governess depends upon herself, all her *comfort* rests with the mother or the mistress of the family in which she resides. It would seem almost unnecessary to enter upon this subject. Every one knows and talks about it. The very fact of the pity bestowed upon the governesses in England shows how universal is the feeling that in too many instances they are not properly cared for, and that their services are not valued and recompensed aright.

The wages of a lady's-maid and of a nursery governess are about equal. The footman may compare with the well-informed governess who cannot undertake accomplishments; whilst the coachman and butler may be placed side by side with the highly educated lady, who is to teach all accomplishments, to know two or three modern languages, to be thoroughly well read, to possess the highest principles, and to be blessed with perfect wisdom and an angelic temper; and who, for a hundred a year, is expected to dress well, to provide her own travelling and holiday expenses, to pay her doctor, to assist her relations, and to lay by enough to make herself comfortable in age.

It is not said that a governess with a hundred a year may not do all this, but there is no doubt that it will be a matter of difficulty, and that with a less sum the hope of providing for the necessities of sickness and age is almost vain. There are very charitable people who would willingly give their twenty pounds a year to the support of charitable institutions which are to assist governesses, and persons of a like class, who have

fallen into, what is called, distressed circumstances; but who would think themselves likely to be ruined if a lady, wishing to be a governess, were to ask for an additional sum of ten pounds, in order that she might never be reduced to such aid.

Our lunatic asylums, our workhouses, and—alas for England that it should be so!—even our penitentiaries, are too often homes for decayed, distressed, destitute governesses. Are these institutions no burden to us? Might it not be wiser and better if, when we are reckoning up our charities, we calculated so much less for the unhappy persons who are already their inmates, and so much more for those who may, sooner or later, be compelled to take refuge in them, if we insist upon driving the hard bargain which we call prudence? Every person must be judge in his own case. There must be a vast number who really have it not in their power to give a larger salary than they already offer; and there must be many governesses who are thankful to take what they can get, and leave the future in God's Hands; but it is, nevertheless, the bounden duty of every one, who engages a governess, to consider what it is *right* to offer; and to measure the question of right by what it is known must be the governess's expenses and needs. If an additional five pounds, denied to a mother's own expenditure (perhaps in dress), would enable the governess to put five pounds into the savings bank; whereas, without it, she would merely be able to provide herself with respectable clothing, and pay her travelling and holiday expenses; then the self-denial ought to be practised, and the governess's salary increased. And so in other cases. Money expended upon luxuries and pleasures, and grudged to the governess, is money denied to Lazurus, and spent by Dives.

And, here again, an appeal may be made to fathers to consider betimes their daughters' future needs, and, so far as it is in their power, to provide for them.

The hope of leaving them even five hundred pounds may be an impossibility; the idea of setting them out in life by

taking pupils in a house of their own may be impracticable; but if they can save *anything*, if they can put by only a few pounds in a savings bank, yet, in pity to their children, let them do it. The difference between starting in life actually penniless, or with only twenty pounds in reserve, is incalculable. So very small a sum it appears to the father, accustomed to the expenses of a household,—it seems scarcely worth while to go through the little self-denials, by which such a trifle is to be saved. And yet that twenty pounds may make all the difference between hope and despair; possibly between sin and salvation! It may bridge over the gulf, into which absolute destitution would have plunged, and give a breathing time, during which rescue may be at hand. Or if no such time of trial should in God's Providence be appointed, yet the possession of even so small a sum will give a sense of support to the young girl first setting out to earn her own independence. It will be something for her to fall back upon; it may be the nucleus to which she will have a pleasure in adding, and assist in the formation of habits of care and economy, which will ultimately place her in a position of independent ease.

How fathers, who neglect to provide for their daughters, when it is in their power—even as they enable their sons to provide for themselves—justify to themselves their singular blindness, it is impossible to say. It is only to be hoped that God sees more excuses for them than their fellow-creatures can. Judging them by the standard of common sense, it would seem that the man is worse than a fool who does not, at all periods of his life, face the position in which his wife and daughters must be left in the event of his death, and prepare for it accordingly. He may have years of prosperity before him, in which he may be able to secure a fortune for them. He may be justified in calculating upon this probability, it may cheer and inspirit him. But at the present moment if he were to die —and what a tremendous "if" that is—they would not have enough to live upon. Painful as the thought is, he may not dare to put it aside. And surely it must compel him to be

economical, to save the utmost he can; to put aside five pounds, if he cannot spare a hundred; to store up shillings, if he cannot lay by sovereigns. If this were done as it ought to be, what a moral revolution it would create in England! Many of the most crying evils of our luxurious age arise from the pressure of poverty upon those who are unprepared to meet it. The sins of the fathers are, by the working of natural laws, visited on the children; and although there are unhappily many cases in which it is absolutely out of the father's power to lay by anything, and in which he can but trust his children to God's care in a spirit of faith, these instances are by no means the majority; and He who has said, "Leave thy fatherless children, I will preserve them alive; and let thy widows trust in Me,"[1] has also said, "If any provide not for his own, and specially for those of his own house, he hath denied the faith, and is worse than an infidel."[2]

It is for the fathers of the present day to take warning; and if they look with surprise and horror at the statistics of our charitable institutions, to remember that, by indulging their own selfish affection, and spending money upon their daughters' amusements, instead of laying it by for their future maintenance, they are doing their best to add to that sickening catalogue of sin and misery which makes the heart of the Christian grow faint, and tempts the blasphemer to ask, "Is there a God in Heaven?"

But to return again to the duties involved in the relation which subsists between the mother of a family and the governess.

The amount of salary is but one amongst many points which the mistress of a household is, in this case, to consider. It is scarcely possible that a governess's services should be adequately remunerated, and therefore she is more entitled to the privileges which are to make amends for the pecuniary disadvantage.

When complaints are made of the smallness of a clergy-

[1] Jer. xlix. 11. [2] 1 Tim. v. 8.

man's income, one of the plausible arguments brought forward on the opposite side is, that the position which is ensured to him makes up for the absence of money; the fact being overlooked that the necessity of keeping up such a position makes the need of money greater, and the want of it the more distressing. But, however unsound this argument may be, the use of it is at least an acknowledgment that social position is somewhat of an equivalent for poverty, and therefore the loss of that position in the case of a governess must be considered as so much additional poverty. We cannot change the state of society at once. There is no magic wand by which we may cause a certain class of persons to be recognized as equal, when English pride and prejudice have decided that they are not equal; but it is in the power of every mistress of a family to do something towards breaking down barriers which exclusiveness has erected; and to define in her own household the position of friendliness and respect which the governess ought to occupy.

As she treats the governess, so, as a rule, will the servants and visitors treat her; and it is from them that the petty annoyances arise which make the position of a governess so trying. And the obligation lies equally upon the master of a family. It is often to please him that the governess is put in the background. He comes home from his day's employment weary, and perhaps irritable, and he wishes to be with his wife and children alone. The presence of a third person is irksome; and, therefore, when the governess undertakes her duties, she is made to understand that she will only be expected to spend the evening in the drawing-room when she is invited. And on those special occasions she is still more of an interruption, because the ordinary family habits are disturbed by her presence. But if parents wish their children to be well educated, they must make personal as well as pecuniary sacrifices. Money will not purchase what they want. They desire a sensible, affectionate, sincere friend, who is to watch over their children when they cannot do it themselves. Kindness

and affection are to be won,—not bought. If they will make the governess one of their family, she will share their interests, and exert herself for them, at all hours, and on all occasions. If they shut her out from it, she must almost inevitably be thrown back upon what will seem to be her own interests. She will feel that for so much money she is expected to undertake so much work; and when she has completed this, she will imagine herself at liberty to provide for her own gratification, leaving it to the mother to do whatever else the children's well-being may require. Parents cannot enjoy the pleasure connected with the companionship of children, unless they undertake the corresponding duties. They may, if they will, bear the whole responsibility of education themselves; but, in that case, they must do the work. If in any degree they devolve this responsibility upon another, then, according to that degree, they must be prepared to yield a portion of their parental privilege; that is to say, they must give up a certain amount of authority, they must be contented to find another sharing their children's respect and affection; and they must be willing to admit the person on whom they depend to fulfil the task which they are unable to undertake themselves, to that position in their family which her important office demands.

Unless this is done, the children will suffer the inevitable result of a false relation. Their governess is their superior, yet not their superior. They are called upon to obey her, yet they see her treated with disrespect. They are told that she is clever and good, but they find that nevertheless she is always kept in the background. They are inclined to be fond of her, but their mother is perhaps jealous of their affections, and they dare not show it. Such an unsettled state of feeling must produce unsettled conduct. Children can never be rightly governed by any one whose right to authority and respect they are at liberty to dispute. They will be disobedient and wilful. The governess will punish them. The children will appeal to their mother, who very probably will take their part. They

will then, of course, be more naughty, and the governess in her turn will appeal. The mother will be fretted with both parties, and lay the blame of the contest on the governess's temper.

A change of dynasty will necessarily follow. But let the new governess be an angel of sweetness and wisdom, still she cannot make her way. The under-current of neglect and want of respect is too strong for her. She will probably resign her post long before her resignation is desired, and a successor will be needful. So it will go on again and again; and at the end the children will come forth from the hands of a series of governesses, critical instead of submissive; self-opinionated instead of humble-minded; having spent the most important years of their young lives in unlearning under one plan of instruction what they had acquired under the preceding; and finding themselves at last standing on the threshold of life, with only one certain conviction, that they have never been taught anything properly, and that governesses are simply a mistake and an imposition. When in after years they have households and families of their own, this early prejudice will almost certainly remain, and they will treat a governess as their parents in former days treated her; and so the tradition of evil is handed down, and the customs of society, which depreciate the position of a governess, are strengthened.

CHAPTER XXXI.

THE TRAINING OF GOVERNESSES.

What has been said hitherto has been based upon the supposition that governesses are always persons who can be admitted to friendship, and are competent to exercise authority. But it may be objected, and with great truth, that in this possibility the whole difficulty of the question lies. If these ideal governesses existed, would society venture to look down upon them? If they do not exist, is society in fault?

The question as to what society would venture to do can only be answered by experience. As a rule it now worships rank, wealth, and talent. Whether it will ever be induced to admit good sense, good breeding, and high principle into the number of its idols remains to be proved. But supposing that it would, it must candidly be acknowledged that English governesses cannot always establish a claim to such honour.

Perhaps it is the same with all professions. The number of those who may be termed first-rate or superior will always be few. And governesses come before the world at a great disadvantage. Very many are ladies who have never been trained for their duties, and are sensitively alive to what they consider the humiliation of their position. Many are persons who have never mixed in good society; whilst a third class will be found to consist of young persons, left orphans at an early age, who have been educated for their work at some public institution, and are sent forth from it into private house-

holds, with scarcely any experience of the world or the needs of domestic life. It is not to be wondered at if, amongst persons so variously circumstanced, there should be found habits and tempers which must render it extremely difficult to admit them all to the intimacies of home life. Yet more—it must be admitted, though with very great regret, that the persons most calculated by their manners and general tone to be agreeable friends and companions are by no means the most likely to teach well.

A good governess, in the ordinary sense, is a quick, clever woman, who is a first-rate musician, an excellent linguist and historian, who can discourse upon any "ology" which happens to be a subject of interest for the moment, and, by dint of indefatigable industry and energy, can enable her pupils to shine somewhat as she shines herself.

Let English ladies answer for themselves, whether, speaking generally, they are at all able to compete with such a candidate. Where is the young lady of three or four and twenty who would like to undergo a searching examination in history, geography, and languages; or who would undertake to answer the questions which are put to boys before they enter the army or the Indian Civil Service? The very small amount of information which enables women to make a fair show in society is really ludicrous. Any one who has had much to do with girls who are supposed to have finished their education must be aware of this. There is no time allowed for real study, at the age when study becomes most important. Our grandmothers thought eighteen quite young enough for an initiation into the mysterious delights of "coming out;" but seventeen is the age which is now more generally fixed upon; and as a natural result, at sixteen the young ladies begin to dream of balls, and to consider lessons a drudgery; and when once fairly launched into the world, the idea of really cultivating the mind is almost, if not altogether, laid aside. If parents are wealthy, the daughters have the claims of a large circle of friends and constant engagements; if they are not, they have

to share household duties and home anxieties. The light literature of the day is all they have leisure to read; and the history and geography which were learnt in the schoolroom are remembered only in their vague outlines. A few prominent names and facts are retained—just sufficient to keep them from committing any gross blunders in conversation, and to enable them to show the requisite amount of interest in the topics of the day; but beyond this all is chaos. Yet, it may be said, they do very well. Women have such a natural readiness, they so soon perceive quicksands in conversations, and are so clever in avoiding them. It is very rarely that even the most ignorant will venture out of her depth. And then information in a woman is, it is supposed, not wanted. It does not attract. Men are rather shy of it. It savours of the pedantic. They like being listened to deferentially, and think argument with a woman beneath them. The clever woman, who has an opinion of her own, is alarming, more especially if she ventures to strengthen her statement by facts. The gentle young girl who looks up with timid admiration, asks a few sensible questions, and says "Yes" and "No" at the right moment, is delightful.

And if the voyage of life could always be made in smooth water—if there were no "changes and chances," no death, no poverty—these refined, timid, ignorant girls might pass the time of their earthly sojourn in rest and happiness. They know enough to please their parents—more than enough to delight their husbands. They will make obedient wives and careful mothers; and as they were instructed themselves, so can their children be instructed. It is all simple, natural, easy of attainment. But, suddenly it may be, storms gather on the horizon, rumours of losses, symptoms of illness: the dark cloud of poverty, though "small but as a man's hand," looms in the distance. Rapidly it widens and spreads, and in a moment it bursts. These pleasant-mannered, interesting young girls are destitute. They have to maintain themselves, and only one profession is open to them. They must be gov-

ernesses. What can they teach? What do they know? They themselves will answer—in all humility and truthfulness—"Nothing." But their friends will answer for them. They have had a good education, they can play a little, and sing a little, and speak a little French, and read a little German; and of course they know something of geography and history. And then they are so thoroughly refined and well-bred, there can be no difficulty in procuring for them good situations. The young ladies are told that they must profess to teach all which they are supposed to know, and they obey. A situation is offered them: a home, in which they are to be quite happy. "They will be so well treated, and made entirely one of the family!"

It is all bright, *couleur de rose*, so far as any such position, under such circumstances, can be; and the young governess is found to be really all that has been said of her, as regards sweet temper, and amiability, and good principle. Only, unfortunately—it is very disappointing—she knows nothing. The bubble of information which in the clear air and the sunshine of prosperity shone so gaily, and floated so lightly, has burst. She is perfectly incompetent for her task. She has but a vague recollection of what she once knew. She feels no certainty about anything she attempts. She has not the slightest idea how to teach so as to interest children. She can but go through a dull routine which makes the daily lessons irksome to herself and her pupils. She is herself wholly dissatisfied, so are the parents. They feel a change must be made; and at length they say so, "with great regret, but they must consider their children's good;" and the poor young girl leaves her situation stamped with the brand of incapacity.

There is no need to follow the sad history of trial and discouragement further. All know what it must be. Refinement of manner, good taste, and good breeding, like everything else, have only a certain marketable value. They are inestimable treasures in themselves, but if the world needs something else they will not find purchasers.

CHAPTER XXXI.

THE TRAINING OF GOVERNESSES.

WHAT has been said hitherto has been based upon the supposition that governesses are always persons who can be admitted to friendship, and are competent to exercise authority. But it may be objected, and with great truth, that in this possibility the whole difficulty of the question lies. If these ideal governesses existed, would society venture to look down upon them? If they do not exist, is society in fault?

The question as to what society would venture to do can only be answered by experience. As a rule it now worships rank, wealth, and talent. Whether it will ever be induced to admit good sense, good breeding, and high principle into the number of its idols remains to be proved. But supposing that it would, it must candidly be acknowledged that English governesses cannot always establish a claim to such honour.

Perhaps it is the same with all professions. The number of those who may be termed first-rate or superior will always be few. And governesses come before the world at a great disadvantage. Very many are ladies who have never been trained for their duties, and are sensitively alive to what they consider the humiliation of their position. Many are persons who have never mixed in good society; whilst a third class will be found to consist of young persons, left orphans at an early age, who have been educated for their work at some public institution, and are sent forth from it into private house-

seeking a remedy. We owe to this acknowledgment the foundation of a college in London, where men of distinguished ability have given time and attention to lectures and classes upon all subjects, which may be attended by young women desirous to qualify themselves for being governesses. We hear also of efforts made to extend the stimulus of examination by university men, to young girls educated either at school or at home. The need is pressing, and each person is tempted to adopt the panacea nearest at hand. And no one can say that such remedial measures have entirely failed, or are certain to fail. There is no doubt that Queen's College is a great assistance in enlarging the minds of those who frequent it, with a real desire to profit by its advantages. It may be expected also that, should the idea of public examinations ever be adopted, it would rouse to the utmost the mental energies of those who have always been inclined to work; but putting aside all other objections to such measures—to the latter especially—it may be permitted to question whether the system pursued in either of these cases can really prove a remedy adequate to the need, because both deal with only one side of a great question. They offer assistance to the mental deficiency, but they leave the moral untouched.

And that for a very plain, almost a self-evident, reason.

They are both worked by men; and men, however earnest, devoted, and intellectual, are not the persons whom nature points out as fitted to be the educators of young girls.

It is indeed one of the good points of the schemes to which reference has been made, that they do not profess to attempt moral training. Yet without it, how is the standard for English governesses to be raised?

But we may go still further, and assert that as English society is at present constituted even the intellectual training of girls by men is not without serious risks; that it works for good only when counteracted by a very strong womanly influence which can guard and check it. Any one who has had much to do with young girls of the educated classes will prob-

ably own that in most instances there are but three points of view in which they are likely to regard their gentlemen teachers. Either they will be afraid of them—or they will quiz them—or they will make romances about them. Fear, ridicule, and romance are not very elevating influences. The last indeed will often be hid under the veil of respect; but if examined it will be seen that underneath lies a very large admixture of vanity and excitement, which cannot fail to do grave injury.

Women can deal with women as men never can. They know the material upon which they have to operate. They are not kept back by any chivalrous feeling from plain statements of truth; and they can enter into innumerable little difficulties which to a man are simply incomprehensible. The most sensible man will now and then give advice to a young girl, at which a sensible woman will lift up her hands in astonishment. Above all, women can give girls sympathy with safety, and sympathy is the great instrument of influence with all young people.

If the standard of governesses in England is ever to be raised, it must, so it would seem, be through the medium of women; of persons gifted with that rare quality—common sense—and who, being well educated, well informed, thoroughly refined, and accustomed to good society, will devote themselves to the training of young governesses under their own eye; giving them all the sympathy and comfort of home friendship, whilst showing them how they may cultivate whatever talents they possess, and make them most serviceable to their pupils. The only way in which anything of this kind is now attempted is in large schools, where the governess receives a pupil teacher, giving her the advantage of masters, whilst making her useful in instructing the younger children. But this, it will be seen at once, is only a question of mutual convenience. The governess wants help, the pupil teacher wants instruction. It is a case of barter. There is nothing

noble in it, nothing winning to the affections, or likely to exercise a permanent influence for good.

Is it a dream of Utopia that at some not distant day we may find training *homes* for governesses established, as well as training schools for National Schoolmistresses? Such an undertaking would demand an outlay of money at first, but, possibly, in the end it might be made self-supporting. The young governesses would be expected to contribute something, and if they could not do it themselves, they would almost certainly find friends who would be thankful, for a small sum, to secure for them permanent advantages. And, perhaps, if the plan were carried out in London, or some large town, by one in whom the world had confidence, parents, with only moderate incomes, might be induced to try the working of a thoroughly superior day-school, attached to the home, in which their children might have the stimulus and interest of competition, and the advantage of good masters, and still be kept under their own eye.

If this plan could once be set on foot, the young governesses, whilst studying themselves, might be practically taught how to make children study. And they would have experience without risk. They would be tried indeed, and their faults would be developed, but they would be made to see them, and be shown how to guard against them. Intellectually, they would have the great benefit of discovering their deficiencies, and remedying them, so far as time and opportunity would allow; and—what is infinitely more important—they would learn how to employ their natural superiority in age and experience, so as to make up for any want of actual information; and by continuing the task of self-teaching, and self-improvement, they would learn how to keep themselves in advance of their pupils, and ensure their respect, even though occasionally they might be forced to own themselves ignorant.

The position of the head of such a home would, indeed, be difficult and arduous. She would have to take care that the school was carefully and well worked, and to superintend and work in it

herself; and when the actual labour of tuition was over, she would have to make herself the friend and guide, the comforter and confidante, of the young inmates of her house. It would be the duty of the mother of a family, added to that of the governess. And there could be no idea of pecuniary remuneration. If not called upon to sacrifice her own fortune, the utmost she could expect would be to save herself from diminishing it. She might cover her expenses; it cannot be expected that she should do more. She must, therefore, be found in the upper classes of society, amongst those who have all that this world can give in comfort and luxury, but are willing to sacrifice that all, if need be—for Christ's sake.

Time was, when the expectation of meeting with such a person would have been pronounced hopeless, but late experience has shown that women are to be found capable of making any sacrifice, and undertaking any amount of labour, if the object can be proved to be worthy of the effort. In the present case, all persons, probably, would agree in the importance of raising the standard of governesses in England, and through these means improving education throughout the whole country. The only difference of opinion would be as to the means to be employed. With regard to governesses themselves, the advantages to be derived from such home training would seem too obvious to be dwelt upon. There is, probably, no one who, on looking round a circle of acquaintances, cannot instantly fix upon some case in which the opportunity for study and experience which it would offer, would be felt to be invaluable as a preparation for the work of tuition.

And it must be remembered that female superintendence and guardianship need not necessarily interfere with the advantages to be derived from the partial instruction of men. No lady would compete, or wish to compete, with the able professors of Queen's College, for instance. She would only be too glad that the young girls under her charge should take advantage of their lectures. All that she could desire would be to render them appreciated; to see that what was taught was

thoroughly worked into the mind; and to show, by practical experience, how it might be made useful for the benefit of younger children.

For the instruction of young children is a subject distinct in itself. The neglect of the lesser regulations which enforce discipline and order in a schoolroom will interfere with their progress, even under a very clever governess; whilst the attempt to give them general information, if it is beyond their power, or if they have no sufficient foundation of elementary facts, will ultimately prove a failure. And a most essential part of good education, also, which nothing but practical experience can teach, is the very small amount of privation and punishment which, judiciously administered, will be perfectly efficacious in keeping any girls in order. Men, accustomed to deal with the more violent and headstrong nature of boys, do not always comprehend this; and women, when they are inclined to be strict disciplinarians, will scarcely believe it. Three parts of the discipline of a schoolroom may be maintained by the mere working of regular and well understood laws, carefully enforced. And should any further interference be required, once gain a young girl's thorough respect, and the mere tone of the voice will be sufficient to touch the heart, and lead it to repentance and amendment.

And though the young people who desire to be governesses are often very unfit for their office, when their actual amount of information is alone considered, yet, if they have anything like common ability, they may, after the training, even of a year, be raised to a much higher level. After all, it is the mind itself, not the information which it has absorbed, that is the efficient engine in instruction. Almost all women who, at the present time, are undertaking to teach, have, probably, felt this. Their task has, most likely, presented itself to them unexpectedly. They were not trained for it. They have been learning all their lives, just as their pupils have been learning; and they have made their mistakes, and have to lament failures, and to grieve over their own incompetency. It has, possibly,

been a matter of surprise to themselves how, with their small amount of actual information, they have been able to teach anything.

It is the mind—the working of thought and experience—which has placed them above their pupils. The children will, probably, remember the dates of the English kings perfectly, whilst the governess is by no means certain of them; but the reason why the knowledge of those dates is an advantage—the use of them as pegs on which to hang other contemporaneous facts, so as to arrange the history of the world in order, and from this history to deduce the great principles of God's Providential government of mankind, and to connect it with what we are permitted to know of the vast scheme of the universe—is quite beyond a child's natural power of thought to originate, though it is not beyond its comprehension when once presented to it. Children are not at all injured by finding their governess ignorant of certain facts, so long as they feel the superiority of her mind. They quite appreciate the distinction between memory and thought; and thus, a comparatively small stock of information, with a really working reflective mind and habits of industry, will enable a young person to teach both agreeably and well, if she can only acquire that preliminary experience which is needed to give her confidence, and with which even a year's judicious training may supply her.

And so, also, the moral powers will be found to multiply the intellectual to an extent which is almost incredible, until it has been actually observed.

A young governess undertakes her first situation, probably, in complete ignorance of her own qualifications for government. She does not even know what qualifications government requires. She has not the least idea that it must first of all begin with self, and that unless it does so it must infallibly fail. Her only idea is that of authority and obedience: the former exercised through the medium of words, the latter exhibited in action. She has no perception of the fact that if she insists upon her pupils being attentive while she herself is list-

less, she is counter-ordering by her behaviour what she is enforcing in her language; neither does she see, that if she is obeyed simply because the children dread punishment, the obedience is not due to the power of a right authority, but to the spirit of fear, and, therefore, is, in reality, no obedience at all.

These things and many more must be learnt before a young governess can educate properly, and they can only be acquired by training and experience. When they are acquired, however, the task of educating ceases to be irksome. Persons always like to do what they feel they can do well; and a great element of happiness in the life of one who has to teach others, is the feeling that she can govern judiciously and instruct with interest.

No wonder, then, that young governesses are unhappy, since, too often, they can do neither. But a little preparatory guidance would go a great way towards remedying these evils. And if a girl has really high religious principle, and can rule and influence rightly, her instruction will, in the end, be worth more than that of a cleverer person who is inferior in moral power. It will make less show, but it will be more durable. What is taught will be taught carefully, conscientiously, thoroughly. The children will feel the elevating influence of the mind to which they are called upon to submit. They will exert themselves heartily; they will feel pleasure in giving pleasure by their improvement; and when once this feeling is introduced into a schoolroom, lessons are no longer a drudgery. But high moral and religious principles will not always work in the right way of themselves. The eccentricities of goodness are quite as remarkable as those of genius. The best of us need common sense; and, perhaps, no advantage which a year or two of careful training would secure for a young governess, would be greater than that which would teach her to make a right use of her virtues, as well as to watch against and check her faults.

Yet more, that which creates a difficulty in admitting governesses to a perfect intimacy in a family, is the fact that they

do not all bear the stamp of perfect good breeding. Some have been accustomed only to second-rate society. Some have been neglected at home; some educated at large schools, where there has been no opportunity of acquiring the little refinements which make familiarity safe and pleasant. A young girl, under these circumstances, does not perhaps understand the difference between ease of manners and freedom. She is apt, unconsciously, to take liberties, and by little unintentional awkwardnesses, or neglect of the conventionalities of the world, to give offence. For it is not the question of birth which makes a person lady-like, or renders it pleasant to live with her. It is education in the little niceties of social life, joined with a habit of thoughtfulness and self-control. Both are equally necessary.

How vulgar polished ladies and gentlemen can be, we have all probably known by experience, when we have seen them thrown off their guard, and giving way to intemperate passion. But we do not always consider that neglect of the little etiquettes of social life will jar and fret every day, whilst the storms of passion may never be heard. Very careful, anxious mothers will let their little girls acquire habits which are inadmissible in society, and think they are doing them no injury, so long as they instil good principles into their minds. But when the little girls become the young governesses, and do what they have been accustomed to do from childhood, they are pronounced vulgar, and *tabooed.*

Now, the training under a thoroughly refined well-bred woman, accustomed to notice and check all these little neglects, would be of untold value to a young girl before entering upon the office of a governess. It would tend to give her the ease and self-possession which will set the persons she is to live with at ease also. The stiff propriety, the *crinoline* of manner, which destroys all grace, and inflicts a blow upon those who come in contact with it, is, in nine cases out of ten, the result of a self-conscious shyness, based upon ignorance. Persons who are afraid of doing or saying something which should not

be said or done, have no refuge but in stiffness; for if once they leave this shelter, they feel that they are in danger of giving offence. And unconscious offence is given perpetually. The young governess perhaps appears late at the dinner-table, and makes no apology; or she reads her letters without begging to be excused for doing so; or she rings the bell because she feels herself at home; or she whispers in company; or yields to some feeling of curiosity; or thrusts herself uncalled for into conversation; and the fastidious lady of the house draws back, and decides that she is ill-bred, and chills her with distant politeness, and so makes her wretched. Perhaps the lady is not to be blamed, but the governess is certainly to be pitied. She cannot know what she has never been taught.

These small matters, how great they are in their effect upon life! and how essential would be the advantage which a young girl would receive if she could be *toned* as well as taught—fitted for the drawing-room as well as prepared for the schoolroom, before she undertook to educate!

And if the happiness of the governess herself is to be considered, we can scarcely overestimate the support which many an otherwise friendless girl would receive from the feeling that her course was watched by friends of position and influence, who were willing to advise her in a difficulty, to sympathize with her in trouble, to restore to her, in fact, though necessarily in an inferior degree, the guardianship of the home which she had lost. How many desolate hearts would be cheered, how many saved from shipwreck on the rocks and quicksands of a perilous life, if only they could feel that they belonged, as it were, to those whom the world respected, and were responsible to them for their conduct!

And yet again the thought arises, is not the idea Utopian?

Even supposing that such a home as has been suggested were to be set on foot, and to be found to work well, how very little it could do! A dozen governesses might perhaps be sent forth from it annually. That is reckoning upon rather a large number, and a complete success. What can twelve good governesses do towards raising the tone of education in England?

The answer to this is—Try.

We are looking at the acorn, so little that it would seem impossible it should ever become an oak. Yet if it is fashioned by God's Providence, in obedience to His law, it will undoubtedly germinate and spread. And the moment it does spread, even in a small circle, its influence must be felt in those beyond. Let one such home work well, and others would follow; and though the number of persons so educated and trained might always be few in comparison, yet we may not therefore decide that their influence would be slight. Few of us perhaps ever realize to ourselves how the existence of a recognized upper class in any society affects the tone of the whole. We see it in the working of social distinctions. The manners of a colony are unlike those of England because, where all believe that they stand on the same level, there is no need for outward deference. That which tends more than anything else to keep up the external refinement of the professional classes in England is the existence of a class above them, with whom they are constantly mingling; and who, from the fact of their position, are accustomed to dictate certain laws for the conduct of society, which all who desire to be admitted to their circle on terms of equality are compelled to observe.

An acknowledged standard of good breeding insensibly affects the whole community. So again, and in a much more important way, the influence of university education tells upon the thousands who carry on their studies elsewhere. According as the standard of the university is high or low, so will be that of public schools; and by the standard of public schools, private schools are compelled to measure themselves.

And in these instances, as in many others of a like kind, it will be found that influence, when directly exercised, is restricted to a few persons. We talk of the will of the people, the power of the people; we say that numbers must always gain the day. And we are right so far as this, that the will of numbers will always be the most effective instrument which

can be used for the carrying out of any purpose. But we shall find, upon inquiry, that the will of the many has in all cases been first moved by that of the few, and that even when aroused, it can never work until its force is concentrated in the hands of a few.

The Reformation changed the current of religious thought throughout all Christendom; it was essentially the will and the mind of the many;—but we can count up the number of the leading reformers on our fingers.

There is, therefore, no reason for distrusting the result of any plan because it must begin upon a small scale, and act only upon a few persons. It is the spirit in which an undertaking is commenced that permeates society. The form under which it may first develop itself may be imperfect, it may even fade and die, and yet it may leave a seed which will eventually spring up and bear fruit. If the educational movement for the improvement of female education in England could be led by a few persons of sufficient position, talent, high principle, and good sense, to impress upon it their own stamp; if it could be home training under their own eye, which should accustom the young girls placed under their charge to the refinements of really good society, whilst at the same time they enjoyed the advantages of good instruction; it would ensure to the governesses who were sent forth a distinction which, it would seem, could not fail to raise them in the social scale. Supported by the friendship and guardianship of such persons, a young girl could scarcely be open to the neglect which is met with by the unknown penniless orphan. And when once this rise was acknowledged, parents in the more polished ranks of society would not be so unwilling to allow their daughters to undertake educational duties, and the daughters would cease to look upon it as a hardship. The few would then become the standard for the many, and ultimately, it might be hoped, the leaven would make its way through all grades.

The work would, indeed, be very slow; for a long time it would scarcely be recognized; but perhaps, in the end, it would

be surer than a more extensive movement which would meet only the intellectual needs of the day, and must leave those belonging to the moral and social relations untouched.

Yet once more it may be objected;—this scheme for raising the standard of governesses can never really operate to any extent, so long as crowds of ill-bred, half-educated young people are pressing into the service, whose only object is to raise themselves from an inferior position, and who undertake to be governesses merely because they think it more "genteel" than to serve in a shop or become lady's maids.

This is very true. But there are two answers to be made to this objection.

In the first place, the very fact of the crowds who seek to be governesses must tend eventually, and is tending even now, to diminish the number. People are opening their eyes to the fact that the profession is overstocked and ill-paid; and the movement made for the employment of women in other ways —though there are enormous difficulties in its path—must ultimately remove into other spheres those who, either from incapacity or want of education, are not fitted to undertake the task of instruction. In the second place, it must be remembered, that there will always be a large class who, from not being refined and fastidious themselves, will be insensible to the defects of others. A second-rate class of governesses will always exist, because there will always be second-rate persons to employ them. The efforts which are made to improve the mental cultivation of the middle classes will, no doubt, in a degree, render them more fit to be teachers; and the fact that when they become governesses they are *rising* in the world, instead of falling, creates an immense distinction between them and the young girl born in a higher grade, and suddenly compelled to take what is called a "situation." They do not want sympathy and commiseration, however much they may guidance.

The need at present under consideration is, that "ladies" should be educated by "ladies;" and the fact to which none

of us can shut our eyes is, that very few ladies are competent to the task; and that if they are, they look upon it as a descent, just as much as the persons beneath them look upon it as an advance in the social scale. Whilst this is the case, the idea of raising the tone of English education in the upper ranks of society is hopeless.

What should we think of the provision made for the education of English boys, hereafter to be English gentlemen, if the only instructors that could be found for them in their youth were either men who, without having had any previous training, were compelled to enter the profession by the pressure of poverty; or persons who undertook the task because they thought that a tutor was a greater man than a clerk in a counting-house?

That which makes an English gentleman what he is, is the respect accorded to those who devote themselves to his education. If we were to lower the social status of the men who work in our public schools, or of the clergymen who take private pupils, we should instantly find that an intellectually inferior class would take their place; and the whole tone of English society would be affected by the change.

But what is to be done with the refined, carefully nurtured, but unintellectual "ladies," who are quite incompetent to teach, and yet must labour for their livelihood?

That is a very large question. Society is working out the answer; slowly, at the risk of much suffering from the delay, and as yet without any prospect of meeting it satisfactorily.

Perhaps in this narrow, exclusive England, the slave of fashion and conventionalities, we have yet to learn that work under any form is noble. The time may come when we shall admit to our social circle the friend who, being poor, undertakes to make our dresses, as we should, if, from the same necessity, she professed to fulfil a duty which she could not perform, and became a governess. So also the religious world (taking the expression in its best sense) may by and by recognize that a woman is not always to be expected to give up time and health, and the brightest years of life, to work in

penitentiaries, and reformatories, and schools, and amongst the most degraded and repulsive of our overgrown population, without some offer of remuneration.

Even an apostle could say, "Who goeth a warfare any time at his own charges? . . . . who feedeth a flock, and eateth not of the milk of the flock?"[1]

They who can give money as well as time to these duties are the happy few. But must the work be necessarily less efficacious or acceptable when undertaken in a Christian spirit by one who sees in it a profession by which she is to support herself? Then is the virtue of a clergyman's work negatived in proportion to the temporal advantages he derives from it!

But if a bishop can be saintly with five thousand pounds a year, and a rector with five hundred, would it be impossible for a deaconess to be saintly with fifty? It is true that women delight in self-sacrifice, and that the educated classes are so little accustomed to the idea of remuneration for any duties they undertake, that many would shrink from it as from insult. But if God tells them, by the events of His Providence, that they cannot live unless they will work for remuneration, then to set themselves against such work is simply pride and rebellion; and the more Christian in spirit a woman is, the more simply, humbly, and naturally will she accept the idea of working for money, where others work for love.

A lady, not in the least fitted to teach, might make an admirable deaconess; but, in the present state of things, she is compelled to undertake what she cannot do, and to give up what she can, because in the one situation she can live, and in the other she must starve.

The suggestions made in this chapter are merely theoretical, they can have no real value until tested, and they may be found wholly unpractical. But when great and crying evils, like those of the inefficiency of governesses, and the non-employment of women, are acknowledged to exist, the very fact of

[1] 1 Cor. ix. 7.

being able to do nothing is a temptation to think the more. And even when ideas are in themselves useless, the very arguments which are used to refute, often tend to lead other minds in the same direction, so that ultimately, the solution of the problem is worked out.

CHAPTER XXXII.

INSTRUCTION.

This then, it will perhaps be said, is all which can be suggested to assist governesses in fulfilling a task for which it is asserted that the greater number are incompetent;—they are told to look upon themselves as having a very important duty to perform, and to content themselves with the dignity thus conferred upon them of working directly for God! But if they are unfitted for their task, there can be no great satisfaction in undertaking it. Can no practical advice be given them? Can they not be instructed how they should teach; what books they should use; how they may best arouse their pupils' energies; under what form information may be given, so as to be most permanently useful? Certainly, this kind of advice would be most helpful, most valuable. Many persons have already attempted it, and yet no one has really succeeded in offering it in a satisfactory form. And, perhaps, for this reason—that no person is thoroughly capable of doing it.

Principles are eternal, and therefore applicable to all ages, and all circumstances. Rules vary according to every phase in which the kaleidoscope of human society presents itself to us. The kind of teaching which is very effective in one case, will be the reverse in another. The books which are recommended to us to-day, will be superseded by others to-morrow. The system which is admirable on paper, when there are no obstacles to interfere with it, is found to be impracticable when an

attempt is made to carry it out amid the interruptions of domestic life.

And this, perhaps, is likely to be one of the great defects of a regularly trained governess, who removes from the schoolroom in which she is a pupil, to that in which she is a mistress, without having had any intermediate experience. She has a system, a bed of Procrustes, and she imagines that by compelling children to fit themselves to it, they will necessarily become all that she desires. Therefore she goes through a certain course of study, makes them repeat certain lessons, and read certain histories, and never suspects that whilst some will come forth from her training well informed, others will remain, as they originally were, buried in ignorance.

And besides this, it must be remembered that no one person can really be expected to give advice upon all subjects connected with instruction. Each individual has his or her own province. If we wish to learn how we may the most easily teach a child of four years old its letters, we shall probably do well to apply to an infant schoolmistress. Arithmetic also is, as a rule, better taught in a boys' national school than in any private schoolroom.

French and German masters will know more about their own languages, and the best method of imparting them, than any English person can do. A professor of history will give us a valuable list of historical books; a clergyman will tell us about catechizing and scriptural instruction. But when any single individual undertakes to teach all these things, or to give advice about them, we may be quite sure that the teaching and the advice will be not the best we could receive; but only that secondary guidance, the result of experience,—gained as much through failure as success,—which, though it may be very well when suggested in conversation between friends, is not at all fitted to be put forth to the world dogmatically. Looking at governesses as they are now—for the most part untrained, unprepared for their work of instruction—that which is most essential is that they should put their hearts into the

duty committed to them, use their intellects to watch the effect of their plans, and not change those plans suddenly, even if they find that they fail to work quite successfully; for frequent change is a confession of weakness, and unsettles a child's mind.

And if, above and beyond the desire for their pupils' mental cultivation, there is a heartfelt desire for their moral and religious improvement, many a question will be at once answered which, though it may appear only to concern instruction, is in reality connected with education.

There is no royal road to learning; because God has appointed that, through the medium of learning, children should be trained in goodness, in obedience, energy, self-discipline—the qualities which are to fit them to be the soldiers of Christ in the great battle of the universe—the contest between good and evil.

To attempt, therefore, to cheat children into learning is to defeat the very purpose for which the task of learning is imposed upon them. It is of the sick child that the poet says—

> Cosi all' egro fanciul porgiamo aspersi
> Di soave licor, gli orli del vaso;
> Succhi amari ingannato, intanto ei beve,
> E dall' inganno suo vita riceve.

The child in health, who is accustomed to accept the bitter only under the form of the sweet, receives not benefit, but injury. Perhaps the safest of all maxims for the training of a child of four years old is—that lessons should be lessons, and play should be play. The little creature who is sent to the nursery to have her hair brushed and her hands washed, and is then brought down to the schoolroom, and made to sit quite still, and attend to her tiny lessons, if only for ten minutes, has, through that rather troublesome process, learnt what is as much more important than reading and spelling, as moral training is than mere information. If she could have learnt ten times as much by scrambling on the floor, in a dirty pinafore,

and playing with pictures, she would still have been the loser. What is the power of distinguishing A from B compared with obedience, reverence, self-restraint, the habit of attention?—all of which are enforced by the mere fact of being prepared each day at a certain hour for a regular lesson, and being compelled to go through it carefully.

So again, people ask, why be so particular in making little children say their lessons perfectly? If they know what they have learnt, if they give the sense in other words, why is not that sufficient? The answer is as before, moral rather than intellectual. Because the sense can be acquired easily, the precise words only with difficulty; because exactness in repetition involves carefulness; because it is a check upon that habit of hastily catching up words which is the bane of so many through their whole lives; because, moreover, it counteracts the tendency to be contented with something short of perfection, which is a most common temptation with us all. Who does not know what it is to strive to a certain point, and then fall short, from the feeling that there is not strength for one effort more? A lesson perfectly repeated must have required a moral effort, and it is that which is the real benefit. Though it may also be remarked that the moral powers are never strengthened without a gain also on the part of the intellectual; and that the lesson learnt according to the words of the book will, from the very effort it has cost, be remembered, when that which has been put into the child's own words will be forgotten. It is the fashion sometimes to depreciate the exercise of memory as being merely mechanical; but any one who has had to deal with young persons whose memory has been neglected will feel what an incalculable loss theirs is, and what an obstacle to their improvement in higher ways. Memory is indeed simply the act of heaping up treasures, not the power of making use of them; but if there are no treasures to use, the power becomes comparatively valueless. This does not, of course, imply that the mere perfect repetition of a form of words is sufficient, without any comprehension or explanation

of the sense ; but merely that it should be the groundwork for explanation, and that the comprehension without it should not be accepted as sufficient.

We may sometimes be inclined to wonder how it was that in former days, when so much less pains were taken to open children's minds and to make them understand what they learnt, there should still have been such powerful and cultivated intellects in the world. The fact may probably be traced to the moral force which, in curious contrast to the paucity of the intellectual instruction, was in those days often exhibited, even under the form of prejudice and severity. We may, perhaps, have known cases ourselves in which the actual amount of information acquired under the strict discipline of an old-fashioned school, has been so small as to be almost absurd; and yet, looking back, we may perceive that the energy and self-discipline which were exerted to learn that little *well*, will have been, even intellectually, of such vast use in life, that the question of how much was actually learnt in childhood has become comparatively of no importance.

Repetition of some lessons, till they are known so that they are never forgotten, is another old-fashioned custom which has a moral benefit concealed beneath it. It creates a feeling of stability and permanence, and gives a sense of possession which is actual strength.

Any one fact which we know quite perfectly, and which we feel that we cannot forget, is a mental possession, valuable as the first treasure in the formation of a cabinet of curiosities. It may be made the germ of a collection of facts.

A child who can repeat perfectly the dates of the English kings is possessed of the nucleus of historical knowledge ; and children unconsciously feel this. The power of arranging and comparing the historical events which they meet with in books depends upon having some certain event to fall back upon. When they find they have these facts thoroughly established in their minds they take a pleasure in making use of them. In this way an interest in history is awakened which might have

lain dormant for ever if the information acquired had been left in the brain in a state of confusion. And an interest in history is a moral as well as an intellectual benefit, because it widens the sphere of sympathy, enlarges the mind, and is a safeguard against the temptations of trashy literature. But apart from this, to know or do anything well is an advantage, especially for weak timid characters. If a little girl, for instance, develops no taste for accomplishments, and is so dull that she cannot be made to study, yet if she can work well with her needle, and the talent is cultivated, so that she is aware she is worth something, and has a power which others possess in a less degree, her whole moral being will be raised by the involuntary self-respect thus engendered. What we thoroughly understand we can speak of with decision and firmness; and the habit of decision in one case accustoms us to it in others.

But all this exactness and mechanical labour in acquisition, of which we have been speaking, must, if we are to make it endurable, begin early. The analogy between mental and moral training is very close. Little children will bear routine lessons just as they will bear strictness in discipline. It can be exercised on a small scale, and they will become accustomed to it insensibly. But if carried on too long, it will stunt them mentally, just as too rigid a restraint in conduct will stunt them morally.

Let a foundation of obedience and self-discipline be laid in early childhood, and freedom may be given in youth; and so also, make a child exact and perfect in its lessons when instruction begins; and, as time goes on, the habit of exact repetition may be, in a great measure, laid aside. Yet not entirely, even as obedience and external restraint may never wholly be given up. The exercise of memory should always be continued in some form. For as years go on, and we find that this faculty is weakened, we begin to appreciate its value, and to wish that we had made more use of it. Poetry learnt in youth is an invaluable treasure for life. The Collects, and a certain number of the Psalms, thoroughly acquired, will be a

comfort unspeakable in sickness and age. Texts of Scripture are helps which we often actually long for, when ill or sorrowful ourselves, or when ministering to those who are suffering; and if we have not learnt them quite perfectly when young, we can never feel that they are ours, so as to make an easy use of them afterwards. Tell young people these things, give them a reason for insisting upon the use of memory, and being particular as to exactness, and they will acquiesce in the tasks imposed upon them. What they do not acquiesce in, is a routine of lessons to be repeated by rote, apparently for no purpose. The memory cultivated systematically, and upon principle, is one of the most important educational instruments we possess. It is a kind of mental savings bank, into which we put our knowledge, with the certainty that, when drawn out again in future years, we shall receive it with interest. For the events of life, and the growth of the moral faculties, will increase, in some instances indefinitely, the value of intellectual knowledge. The twenty-third psalm learnt as a Sunday lesson in the schoolroom, and the same psalm repeated in dying ears—how vast is the difference! And yet but for the schoolroom lesson, the words might never suggest themselves so readily and perfectly as to be a support in such an hour of anguish and mental disturbance.

The whole value of early instruction, indeed, depends upon the use which can be made of it in after years. An evident truism, and yet singularly neglected, or misunderstood. For if it were not, why should we perplex ourselves, as we do, with discussions as to the comparative powers of boys and girls? What does it signify whether or not a girl is capable of the same mental work as her brothers? She is not meant to be a man, but a woman, with a woman's duties; and the best kind of education which can be given her, is that which will most obviously fit her for those duties. Suppose that she can understand political economy, and master the problems of Euclid; she will never sit in Parliament, or be a Cambridge Professor. And she has lessons of her own to attend to, and

these things, except so far as they exercise the mental powers (and in this respect they may, no doubt, be helpful), can, at the best, only be adjuncts. She may learn them, they may be useful to her, just as a boy may learn drawing or music, and find such accomplishments profitable acquisitions; but even if she had a decided talent for them, she could never devote sufficient time to them to enable her thoroughly to master them. The very utmost that will ever be said of her is, "she is surprisingly learned for a woman." The idea of making a boy's attainments the standard by which to measure a girl's, is indeed obviously unfair. To render the comparison equal, boys should be required to play brilliantly on the piano, to sing well, to dance gracefully, to draw cleverly and with facility, to be skilled in every kind of needlework; for all these things are more or less required of girls, in addition to their intellectual acquirements; and they cannot be taught or learnt, unless time is devoted to them; and time given to one branch of instruction is so much taken from another. Yet further, if there is to be any fair competition between the two sexes, a girl must have a boy's physical strength. It is very easy for studious men, who have never had to deal with delicate girls, to suggest a course of instruction which shall bring them on a level with their brothers. There is no doubt that girls can, up to a certain point, be made to learn just as much, and as well, as boys. Take a school of little boys and little girls, and compare them, and the probability is that the latter will be found the superior. There is a quickness, a kind of intuitive perception about them, in which boys are wanting. They develop at an earlier age, and more rapidly. But take those same boys and girls at seventeen and eighteen, and the boy will have advanced far beyond the girl. Even in those things which he does not know, he will show a power of ready acquirement, in which she will be wanting. Not one girl in a hundred would be able to work up the subjects required for an Indian Civil Service Examination, in the way which boys do. And for one very obvious reason, putting aside all others. Her health

would break down under the effort. And health is the obstacle, which, even under the most favourable circumstances, must stand in the way of a girl's acquiring the intellectual strength, which, at this age, is so invaluable to a boy. He has been tossed about the world, left in a great measure to his own resources, and been inured to constant physical exertion. He has been riding, and boating, and playing cricket, and both body and mind have been roused to energy; and so, when he comes to study, he has a sense of power, which acts mentally as well as physically, and enables him to grasp difficulties, and master them. The girl, on the contrary, has been guarded from over fatigue, subject to restrictions with regard to cold, and heat, and hours of study, seldom trusted away from home, allowed only a small share of responsibility;—not willingly, with any wish to thwart her inclinations—but simply because, if she is not thus guarded, if she is allowed to run the risks, which, to the boy, are a matter of indifference, she will probably develop some disease, which, if not fatal, will, at any rate, be an injury to her for life.

This question of health must be a primary consideration with all persons who undertake to educate girls. It will be a perpetual interruption to their plans for study and mental improvement, but it is one which can never be put aside. Parents in private, and the intellectual world in public, will demand that girls should be brought forward, and taught all that an age which makes intellect its idol thinks fit to require, and the attempt to satisfy them must be met in one of two ways. Either by the over mental exertion which ends in a break-up of health, or by a superficial intellectual show which resembles actual knowledge and moral power only as the veneered table resembles solid wood.

Any strain upon a girl's intellect is to be dreaded, and any attempt to bring women into competition with men can scarcely escape failure. And if this be so, and if, as has before been said, the value of a girl's acquirements can best be measured by a girl's necessities, by the needs of her after-life, then it is

probable that women will know better than men what those needs are, and will therefore prove more suitable instructors. And yet an exception must, under certain limitations, be made to this assertion.

It will generally be found that a father's instruction, supposing him, of course, to be a man of intellect, is far more advantageous to a girl mentally than that of the very best governess she could have. There will be a peculiarity about it, a certain one-sidedness, some necessary things will be neglected, which must be acquired in after years; but under such teaching the mind does gain a largeness and strength which are too often wanting under that of a woman.

Does the fact bring us to a different general conclusion from that which we arrived at before?

It would seem not.

In the case under consideration, the instructor is a father, and a father is less liable to the temptation to overwork his child, or to expect too much of her; so that under his care health is not likely to be sacrificed. By taking the education of his daughter into his own hands, he gives up the peculiarly feminine accomplishments. He makes her perhaps a first-rate historian, an excellent linguist, and a cautious thinker. But music, drawing, needlework, are considered secondary. Experience shows him that young people cannot learn everything, and he chooses the studies in which he desires his child to excel, and is successful. And with good cause. He has everything to aid him. Absolute authority, the reverence which is naturally his due, the affection which makes it a pleasure to work for him. And yet, after all, he feels that there is something wanting, and after a time he sends his daughter to school, to be under the influence of a person in all probability greatly inferior to himself, because she needs a woman's influence.

Well trained, well informed though she is, she is not feminine, and a woman who is not feminine is a monster in creation.

Under the very best circumstances, therefore, the teaching of a man is not, as it would appear, all that a girl requires.

But if women could discover the secret of the power which, in the case under consideration, is wielded by a father, they might perhaps do something towards acquiring it themselves.

A clever man—one who has thought as well as studied—will almost always make his knowledge tell more than a woman, from the fact that he has mixed more in the world, and, therefore, knows better how to turn his information to account by bringing it to bear upon the present day. He has seen more, noted and compared more, and his interests are on a larger scale. If he reads ancient history, for instance, it is not simply as a record of the past, but as an influence which has come down to modern times. If he reads modern history, he connects it with the politics of his own period. Facts are to him not mere facts, but the materials for thought. And thus it is, that whilst he is instructing his child by reading with her, he is educating her by talking with her ; whereas, a governess will, too often, be contented with the former, and quite put aside the latter. The father is, himself, interested in the subject of study, and he communicates his interest to his child ; and the governess, if she is to compete with him, must do the same.

To teach well, we must be learning at the same time. There must be a feeling of sympathy between the instructor and the scholar, based upon the fact that both are travelling upon the same road, only that one has advanced rather further than the other. It is in this way that a young governess, though conscious of her own deficiencies, may hopefully undertake the task of education. If she will only study with her pupil, as well as teach her, she will, perhaps, in the end, do quite as much towards forming the mind as a person of distinguished attainments could.

Governesses are sometimes afraid of confessing themselves ignorant upon any point. They think that if they do they will lose their pupils' respect ; and so they have recourse to little

subterfuges which a child's quick eye will almost invariably discover. An exercise, for instance, will be corrected by the aid of a key, only the key must not be seen. Yet when such assistance is openly acknowledged, it will be found that the child receives it as a matter of course, without any surprise; and the only thing the governess has then to guard against is putting the book in her pupil's way, so as to be a temptation. This does not require any mystery or locking up, but merely keeping it apart from other school books. The child's sense of honour must be trusted for everything beyond this. There are very few cases in which it will be found to fail; if it should, it is far better that such a tendency should be discovered and corrected, than left to work out its fatal course in after life. Truth, sincerity! there is, in fact, no other foundation for good education.

And even apart from this consideration, acknowledgment of ignorance or doubt need not necessarily be injurious. To say to a child, "I do not know such a thing, but I will find it out;" and to set the example of searching, and not being contented until the point in dispute is discovered; is a lesson tenfold more important to a young girl's mind than any fact or series of facts can possibly be. It is setting before her what she must be resolved to do in after life, if she is ever to be really well informed. For the truth, which all persons who are interested in female education must, sooner or later, acknowledge, is, that at the age at which girls are taken from the schoolroom, and introduced into the world, their education, instead of being completed, has only just, to any real purpose, begun; and that if they have not the energy and good sense to carry it on for themselves, in spite of all the interruptions which throng them, they must eventually forget one-half of what they have learnt, and be incapable of making any satisfactory use of the other half.

Again, we must place the boy of eighteen and the girl of the same age side by side, and inquire in what light society regards them.

The boy of eighteen is only just beginning his college career. He is not yet fit for any profession; he has several years of hard study to go through before he can be a clergyman, a physician, a barrister, before, in fact, he can ordinarily undertake any independent responsible position. What he knows now is the foundation for what he is to know and carry out hereafter.

The girl of eighteen is ready to be married, to become the mistress of a household, to control servants, to bring up children, to take a definite place in society. All that she has learnt in the schoolroom, instead of being improved and made useful, may now be put aside. She is *finished.* So much history, so much geography, so many dates, so much arithmetic acquired; and to be laid by, like jewels in a box, to be taken out when wanted. Being *finished*, of course she has enough. If she should happen to have a taste for these things, she may collect more at leisure; but there is no real necessity for it. When married to the world (as how many young girls are married to it—pledged to "love, honour, and obey" it!) she was provided with her intellectual *trousseau*, and it will last her for some years at least; and when it is worn out she will be able to replace it by that knowledge of life, that *savoir faire* which covers a mine o ignorance.

False! utterly false! And yet, if a girl is taught to look upon the day when she leaves the schoolroom as the day of emancipation, how can she think otherwise? It is not she who is to blame, but the parents and teachers—the former, perhaps, more than the latter. For any governess who is worthy the name, and really has her pupils' interests at heart, will sigh over the shortcomings which she has no time to remedy; and urge, with an earnestness which will probably meet with very little sympathy, that education is a condition of life, and that the years spent in the schoolroom have been but its first stage; that information is nothing, and cultivation of the mind everything; and that, next to religious principle, there is no moral safeguard equal to that of a steady determination, if possible, to

let no day pass without having done something towards such cultivation.

And the mother will agree to all this in theory. But how is it too often in practice? The world's joys are dangled before the young daughter's imagination as the glittering bauble is dangled before the eyes of an infant. To be introduced into society—or, as it is called, to "come out;"—to be presented at Court, perhaps, and enjoy the rush of a London season; and eventually to be married to a man of rank, wealth, and—of course, if possible!—of high character, these are the things hinted at—produced, as it were, like choice treasures, tempting morsels, to stimulate the worldly appetite. In preparation for these delights, there must necessarily be accomplishments, music especially. It is the one grand desideratum, for music is showy—every one talks of and notices a girl who plays and sings beautifully; and therefore before everything else so many hours a day must be devoted to music. French, too, is quite necessary, though unfortunately it is very seldom thoroughly acquired without a residence abroad; and as the world is rather linguistic-mad at this time, German, too, must be learnt. But thoroughness in German is not requisite. To be able to ask for what is needed at a German *table d'hôte* is sufficient to enable a girl to say she knows German, and the saying is all which is required. Italian, too, is desirable—it is such a graceful, sweet-sounding language; but here again it is the appearance which is of importance. The world does not exactly expect Italian, though it looks favourably upon it. If the words of an Italian song can be pronounced it is satisfied, whether they are understood or not. But the world is literary and scientific, as well as accomplished; and therefore into the interstices left by the accomplishments are to be inserted all those duller, less showy acquirements, which, like the literary *padding* of a review, serve to fill out the educational volume to its fitting size. Still, like the accomplishments, they are not to be valued for themselves, but only for the effect they may produce; and as they will be required for immediate use

when the young lady is "introduced," they must be got up for the occasion, at the shortest notice, and on the most approved fashion.

Very hard work all this requires; but then it is only for a short time. A year or two more, and then it will all be over! The fortune will be made, and nothing more will be required but to spend it—or rather to invest it to the greatest profit. The dear children are urged to be diligent—to make the best use of their time; they are assured they will have no more such opportunities; and if dispirited by the strain put upon them, they are sympathized with. "Lessons are very trying, and discipline is detestable, and they must exert all their high principle to bear with it." And so the children do bear with it, as the ox submits to the yoke, and the horse to the halter; but they never cease to feel that it is a yoke, and to sigh for the day when they are to be freed from it. And the governesses feel the yoke too. Accomplishments and information are expected to be ready by a certain hour, and if they cannot produce the reality, they must at least be prepared with a well got-up sham. They cannot consult the tastes or powers of their pupils, because that hardest of all tyrants, the world, insists that young girls shall know certain things, or else they shall not be accepted as well educated. Perhaps at the present moment it is in vain to endeavour to stem the tide. It may be better to sail with it. Parents will not be contented unless there is something to *show* in their children's education; and though they expect them to learn a great deal more than it is possible to learn thoroughly in the time given, there is no alternative but to follow out their wishes. The various acquirements must be attempted, and the only thing to be done is to point out to the children, and to urge upon them, with all possible earnestness, that school-time is only seed-time; and, as has been said before, if they do not carry on their own education when they leave the schoolroom, the seed will never spring up and bear fruit.

If this idea can be thoroughly rooted in their minds, the

fact of beginning so many studies may even be turned to good. For to know the first steps of any science or language will often lead to its being pursued; whereas if those steps had never been taken, the study would never have been attempted. In like manner, a little music, and a little drawing, though very unsatisfactory to persons who wish to make a show with them, may be invaluable as resources to the individual. It is not the small amount of any knowledge, or the absence of facility in an accomplishment, which is to be lamented, but the looking upon the labour of learning as completed when it is only just begun.

And if governesses will only bear this in mind, and act upon the idea that their business is less to educate their pupils, than to lead them to educate themselves, they will be saved much of the vexation which must arise from the sense of the incompleteness of their work. In some few cases a governess has the training of a child from infancy, and is able fully to pursue her own plans, but this is very rarely the case. As a general rule, a child has, from various circumstances, several governesses, and each can only carry out her own ideas, whatever they may be, to a certain point. So it will happen continually that the actual amount of instruction which any one individual is able to give, will be provokingly small; but if she has been able to awaken interest in the subject taught, she has conferred on her pupil a very great benefit, and the deficient information will be supplied in after years. Conversation upon the subjects of the lessons is one of the surest modes of awakening interest, and it is in this way that much is lost by the numbers who congregate at the dinner-table in a large school, and are compelled when they speak to express themselves in a foreign tongue. The restriction may be a very necessary safeguard against the tumult which would ensue if twenty or thirty girls were allowed to chatter indiscriminately; and it may teach them the French or German for mutton and beef; but free discussion of some subject which has been suggested during the morning's study, when carried out by a

small party having the use of their mother-tongue, will do infinitely more for the improvement of the mind. It will show to young people the use of their lessons, the value of conversation; it will make them appreciate the society of persons of sense and information; and when they have once acquired a taste for superior society, they will never sink down to the level of the shallow, gossiping, slanderous world. Historical questions are often quite exciting, when brought forward in this way, and the foreign politics of the day may be a continual subject of interest.

Only one caution must be given. There must be no effort in such conversation, no talking for effect. The young detest this quite as much as their elders, perhaps more.

In order to make useful conversation agreeable, the person who leads it must be really interested in it; and when this is the case, a little ignorance on the part of the governess is often no disadvantage, because it brings her down to a more sympathizing level, and enables her to show how knowledge may be acquired.

Neither may it be forgotten that young persons—indeed all persons—require complete definite relaxation just as much as they do definite instruction; and the cultivation of a sense of humour, and a refined perception of the ludicrous, can no more be omitted as parts of good education than languages and science. A sense of the ludicrous is in fact really necessary as a safeguard against unnumbered mistakes which persons fall into who have excellent intentions, but fail to perceive the fitness, and right proportion, and relation, of the persons and things with which they are brought in contact. To be able to take part in a light, merry, witty conversation, and yet never to go beyond the bounds of reverence, kindness, and propriety, is a gift which comparatively few persons possess, and it is certainly most heartily to be desired. If, making no provision for this need, we think it necessary to be always teaching, we shall end by dulling instead of sharpening our pupils' intellects. And we can never remedy the deficiency

of real mirth and fun by dressing up information and calling it amusement. A very pleasant lesson is a very dreary play.

With this view of arousing interest, and making lessons pleasant, it may perhaps be advisable to take rather a less rigid view of the course of study to be pursued, especially with regard to history. Certain main facts, and dates it has been said, must be thoroughly impressed in the memory, as the pegs on which to suspend others. If this is neglected, the ground of the mind will be strewed with knowledge, important in itself, but, from the confusion in which it lies, almost as useless as rubbish. These main facts ought to be acquired in early childhood. But when this is past, it is often supposed necessary to begin some standard work, consisting probably of some four or five thick volumes. Now any one who is at all acquainted with the routine of a young girl's schoolroom life, will know that months and months will be needed to go through these volumes. So many other things are to be attended to, that it is quite impossible to give up more than a small portion of the day, and that probably not every day, to this special book. For there are other histories to be studied—Greece and Rome, Egypt and Assyria—the whole of modern Europe in general, and the principal countries in detail. Few girls of fourteen and fifteen know more than the merest shadowy outline of universal history; and if they are intelligent and interested in their studies, they are eager to know more. And thus the lengthy work, though it may be in itself clever and interesting, becomes irksome. The thread of the history is too often interrupted, and it is drawn out to too great a length. The young people wish to finish the book, merely in order that they may say they have read it. And if, as is very often the case in schools, the whole period of a pupil's residence is but a year, or a year and a half, it is evident that in this way nothing like a real interest in history generally is likely to be awakened. The impression left upon the mind is that of dulness; and when emancipated from the schoolroom,

history will very likely be put aside. But if the study of history could be brought before the mind in shorter portions, and, with the help of extracts from standard writers, be made to embrace larger interests, a different result might be expected.[1]

Such discursive reading as this will not enable a young girl to give a satisfactory answer to the question, What have you read? or, what are you reading? Should such an inquiry be made, she would probably reply, "We read bits of different books just as it happens," and the answer might sound unsatisfactory; but there is very little doubt that the interest in these historical subjects, awakened by such varied and contemporary reading, would be tenfold greater than if the history of any one nation had been read for months, through the medium of five or six thick octavo volumes; and by degrees, as the mind enlarged, those deeper and more philosophical writers would be read with an appreciation which would be utterly impossible, if they had made part of the schoolroom routine.

[1] An illustration of what is meant may be given from books taken at random. The History of England must, to an Englishman, be the thread on which he is to string the history of other countries. Some School Compendium may be taken, and the life of William the Conqueror read; this will be an introduction to Lanfranc and his Life in Dr. Hook's "Lives of the Archbishops;" and this again will lead to the eventful history of Gregory the Seventh, which will be found in a most fascinating form in Sir James Stephen's Essays. If Dean Milman's "Latin Christianity" should be at hand, most valuable extracts may also be made from it, though it is a work too voluminous for the generality of young people, and which from its details it is not desirable to put into their own hands. From this will arise the question of the settlement of the Normans in Italy, of which a short graphic account will be found in a regular school-book, Miss Yonge's "Landmarks of History" (the Middle Ages), whilst still further light may be thrown upon the period by the very interesting and most useful papers by the same author, called "Cameos of History," which are to be met with in the well-known periodical called *The Monthly Packet;* to say nothing of Miss Strickland's "Lives of the Queens of England," which tell almost all that can be told of the domestic life and habits of English Royalty.

It may, probably, be urged as an obstacle to this suggestion, that many persons have not the books they need at command; but if the principle is acknowledged, there will always be some means of carrying it out. If one author is not at hand, another is. Even regular school books may be made use of, so as to give variety and interest by reading contemporary reigns; whilst the best magazines and reviews often contain essays of the greatest value upon historical subjects. If a governess has it really at heart to interest her pupils, she will be constantly picking up, as it were, suggestions as to books, and poetry, and tales, which may be made useful; and the variety of the authors bringing out their various views of the events and the persons they describe, will give rise to conversation, not only agreeable and exciting, but which will throw a light upon the children's characters, and be a material help in the formation of their principles.

And so with regard to geography. A discussion upon the foreign political events of the day will necessarily lead to geographical questions. When all Europe interests itself in the affairs of Italy, the map of modern Italy, as compared with the Italy of the middle ages, becomes an engrossing study. Or, again, when the probable fate of Denmark and Schleswig-Holstein is a subject introduced into every drawing-room, the map of Denmark and Germany becomes an object of almost personal importance. There must, of course, be regular lessons independent of these episodes. Young people must know what they have to do, and be made to do it; but it is by seizing upon the events transacting at the present moment, and connecting them with the past, that interest is awakened; and this, it must be repeated, is the great object of female instruction.

A boy requires a definite amount of information to enable him to pass a certain examination. He may or may not afterwards follow up the subjects proposed. His path in life is marked out, and probably he will devote himself only to those studies which bear upon it. But a woman's mind needs a more

general cultivation. She is to be her husband's companion and friend, to entertain his guests, to be sensible and agreeable, to raise the tone of conversation; and she can only be and do all this, by having that general acquaintance with history, geography, and science, which will enable her to draw out the knowledge that men possess. A woman who declaims, instructs, or preaches in society, has forgotten her vocation, and is utterly out of place; but when she makes use of her own sense and information to make others talk well, her influence is of inestimable use.

Public and private lectures will also aid greatly in the general cultivation of mind of which we have been speaking; but they will lose nearly all their value, unless a groundwork of information has been previously laid, and pains are taken to imprint the facts of the lecture upon the memory after it has been heard. Private lectures should always be accompanied with examination questions upon the subject that has been treated of. It is singular how very little definite information may be derived from oral instruction, even when a clear impression of its general purpose may be retained. At first this impression will be taken for knowledge; but it will be found to vanish too speedily to be worthy of the name, unless it is imprinted upon the memory by some personal mental effort. These general suggestions, with regard to instruction considered apart from education, are all which it seems needful to give. The materials with which, and upon which, a governess (especially in a private family) is required to work, must vary continually, and if bound down to a certain system, she will be entirely thrown out by the loss of the instruments with which she has been accustomed to work, and the variety of minds which she is expected to influence. Experience and observation, especially if aided by suggestions from persons who are well practised in some peculiar branch of study, will do far more for a governess than any system; for they will show not all that can be done with the best helps—books of reference, intellectual society, first-rate masters and mistresses for accomplishments;—

but the good that may be obtained by just taking what is placed within reach, and by personal energy and earnestness rousing the young intellect, and exciting the interest, so that when greater advantages are bestowed, greater profit may be derived from them.

CONCLUSION.

All that has been said, both upon education and instruction, has been founded upon the idea that governesses are really putting their hearts into their duty, and not merely going through it as a drudgery from which they are longing to escape.

Whether this is the case or not, each must answer for herself. But, supposing it to be so, supposing the work to be thus undertaken for God, and carried on with all the ability which He has bestowed, what is the reward to be expected?

In the great majority of instances, more or less, Disappointment. It is better to own it: better to read the word which God has inscribed upon all human efforts. So far as they are human, so far as their object is to be fulfilled in this world, we shall never thoroughly attain that for which we labour.

We set an ideal before our eyes; we work for it by day and night; we bend all the powers of our mind to its completion; and God, in the ordering of His Providence, is constantly permitting thwarting influences to cross our path: influences which seem to us, perhaps, unmitigated evil; which check and harass us, and undo our work, and cut it short; and at length it may be He takes it finally out of our hands, so that we are not able to perceive that it has in any true sense been work at all.

And why?

Surely, because the truth which the parent has to own in

the nursery is one which the governess has to recognize in the schoolroom. As we begin, so we must continue, and end, by acknowledging that God has a scheme of education beyond ours,—a purpose, vast, unfathomable, hidden in the Mysteries of the Universe; that He commands us to work for Him with the materials which He gives us—that He points out by the instrumentality of nature, reason, and revelation, what this work is to be; but that He does not tell us the end which is ultimately to be reached; and, therefore, when He takes from us the materials with which we desire to labour, or changes our occupation, or puts a stop to it, or even suffers it to appear null and void, He is not really thwarting us, but only carrying out this great hidden scheme by the means which, in His Almighty Wisdom, He sees will most surely conduce to its accomplishment.

We can never remind ourselves of this truth too frequently or too earnestly.

God's Will is one thing, God's Purpose is another. We obey God's Will when, in simple faith, we set ourselves "to do our duty in that state of life to which He has called us." Having done this, we may commit our efforts to Him and rest satisfied. Successful or unsuccessful, as regards ourselves, it matters not. Or rather we can never be unsuccessful. We may fail in influence, we may see our most cherished hopes shipwrecked, but the work done for God is accepted and stored up by God. It will, hereafter, be acknowledged before angels and men, and through the ages of Eternity the echo of those blessed words of approbation, "Well done, good and faithful servant," will ring as sweetly in the ear of him who on earth missed his object, as in the ear of him who attained it.

But we are human; we grow weak without encouragement; we are chilled at heart by constant failure. Is there not some way by which we may secure to ourselves an earthly as well as a heavenly reward? Undoubtedly there is; but the first thing to be done with this view is to guard against expecting too much.

We must remember that we cannot demand of the young a consistency and earnestness which we have failed to acquire ourselves. If, as we must all know, life has been to us a school of severe discipline, and nevertheless we are still miserably faulty, it is folly to suppose that those who are only at the beginning of their course can possibly be perfect. And yet this is really the kind of expectation which very good people sometimes seem to cherish. They fret, and fume, and vex themselves because they are obliged to repeat the same warning again and again; because words seem to make no impression; because the simplest, easiest commands are disobeyed. It is very vexatious, extremely trying; but how is it between themselves and God? What careless habits, petty faults—negligence, inattention—not to speak of sins of graver character—has not God been warning them against for years; and still they give way to them; and still He is patient. Our Blessed Lord taught His disciples during the whole of His ministerial life that His Kingdom was not of this world; and yet, after being spectators of His Death and witnesses to His Resurrection, they asked, "Lord, wilt Thou at this time restore the kingdom again to Israel?" We do not hear that He was impatient with them for their question. He reminded them, as He had done before, that it was not for them "to know the times or the seasons which God had put into His own power;" and then He cheered them by encouragement.

Patience and Hope! Nothing can be done in education without these virtues. Youth is the seed-time, not the harvest. If we expect to reap in the seed-time, we must be disappointed.

But it is also very important to be prepared for the sources from which disappointment will be derived, and these it may be as well, before concluding, to consider.

And first we must, in some form or other, inevitably be disappointed in ourselves. The assertion seems almost a truism, so willing are we all to acknowledge that it is impossible to come up to our own ideal standard. And yet, strange to

say, moral deficiencies are not those which press the most heavily upon persons who attempt, in earnest dependence upon God's help, to educate the young. Whatever our faults may be, a constant check is kept upon them when we know that we are called upon to set an example. They who are really striving to walk in God's ways must be able, to a great extent, to control the outward exhibitions of temper, pride, vanity, and selfishness before the young. Reverence for a child is a strong instinct in the human breast, and it is peculiarly cultivated by the spirit of Christianity. If the one object of our lives is to do our Lord's work on earth, we can never forget His awful warning, "Whoso shall offend one of these little ones which believe in Me, it were better for him that a millstone were hanged about his neck, and that he were drowned in the depth of the sea."[1] No doubt the lesser faults of hastiness, procrastination, unpunctuality, indolence, forgetfulness, or even involuntary coldness or absence of manner, will ocasionally fret ourselves, and work injuriously for our pupils ; but the remedy for these defects lies, to a certain extent, in our own power. Leaning upon God, and exerting our own will, we may hope eventually to neutralize their effects, even if we do not succeed in entirely overcoming them. But mental deficiencies are not equally within our grasp, and the moment we test our acquirements by teaching we find how shallow they are. Natural incapacity for certain branches of knowledge, carelessness in earlier years, want of a sure foundation, absence of opportunities for instruction, have, in all probability, each or all, left their mark upon us. If we can do a few things well, we do a great many other things badly ; if we know a little, we are ignorant of much ; and in the act of blaming our pupils, we shall often be much more inclined to blame ourselves.

Notwithstanding this self-dissatisfaction, we may, however, be by no means actually incompetent teachers. Power of mind, energy, the love of knowledge, and a determination to seek for it, are the really efficacious instruments of instruc-

[1] St. Matt. xviii. 6.

tion. If we possess these, we shall manage to make more use of our small knowledge, than a much better informed person would, without them, make of his or her large knowledge.

But the secret consciousness of the deficiency will continually be present with us; all the more if we happen to be placed in a position of responsibility, and are supposed to know, and to be able to do everything.

And the remedy for this evil can scarcely be said to be within our reach. In the middle of life, and in the full tide of work and anxiety, there is neither the time nor the spirit necessary for much effective study. And even supposing the contrary, there will, most frequently, be something wanting in the faculties which are our instruments for acquiring knowledge.

If we omitted to learn the dates of the English kings when we were ten, we shall scarcely be able to acquire them when we are forty. And, though we may find our matured intellect very helpful when we wish to grasp the meaning of a German sentence, we shall long for the clearness and exactitude of a youthful memory, when we are called upon to master the German declensions.

It is the foundation which is so needful—and it is this which can only be laid in youth.

Unimportant as such mental deficiencies may seem to those who look on, the perception of them is very harassing when we are actually engaged in teaching; and a morbid yielding to regret on account of them, may be really paralyzing to our intellectual vigour. In such cases, the only thing to be done is to accept our ignorance even as we do our poverty, and since God has pointed out that it is our business to teach, to do the best we can, and trust to His blessing upon the result.

But next to our own deficiencies, a great source of disappointment will be those of the persons who work with us. For scarcely any governess undertakes to educate entirely alone. If she is in a private family, indeed, she may do so for some

years; but after that time masters will generally be called in to assist her. But in a school, or even with a few private pupils, this assistance must almost always be required. And it will never be quite what is needed; often it will be much the reverse; and we shall find our best plans upset simply because we cannot prevail upon others to do as we wish. And one requirement will continually be sacrificed to another. It will often be necessary to put up with the absence of talent for the sake of good principle; or again, we may be compelled to accept something which, if not bad, is at any rate inferior in principle, for the sake of some particular talent. These things are most vexatious. They act positively as well as negatively. As a bad nurse will do injury in the nursery which the wisest of mothers cannot undo, so it will be in the schoolroom. And this is the reason why the moral tone of large schools is often so unsatisfactory, notwithstanding the possible superiority of the lady at the head. She is obliged to delegate her authority to subordinates who are inferior, and as they are more constantly with the children, their influence necessarily acts in the end more powerfully. And again, there is health, a most frequent trial and source of disappointment. We could do so much more if we had only physical strength! If we could rise earlier, and sit up later, and work more continuously, and did not need so much relaxation! Persons who are entering with anything like enthusiasm upon a career of usefulness never sit down to consider the obstacles likely to arise from their not having herculean powers. Perhaps it is as well they should not, or they would probably never attempt to be useful at all; and God will help them, and enable them often to do more than they could possibly have calculated upon beforehand. But it is, nevertheless, desirable to remember generally, that interruptions from want of health and strength must be expected; because we shall then be less troubled when they arise, but shall look upon them as Providential arrangements, pointing out God's Will for us, and reminding

us that active duties are not the only ones which He demands of us, but that "they also serve who stand and wait."

Again—there must frequently be very great disappointment from the varieties of character and intellect which are subject to our influence. We use the same efforts for all, and, at first, are apt to expect the same results. But we shall soon find out our mistake, especially when we desire to improve the mind and excite a taste for study.

We may make young people learn, but strive as we will we cannot make them like learning. There are, indeed, many persons, both young and old, by no means dull in intellect, to whom reading is such a task that they will never undertake it except as a duty. They pick up information in some singular way of their own, but a book is a thing scarcely ever seen in their hands. It is very disappointing to find that this apparent indifference to study is the end of our labours. It seems, at first, that they have been thrown away, but we must remember that, after all, reading is only a means to an end. If the mind is awake to what is passing around it, and if right principles are rooted in it, information will be acquired, and useful work will be done, though it may not be in the way of study. Young people who can scarcely be induced to read, will often be most sensible and useful in other ways. They will be pleasant in their homes, and visit the poor, and tend the sick; and in God's sight these labours are, doubtless, quite as important as studying Schiller or Dante; though it must not be forgotten, that mental work is necessary for the balance of character, and, therefore, reading in some form, and to a certain degree, ought always to be urged upon young people, though we cannot really excite their interest in it. In this, as in every case, our disappointment is the result of a mistaken aim. We put our own wishes in the place of God's manifest intention, and so, instead of taking the materials He has given us, and doing the best we can with them, in the mode which nature points out; we decide for ourselves what children ought to be, and then set to work to make them such; without troub-

ling ourselves to ask whether God has placed the means of doing so within our reach.

This must not be interpreted to imply that children should never be made to learn anything for which they have not a decided bias, for there is a certain amount of general information which is needful for all; and when once the first difficulties are mastered, an interest will constantly be aroused in studies, which at the beginning were almost disliked. But it does imply that it is no use to battle against decided tastes, or (after a certain effort has been made to conquer them) against decided distastes. Children often dislike the trouble of learning music; yet some knowledge of it is so useful that it is by no means wise to give way at once to the fancy; but if there is really no ear and no musical faculty, the time and money bestowed upon the acquirement of music are absolutely lost. These things are matters of observation. In childhood, therefore, we have to watch, and examine, and find out what the natural inclinations and powers are; but in youth we can only accept them, and do our utmost to train them in a right direction, and make them useful in the way which God has appointed. When we have done this we have nothing to reproach ourselves with; and there need be no disappointment, although the character and pursuits may be wholly unlike what we had pictured to ourselves as desirable.

And once more, as a source of disappointment, there are too often home influences—influences which, whether good or evil, are so strong, that after long experience most governesses will probably arrive at the general conclusion that the pupils who come from good homes would have been good without their efforts; and those who come from unsatisfactory homes will scarcely ever be anything but unsatisfactory, even with them.

A private governess must indeed be so alive to the power of this domestic influence that, supposing it to be injurious, it can scarcely be a matter of disappointment, though it may be a great vexation to find that she is unable to make head

against it. But she has one advantage—she can throw herself into it, and work in a measure with it. And she can understand her pupils' trials and temptations, and guard them against them; whereas the governess who receives pupils in her own house is comparatively ignorant of their difficulties. She knows only what she is told, and it is next to impossible to give good advice upon one-sided information.

So it is that young people who are troublesome and wilful at home, will often be amiable and agreeable away from it, and will even develop really charming qualities, and appear to act upon religious principles; and yet, when they return home, the old faults will show themselves again as if they had never been corrected. It must not be thought from this fact that no good has been effected by the school training. The faults do indeed exhibit themselves in a very disappointing way; but they will not do so now, as they did probably heretofore, without a strong check from conscience. The child may do wrong, but she is no longer ignorant of it; and there will be an inward struggle in consequence, which, though it may fail to result in any marked improvement at the time, is the beginning of the effort which is to last through life, and, through God's help, must be finally victorious.

But the disappointment is unquestionably great to the governess. To strive, and pray, and warn, and entreat, and to believe that God's blessing has so rested upon our efforts that the heart is really touched, and the work will be permanent; and then to find that it is apparently nothing more than the effect of extraneous influences; is so disappointing that it almost tempts us to distrust all outward appearances. Certainly, it tends to make an earnest mind very cautious as to subjecting the young for a continuance to what may be called the excitements and luxuries of religion, likely as they are to produce a semblance of good, ending in self-deceit. Where there is actual unreality the heart is fatally injured, and it may require years of suffering and bitter experience to restore it to simplicity. But in very many cases there is no unreality, only

the principle is young and weak, and requires support; and when the scenes and circumstances in which it is to be exercised are untoward, it seems for a time to fail.

But it is only seeming—only for a time. We must ever remember that the result of our labours can never be estimated in this life, and therefore to judge of our work by its apparent success is most surely to open the door to discouragement. In the Day when all things are revealed, we shall see and know better; and in that Day, as we shall have to bear the sight of the consequences of our sins and neglect, so shall we also be gladdened by seeing the consequences of our efforts for good. The seed which is now buried in a hard dry soil will, when the ground is harrowed by affliction, or by some other discipline of God's Providential grace, spring up and bear fruit. We may never know it in this life, but we shall know it after death. And in the mean time we may safely trust our work in God's Hands, with the certainty that if even the cup of cold water, given in the name of Jesus, shall not lose its reward, much less shall the "word spoken in season," or the watchful care exercised when none was near to notice or to praise.

And assuredly there is, in many cases, a reward even on earth. It may not come to us in the form which we have pictured to ourselves;—there, where our hearts were most centred, the blight may fall witheringly;—but it will sometimes be given in cases in which we could least have anticipated it.

In so far as we have in any way been permitted to strengthen the young heart, and guide it on its Christian course, it will look to us with a loving gratitude which will bind it to us to its latest day. Earth's bereavements are many, but the gap which death makes, life—the life of the young—can in a measure fill up. If when that life is given into our hands to cherish and train for Heaven, we carry on our work in dependence upon God's grace, the tie is no longer natural, but spiritual. The life becomes one with ours, to remain united with ours for ever. Though scattered over the face of the earth—perchance in other lands, perchance in scenes and circles removed from our own, yet those

whom we have tended for God and led to Him will still turn to us as their best and truest friends; and whilst these interests are secured to us there can be no lasting dreariness, no real loneliness. Travelling, as we trust we are ourselves, towards Heaven, we shall watch with a satisfaction which no mere human bond can inspire the course of the young who thus belong to us, and are following us. Their joys will be in a measure our joys, their sorrows our sorrows. The brief moments of meeting will from time to time renew their eager sympathies, and recall the first freshness of their young affections. Others may indeed be nearer and dearer, but none can go back to the days "lang syne gone by," and be to them what we have been. What the importance of those memories may be, we may not venture to imagine. Each separate soul has its own secret history, and God alone can tell how far any single influence has been used as the means through which His Grace has effected its conversion; but of one fact we may be certain, that of all the influences which surround the young there is none so powerful, so abiding, as that of thorough, devoted, Christian earnestness. Only give them faith in this—only convince them that it exists; and we have provided them with a shield for their future life, the value of which will only be appreciated at its close.

The half-heartedness, the lukewarmness, the inconsistency of the professing Christian world it is, which drives the young to indifference, and too often to scepticism. There is a mournful, a most heart-sickening confession, which perhaps it may have been ours to hear from the lips of one whom we have sent forth to face the battle of life—"I have lost all confidence in goodness. The people whom I meet are heartless; I see no high principle. I can scarcely realize its existence. It is in vain to struggle against the current, and therefore I go with it."

One cure is to be found for that terrible distrust. A recall to the scenes of former holy joys and the society of friends, the evidence of whose sincerity cannot be doubted.

The sight or the memory of one holy life will then be a shield

against unbelief, from which the darts of Satan will fall powerless. To behold "how a Christian can die" is a great privilege; but to behold how a Christian can live is a yet greater one. And it is this shield, this inestimable safeguard, which it is in the power, as it is the paramount duty, of every one to whose guardianship the Redeemer has confided the young, to provide.

Once let us be told that our efforts have not been in vain;—once let us hear it said, "But for you I should never have known the reality of religion. The example of your life made me feel what it is to give the heart to God;" and we may exclaim, "Lord, now lettest Thou Thy servant depart in peace," for on earth we shall have had our reward, and no purer joy will here be awaiting us.

Yet more will that reward be intensified if it shall have been secured to us by the irrev ocable seal of death.

No risk of change! No dread of future temptations! No fear of backsliding! But the soul—the spirit we loved so dearly—the heart which responded to ours so tenderly—safe—safe for ever!

To God be the glory, as to us will be the joy. Precious beyond all other treasures are those which we have thus given to His care, and loving is the watch which in Paradise He keeps over them.

Their home is a home of waiting rest—of peace unutterable. A time will soon come—God grant it!—when we shall join them there; and when the long twilight day is ended, and the Morning of the Resurrection breaks upon us, once more we shall be permitted to claim them for our own; as in the sight of angels and of saints we bow before the Throne of the Redeemer, and in humblest thankfulness say, "Lord, here are we, and the children whom Thou hast given us."

THE END.

Greek Ollendorff;

Being a Progressive Exhibition of the Principles of the Greek Grammar. By ASAHEL C. KENDRICK, Professor of the Greek Language and Literature in the University of Rochester. 12mo, 371 pages.

The present work is what its title indicates, strictly an *Ollendorff*, and aims to apply the methods which have proved so successful in the acquisition of the modern languages to the study of Ancient Greek, with such differences as the different genius of the Greek, and the different purposes for which it is studied, suggest. It differs from the modern Ollendorffs in containing Exercises for reciprocal translation, in confining them within a smaller compass, and in a more methodical exposition of the principles of language.

The leading object of the author was to furnish a book which should serve as an *introduction* to the study of Greek, and precede the use of any grammar. It will therefore be found, although not claiming to embrace all the principles of the Grammar, yet complete in itself, and will lead the pupil, by insensible gradations, from the simpler constructions to those which are more complicated and difficult. The exceptions, and the more idiomatic forms, it studiously avoids, aiming only to exhibit the regular and ordinary usages of the language as the proper starting-point for the student's further researches.

In presenting these, the author has aimed to combine the strictest accuracy with the utmost simplicity of statement. His work is therefore adapted to a younger class of pupils than have usually engaged in the study of Greek, and will, it is hoped, win to the acquisition of that noble tongue many in our academies and primary schools who have been repelled by the less simple character of our ordinary text-books.

Exercises in Greek Composition.

Adapted to the First Book of Xenophon's Anabasis. By JAMES R. BOISE, Professor of Greek in the University of Michigan. 12mo, 185 pages.

These Exercises consist of easy sentences, similar to those in the Anabasis, having the same words and constructions, and are designed by frequent repitition to make the learner familiar with the language of Xenophon. Accordingly, the chapters and sections in both are made to correspond. No exercises can be more improving than those in this volume; obliging the student as they do, by analysis and synthesis, to master the constructions employed by one of the purest of Greek writers, and imbuing him with the spirit of one of the greatest historians of all antiquity

Xenophon's Anabasis:

With Explanatory Notes for the use of Schools and Colleges in the United States. By JAMES R. BOISE, Professor of Greek in the University of Michigan. 12mo, 393 pages.

A handsome and convenient edition of this great classic, really adapted to the wants of schools, has long been needed; the want is here met by Professor Boise in a manner that leaves nothing to be desired. Decidedly the best German editions, whether text or commentary be considered, have appeared within the last few years; and of these Mr. Boise has made free use; while, at the same time, he has not lost sight of the fact that the classical schools of this country are behind those of Germany, and that simpler and more elementary explanations are therefore often necessary in a work prepared for American schools. Nothing has been put in the notes for the sake of a mere display of learning—pedantry is out of place in a school-book; and nothing has been introduced by way of comment except what can be turned to practical use by the reader.

An historical Introduction, which will enable the pupil to enter on his task intelligently, is prefixed. An abundance of geographical information, embodying the latest discoveries of travellers, is supplied; and the whole is illustrated with Kiepert's excellent map, showing the entire route of the ten thousand on their retreat.

The First Three Books of Anabasis:

With Explanatory Notes and References to Hadley and Kühner's Greek Grammars, and to Goodwin's Greek Moods and Tenses. A copious Greek-English Vocabulary, and Kiepert's Map of the Route of the Ten Thousand. 12mo, 268 pages.

Xenophon's Memorabilia of Socrates:

With Notes and an Introduction. By R. D. C. ROBBINS, Professor of Languages in Middlesex College, Vermont. 12mo, 421 pages.

This will be found an exceedingly useful book for College classes. The text is large and distinct, the typography accurate, and the notes judicious and scholarly. Instead of referring the student to a variety of books, few of which are within his reach, the editor has wisely supplied whatever is necessary. An admirably treatise on the Life of Socrates introduces the work, and English and Greek Indexes render it easy to refer to the text and notes.

Plato's Apology and Crito;

With Notes. By W. S. TYLER, Graves Professor of Greek in Amherst College. 12mo, 180 pages.

This edition of the Apology and Crito has been prepared to meet the largely felt want among students of the Dialogues of Plato, now mostly superseded in Academic Courses. It is in the main an exact reprint of Stallbaum's Third Edition—though the author has had before him, and used, whenever it seemed best, the editions of Bekker, Forster, Ast, Schleiermacher, and others. The Notes are particularly full and clear; and errors in the text have been guarded against with the very greatest care.

From J. B. GARRITT, *Professor of Greek, Hanover (Ind.) College.*

"I can most heartily say that I am much pleased with the book. Prof. Tyler seems to have hit the happy medium between too profuse and too scanty notes; and also to have known the *kind* of notes needed in our American institutions, better than the great majority of those who have given us editions of the ancient classics. I have adopted the work this year, in place of the Georgias, and anticipate much pleasure in reading it in connection with the class."

From JACOB COOPER, PH.D., *Professor of the Greek Language and Literature in Centre College, Danville, Ky.*

"I have examined Prof. Tyler's edition of the 'Apology and Crito,' and am highly pleased with its execution. It bears the marks of the editor's well-known scholarship, and is an acceptable addition to our college text-books. The typography is also accurate and very beautiful. I purpose to introduce it into Centre College."

From ALPHEUS S. PACKARD, *Professor of the Greek Language, Bowdoin College.*

"I received, a short time since, Plato's Apology and Crito, edited by Prof. Tyler. I am much pleased with the edition, and shall introduce it into my classes as soon as I have opportunity. I have no doubt it will prove a most acceptable addition to the classics read in our colleges."

From W. H. YOUNG, *Dept. Anct. Languages, Ohio University, Athens.*

"It will meet a pressing want with us, and shall be introduced at once. The type is beautiful indeed, and the earnest teacher of the classics needs no better recommendation of a text-book than the name of Prof. Tyler."

From the New York Observer.

"A valuable service to classical learning and letters in general has been rendered by Prof. Tyler, in giving to the American student this edition of Plato's Apology and Crito. Hitherto, the scholars of our country have had no access to this work of Plato, except in foreign editions, or as in fragmentary form they found it in the old and now obsolete Græca Majora. It is now placed within their reach, in a form both convenient and beautiful, and accompanied by such notes and illustrations as to remove all serious difficulties in ascertaining the meaning of the text. One of the most valuable features of this edition is the introduction, which occupies some forty pages, and contains a clear and scholarly analysis of the Defence of the great philosopher before his judges, who had already determined on his death."

Selections from Herodotus;

Comprising mainly such portions as give a Connected History of the East to the Fall of Babylon and the Death of Cyrus the Great. By HERMAN M. JOHNSON, D.D., Professor of Philosophy and English Literature in Dickinson College. 12mo, 185 pages.

The present selection embraces such parts of Herodotus as give a connected history of Asiatic nations. These portions are not only particularly interesting in themselves, but open to the student a new field, inasmuch as the other Greek and Roman authors commonly put into his hands leave this period of history untouched.

Herodotus is peculiarly adapted to academical reading. It has charms for the student which no other text-book possesses, on account of the simple elegance of the style and the liveliness of the narrative. In preparing his notes, the editor has borne in mind that they are intended for learners in the earlier part of their classical course; he has therefore made the explanations in the former part of the work quite full, with frequent references to such grammars as are in the hands of most students.

The notes proper are purely explanatory and grammatical. Other remarks, in the way of criticism or investigation, are appended to the several chapters, for the sake of awakening reflection and inciting to further inquiry.

A condensed treatise on the Ionic Dialect, and the peculiar forms of declension and conjugation used by Herodotus, removes one of the most serious difficulties that has heretofore embarrassed the student in reading this author. If this chapter is learned in advance, the dialectic forms, otherwise so troublesome, will be recognized without the slightest difficulty.

The text is printed in large, bold type, and accompanied with a Map of the regions described.

Sophocles' Œdipus Tyrannus.

With English Notes, for the use of Students in Schools and Colleges. By HOWARD CROSBY, A.M., Professor of the Greek Language and Literature in the New York University. 12mo, 138 pages.

The object had in view in this publication is to furnish to college-students the masterpiece of the greatest of Greek tragic poets in a convenient form. No learned criticism on text was needed or has been attempted. The Tauchnitz edition has been chiefly followed, and such aid is rendered, in the way of notes, as may assist, not render needless, the efforts of the student. Too much help begets indolence; too little, despair, the author has striven to present the happy mean.

The inviting appearance of the text and the merit of the commentary have made this volume a favorite wherever it has been used.

www.ingramcontent.com/pod-product-compliance
Lightning Source LLC
LaVergne TN
LVHW020921110826
845150LV00004B/731
9781425554651